The Anthropology of Religion

To my teachers, colleagues, and students, with grateful thanks to them all.

The Anthropology of Religion

An Introduction

Second Edition

Fiona Bowie

BLACKWELL PUBLISHING
350 Main Street, Malden, MA 02148-5020, USA
9600 Garsington Road, Oxford OX4 2DQ, UK
550 Swanston Street, Carlton, Victoria 3053, Australia

First edition published 2000
Second edition published 2006 by Blackwell Publishing Ltd

6   2009

Library of Congress Cataloging-in-Publication Data

Bowie, Fiona.
    The anthropology of religion : an introduction / Fiona Bowie.—2nd ed.
      p. cm.
    Includes bibliographical references and index.
    ISBN 978–1–4051–2104–0
    ISBN 978–1–4051–2105–7
1. Ethnology—Religious aspects. 2. Religion. I. Title.
    BL256. B69 2005
    306.6—dc22

                                                                      2005019722

A catalogue record for this title is available from the British Library.

Set in 10/12.5pt Goudy
by SPI Publisher Services, Pondicherry, India
Printed and bound in Singapore
by Utopia Press Pte Ltd

The publisher's policy is to use permanent paper from mills that operate a sustainable forestry
policy, and which has been manufactured from pulp processed using acid-free and elementary
chlorine-free practices. Furthermore, the publisher ensures that the text paper and cover board
used have met acceptable environmental accreditation standards.

For further information on
Blackwell Publishing, visit our website:
www.blackwellpublishing.com

Contents

References and Further Reading   197

8   **Witchcraft and the Evil Eye**   200
    Introduction   200
    Witchcraft in Africa   202
    Witchcraft in Rural France   212
    The Evil Eye   215
    The Mentalities Debate   220
    Notes   229
    References and Further Reading   232

9   **Pilgrimage**   237
    Introduction   237
    Approaches to the Study of Pilgrimage   238
    The Politics of Religious Synthesis   252
    Conclusion   258
    Notes   259
    References and Further Reading   262

10 **Myth**   267
    Introduction   267
    Myth and Ritual   269
    Malinowski and the Function of Myth   272
    The Power of Myth   275
    The Structural Study of Myth   279
    Joseph Campbell and the Monomyth   284
    History, Myth, and Memory   291
    Conclusion   298
    Notes   298
    References and Further Reading   301

    Appendix: Film and Video Resources   305
    Index   324

Preface to the Second Edition

This second, updated and extended edition of *The Anthropology of Religion* has two additional chapters. Chapter 9, dealing with Pilgrimage and the theme of religious syncretism was originally intended for the first edition, and excluded on the grounds of length. The final chapter, on Myth, is new and comes as a response to readers' comments. In addition to those acknowledged in the first edition I would like to thank Joel Dudley, Isabel de Salis, and above all Robert Segal for reading and commenting on the final chapter. While all mistakes are my own, the chapter on Myth certainly benefited from Robert Segal's careful reading and perceptive comments. I would like to thank the editors at Blackwell for giving me the chance to extend the text, and for their professionalism in seeing the book through the production process.

Fiona Bowie
Bristol 2005

Preface to the First Edition

The Anthropology of Religion is intended as an introductory text for under-graduate students and for anyone who wishes to know something about the subject. The book combines discussion of the origin and development of ideas and debates within the anthropology of religion with a look at where the subject is going today – the interests and preoccupations of current practitioners. Links with other disciplines, particularly religious studies, are discussed wherever possible. Although there is a development of ideas throughout the book, each chapter is self-contained, with its own bibliog-raphy, and the chapters could be approached in any order. The appendix consists of a list of ethnographic films and videos that could be used to illustrate or extend the issues raised in the various chapters.

Each chapter aims to introduce central theoretical ideas in the anthro-pology of religion and to illustrate them with specific case studies. Links are made between the work of nineteenth- and early twentieth-century scholars, the founding figures or "ancestors" of modern anthropology, and contempor-ary ideas and practices. Chapter 1, Theories and Controversies, provides a key introduction to many of the debates and issues that follow, and could usefully be read at both the beginning and the end of the book. Both methodological issues in the study of religion and the historical development of the subject are discussed. Chapters 2 and 3, The Body as Symbol, and Maintaining and Transforming Boundaries, focus on symbolism, embodi-ment, politics, and gender. Symbolic classification is a key theme in both chapters, looking in particular at ways in which the body expresses the relationship between individual and physiological identity, and the forma-tion of groups, cultures, and societies. Although the sociological influence of Durkheim and Mary Douglas is much in evidence, psychological and cultural approaches are also included. Chapter 4, Sex, Gender, and the Sacred, takes a slight detour in order to look more closely at gender and sexuality, and the influence of feminist theory on the anthropology of religion. Chapter 5, Religion, Culture, and Environment, introduces various cosmological systems and interpretations of cosmologies as being either adaptive or dysfunctional, as well as exploring the links between mythology, gender, and the environment. Chapter 6, Ritual Theory, Rites of Passage, and Ritual Violence, forms a central part of the book. Ritual is a major theme in the anthropology of religion, and after some theoretical discussions, rites of passage, and in particular women's initiation ceremonies, are taken as an example to illustrate some of the ways in which anthropologists have approached this topic. Chapter 7, Shamanism, deals with another key issue in anthropological studies, although one in which there is little agreement. Both "classical" shamanism in the Arctic and contemporary "neo-shamanism" are discussed, raising questions concerning the effects of globalization and the exchange of cultural ideas between so-called "indigenous" and industrial societies. Chapter 8, Witchcraft and the Evil Eye, introduces three interrelated themes. First, witchcraft in Africa is illustrated via Evans-Pritchard's famous study of the Azande and witchcraft in modern Cameroon. We then look at contemporary discourses of witchcraft in France, which lead on to related discussions concerning belief in the Evil Eye in Europe and elsewhere. The final section of the chapter introduces the debate on "mentalities," the nature of cognition and its universal or relative expressions in different cultures.

I am conscious that most if not all of the themes discussed could equally have been introduced using quite different topics and ethnographic examples. The book could have been arranged differently, so as to highlight issues such as globalization, agency, colonialism and post-colonialism, notions of the self, and so on. Equally, I could have approached the subject via chapters focusing on different theoretical schools – evolution and diffusion, structural functionalism, psychological approaches, structuralism, post-structuralism and postmodernism. All these themes are present, either explicitly or implicitly, and in the end the particular arrangement of the book is a matter of personal choice. The bibliographies are fairly extensive and should be useful in following up both texts referred to in the chapters and related themes that I have not been able to discuss in any detail. Finally, I hope that this introduction to the anthropology of religion will inspire people to explore the subject more fully. Anthropology is not just about reading or doing fieldwork; it is a way of looking at the world, of appreciating its richness and variety, and of becoming self-conscious practitioners within our own culture. While this process may be unsettling, it is certainly never dull. May you enjoy the challenge of always asking "Why?"

Fiona Bowie
Lampeter

Acknowledgments

The Anthropology of Religion grew out of my introductory lecture course at the University of Wales Lampeter. My thanks must therefore go first and foremost to former and current students in anthropology and religious studies whose interests, queries, challenging questions, and enthusiasms have been the inspiration for this book. I am also indebted to numerous colleagues who have kindly given their time and expertise to read and comment on various chapters. While they have no doubt saved me from many minor and not so minor errors of fact and judgment, any mistakes remain my own. In particular I would like to thank Simon Coleman, Paul Cooper, Penny Dransart, John Eade, Graham Falvey, Gavin Flood, Merete Jakobsen, Lucy Rushton, Veronica Strang, and Dimitris Theodossopoulos, for both encouraging comments and necessary corrections. The Tairona Heritage Studies Centre and Veronica Strang have kindly lent me photographs to illustrate the text. I am grateful to Martin Davies at Blackwell Publishers, who originally commissioned the book, to Alex Wright, who succeeded him, and to Joanna Pyke and Clare Woodford, who waited so patiently for the manuscript. The book has benefited from the comments of anonymous readers, although it proved impossible to encompass adequately their somewhat conflicting suggestions. I trust that each will find enough of interest in the current work, and not too much that displeases them. I could not have completed the work if the University of Wales Lampeter had not given me study leave, and I am grateful to Clare Hall in Cambridge for their hospitality in providing a peaceful working environment. Last but not least, my thanks go to my husband Oliver Davies and sons Isaac and Rory for their support, love and laughter.

Chapter 1

Theories and Controversies

Introduction

The unfortunate fact is that man has been created with a body and a soul as well, and this original sin, after having incessantly haunted the reflective mind through myth, religion, theology, and metaphysics, comes now to lay its curse on anthropology. Physical and cultural anthropology are divided by a deep rent between soul and body, mind and matter, which is no easier to bridge over in science than in the somewhat looser speculations which precede it. (Malinowski, 1923, p. 314)[1]

Anthropology claims to be an inclusive discipline, with *anthropos*, "human kind," as its object of study. The natural sciences, philosophy, history, theology, classical studies, and even jurisprudence have all been called upon in order to throw light on this exploration of human beings in all their complexity. In studying human society we are looking at both ourselves and others, and the dialectical relationship between self and other, the individual and the group, lies at the heart of anthropology. Who is this "other"? And what can the other tell us about ourselves, our culture, our society? Are the others human? And what does this mean? Do small-scale "primitive" societies mirror the evolutionary past of the "civilized" world? What if any are the underlying similarities between peoples? Are we all so different that each culture and society can only be looked at in isolation – with little or no basis for comparison? Is religion a product of society, merely a human invention and projection? Or is there "more in heaven and earth" than the material or social scientist can explain? Are religious motivations and impulses a response to external spiritual energies and revelations, or the result of a deluded mind and false consciousness? Is religion universal, or will it soon disappear under the weight of technology and reason?

These conflicts, noted by the great Polish ethnographer Bronislaw Malinowski over 60 years ago, are still the stuff of current and heated debate.

It will become obvious that there is no one anthropological approach to the study of religion, and those who in reading this book are looking for a "right answer" are bound to be disappointed. The onus is on readers to examine the data, draw their own conclusions and build their own bridges "between soul and body, mind and matter."

The first part of this chapter plunges straight in with an examination of various *issues in the study of religion*. These include the differing perspectives of positivistic scientific anthropologists on the one hand, who feel obliged to point out that all religion is irrational, and on the other those whose belief in Western concepts of truth and order has been profoundly shaken as a result of contact with alternative "indigenous" cosmologies. I also look at the assumptions and methodologies characteristic of anthropological approaches to religion, and their relation to the phenomenological method of religious studies. Theories concerning the *origins* of religion preoccupied many nineteenth- and early twentieth-century thinkers, and affected the type of definition they favored. Some of these themes are examined in the second part of the chapter. The final section looks in more detail at *definitions* of religion and at attempts to *categorize* religion – both of which are less straightforward than someone with a tidy mind might wish!

In looking at and trying to understand the "other" we do so as in a mirror, seeing our own interests and assumptions reflected in the questions we ask and the answers we receive. Anthropologists have for many years been engaged in an analysis of their own practice. The discussions therefore include an account of some attempts to overcome the distorting effects that result from imbalances of power between the anthropological author and the subject, and efforts to "decenter" the authority of the ethnographic text, with its explicit or implicit claims to "tell it like it is."

Issues in the Study of Religion

Medieval Europe may have been a turbulent place at times, with different political and religious interests vying with one another for dominance, but there was a certain unity of belief in the existence of God and the just claims of secular authority.[2] With the Enlightenment these basic assumptions were challenged. The Scottish historian and philosopher David Hume (1711–76), for example, argued that empirical observation (based on what one can know from experience) should form the basis of the "moral sciences," while the German philosopher Immanuel Kant (1742–1804) insisted that all knowledge is constructed and that we cannot know "the world in itself." For Ludwig Feuerbach (1804–72) Christianity was an illusion, and the proper object of theology and philosophy the study of human beings, rather than metaphysical speculation concerning the nature of God.

> **The Enlightenment:** a movement in seventeenth- and eighteenth-century European philosophy concerned with the role of reason and the progress of human civilization. Enlightenment philosophers were prepared to reject tradition and to question existing sources of authority. A leading Enlightenment figure was the French philosopher Jean-Jacques Rousseau (1712–78), famous for his depiction of "the noble savage." Unlike Thomas Hobbes (1588–1679), who held that human life in its natural state is "solitary, poor, nasty, brutish and short," Rousseau believed that so-called civilization, with its increased inequalities, actually represented degeneration from an original harmonious collective social life. Education and the reimposition of the *social contract* – the collective will of the people – were necessary in order to assume an orderly progress. Rousseau's ideas of social collectivity were later to influence Émile Durkheim.

While these brave new ideas were debated in intellectual circles, and philosopher Friedrich Nietzsche (1844–1900) proclaimed the "death of God," the majority of the population of Europe continued to hold traditional Christian (or Jewish) beliefs and values. Seminal ideas regarding the nature of religion put forward by nineteenth- and early-twentieth-century scholars (and, indeed, many anthropologists today) can only be understood against the background of formal religion, which provided both the vocabulary and template for thinking about the religions of others, and a model to reject. Evans-Pritchard, a convert to Catholicism, pointed out in his lectures on "primitive religion" that many of the founding fathers of European social science had been raised within the Christian or Jewish faiths, but had reacted against their religious upbringing:

> Tylor had been brought up a Quaker, Frazer a Presbyterian, Marett in the Church of England, Malinowski a Catholic, while Durkheim, Lévy-Bruhl, and Freud had a Jewish background; but with one or two exceptions, whatever the background may have been, the persons whose writings have been most influential have been at the time they wrote agnostics or atheists. Primitive religion was with regard to its validity no different from any other religious faith, an illusion. (Evans-Pritchard, 1972, pp. 14–15)

I will return briefly to some of these thinkers and their theories of religion later in the chapter,[3] but first we will look at what for many has become the standard approach to the study of religion in both religious studies and the social sciences, the *phenomenological method*.

Phenomenology and methodological agnosticism

> **Phenomenology:** from the Greek *phainomenon*, "that which shows itself." The term was used by Kant to describe what one can know from experience, and by Husserl to refer to a description of the world (phenomena). The term "*phenomenology of religion*" was coined by the Dutch scholar P. D. Chantepie de la Saussaye in 1887 to refer to a systematic description of religious phenomena.[4]

Whether or not they subscribe to a religion or consider themselves to be "spiritual" people, most social scientists and historians of religion would regard Evans-Pritchard's evaluation of the role of the anthropologist as valid:

> What I have said does not imply that the anthropologist *has* to have a religion of his own, and I think we should be clear on this point at the outset. He is not concerned *qua* anthropologist, with the truth or falsity of religious thought. As I understand the matter, there is no possibility of his *knowing* whether the spiritual beings of primitive religions or of any others have any existence or not, and since that is the case he cannot take the question into consideration. The beliefs are for him sociological facts, not theological facts, and his sole concern is with their relation to each other and to other social facts. His problems are scientific, not metaphysical or ontological. The method he employs is that now often called the phenomenological one – a comparative study of beliefs and rites, such as god, sacrament, and sacrifice, to determine their meaning and social significance. (Evans-Pritchard, 1972, p. 17)

This methodological neutrality or agnosticism[5] allows, in theory at least, anthropologists of any or no religious persuasion to examine the religious beliefs and practices of others without bias. Any cosmological statement or ritual practice is of interest not because it might or might not be true, but for what it reveals of a coherent body of thought that constitutes a culture and its social structure. As we will see, there are both ethical and methodological problems with this assumption, even if it is the "rule of thumb" by which most anthropologists today operate.

Within religious studies and the history of religions the phenomenological method has served the function of separating the discipline from its elder brother, theology. While there are those who argue that the teaching of theology is a "teaching about" rather than a catechesis (a "how to"), nevertheless, there is often a presumption that a religion will be taught, or a book written, from within a particular faith position – probably (but not necessarily) shared by teacher and pupil or author and reader. From a theological perspective, the study of religions other than one's own may consist of a search for points of comparison, probably, even if unintentionally, to the detriment of the other religion (after all, to accept that all are equally true or valid would undermine the logic of most religious positions). Almost certainly, other religions will not be studied on their own merit without presumption as to what to look for. Roman Catholic missiologists and theologians involved in "inculturation," for example, may examine African religions in order to discover the "seeds of the gospel" (i.e. elements of culture compatible with Christianity), and use these as an aid to conversion or with the intention of strengthening the faith of converts.[6] In reaction to this approach, religious studies has embraced the phenomenological method, which in practice usually means describing other people's customs and doctrinal beliefs and translating their sacred texts with as little comment and judgment as possible.[7]

The philosopher **Edmund Husserl** (1859–1938) is recognized as the founder of the *phenomenological movement*. Husserl was born into a Jewish family in Moravia in the modern Czech Republic. He is best known within the social sciences and religious studies for developing the methodological practice of epochē (a Greek word meaning to "check" or "cease"). In effect what Husserl suggested was that instead of concerning ourselves with the question of whether or not something is true or actually exists, we should "bracket out" or "put in parentheses" what cannot be demonstrated or proved. This allowed attention to be paid to the "appearances" that can be observed without prior assumptions, and further allowed the intuition of the essence or *eidos* (from the Greek, meaning "form," "idea," or "essence"). This method opened the door to the creation of typologies by phenomenologists of religion such as Gerardus van der Leeuw (1890–1950).[8] The emphasis in Husserl's thought was on the *cogito* or conscious observer, but he avoided questions concerning the identity of this conscious mind, its authority, and its relation to language. These weaknesses are characteristic of much scholarship that identifies its approach as phenomenological. There is a failure to address questions of subjectivity, reflexivity, and textuality – treating the scholar as a "fly on the wall" rather than as a thinking, relating individual who is implicated in the phenomenon he or she describes.[9]

Rationality and religion

One anthropological critique of the phenomenological method comes from those who hold that anthropology should regard itself as a science, based on empiricism and rationality. If something is demonstrably false, the anthropologist should say so. James Lett is one of the more vociferous exponents of this approach, arguing in a recent handbook on the anthropology of religion that, "anthropologists have an intellectual and ethical obligation to investigate the truth or falsity of religious beliefs" (Lett, 1997a, p. 105). For Lett, "scientific knowledge" is defined as objective propositional knowledge that can be publicly verified and tested – which does not of itself rule out the possibility of incorporating non-empirical knowledge. Religion, on the other hand, is defined by its non-empirical nature. It lies in the realm of faith rather than fact and is therefore by definition unverifiable. If it cannot be falsified, it cannot be proved. Religion is *ipso facto* irrational. While many people, including anthropologists, are content to leave a space for the existence of the unprovable, and even the improbable, to "bracket it out" or simply to examine its social dimensions, not so James Lett, who feels that it is incumbent on anthropologists to take a stand on the side of rationality:

> It seems to me that the obligation to expose religious beliefs as nonsensical is an ethical one incumbent upon every anthropological scientist for the simple reason that the essential ethos of science lies in an unwavering dedication to truth. . . . In science there is no room for compromise in the commitment to candor. Scientists cannot allow themselves to be propagandists or apologists touting convenient or comforting myths. . . . When anthropologists fail to publicly proclaim the falsity of religious beliefs, they fail to live up to their ethical responsibilities in this regard. (Lett, 1997a, pp. 111–12)

Such explicitly materialist zeal is unusual in anthropology, even if the underlying skepticism is not. In the same volume, for instance, Stewart Guthrie sets out to "prove" that all religion is a result of anthropomorphism, and therefore illusory. Guthrie argues that people "bet high" – that is, there is less to be lost by attributing human characteristics to other creatures and phenomena than by getting it wrong. "In consequence, our practice in the face of uncertainty is to guess at animacy over inanimacy and humanlikeness over its absence. Betting on these possibilities and often erring, we chronically animate and anthropomorphize the world" (Guthrie, 1997, p. 495).

At the other end of the spectrum we have those who have approached the study of religion from within a particular faith. The Swedish Lutheran missionary Bengt Sundkler, for instance, was well aware of both the advantages and disadvantages of his own position. In his celebrated account of Bantu prophets in South African Independent churches, Sundkler reflected that:

> Prior to undertaking this study, I had certain forebodings that in my capacity as a missionary of one particular church I should be handicapped in establishing friendly contacts with Independent church leaders – contacts without which

they would not give information about themselves, their work, ambitions and aspirations. But my fear on this point was unnecessary. In an overwhelming number of cases I found that the very fact that I was known as a missionary, genuinely interested in their church life as well as in their personal life-histories and activities was a help when trying to elicit the information I wanted. . . . Experience of related problems in the work of one's own mission church opened up new avenues of inquiry and research. (Sundkler, 1961, pp. 15–16)

Sundkler goes on to reflect on the inevitable bias in all anthropological investigations, whether the fieldworker is a Christian believer or an atheist, noting that: "Obviously the writer's valuations and ideals enter into the investigation – from the collecting of the material itself, which is the fundamental stage, to the final presentation with its balancing of one viewpoint against another" (Sundkler, 1961, p. 16). The notion of disinterested social science is a myth.

Value premises do enter into our arguments. So they should not be hidden, as tacit assumptions, but explicitly stated. A subjective emphasis is bound to affect the valuations of any missionary dealing with a problem of this nature, implying a definite criticism of his own ideals and life-work. No doubt, I am myself, both as a Protestant missionary and as an investigator, a part of the problem, and I affect its future development by my missionary activity or inactivity. (Sundkler, 1961, p. 16)

Most anthropologists would endorse such sentiments, which were unusually perceptive, honest, and reflexive for a book originally published in 1948.

Increasingly common are anthropological accounts in which the fieldworker may approach other cultures secure within a Western positivist framework, with the intention of "bracketing out" the truth or falsity of others' beliefs, but who then finds that an alien view of the world can indeed "work" much as its advocates describe. Evans-Pritchard, in his study *Witchcraft, Oracles and Magic among the Azande*, stated baldly that "Witches, as the Azande conceive them, clearly cannot exist" (1976, p. 18), but he nevertheless discovered that living as if they did exist was no better or worse a manner of organizing his affairs than any other. Merete Jakobsen (1999), taking part in New Age shamanic workshops, was happy to record soul journeys in which she encountered guardian animal spirits, without necessarily "believing" in them, or in the explanations given by the workshop leaders. Tanya Luhrmann (1989) joined a witch's coven and cast spells without actually sharing the worldview of her co-witches. In each instance the fieldworker had a personal philosophy that could account for new or strange experiences, thus avoiding any great rupture or challenge to his or her understanding of the world and sense of self.

Where, on the other hand, the fieldworker, originally skeptical, finds himself or herself subject to a series of misfortunes for which they have no rational explanation, faith in a Western scientific worldview may be profoundly shaken. One such ethnographic account is Jeanne Favret-Saada's study of witchcraft in northern France (1980). While Favret-Saada does develop a series of logical explanations for witchcraft beliefs in rural Normandy, she also, having been "caught" in the discourse of witchcraft through falling victim to a series of unfortunate events, takes magic forces extremely seriously (if only at a psychological and linguistic level, and as a form of explanation).

Michael Kearney was drawn to his fieldwork in southern Mexico by a fascination with the differences between the Indians' cosmological system and his own. The people of Ixtepejano lived in a world "saturated with harmful, even lethal immaterial forces," which included "bad airs" that could be sent into a victim by witches (Kearney, 1992, p. 48). Kearney attributed the unscientific and irrational views of the people to the insecurity and poverty of their lives, until he became unwittingly involved in supernatural dispute between neighbors. On discovering that he had been afflicted by sores, one of the weapons in the witches' armoury, Kearney panicked:

> My mind began to race like a motor with its throttle stuck while I witnessed the disintegration of my own rational, scientific, materialist world view. The unsuppressable assertion rose into my mind that it was all false, that the people among whom I had been living with what I had assumed were quaint backward customs and superstitions were aware of and in touch with knowledge of forces with which I was in no way prepared to deal. I feared for my life as I never had before. (Kearney, 1992, pp. 53–4)

Suspended between the world of rural Mexican Indians and the safety of abstract intellectual life in Berkeley, Kearney gained a new understanding of the terrors of witchcraft and its reality in people's lives – even if he eventually succeeded in rationalizing the experience.

In my final example, the transformation from Western skeptic to "believer" is more complete and permanent. Paul Stoller became a sorcerer's apprentice during his fieldwork in the Songhay region of West Africa. In his first account of Songhay, Stoller edited out the personal accounts that he felt contravened the conventions of the ethnographic text. This included the abrupt end to his fieldwork in 1984, when he fled from an attack of spirits sent by a priestess who intended to harm him. For Stoller, however, fieldwork is both a science and "a profoundly human experience," and he did not shrink from entering as fully as possible into the cosmological understandings of the Songhay.

> As anthropologists we must respect the people among whom we work. . . . For me, respect means accepting fully beliefs and phenomena which our system of

knowledge often holds preposterous. I took my teachers seriously. They *knew* that I used divination in my personal life. They *knew* that I had eaten powders to protect myself. They *knew* I wore objects to demonstrate my respect for the spirits. They *knew* I had an altar in my house over which I recited incantations. They liked the way I carried my knowledge and power and taught me more and more. (Stoller, 1989, p. 229)

Eventually, however, Stoller overstepped the mark between participant-observation and active sorcery and was forced to flee. Although Stoller remains a Western-trained anthropologist, he did not slough off the insights he had gained in Songhay, even when he finally managed to rid himself of the magically induced illness that had precipitated his departure:

The Songhay world challenged the basic premises of my scientific training. Living in Songhay forced me to confront the limitations of the Western philosophical tradition. My seventeen-year association with Songhay reflects the slow evolution of my thought, a thought profoundly influenced by Songhay categories and Songhay wisdom. (Stoller, 1989, p. 227)[10]

The politics of representation

We have moved a long way from the methodological agnosticism propounded by proponents of the phenomenological method. Or have we? It is certainly possible to remain open to another culture and its beliefs, and perhaps be profoundly affected by them, without feeling it necessary to enter into discussions of truth or falsity. One of the key differences between anthropological participant observation and the data gathering of earlier "armchair anthropologists" or survey ethnographers is the potential for physical, emotional, and spiritual involvement in the lives of others. Ethnographers who submit themselves to periods of immersion in another culture inevitably take the risk that their own way of looking at the world will be challenged, transformed, and perhaps destroyed. The degree of dissonance the anthropologist can tolerate between one worldview and another will be largely an individual affair, and a combination of respect, skepticism, and agnosticism toward the "reality" of other people's explanations of the world is not uncommon.[11] Anthropologists do tend to bracket out questions of truth and rationality, and may write themselves out of the fieldwork altogether, with the result that ethnographic texts often appear rather dry and lifeless beside the intensity of the original experience. The gap between the vivid retelling of fieldwork tales to friends and colleagues and the published monograph in academic anthropology is for this reason probably greater than the gap between research and text in most other disciplines.[12]

An emphasis on methodological agnosticism can encourage scholars, whether anthropologists, sociologists, or historians of religion, to assume that they are somehow neutral in their observations. We may wish to believe that sensitivity and empathy with our hosts is sufficient to produce a balanced monograph, or delude ourselves into believing that including verbatim accounts of conversations, or discussing the final text of a book with informants, somehow leads to a shared authorship. Those who duck questions of language, power and translatability merely leave the authority of the authorial voice implicit and unchallenged.[13] Rijk van Dijk and Peter Pels (1996, p. 245) point out that "Ethnographic dialogue is always contextualised by a dialectics of power relationships that conditions and inhibits it." The authority of the fieldworker to ask questions and edit the answers is part of the process of anthropological production. Even in an "experience near" text, perhaps consisting of transcribed conversations, film, photographs, first-hand accounts of informants, and the reflexive journals of the fieldworker, the final production is crafted by the interests, skill, and aesthetic judgments of the anthropologist in relation *not* to the fieldwork subjects, but to an imagined and intended audience.[14] This is not in itself "bad," but it should be made explicit. The anthropologist is a translator of culture, and the translation should not be mistaken for the original.

Van Dijk and Pels go a step further than most anthropologists, and certainly beyond the practice of *epochē* as commonly understood and practiced by scholars of religion, in suggesting "a 'democratising' of the capacity to deconstruct authoritative statements in the study of religion" (1996, p. 246). When encountering religious specialists in the cultures they study, anthropologists commonly attempt to "explain away" their claims by situating them in terms of social structure, history, psychology, and so on. They are seldom taken at face value in the way Paul Stoller accepted the "truth" of Songhay sorcery. The reflexivity recommended by most contemporary authors merely involves focusing attention on the anthropologist rather than the host community, through a process of reflexivity, and carries no guarante of a shared ability to set the terms of the debate. Van Dijk and Pels make the claim, with rather uncomfortable and perhaps unacceptable implications for most scholars, that:

> it is necessary to democratise deconstruction in this way, if not to unsettle anthropological claims to authority, then at least to restore agency to those whom these claims commonly reduce to "objectivity" (or a "voice"). We think that such a step is necessary for the reorientation of research into religion in a postcolonial world. (van Dijk and Pels, 1996, p. 246)

Van Dijk and Pels give an example, taken from van Dijk's fieldwork among young Born Again Christian preachers in Blantyre, Malawi, of the implications of such an approach. After gaining their trust, van Dijk published an article on the preachers in a national monthly magazine. The article included the following description, which makes clear the author's distanced and authoritative stand:

> With the "infilling" of the Holy Spirit, as many youngsters have been explaining, one suddenly feels as having stepped into the world of light. Every meeting, therefore, is filled with ecstatic prayers, shouting and speaking in tongues to create the exact state of mind wherein the baptism by the Holy Spirit can take place. (van Dijk and Pels, 1996, p. 258)

Most anthropologists would probably regard van Dijk's style as appropriate and "normal," yet the young preachers took grave exception to the article, above all to the manner in which it was written, summoning van Dijk to a private meeting to explain himself. The use of inverted commas around the word "infilling," for instance, was seen to lessen the authority of the preachers by reducing what was for them a reality to a position of relativity. By his acceptance of their hospitality and participation in their meetings, the young men had assumed that van Dijk also accepted their status as inspired prophets. By appearing to deny, or at least to distance himself from, the truth of their message by using "outsider" language, van Dijk had jeopardized his position within the community. Was he a spy of the Pope, they demanded? In order to restore the goodwill that had been forfeited by this pretence of authorial neutrality, van Dijk was obliged to acknowledge the power of inspiration by the Holy Spirit at a public meeting. In a country in which challenge to political authority was dangerous, the poorly educated young preachers needed to stress the orthodoxy of their message, as well as the source of its inspiration. Theirs was an oral, tactile culture and the written word was suspect, associated with an older, corrupt generation that had hung onto power for too long.[15] What appeared fair, balanced, and innocuous to the academic anthropologist constituted a threat to the community he was studying.

Despite their valuable role in challenging anthropological ethnocentrisms, Van Dijk and Pels's recommendations do not really point a way forward. In describing his experiences, for instance, van Dijk adopts the authorial tone appropriate to an academic readership, but dismissed by his informants. The logic of van Dijk's position would be that the anthropologist becomes a mouthpiece or apologist for the views of interlocutors in the field but nothing more. Even if this were appropriate, it would not solve the problem of whose views one is to represent. The perspective of women may be different from that of men, members of one church may disagree with the interpretation of their views given by members of another, and so on. The task for the ethnographer remains to interpret the views of others in as honest and responsible a manner as possible and to place these views and practices within a broader theoretical framework. To make a difficult job even harder, the anthropologist is also trying to address simultaneously a number of different audiences, including academic colleagues and students, people from the fieldwork area, and perhaps non-governmental organizations, commercial sponsors, and the media.

We will now return to some older debates and examine attempts to understand the nature of religion by reference to its origins; debates that once more took shape in the nineteenth century, but continue to reverberate in academic circles today.

The Origins of Religion

When Charles Darwin (1809–82) published his controversial account of human evolution, *The Descent of Man*, in 1871, the Church was outraged. Darwin appeared to claim that human beings were descended from apes, and to leave no room for God in his account of natural selection and species adaptation. Where was the order in creation if a random interaction between the natural environment and biological organisms led to the variety of living creatures now in existence? While Darwin's ideas appeared as an affront, the notion of *social evolution* (later known as social Darwinism) was well established by the 1870s, and much less objectionable. Herbert Spencer (1820–1903), a prominent British social and political thinker, propounded the theory that all things, animate and inanimate, move from simpler to more differentiated complex forms, from homogeneity to heterogeneity. In *The Principles of Sociology* (1876), Spencer developed his thesis of universal evolution – which included his notion of the "survival of the fittest." This view of human society was more flattering to the Victorian mind. After all, human beings represented the grand climax of evolution, and Great Britain, leader of the Industrial Revolution, was arguably the most complex society in the world and therefore at the very peak of the evolutionary pyramid.

Unlike some of his contemporaries, who could see little kinship with "rude and savage peoples," Spencer firmly believed that all human beings, however simple their technology, were equally rational. According to Spencer, religion arose from the observation that in dreams the self can leave the body. The human person therefore has a dual aspect, and after death the spirit or soul continues to appear to living descendants in dreams. The ghosts of remote ancestors or prominent figures eventually acquired the status of gods (an idea known as *euhemerism* after the Sicilian writer Euhemerus, *c.*315 BCE). The widespread practice of pouring libations on the graves of ancestors and offering them food developed into sacrifices for the gods. Ancestor worship was therefore at the root of every religion.

British anthropologist Edward Burnett Tylor, who gave the anthropology of religion some of its key terminology, agreed with Spencer's social evolutionary views and his notion of the dream origin of religion. Tylor, however, preferred to emphasize the role of the soul (Latin *anima*) in his account of religious origins, giving rise to the term *animism* to describe the belief that animate and inanimate objects, as well as human beings, can have a soul (or life force and personality). The term is still used with different nuances as a general descriptive term for "primitive," "indigenous" or "tribal" religions.

Sir Edward Burnett Tylor (1832–1917) was from a London Quaker family (which, due to the religious tests still in operation, prevented him from attending a university) and came to anthropology by chance. He traveled to Mexico and the United States for the sake of his health, and became fascinated by the lives of the indigenous inhabitants. On the basis of his observations, Tylor formulated his theories of ancient and simple societies, which were published in numerous works, including *Primitive Culture* (1871) in the year in which he was elected a Fellow of the Royal Society. In 1884 he became a Reader in Anthropology at Oxford University, the first recognized university position in anthropology in the English-speaking world. In *Primitive Culture* Tylor developed the notion of three stages of social evolution, from:

animism → polytheism → monotheism

Tylor also formulated a concept of culture (which was to become influential in the USA) and the notion of *diffusion*, the transmission across time and space of cultural elements or *traits*. Where these elements commonly coincided they were referred to as *adhesions*. Supposedly primitive traits found in a more "advanced" society were thought to be *survivals* from an earlier evolutionary stage.

Sir James Frazer (1854–1941), a Scottish classicist with a passion for amassing information on other cultures, is one of Britain's best-known scholars of religion. Drawing on classical sources and the tales of missionaries and explorers, Frazer compiled a two-volume compendium in which he attempted to construct a universal theory of magic, religion, and society, published under the title *The Golden Bough* (1890). Despite its erudition, Frazer's work has had less theoretical impact than that of Tylor. The "butterfly collecting" methodology, which juxtaposes information, often of very dubious provenance, totally out of context, allows the author to "prove" almost any point he cares to make. This has not prevented *The Golden Bough* in its abridged edition from remaining almost constantly in print.

Frazer believed that magic preceded religion. As magic was perceived to be fallacious, people looked for other means of psychological support, and had the illusion that spiritual beings could help them. When people see that religion does not work either, they turn to science. Both science and magic are based on faith in the manipulation of natural laws (although only the former is true), whereas religion is based on a belief in spirits. The scientist and magician can perform their rites with confidence, whereas the priest makes offerings with fear and trembling.

There was considerable debate in the nineteenth century between those who saw all or most human culture resulting from the *diffusion* of ideas via population movement and contact, and those who believed that cultures evolved independently from one another. Because all human beings have a similar psychological make-up it was held that they tend to come up with the same solutions to cultural problems independently. Tylor argued for a social evolutionary perspective, whereas Franz Boas in the United States adapted Tylor's methodology and vocabulary to argue a predominantly diffusionist position.

Evans-Pritchard (1972) eloquently described the intellectualist positions of scholars such as Spencer, Tylor, and Frazer as the "if I were a horse" fallacy, and their tales on the origins of religion as "just so" stories, analogous to Rudyard Kipling's "How the leopard got its spots." Lacking any real evidence, Spencer, Tylor, and Frazer (and others) resorted to asking themselves what they would have done had they been a "primitive," how they would have rationalized the world. As Evans-Pritchard points out, if these scholars were correct, as civilization progressed such rational but fallacious reasoning would die out, whereas instead animistic and magical views of the world, ancestral cults, and beliefs in a Supreme Being all continue to exist, and often to coexist, even in industrialized settings.

A less intellectualist and more *emotionalist* view of religion characterizes the work of Bronislaw Malinowski (1884–1942), one of the founders of the *functionalist* school of anthropology. Functionalism emphasized the interrelations between the various elements of a social system, and therefore paid less attention to evolutionary origins and the notion of "survivals" – the continuation of primitive elements in a culture. Society was seen as a self-regulating system in which religion, economic organization, and kinship formed parts of an organic whole. The realm of the sacred is defined by the attitude people have toward it – rituals are sacred if they are performed with reverence and awe. Malinowski, like Frazer, distinguished magic from religion. A religious act aims at something beyond itself. Its object is not performance of the rite. A mortuary ritual, for instance, is intended to release the soul and prevent it from returning to haunt the living. In magic the end is the efficacious action itself.[16] Both magic and religion, however, serve the same psychological function, the alleviation of anxiety in the face of life's uncertainties. As with the intellectualist arguments, the emotionalist theories of Malinowski (and Freud) are simply guesswork. Evans-Pritchard (1972, pp. 43–7) observes that while emotions, desires, and impulses undoubtedly play a part in religion, it is not the case that the performance of a religious or magical act automatically produces the psychological effects Malinowski supposes. We have another example of the "if I were a horse" arguments: "If we were to perform rites such as primitives do, we suppose that we would be in a state of emotional turmoil, for otherwise our reason would tell us that the rites are objectively useless" (Evans-Pritchard, 1972, p. 43).

A very different approach to religion was taken by the French sociologist Émile Durkheim. Religion was not seen as an explanation of the world, but as a means of making symbolic statements about society. Durkheim was less interested in finding the origins of religion than in describing its function. Unlike Malinowski (and Freud), however, his emphasis was not on the individual psyche but the social group. The *collective representations* of a society exist within and beyond an individual. Religion, for Durkheim, is a projection of the social values of society. It is real because its effects are real, even if its social origins are disguised, and the explanations and beliefs for a religion false.

Émile Durkheim (1858–1917) was a pupil of Fustel de Coulanges at the elite *École Normale* in Paris, and is thought of as one of the founding fathers of both modern sociology and anthropology. Drawing on data primarily from Australian Aboriginal peoples (in the belief that they represented the simplest form of society and could therefore tell us something about the origins of more complex societies), Durkheim developed his ideas on the social nature of religion. These are most fully developed in *The Elementary Forms of the Religious Life* (1915). One of Durkheim's key distinctions was between the *sacred* and the *profane*. The collective life of society gives rise to both the profane world of everyday activities and the sacred world of ethical and moral values – the ideals by which societies seek to live.

Anthropology in North America followed a rather different course, drawing on elements of both continental European and British scholarship, but with a specific emphasis on the notion of culture. A key figure, who influenced several generations of later anthropologists, was Franz Boas.

Franz Boas (1858–1942) carried out fieldwork among the Inuit of Canada, and developed a school of anthropology that stressed cultural differences, eschewing attempts to fit data from different societies into some grand scheme. This *historical particularism*, as it is sometimes known, combined Durkheim's emphasis on the social with Malinowski's stress on individual psychology. Both material culture and personality define a characteristic cultural style unique to each society. Boas was not particularly interested in the social functioning of institutions, which developed into a major theme of British social anthropology under Radcliffe-Brown in the United Kingdom. Like Durkheim, Boas had an interest in *totemic* systems, and the way in which symbols linked religious activities with other aspects of social life.

Alfred Reginald Radcliffe-Brown (1881–1955) was one of the first British social anthropologists to engage in fieldwork. At Cambridge University Radcliffe-Brown studied psychology under W. H. R. Rivers (1864–1922) who had taken part in the *Torres Straits Expedition* of 1898 with another founding figure of Cambridge anthropology, Alfred C. Haddon. From 1906 to 1908 Radcliffe-Brown carried out research in the Andaman Islands in the Bay of Bengal.[17] The resulting monograph, *The Andaman Islanders* (1922), is primarily an account of Andamanese religious beliefs and ceremonies, and therefore represents one of the first fieldwork monographs in the anthropology of religion. Radcliffe-Brown held academic posts in many parts of the world, including Australia, South Africa, Egypt, Brazil, the United States (Chicago), and England (Manchester and Oxford). He was a gifted teacher and influential in propagating what is sometimes described as the British school of functionalist anthropology.

The Andamanese were "tribal" hunter-gatherers (that is, they were neither Hindus or Muslims, nor part of the Hindu caste system), who had been relatively isolated until a penal settlement was established on South Andaman Island in 1858 (Tomas, 1991, p. 77). They were therefore held up as representatives of "racial purity," and their society as a kind of living fossil that could reveal something about the origins of religion and of human culture. Radcliffe-Brown asserted that the Andaman Islanders' main supernatural beings were spirits of the dead, associated with the sky, forest, and sea, and nature spirits, which were thought of as personifications of natural phenomena. He applied a Durkheimian analysis to his Andaman material, looking for correlations between Andamanese religion and social structure. Although he is usually referred to as a functionalist (because of his interest in the ways in which institutions presented an organic picture of society),

Radcliffe-Brown's method also anticipated the type of structural analysis pioneered by Lévi-Strauss. He divided Andamanese cosmology into a tripartite schema – sea/water, forest/land, and sky/trees – with spiritual agencies, dietary restrictions, ceremonies, subsistence activities, flora, and fauna all corresponding to one of these three categories.

Arthur Maurice Hocart (1883–1939) was an Oxford-educated anthropologist who carried out extensive fieldwork in the South Seas. He adopted Boas's detailed fieldwork methods, while continuing to hold a basically evolutionary perspective. He was not interested in finding the origin of religion, as he regarded it as an impossibility, although he did concern himself with the origins of monotheism. Hocart also rejected Malinowski's individual psychological approach, favoring a more Durkheimian social view of religion. According to Hocart (1973, p. 67), "the facts are that our earliest records show us man worshipping gods, and their earthly representatives – namely kings." This led him to a rather contemporary conclusion (developed by Maurice Bloch, for instance, in his work on Madagascar), namely that:

> religion and politics are inseparable, and it is vain to try to divorce them. . . . Monarchists must necessarily uphold the Church and ardent believers in one God will help build up large nations. The belief in a Supreme God or a Single God is no mere philosophical speculation; it is a great practical idea. (Hocart, 1973, p. 76)

The solution to the origins of religion and society proposed by Lévi-Strauss is of a totally different nature. Lévi-Strauss has been unswerving in his search for the universal structures of human thought and social life. Taking his cue from structural linguistics, in particular the work of Noam Chomsky and Ferdinand Saussure, together with the Russian formalists, such as Vladimir Propp, who collected fairy tale motifs, Lévi-Strauss has sought to reveal a grammar of the mind, a kind of universal psychology with a genetic base, which gives rise to social structures. Just as there are limits to linguistic variation, so there are certain basic innate patterns of culture based on a series of binary oppositions. Thus, all societies distinguish between the raw and the cooked, the raw standing for nature (and women) and the cooked for culture (and men). Myths reveal common story lines that can be used to understand the limited number of ways in which human beings interpret the world.[18]

Claude Lévi-Strauss (1908–) was born in Belgium, but has spent most of his working life in France. He is one of the founders of *structuralism*, an intellectual movement derived from linguistic theory that focuses on the structures of societies, texts, languages, and cultural life. The interrelations between elements in the present are stressed, at the expense of historical change. Apart from a couple of brief excursions in the Amazonian regions of Brazil, Lévi-Strauss has not been a fieldwork anthropologist. Lévi-Strauss's interest in and knowledge of South America is, however, considerable, and his four-volume series *Mythologiques*, in English translation *Introduction to a Science of Mythology* (1970–81), draws on this material. His other major works include a personal account of his journeys in Amazonia, *Triste Tropiques* (originally published in 1955), *Totemism*, a discussion of human symbolic thought (originally published in 1962), and a series of influential essays, *The Savage Mind* (originally published in 1962).

While structural theory was popular in Britain for a period in the 1960s and 1970s, its influence within anglophone social and cultural anthropology has been less marked than the Durkheimian symbolist approach. As with the earlier search for universals, the innate structures proposed by Lévi-Strauss remain speculative and (like Frazer's *Golden Bough*) there is a danger of simply amassing data that repeat an argument without actually strengthening it. For Lévi-Strauss, individual experience and emotions such as love, hate, fear, and desire are subsidiary to the basic underlying structures that give rise to society, which have a biological basis. Many critics have in the end found that such an approach leaves too many important questions unanswered.[19] We may unravel the structures of the mind and of society, but do we know what it is to live and feel as a human being? If history and agency take a back seat, can we see ourselves as self-determining individuals and can we understand the complexity of interactions between humans and their physical and social environment?

We have surveyed a number of approaches to the study of religion without thus far attempting to define "religion" itself. In the next part of the chapter we will therefore look at some of the most widely quoted definitions of religion, although the reader may conclude that they are so vague or contradictory that the attempt has limited utility.

Defining Religion

Whatever religion may or may not be, there was no shortage of Victorian explorers, traders, and missionaries who could declare with confidence that "savages" did not have it. A famous explorer, Sir Samuel Baker, addressed the Ethnological Society of London in 1866 on the topic of the Northern Nilotic peoples of Africa, stating that: "Without any exception, they are without a belief in a Supreme Being, neither have they any form of worship or idolatry;

nor is the darkness of their minds enlightened by even a ray of superstition. The mind is as stagnant as the morass which forms its puny world."[20]

Henry Drummond, a widely traveled Evangelical Christian, attempted to combine evolutionary theory with more charitable and romanticized sentiments in his view of "primitives." In Rousseauesque terms, Drummond (1894) states that "here in his virgin simplicity dwells primeval man, without clothes, without civilization, without learning, without religion – the genuine child of nature, thoughtless, careless and contented. This man is apparently quite happy; he has practically no wants."[21] Such gross and obvious mistakes depended on an ignorance of the lives and languages of the peoples under discussion. European observers (as with all travelers) looked for points of contact with their own culture, and often failed to recognize what we might wish to term "religion" when it presented itself in unfamiliar guises.[22] Even when Europeans and Africans, or other "natives," spoke the same language (such as a Pidgin English), this was no guarantee that the meanings attached to words corresponded. As Evans-Pritchard (1972, p. 7) observed:

> Statements about a people's religious beliefs must always be treated with the greatest caution, for we are then dealing with what neither European nor native can directly observe, with conceptions, images, words, which require for understanding a thorough knowledge of a people's language and also an awareness of the entire system of ideas of which any particular belief is part, for it may be meaningless when divorced from the set of beliefs and practices to which it belongs.

Friedrich Max Müller (1823–1900), a German philologist, who spent most of his academic life in Oxford, is regarded as one of the founding fathers of comparative religion. Müller, in his *Introduction to the Science of Religion* (1873), argued that belief in a divine being was universal, and that however childish or primitive a religion might appear, it still served to place the human soul in the presence of God. Müller predicted that the truths present in all religions would one day give rise to a new form of religion, which might still be called Christianity, that would preserve the best of each revelation of the divine.

Definitions

When we come to look at various definitions of religion, we need to remember that we are constructing a category ("religion") based upon European languages and cultures, and that the term has no necessary equivalent in other parts of the world. At best we are therefore looking at a clumsy process of translation – translation of other peoples' languages and cultures into categories that Westerners can understand and interpret in terms of their own experience.[23]

> The word **"religion"** in Western European languages probably derives from the Vulgate, the Latin translation of the Bible from Hebrew and Greek attributed to Saint Jerome (c. 345–420). The Greek term *threskeia* was translated with the Latin *religio*. Latin-speaking church fathers, unlike their Greek counterparts, spoke of "true" versus "false" religion (Pieris, 1988).

Tylor (1958, p. 8) argued that a minimum definition of religion was "the belief in Spiritual Beings." In one form or another this definition, with various embellishments, has proved remarkably durable, despite the fact that it begs the question, "what are Spiritual Beings?" For Tylor, religion is an attempt by human beings *to make sense of their experiences* and of the world in which they live (sometimes called an *intellectualist* approach to religion).

A rather different but equally influential definition of religion is given by contemporary American anthropologist Clifford Geertz, who is often seen as a representative of the *symbolist* approach to religion, with its focus on *what religions represent*. Symbolists look at the ways in which symbols and rituals act as metaphors for social life, rather than at what religions seek to explain.

> For Clifford Geertz religion is:
>
> (1) a system of symbols which acts to (2) establish powerful, pervasive, and long-lasting moods and motivations in men by (3) formulating conceptions of a general order of existence and (4) clothing these conceptions with such an aura of factuality that (5) the moods and motivations seem uniquely realistic. (Geertz, 1973, p. 4)

Also in the symbolist camp is Melford Spiro, who, in a long article on problems of definition, defined religion as "an institution consisting of culturally patterned interaction with culturally postulated superhuman beings" (Spiro, 1973, p. 96).

One of the most vociferous critics of symbolist definitions of religion is Robin Horton, who claims that:

> defining religion as structural symbolism comes to much the same thing as defining the substance of "linen" in terms of its occasional use as a flag: the

symbolic function is as incidental to the nature of the first as it is to the second. (Horton, 1994, p. 23)

Horton's own definition of religion is "an extension of the field of people's social relationships beyond the confines of purely human society," in which human beings see themselves as being in a dependent relationship vis-à-vis their "non-human alters." The qualification is necessary to exclude relationships with domestic animals from the definition – after all, every time someone feeds the cat or walks the dog he or she is involved in social relationships "beyond the confines of purely human society" (Horton, 1994, pp. 31–2). While Horton identifies himself with the intellectualist position associated with Tylor, his definition also contains Durkheimian elements in its view of religion as an extension of social relationships, i.e. its approach is *inductive* rather than *deductive*, starting from human beings and their experience, rather than looking down from the position of God. For Horton, who has spent most of his academic life living and working in Africa, symbolist interpretations betray the ethos of Western universities: "The reality of spirits is apt to fade, to be replaced by visions of people engaging in elaborately veiled power-plays, composing secular poetry, or participating in complicated semiological parlour games" (Horton, 1994, p. 386).

Leaving aside for the present the intellectualist/symbolist debate, Arthur Lehmann and James Myers have proposed an extended version of Tylor's and Spiro's definitions that in practice covers most of what anthropologists might wish to include in a book such as this on the anthropology of religion:

> Expanding the definition of religion beyond spiritual and superhuman beings to include the extraordinary, the mysterious, and unexplainable allows a more comprehensive view of religious behaviors among the peoples of the world and permits the anthropological investigation of phenomena such as magic, sorcery, curses, and other practices that hold meaning for both preliterate and literate societies. (Lehmann and Myers, 1997, p. 3)

An influential definitional approach to religion from within religious studies is Ninian Smart's analysis of religion according to various "dimensions." These too are intended to apply to all religions, and can be seen as a reminder to theologians and historians of religion not to forget the practical, aesthetic, and emotional aspects of religion in their concentration on scriptures and doctrinal formulae. Too often what are taken as authentic or correct forms of religion are the representations of priestly elites, interested in what their religion *ought* to be, rather than how it is actually lived by the majority of its adherents. Smart's dimensions have gone through several incarnations over the years, and have reached their most developed form to date in *Dimensions of the Sacred*. To his most widely cited "seven dimensions" Smart has added an eighth, the political and economic, giving us the following list (Smart, 1996, pp. 10–11):

1   Ritual or practical.
2   Doctrinal or philosophical.
3   Mythic or narrative.
4   Experiential or emotional.
5   Ethical or legal.
6   Organizational or social.
7   Material or artistic.
8   Political and economic.

Smart's dimensional approach is within the comparative, phenomenological tradition, looking for points of similarity and contact between the world's religions, rather than the more traditional anthropological focus on the social nature of religion within a specific host community or sub-group. Where most anthropologists would agree with Smart is on the utility of regarding religion as a multifaceted phenomenon with overlapping spheres, rather than a single "thing" that can be readily identified and studied in isolation. Religions differ in their emphasis on these dimensions, as do groups within a single religious faith. The doctrinal and legal aspects of Islam and Judaism, for instance, are well developed, whereas societies without written scriptures are more likely to emphasize the role of myths, perhaps enacted in dance or through "shamanic" trancing. Within Christianity some branches of Protestantism place great emphasis on personal experience and emotion, whereas Orthodoxy and Roman Catholicism are more focused on liturgy and ritual, and have in many places a highly developed material and artistic dimension (churches, icons, vestments, music, and so on).

Some of these descriptions of religion, such as Smart's, are just that – attempts to categorize and classify religion without really addressing the question as to just what it is we are looking at. Other definitions are dependent on a view as to what function religion serves, or relate to ideas concerning the genesis of religion. In this final sub-section we will look at attempts to categorize various religions, and at some problems with these categories.

Categories

When nineteenth-century scholars turned their attention to the study of religion they not unnaturally used their own experience as a base for comparison. The most enduring division that arose was between the so-called "world religions" and the others. Whatever a world religion might be, the religion of "primitives" or "savages" must be different, its mirror image. World religions themselves were divided into "higher" and "lower" forms depending on their perceived similarity to or difference from the main three Semitic religions, Judaism, Christianity, and Islam. The view of each religion was largely based on its elite or doctrinal and scriptural forms, rather than its more popular "folk" manifestations. While the racist and hierarchical over-tones of such thinking are no longer considered acceptable, the original classifications have proved remarkably enduring, particularly within the fields of theology and religious studies.

The supposed features of a "world" religion

1   It is based on written scriptures.
2   It has a notion of salvation, often from outside (a "coming deliverer").
3   It is universal, or has universal potential.
4   It can subsume or supplant a "primal" religion.
5   It often forms a separate sphere of activity.

By way of contrast, "primal" religions are often seen as a mirror image of the world religions.

The supposed features of "primal" religions

1   They are oral – if the culture is literate, the religion lacks written scriptures and formal creeds.
2   They are "this-worldly" in orientation.
3   They are confined to a single language or ethnic group.
4   They form the bases from which world religions have developed.
5   Religion and social life are inseparable and intertwined, and there is no clear division between the "sacred" and "profane" or natural and supernatural.

These categorizations are not without utility, or they would not have survived so long. They do, however, as numerous scholars have pointed out, beg many questions, and are at best intellectual constructs rather than descriptions of reality. To take the world religions first, to what extent can Taoism or Confucianism be considered to have universal potential? They are both commonly referred to as world religions, but are largely confined to

South East Asia. Confucianism is as inseparable from Chinese notions of social order as the concept of *dharma* ("law") is from the Hindu caste system. The Vedic (scriptural and priestly) elements of Hinduism are indeed only one strand, and most "village" Hinduism would more closely fit the description of a primal religion. To what extent can Judaism, with its notion of membership via descent in the female line, really be seen as a universal religion? Islam places great emphasis on the sanctity and authority of the holy Qur'an, but the scriptures were originally *recited* to Muhammad, and the recitation of the Qur'an from memory in Arabic remains central to Islamic worship. Most fervent practitioners of "religions of the book" claim that religion penetrates all aspects of their lives – there is no experience or part of the day that does not come under its jurisdiction.

What, apart from the rather arbitrary list of elements (which derive mainly from Western Christianity), do these world religions have in common? Is there any descriptive utility in ranging the Semitic and Asian religions on the one hand against the world's "tribal" religions on the other? Many African religious cults, for example, have crossed linguistic and ethnic boundaries.[24] There is always a relationship between religion and other aspects of culture, but among both "primal" and "world" religions we find several cultures sharing one religion as well as several religions within one culture.[25] David Turner has argued that Aboriginal Australian religions could equally well be classified as world religions in the sense that their method of relating to the world is "applicable to all times and places and all peoples independently of inherited membership in a defined kinship or ethnic group" (Turner, 1996, p. 80).

The past few decades have seen a rapid growth in the number of Americans and Western Europeans calling themselves Pagans – usually drawing on indigenous small-scale societies (particularly Native American), Eastern religions, and pre-Christian European traditions in an eclectic mix. The oral and local are emphasized over the written and the universal (or abstract) – but here we have forms of religious belief and practice defying classification according to the schemes outlined above. Contemporary Western Paganism crosses cultures and languages, but usually emphasizes the importance of locality and of "spirits of place," as in primal religions. Paganism attracts former Jews and Christians, as well as those without foundations in another faith, a characteristic usually associated with world religions. Aloysius Pieris has argued persuasively that:

> mass conversions from one soteriology to another [e.g. from Christianity to Islam] are rare, if not impossible, except under military pressure. But a change-over from a tribal religion to a metacosmic [world] soteriology is a spontaneous process in which the former, without sacrificing its own character, provides a popular base for the latter. (Pieris, 1988, p. 99)

With contemporary Western Paganism, however, there is a reverse trend. Perhaps the numbers involved at present hardly qualify for the term "mass conversion," but we do see a process in which substantial numbers of people are rejecting metacosmic religions that offer a notion of final salvation (a soteriology), turning instead, not to materialism and scientific explanations of existence, as both Frazer and Malinowski would have assumed, but to a pantheistic, magical view of the world.

James Mackey, a Christian theologian, complains of the "silliness of anthropology" in seeking at times to "draw clear lines between animism or magic and religion" (Mackey, 1996, p. 9). The implication is that anthropologists should have known better, but whatever position people start from they feel impelled to classify, define, exclude, and label human experience. Mackey quotes Ludwig Feuerbach's dictum that "what today is atheism tomorrow will be called religion,"[26] and makes a plea for a much more fluid and less dogmatic approach to definitions of religion, arguing that:

> Of course people who have somehow pre-defined the nature of divinity, and more particularly those who treat the notes of immanence and transcendence in relation to a divine dimension as contraries instead of what they always are in fact, namely, coordinates, can also appear to specify with great accuracy what is to count as religion, as a truly religious dimension of life and knowledge, and what is not. It is interesting to note that this alleged ability is so often shared by those who are most dogmatic about religion and those who, allegedly on scientific grounds, are most dismissive of it. (Mackey, 1996, pp. 8–9)

While definitions, categories and theories of origin have all influenced what anthropologists have studied and how they have interpreted what they found, I am not primarily concerned with such questions in the chapters that follow. This is not due to a lack of respect for analytical rigor, but stems from a recognition that religion as a category is fluid and contextual, and that any attempt to define the subject matter too narrowly risks giving a positivist stamp to what in fact is an interpretative process.

Conclusion

Anthropologists do not start their theorizing *de nuovo*, from scratch, but build on and react to the work of their predecessors. In the following chapters we will see how contemporary anthropologists develop their understanding of religion through a dialogue between earlier anthropological ideas and methods and contemporary culture. The various themes dealt with in each chapter are chosen for their relevance not just to the anthropology of religion, but also to related disciplines, in particular religious studies. The examples used to illustrate each theme are not exactly chosen at random, but numerous alternative possibilities could equally have been selected. My own Christian upbringing, my anthropological education, and the experience of doing fieldwork in Africa have all no doubt influenced the tenor and subject matter of the book. Equally important, however, have been the interests of students and colleagues, and the availability of material. My hope is that readers will find this introduction to the anthropology of religion sufficiently stimulating to continue their own explorations and reach their own conclusions regarding a fascinating and central area of human experience.

Notes

1 Quoted in Urry (1993, p. 12).
2 Secular and religious authority often merged, as indicated by the title "Holy Roman Emperor" given to the successors of Charlemagne (c.742–814) and the assumption of political power by the papacy.
3 There are numerous excellent works available on the history of Victorian anthropology and on the historical development of anthropological theories (see the References and Further Reading list at the end of this chapter), so here I attempt to do no more than give the reader some brief pointers.
4 Compare Sharpe (1998, pp. 222–3).
5 The term "methodological agnosticism" was coined by the religious studies scholar Ninian Smart in order to distinguish it from sociologist Peter Berger's "methodological atheism." I am indebted to Gavin Flood for drawing my attention to this distinction.
6 See Bowie (1999). The debate on inculturation may include a more explicitly nationalist agenda. See, for instance, Paul Gifford's (1998, pp. 259–62) discussion of Bishop Nkuissi in the Cameroonian diocese of Nkongsamba.
7 A phenomenological or scientific stance has been challenged by theologians and philosophers as well as by anthropologists. The philosopher of religion Roger Trigg, for example, has argued that a focus on the social dimensions of religion "does violence to important features of religion," as it "appears to ignore the claim that religious beliefs can themselves be held on rational grounds and hence have a right claim to truth" (Trigg, 1998, p. 29).
8 Van der Leeuw acknowledged his debt to Lucien Lévy-Bruhl, despite the tensions between an evolutionary and phenomenological stance. Van der Leeuw also remained primarily a Christian theologian for whom phenomenology was a tool that could aid theological speculation. For the anthropologist of religion, the main interest in van der Leeuw's work lies in his attempt to combine description with psychological insights, emotion, experience, and the creation

of meaning. He was not a fieldworker, but these issues lie at the heart of ethno-graphic practice and of debates on how to understand and represent other people's experience. In "Confession Scientifique" (*Numen*, I, 1954, p. 10), for instance, van de Leeuw wrote that the phenomenology of religion "consisted not merely in making an inventory and classification of phenomena as they appear in history, but also a psychological description which necessitated not only a meticulous observation of the religious reality, but also a systematic introspection; not only the description of what is visible from outside, but above all the experience born of what can only become reality after it has been admitted into the life of the observer himself" (cited in Sharpe, 1998, p. 231).

9   For a description of the history of the use of phenomenology in religious studies and a critique of it, see Sharpe (1998, pp. 220–50), Erricker (1999), and Flood (1999). James Cox (1992) provides a clear account of the phenomenological method as applied to the study of religion, using Maurice Merleau-Ponty (1908–61) to introduce a rather more nuanced notion of the interaction of the observer with the phenomenon observed. An account of several phenomenological thinkers, including Malinowski and Eliade, can be found in Bettis (1969).

10 For a critique of Stoller and Olkes see Geschiere (1997, p. 281) and Oliver de Sardin (1988).

11 Pierre Bourdieu outlines three stages in the transformation of empirical experience to anthropological theory. First, we have the rules and theories of the people being studied. At the next level there are the rules and theories of the ethnographer, and, third, the rules and methods governing the discipline as a whole (even if these do not form a single pattern of ideas) (Bourdieu, 1977, pp. 3–9). While many anthropolo-gists may succeed in keeping these three levels conceptually distinct, others may find the boundaries becoming confused, which can lead to a sense of disorientation. At one extreme the anthropologist may "go native" and abandon any attempt to maintain his or her previous assumptions and values, while at the other extreme the fieldworker may withdraw, physically or psychologically, or erect barriers around each discourse to maintain his or her separateness. Most, however, accept the uneasy challenge of moving between the worlds of informants, the academy, and the self, perhaps consciously using the self as an ethnographic tool.

12 Those who attempt to bridge this gap often write under a pseudonym, such as Laura Bohannan, who adopted the *nom de plume* Eleanor Smith Bowen in her personal account of life with the Tiv in northern Nigeria (1954). Those who do stick their head above the parapet risk having it knocked off, being dismissed as popularists, a fate that befell Nigel Barley's immensely successful (outside aca-demia) stories of fieldwork among the Dowayo of Cameroon (1983, 1986).

13 Compare Parkin (1982), Clifford and Marcus (1986), Bowie (1998), and Flood (1999) on reflexive trends in anthropology and religious studies.

14 The anthropological subjects may be one intended audience of the academic monograph, but no commercial publisher would accept a manuscript written *primarily* for a limited, specialist group of readers (except an academic one – with guaranteed library sales).

15   Women and others in a structurally weak position commonly resort to claims of divine inspiration in order to pass on their message without directly challenging those in authority (which is not to deny the truths of these claims). A classic example of this is the German medieval abbess, Hildegard of Bingen, who, although extraordinarily talented and influential, nevertheless insisted that she was but a "feather on the breath of God" and that her writing came from the "living light" rather than her own creative mind (see Bowie and Davies, 1990).

16   The distinction between religion and magic is often less clear-cut in practice than Malinowski's distinction would suggest. Is a rain dance an efficacious magical act, or implication of a deity to act on behalf of those making the request? Most magical acts involve the action of an intermediary power between the performer of the rite and its intended result. The words of consecration used by a Roman Catholic priest during the Mass can be seen as an end in themselves – making Christ present in the Eucharistic bread and wine.

17   David Tomas (1991) gives an interesting account of the colonial background to the administration of the Andaman Islands prior to and during Radcliffe-Brown's fieldwork, and of attempts by the British to "tame" the "primitive and savage" tribal peoples in this remote corner of the Empire.

18   According to Lévi-Strauss motifs in myths or folk tales recur and the elements within them are transformed in a limited number of fairly predictable ways. A myth is not defined by a single, original, or correct version, but by the sum of its many variations and transformations.

19   In *The Naturalness of Religious Ideas* (1994), Pascal Boyer argues that there are cognitive (genetic) constraints on the cultural acquisition and transformation of religion. This accounts for the recurrence of universal themes in religious beliefs and practices (in a way similar to Chomsky's innate grammar and Lévi-Strauss's universal mythic themes). For Boyer, "culture" as a concept is too vague and relativistic to account for religious transmission. We are predisposed to accept certain concepts and to ignore others. Mimesis (imitation) alone cannot account for the continuity of religious practices. Boyer admits that his cognitive approach ignores most features of religion that human subjects actually find interesting or important (such as emotions and experience, power and the operation of political relations, and aesthetics). Maurice Bloch (1998) also argues that culture and cognition need to be separated, and that because anthropologists tend to focus on the explicit and the unusual, cultural variation is often exaggerated. For Bloch, everyday knowledge is implicit or "inexplicit," and therefore anthropology cannot afford to ignore the work of cognitive psychologists when trying to give an account of human societies. Boyer and Bloch, in their views on religion and cognition, represent the experience-far or etic end of the spectrum, although Bloch also argues passionately for the value of participant observation.

20   Baker (1867), quoted in Evans-Pritchard (1972, p. 7). This statement is particularly ironic, as the subsequent fieldwork of Evans-Pritchard (1974) among the Nuer and Godfrey Lienhardt (1978) among the Dinka – both Sudanese Nilotic

peoples – depict rather pious peoples whose devotions center on a Supreme Being (known as *kwoth* and *nhialic* respectively).

21 Cited in Jahoda (1999, p. 142), who is in turn citing Cairns (1965, p. 94).

22 Tylor was responsible for the questions on religion in the 1874 edition of *Notes and Queries* – which became a standard manual for aspiring fieldworkers. He urged detailed and careful observation, with prefaces that were "clearly intended to counteract the effects of monotheistic ethnocentrism – to enable observers reared in the Christian tradition to recognize animistic religion where otherwise they might simply have reported some form of degenerate 'devil worship,' or even that their particular 'savage' group had no religion at all" (Stocking 1996, p. 15). Jahoda (1999, p. 227) points out that some Victorian descriptions of the Irish and Highland Scots as primitive savages resembled accounts of African and other non-Western "primitive" peoples. Although color and race were (and remain) important elements in defining the "other," poverty, the use of a minority language, remoteness from urban centers, and a lack of English manners were sufficient to earn the appellation "savage." See Smith (1999) for a perspective from "colonized" peoples.

23 Pieris (1988, p. 90) claims that "None of the Asian soteriologies [from the Greek *soter*, 'savior'] . . . has offered us a comprehensive word for, or a clear concept of, religion in the current Western sense."

24 See Shaw (1990) and Cox (1996).

25 See Pieris (1988, p. 97). This really just begs the same definitional questions. What is a religion? What is a culture? Who has the power to classify a religion? There has been considerable debate in Africa, for instance, as to whether African Independent Churches and various African new religious movements should be considered Christian or not. As religions always change and develop, drawing on different elements at different times, we are left with a shifting field of contested definitions.

26 Feuerbach (1957, p. 32), cited in Mackey (1996, p. 9).

References and Further Reading

Barfield, Thomas (ed.) (1997) *The Dictionary of Anthropology*. Oxford: Blackwell.

Barley, Nigel (1983) *The Innocent Anthropologist: Notes from a Mud Hut*. London: Colonnade Books, British Museum Publications.

Barley, Nigel (1986) *A Plague of Caterpillars: a Return to the African Bush*. London: Viking.

Bettis, Joseph D. (ed.) (1969) *Phenomenology of Religion: Eight Modern Descriptions of the Essence of Religion*. London: SCM.

Bloch, Maurice E. F. (1985) *From Blessing to Violence: History as Ideology in the Circumcision Ritual of the Merina of Madagascar*. Cambridge: Cambridge University Press.

Bloch, Maurice E. F. (1998) *How We Think They Think: Anthropological Approaches to Cognition, Memory and Literacy*. Boulder, CO, and Oxford: Westview Press.

Bourdieu, Pierre (1977) *Outline of a Theory of Practice*. Cambridge: Cambridge University Press.

Bowen, Eleanor Smith (1954) *Return to Laughter*. New York: Harper and Row.

Bowie, Fiona (1998) Trespassing on sacred domains: a feminist anthropological approach to theology and religious studies. *Journal of Feminist Studies in Religion*, 14(1), 40–62.

Bowie, Fiona (1999) The inculturation debate in Africa. *Studies in World Christianity*, 5(1), 67–92.

Bowie, Fiona and Davies, Oliver (1990) *Hildegard of Bingen: an Anthology*. London: SPCK; New York: Crossroad.

Boyer, Pascal (1994) *The Naturalness of Religious Ideas: a Cognitive Theory of Religion*. Berkeley: University of California Press.

Cairns, H. A. C. (1965) *Prelude to Imperialism*. London: Routledge and Kegan Paul.

Clifford, James and Marcus, George E. (eds) (1986) *Writing Culture: the Poetics and Politics of Ethnography*. Berkeley: University of California Press.

Cox, James L. (1992) *Expressing the Sacred: an Introduction to the Phenomenology of Religion*. Harare: University of Zimbabwe Publications.

Cox, James L. (1996) The classification of "primal religions" as a non-empirical Christian theological construct. *Studies in World Christianity*, 2(1), 55–76.

Cunningham, Graham (1999) *Religion and Magic: Approaches and Theories*. Edinburgh: Edinburgh University Press.

Darwin, Charles (1897) *The Descent of Man, and Selection in Relation to Sex*. London: Murray.

Davis, John (ed.) (1982) *Religious Organization and Religious Experience*. ASA Monograph 21. London and New York: Academic Press.

Drummond, Henry (1894) *The Lowell Lectures on the Ascent of Man*. New York: Pott.

Durkheim, Émile (1976) *The Elementary Forms of the Religious Life*. London: George Allen & Unwin (originally published 1915).

Erickson, Paul A. and Murphy, Liam D. (2001) *Readings for a History of Anthropological Theory*. Ontario and New York: Broadview Press.

Erricker, Clive (1999) Phenomenological approaches. In Peter Connolly (ed.), *Approaches to the Study of Religion*. London and New York: Cassell, pp. 73–104.

Evans-Pritchard, E. E. (1972) *Theories of Primitive Religion*. Oxford: Oxford University Press (originally published 1965).

Evans-Pritchard, E. E. (1974) *Nuer Religion*. Oxford: Oxford University Press (originally published 1956).

Evans-Pritchard, E. E. (1976) *Witchcraft, Oracles and Magic among the Azande*. Abridged with an introduction by Eva Gillies. Oxford: Clarendon Press (originally published 1937).

Evans-Pritchard, E. E. (1981) *A History of Anthropological Thought*. London: Faber.

Favret-Saada, Jeanne (1980) *Deadly Words: Witchcraft in the Bocage*. Cambridge: Cambridge University Press; Paris: Editions de la Maison des Sciences de l'Homme.

Feuerbach, Ludwig (1957) *The Essence of Christianity*. New York: Prometheus Books.

Flood, Gavin (1999) *Beyond Phenomenology: Rethinking the Study of Religion*. London: Cassell.

Frazer, James (1890) *The Golden Bough: a Study in Comparative Religion*, 2 volumes. London: Macmillan.

Geertz, Clifford (1973) Religion as a cultural system. In Michael Banton (ed.), *Anthropological Approaches to the Study of Religion*. ASA Monographs 3. London: Tavistock, pp. 1–46 (originally published 1966; reprinted in C. Geertz (1993), *The Interpretation of Cultures*. London: Fontana, pp. 87–125).

Gellner, David (1999) Anthropological approaches. In Peter Connolly (ed.), *Approaches to the Study of Religion*. London and New York: Cassell, pp. 10–41.

Geschiere, Peter (1997) *The Modernity of Witchcraft: Politics and the Occult in Post-colonial Africa*, translated by Peter Geschiere and Janet Roitman. Charlottesville and London: University of Virginia Press.

Gifford, Paul (1998) *African Christianity: Its Public Role*. London: Hurst and Company.

Guthrie, Stewart Elliott (1997) The origin of an illusion. In Stephen D. Glazier (ed.), *Anthropology of Religion: a Handbook*. Westport, CT: Greenwood Press, pp. 489–504.

Hocart, A. M. (1973) *The Life-giving Myth and Other Essays*. London: Tavistock/Methuen (originally published 1952).

Horton, Robin (1994) *Patterns of Thought in Africa and the West*. Cambridge: Cambridge University Press.

Jahoda, Gustav (1999) *Images of Savages: Ancient Roots of Modern Prejudice in Western Culture*. London: Routledge.

Jakobsen, Merete Demant (1999) *Shamanism: Traditional and Contemporary Approaches to the Mastery of Spirits and Healing*. Oxford: Berghahn.

Kearney, Michael (1992) A very bad disease of the arms. In Philip R. DeVita (ed.), *The Naked Anthropologist: Tales from Around the World*. Belmont, CA: Wadsworth, pp. 47–57.

Kuklick, Henrika (1993) *The Savage Within: the History of British Anthropology, 1885–1945*. Cambridge: Cambridge University Press.

Kuper, Adam (1988) *The Invention of Primitive Society: Transformations of an Illusion*. London and New York: Routledge.

Lehmann, Arthur C. and Myers, James E. (eds) (1997) *Magic, Witchcraft and Religion: an Anthropological Study of the Supernatural*, 4th edn. Mountain View, CA: Mayfield Publishing Co.

Lett, James (1997a) Science, religion and anthropology. In Stephen D. Glazier (ed.), *Anthropology of Religion: a Handbook*. Westport, CT: Greenwood Press, pp. 103–20.

Lett, James (1997b) *Science, Reason and Anthropology: the Principles of Rational Inquiry*. Lanham, MD and Oxford: Rowman and Littlefield.

Lévi-Strauss, Claude (1969) *The Elementary Structures of Kinship*. London: Eyre and Spottiswoode (originally published 1949).

Lévi-Strauss, Claude (1970) *The Raw and the Cooked. Introduction to a Science of Mythology, volume 1*. London: Jonathan Cape.

Lévi-Strauss, Claude (1973a) *Tristes Tropiques*. London: Jonathan Cape (originally published 1955).

Lévi-Strauss, Claude (1973b) *Totemism*. Harmondsworth: Penguin (originally published 1962).

Lévi-Strauss, Claude (1975): *From Honey to Ashes. Introduction to a Science of Mythology, volume 2*. London: Jonathan Cape.

Lévi-Strauss, Claude (1976) *The Savage Mind*. London: Weidenfeld and Nicolson (originally published 1962).

Lévi-Strauss, Claude (1977a) *Structural Anthropology*. Harmondsworth: Penguin (originally published 1958).

Lévi-Strauss, Claude (1977) *Structural Anthropology, volume II*. London: Allen Lane.

Lévi-Strauss, Claude (1978) *The Origin of Table Manners. Introduction to a Science of Mythology, volume 3*. London: Jonathan Cape.

Lévi-Strauss, Claude (1981) *The Naked Man. Introduction to a Science of Mythology, volume 4*. London: Jonathan Cape.

Lienhardt, Godfrey (1978) *Divinity and Experience*. Oxford: Clarendon Press (originally published 1961).

Luhrmann, Tanya (1989) *Persuasions of the Witch's Craft*. Oxford: Basil Blackwell.

Mackey, James P. (1996) Christianity and cultures: theology, science and the science of religion. *Studies in World Christianity*, 2(1), 1–25.

Malinowski, Bronislaw (1923) The unity of anthropology. [Review of P. Hinneberg (ed.), *Die Kultur der Gegenwart*.] *Nature*, 112, 314–17.

Malinowski, Bronislaw (1974) *Magic, Science and Religion and Other Essays*. London: Souvenir Press (originally published 1948).

McGee, R. Jon and Warms, Richard L. (2004) *Anthropological Theory: an Introductory History*, 3rd edn. Boston: McGraw Hill.

Morris, Brian (1987) *Anthropological Studies of Religion: an Introductory Text*. Cambridge: Cambridge University Press.

Müller, F. Max (1978) *Introduction to the Science of Religion*. New York: Arno Press (originally published 1873).

Oliver de Sardan, Jean-Pierre (1998) Jeu de la croyance et "je" ethnologique: exotisme religieux et ethno-centrisme. *Cahiers des études africaines*, 28(3/4), 527–40.

Parkin, David (1982) Introduction. In David Parkin (ed.), *Semantic Anthropology*. ASA Monograph 22. London and New York: Academic Press, pp. xi–li.

Pieris, Aloysius SJ (1988) *An Asian Theology of Liberation*. Edinburgh: T & T Clark.

Radcliffe-Brown, Alfred Reginald (1922) *The Andaman Islanders: a Study in Social Anthropology*. Cambridge: Cambridge University Press.

Seymour-Smith, Charlotte (1986) *Macmillan Dictionary of Anthropology*. London: Macmillan.

Sharpe, Eric J. (1998) *Comparative Religion: a History*, 4th impression. London: Duckworth.

Schweder, Richard A. (1996) *Thinking through Cultures: Expeditions in Cultural Psychology*. Cambridge, MA and London: Harvard University Press.

Shaw, Rosalind (1990) The invention of African traditional religion. *Religion*, 20, 339–53.

Smart, Ninian (1996) *Dimensions of the Sacred: an Anatomy of the World's Beliefs*. London: HarperCollins.

Smith, Linda Tuhiwai (1999) *Decolonizing Methodologies: Research and Indigenous Peoples*. London and New York: Zed Books.

Spencer, Herbert (1876) *The Principles of Sociology*, 3 volumes. London: Williams & Norgate.

Spiro, Melford E. (1973) Religion: problems of definition and explanation. In Michael Banton (ed.), *Anthropological Approaches to the Study of Religion*. ASA Monographs 3. London: Tavistock, pp. 85–126.

Stevens, Phillip Jr (1996) Religion. In David Levinson and Melvin Ember (eds), *Encyclopedia of Cultural Anthropology, volume 3*. New York: Henry Hold and Company, pp. 1088–100.

Stocking, George W. Jr (1987) *Victorian Anthropology*. New York: The Free Press.

Stocking, George W. Jr (ed.) (1991) *Colonial Situations: Essays on the Contextualization of Ethnographic Knowledge*. History of Anthropology, volume 7. Madison: University of Wisconsin Press.

Stocking, George W. Jr (1996) *After Tylor: British Social Anthropology 1888–1951*. London: Athlone Press.

Stoller, Paul and Olkes, Cheryl (1989) *In Sorcery's Shadow*. Chicago and London: University of Chicago Press.

Sundkler, B. G. M. (1961) *Bantu Prophets in South Africa*. London: Oxford University Press (originally published 1948).

Thrower, James (1999) *Religion: the Classical Theories*. Edinburgh: Edinburgh University Press.

Tomas, David (1991) Tools of the trade: the production of ethnographic observations on the Andaman Islands, 1858–1922. In George W. Stocking Jr (ed.), *Colonial Situations: Essays on the Contextualization of Ethnographic Knowledge*. History of Anthropology, volume 7. Madison: University of Wisconsin Press, pp. 75–108.

Trigg, Roger (1998) *Rationality and Religion*. Oxford: Blackwell.

Turner, David H. (1996) Aboriginal religion as world religion: an assessment. *Studies in World Christianity*, 2(1), 77–96.

Tylor, Edward Burnett (1871) *Primitive Culture: Researches into the Development of Mythology, Philosophy, Religion, Art, and Custom*, 2 volumes. London: Murray.

Tylor, Edward Burnett (1958) *Religion in Primitive Culture* (reprint of volume 2 of Tylor, 1871). New York: Harper & Row.

Urry, James (1993) *Before Social Anthropology: Essays on the History of British Anthropology*. Reading, MA: Harwood Academic Publishers.

van Dijk, Rijk and Pels, Peter (1996) Contested authorities and the politics of perception: deconstructing the study of religion in Africa. In Richard Werbner and Terence Ranger (eds), *Postcolonial Identities in Africa*. London: Zed Books, pp. 245–70.

Whaling, Frank (ed.) (1983) *Contemporary Approaches to the Study of Religion*, 2 volumes. Amsterdam: Mouton.

Chapter 2

The Body as Symbol

Introduction

The German sociologist Max Weber (1864–1920) described human beings as "meaning makers." It is fundamental to all human societies to impose meaning on the environment, to order, classify, and regulate. The term *symbolic classification*, a central theme both of this chapter and in the anthropology of religion, refers to this attempt to create worlds and webs of meaning. Language is an important, but not the only, classificatory tool. Age, sex, ethnic and cultural features, health, and disability are all used as markers in the classificatory process. When we meet other human beings we immediately, if unconsciously, classify them, but how they are classified and the significance of these categories varies from one culture to another. Some people will be classed as kin (either marriageable or non-marriageable), with certain prescribed types of behavior due to them. Other people may be seen as trading or exchange partners, as patrons, teachers, people from whom services are due, as enemies, or as companions, or simply as strangers – to be either ignored or seen as potentially harmful and in need of control. Most societies have groups that are considered to be virtually outside the limits of the "human" category. These may include the "Untouchables" who are outside the Hindu caste system, Jews in Nazi Germany, even Gypsies or Travelers when viewed by the dominant house-dwelling majority. To some people, homosexual men or women, or those of a different color or religious persuasion, may be considered "beyond the pale." In cases of war and other conflicts the enemy must be "dehumanized" before they can be killed. In each instance we are dealing not with biology *per se* but with symbolic classification. It is what these categories mean or represent to us that determines our behavior toward others.

This chapter looks at different but related aspects of the relationship between symbols, religion, the body, and society. In the first section,

"Symbolic Classification and the Body," the concept of the body as a vehicle for symbolizing society is introduced through the work of Robert Hertz and Mary Douglas. A rather different conceptualization of the symbolic body is illustrated in the work of Peter Reynolds, who sees the Manhattan Project, dedicated to the production of the world's first atomic bomb, as the realization of a social myth – that of the idealized male body. In the second section, "Training the Body and Social Control," the link between culture, biology, and the symbolic is explored via the writings of Marcel Mauss and Judith Okely. The concept of *habitus* and the regulation of society by monitoring and restricting physical movement (themes also found in the work of Michel Foucault and Pierre Bourdieu), are central in Mauss's and Okely's work. The third section, "Personal and Cultural Symbols," focuses on the generation of personal symbols located in the body, and the wider cultural meanings they convey. In the world of contemporary Sri Lankan ascetics described by Gananath Obeyesekere, the rejection of sexual relations with a man can lead in some instances to culturally understood symbolic forms of female virtuosity, symbolized by matted locks. Obeyesekere argues that there is no intrinsic reason to suppose that public symbols are devoid of personal content, or that private symbols cannot also constitute part of a symbolic language that is understood by the wider society.

Symbolic Classification and the Body

In this first section we explore some of the ways in which the human body is used as a classificatory mechanism. We all have bodies but we do not necessarily speak the same language, share a dress code, practice the same (or any) religion. The commonality of our bodies makes them particularly useful tools for "saying things" about society. Both gender and politics are themes which run through virtually all discussions of religion. An anthropological approach to religion involves seeing how symbols, myths, rituals, ethics, and experiences of "the sacred" operate within, and are produced by, society. To classify someone as morally deviant, for example, is clearly an act that can have social and political repercussions. A person or group stigmatized by being denied citizenship (an illegal immigrant for example), regarded as "disordered" (perhaps because they espouse gay rights), or refusing to conform to dominant values (such as New Age Travelers) may find their access to health and welfare services, to the justice system, or to leisure facilities removed or curtailed. In these instances a classificatory act, which always stems from a particular view of the world and notions of what is "pure" and what is "polluted," can have profound implications for people's lives.

What is a symbol?

Human beings live in a symbolic world. Even the most literally minded among us constantly makes use of and recognizes symbols. Wearing a religious habit can symbolize an individual's consecration to God. A colored ribbon worn on the lapel may indicate solidarity with AIDS sufferers. A single earring may signify membership of the gay community. National pride, group membership, or support for one's team can be evoked by saluting a flag, singing an anthem, wearing a football strip, a uniform, or a particular costume.

> **Symbol:** from two Greek words, *syn*, together, and *ballein*, to throw. One thing standing for or representing another. Almost anything can be used as a symbol if custom and convention allow.

Symbols are cultural constructs and most do not have universally recognized meanings. A ring, for instance, may symbolize eternity and commitment when placed on the finger of a bride in a Western marriage ceremony. Among the Bangwa of Cameroon, however, a ring on a woman's ankle indicated that she was a slave. The Eucharistic bread and wine, symbolizing the body and blood of Christ, may be spiritual food to Christians, but has scandalized Hindus among others with its cannibalistic resonance. The meaning of a symbol, therefore, is not intrinsic; it does not emanate from it as if it were some special quality that it possessed. A symbol can only be understood when seen in relation to other symbols that form part of the same cultural complex. Sea shells may be used as ornamentation by a white Australian, but to a Trobriand Islander the same shells could symbolize a particular set of exchange relationships, a detailed history, social status, and wealth.[1] In a Western museum that same string of shells could have yet another set of associations, evoking the exotic "other," or symbolizing colonial relationships and the expropriation of one culture by another.[2]

Although rings or shells may have richly symbolic meanings in some societies while being devoid of signification in others, all peoples and cultures have one object to hand which, because of its ubiquity and malleability, carries a particularly heavy symbolic load – the human body. It is simultaneously experienced subjectively and objectively, it belongs both to the individual and to the wider social body. Above all, *we all have bodies*. As Rodney Needham put it:

> there is one specific kind of natural resemblance among men [and women] that all human beings recognise, and which permits effective comparison across the

divides of culture and language. The locus of this resemblance is provided by the human body, the one thing in nature that is internally experienced, the only object of which we have subjective knowledge. (Needham, 1972, p. 139)

Right and left

Robert Hertz was a pupil of the great French sociologist Émile Durkheim, one of a group of brilliant young scholars referred to collectively as the *Année Sociologique*, after the journal of that name founded by Durkheim. Hertz was born in 1881, and briefly held a post at the École des Hautes Études. Like so many others of his generation he died in the trenches during the First World War in 1915, depriving France of an original and creative thinker. His essay, "The pre-eminence of the right hand: A study in religious polarity," originally published in 1909, reflected Durkheim's influence in the importance accorded to the distinction between the *sacred* and the *profane*. It was Rodney Needham's translation of the essay in *Right and Left: Essays on Dual Symbolic Classification* (1973) which brought Hertz's essay to the wider attention of an English-speaking audience.

Hertz noted that a small biological asymmetry was grossly exaggerated by training, and that most societies encourage right-handedness at the expense of the left. Left-handed children may be discouraged from using their left hand (or foot). They may be punished, ridiculed, have their hand bound or otherwise restricted. It is common in many societies to eat with the right hand, and to greet someone with the right hand. The left hand may be associated with defecation, and symbolize uncleanliness.

The values and associations attributed to the right hand differ markedly from those of the left. As Hertz observed at the beginning of his essay:

> What resemblance more perfect than that between our two hands! And yet what a striking inequality there is! To the right hand go honors, flattering designations, prerogatives: it acts, orders and *takes*. The left hand, on the contrary, is despised and reduced to the role of a humble auxiliary: by itself it can do nothing: it helps, it supports, it *holds*. The right hand is the symbol and model of all aristocracies, the left hand of all plebeians. What are the titles of nobility of the right hand? And whence comes the servitude of the left? (Hertz, 1973, p. 3)

The body gives societies a cue – left-handedness is everywhere less common than the dominance of the right. It is a convenient marker on which cultures have erected an edifice of symbolic associations that are as nearly universal as any symbol can be. In any language a useful exercise is to think about, or write down, the words, phrases, and customs which have a left–right polarity. When compared cross-culturally, as Hertz demonstrated, there is a striking uniformity. One is not surprised, therefore, to learn that:

> Among the Maori the right side is the sacred side, the seat of good and creative powers; the left is the profane side, possessing no virtue other than, as we shall see, certain disturbing and suspect powers . . . the right side is the "side of life" (and of strength) while the left is the "side of death" (and of weakness). Fortunate and life-giving influences enter us from the right and through our right side; and, inversely, death and misery penetrate to the core of our being from the left. (Hertz, 1973, p. 12)

Hertz also notes that among the Maori the right side is regarded as male and sacred and the left side as female and profane.

When it comes to explaining why a polarity in dexterity should bear such weighty symbolizations, Hertz rehearses the arguments that link the human body to the natural world and to religious observance.

> According to some authors the differentiation of right and left is completely explained by the rules of religious orientation and sunworship. The position of man in space is neither indifferent nor arbitrary. In his prayers and ceremonies the worshipper looks naturally to the region where the sun rises, the source of all life. Most sacred buildings, in different religions, are turned towards the east. Given this direction, the parts of the body are assigned accordingly to the cardinal points: west is behind, south to the right, and north to the left. Consequently the characteristics of the heavenly regions are reflected in the human body. The full sunlight of the south shines on our right side, while the sinister shade of the north is projected on to our left. The spectacle of nature, the contrast of daylight and darkness, of heat and cold, are held to have taught man to distinguish and to oppose his right and his left. (Hertz, 1973, p. 20)

While this may seem persuasive, Hertz rightly points out that the human orientation to the sun (and its association with the sacred) is an act of culture – and is therefore another fact in need of explanation. It is the human ability to use the body as symbol, as a cipher with which to think and to impose meaning on the world, which gives the left–right polarity its signification. "The slight physiological advantages possessed by the right hand are merely the occasion of a qualitative differentiation the cause of which lies beyond the individual, in the constitution of the collective consciousness" (Hertz, 1973, p. 21). And precisely because the cue to elab-orate social constructions is the body, cultural rules can be made to appear natural. It seems ordained by nature that only men may enter by the east door, that the women's quarters are on the left of a house, or village, or that children be taught to write with their left hands tied behind their backs.

The symbolic weight given to the right–left polarity is decreasing in Western societies, but this does not mean that the categories associated with left- and right-handedness necessarily disappear. They may merely attach themselves to new symbols. On the other hand, a decrease in emphasis on right- and left-handedness could signal an increase in secularization (reduced investment in distinguishing between the "sacred" and "profane"), or a lessening of gender role differentiation. Hertz ended his essay with a declaration that has a strikingly contemporary ring to it. Having recognized the significance of right–left brain polarity, Hertz makes a plea that human beings be allowed to develop their full potential – the left hand (associated with the right brain and creativity) as well as the right hand (associated with the left brain and language).

> If the constraint of a mystical ideal has for centuries been able to make man into a unilateral being, physiologically mutilated, a liberated and foresighted society will strive to develop the energies dormant in our left side and in our right cerebral hemisphere, and to assure by an appropriate training a more harmonious development of the organism. (Hertz, 1973, p. 22)

Hertz's insights into the relationship between biological and sociological processes have been echoed by other social scientists and philosophers. The French thinker Maurice Merleau-Ponty (1908–61), for instance, stressed the embodied nature of perception. We do not have passive bodies that see and understand an objective world "out there." All experience of the world is mediated through our perception of it – via biological, psychological, and spiritual mechanisms, or senses. As the world acts on our bodies, so our experience of being in the world affects and shapes the phenomena we perceive. There is a continual interaction between the embodied individual and the social and natural world of which the individual is a part. While these interrelationships may seem obvious to many people today, they represented a radical move away from a *Cartesian* view of the universe as a mechanical object, observed by the rational mind of the conscious individual.[3]

Purity and danger

One of the best known contemporary anthropological writers on symbolic classification and the body is Mary Douglas, whose work has had a considerable impact on disciplines other than anthropology, particularly through the collection of essays published in 1966 under the title *Purity and Danger*.

Mary Douglas was born in England in 1921, and studied anthropology in Oxford with Max Gluckman, Meyer Fortes and Evans-Pritchard. Her fieldwork among the Lele of Central Africa (in the former Belgian Congo) formed the basis for her later and better-known writings on classificatory systems and anomalies. As a practicing Roman Catholic, Mary Douglas also applied her anthropological training to the Bible, and over her long career has returned many times to biblical themes. The *structural-functionalism* of Evans-Pritchard and the British school of social anthropology and the *structuralism* of Claude Lévi-Strauss are combined in a fruitful manner in much of Douglas's writing on religion and in her reflections on social institutions.[4]

Mary Douglas has dealt at length with the ways in which the human body is used as a social and religious symbol. In *Purity and Danger* Douglas, like Needham, points to the universality of the human body, which makes it such a useful source of shared meanings:

> No experience is too lowly to be taken up in ritual and given a lofty meaning. The more personal and intimate the source of the ritual symbolism, the more telling its message. The more the symbol is drawn from the common fund of human experience, the more wide and certain its reception. (Douglas, 1976, p. 114)

Douglas goes on to stress the importance of the body as a symbol system in which social meanings are encoded:

> The body is a model which can stand for any bounded system. Its boundaries can represent any boundaries which are threatened or precarious. The body is a complex structure. The functions of its different parts and their relation afford a source of symbols for other complex structures. We cannot possibly interpret rituals concerning excreta, breast milk, saliva and the rest unless we are prepared to see in the body a symbol of society, and to see the powers and dangers credited to social structure reproduced in small on the human body. (Douglas, 1976, p. 115)

Just as Hertz demonstrated the way in which a biological differentiation between right- and left-handedness has been used to build a range of symbolic and social associations, so Douglas has shown how the most lowly and intimate of bodily processes can be given the most elaborate and metaphysical of interpretations. Purity rules derive their universality and power from their focus on shared biological experiences of alimentation and excretion.

In the Introduction to *Purity and Danger* Douglas reflects on the humble matter of dirt and its relationship to other areas of human experience: "Reflection on dirt involves reflection on the relation of order to disorder, being to non-being, form to formlessness, life to death. Wherever ideas of dirt are highly structured, their analysis discloses a play on such profound themes" (Douglas, 1976, pp. 5–6). It may seem fanciful to link something as basic as dirt with such abstract and philosophical notions as being and non-being or life and death, but that is how purity rules and ideas of pollution operate. As Douglas points out, purity rules therefore form an excellent way into the study of religion.

In chapter 2 of *Purity and Danger*, entitled "Secular Defilement," Douglas starts by outlining what is known as *medical materialism* (a term attributed to William James). Medical materialism attempts to explain, or to explain away, purity rules by reference to scientific, medical, or hygienic principles. An example of such an approach would state that Jewish avoidance of pork is due to the danger of tapeworm infestation. This sounds reasonable, but if the desire to avoid tapeworm was the reason why the Hebrews drew up this rule, why did neighboring peoples, in similar conditions with a similar level of knowledge and standards of hygiene, continue to eat pork? Why do Jews, and Muslims for that matter, continue to avoid pork when the dangers of tapeworm are minimal or non-existent? The opposite of medical materialism, which attributes purely rational, scientific explanations to purity rules, is the view which sees the rituals and regulations of so-called "primitive" peoples as wholly irrational. At this opposite extreme it is held that the ideas of Westerners have nothing whatsoever in common with those of simpler societies. Douglas characterizes this view, to which she does not herself subscribe, in the following terms: "Our practices are solidly based on hygiene, theirs are symbolic: we kill germs, they ward off spirits." The problem with this type of argument is that, as Douglas puts it, "the resemblance between some of their symbolic rites and our hygiene is sometimes uncannily close" (Douglas, 1976, p. 32).

Medical materialism attempts to explain away purity rules by reference to scientific, medical, or hygienic principles.

Mystical participation describes the assumption that all rituals and regulations of "primitive" peoples are wholly irrational, and have only a magical or mystical significance.

One of the examples Mary Douglas uses to illustrate the connection between purity rules and social structure is a Brahmin group in India known as the Havik, and their relationship with Untouchables. Hinduism traditionally operates on a hierarchy of *endogamous* groups. That is, people are expected to marry within their group or caste, and relations between castes are carefully regulated. The Brahmins, or priestly caste, are at the top of the hierarchy. Untouchables are occupational groups who, because of the work they do, are so polluted that they are outside the caste system altogether. They deal with defecation, death, and other aspects of life avoided by those within the caste structure.[5] Although Brahmins and Untouchables depend upon one another for the maintenance of their respective societies, their contacts are very carefully regulated, set in the idiom of purity versus pollution. By way of illustration, Douglas explains that:

> Precise regulations give the kinds of indirect contact which may carry pollution. A Havik, working with his untouchable servant in his garden, may become severely defiled by touching a rope or bamboo at the same time as the servant. It is simultaneous contact with the bamboo or rope which defiles. A Havik cannot receive fruit or money directly from an Untouchable. But some objects stay impure and can be conductors of impurity even after contact. Pollution lingers in cotton cloth, metal cooking vessels, cooked food. Luckily for collaboration between the castes, ground does not act as a conductor. But straw which covers it does. (Douglas, 1976, p. 34)

Douglas states that, "The more we go into this and similar rules, the more obvious it becomes that we are studying symbolic systems," and she asks the question: "Are our ideas hygienic while theirs are symbolic?" Her answer is an emphatic "No!" Mary Douglas, together with Lévi-Strauss and others, asserts that "our ideas of dirt also express symbolic systems and that the difference between pollution behaviour in one part of the world and another is only a matter of detail" (Douglas, 1976, pp. 34–5).

It is also important to note, however, that our ideas of dirt have been transformed in the past one hundred years or so by a knowledge of *pathogenicity* – the existence of germs and their role in the transmission of disease – hence the medical materialist model and our perception of dirt as a matter of hygiene. This is, however, only part of the story. It does not account for much of our behavior and systems of classification of dirt and pollution. Nor did these notions of dirt and pollution only come into existence with knowledge of germ theory. This observation leads Douglas to one of her most widely quoted conclusions: "If we can abstract pathogenicity and hygiene from our notions of dirt, we are left with the old definition of *dirt as matter out of place*" (Douglas, 1976, p. 35; emphasis added). This definition of dirt as "matter out of place" implies two conditions, states Douglas, a set of ordered relations and a contravention of that order.

> Dirt then, is never a unique, isolated event. Where there is dirt there is a system. Dirt is the by-product of a systematic ordering and classification of

matter, in so far as ordering involves rejecting inappropriate elements. This idea of dirt takes us straight into the field of symbolism and promises a link-up with more obviously symbolic systems of purity. (Douglas, 1976, p. 35)

So dirt is not a "thing-in-itself" but a symbolic category. It is a relative idea, as Douglas illustrates with the following example:

Shoes are not dirty in themselves, but it is dirty to place them on the dining-table; food is not dirty in itself, but it is dirty to leave cooking utensils in the bedroom, or food bespattered on clothing; similarly, bathroom equipment in the drawing room; clothing lying on chairs; out-door things in-doors; upstairs things downstairs; under-clothing appearing where over-clothing should be, and so on. In short, our pollution behaviour is the reaction which condemns any object or idea likely to confuse or contradict cherished classifications. (Douglas, 1976, pp. 35–6)

As human beings we continually create patterns of meaning out of our individual and collective experience. Once a pattern is established it is often reinforced and we become blind to or consciously ignore what does not fit into it. There is an in-built filtering mechanism – human beings don't like ambiguity and anomaly, as they upset and challenge the foundations of our systems of meaning. An example of the ability of people to ignore what they dislike is the attitude of some cultures to faeces. Referring to the Hindu caste system, Douglas points out that:

In the ritual we know that to touch excrement is to be defiled and that the latrine cleaners stand in the lowest grade of the caste hierarchy. If this pollution rule expressed individual anxieties we would expect Hindoos to be controlled and secretive about the act of defecation. It comes as a considerable shock to read that slack disregard is their normal attitude, to such an extent that the pavements, verandahs and public places are littered with faeces until the sweeper comes along. (Douglas, 1976, p. 124)

This, for Douglas, is a convincing demonstration that caste operates as a symbolic system. Its *raison d'être* is the maintenance of hierarchical social relations, not physical hygiene. In a similarly graphic example, Sjaak van der Geest, describing his experience of conducting fieldwork among the Akan of Ghana, ponders the paradox of the Akan manner of dealing with human faeces.

On the one hand, they are extremely concerned with cleanliness and removing dirt from their bodies. On the other hand, the way they actually get rid of human waste is so inefficient that they are continuously confronted with what they most detest: filth, in particular, faeces. (van der Geest, 1998, p. 8)

Having puzzled over the contrast between the spotless wards and nurses and filthy fly-infested latrines of an Akan hospital, where he was taken suffering from dysentery, van der Geest suggested to a Ghanaian colleague that:

> Maybe . . . you are so afraid of shit that you do not only want to remove it from your bowels but also from your heads. You don't want to think about it and you don't even tolerate it near your house. The fact that you have to pass through dirty places and faeces is a consequence which you simply put out of your mind. You don't greet anybody on your way to the place, you pretend nobody sees you and you see nobody. You go silently, as a thief in the night, and forget about it: a mental solution for a very physical problem. (van der Geest, 1998, p. 12)

If ignoring *anomalies* is one way of dealing with them, there are others. Douglas outlines several possible reactions to ideas, objects, behaviors, or people who don't fit into dominant classifications. Reactions may be primarily negative, by mentally rendering the anomaly invisible (as the Akan do with human faeces, or as exemplified in Queen Victoria's apparent denial of the existence of lesbianism), or they may be perceived and condemned (as homosexual activity is condemned by many religious groups today). A more positive approach is to recognize the anomaly and to try to reorder our pattern of reality in order to accommodate it, perhaps leading to a paradigm shift in classificatory values.[6]

Individual classifications are much less powerful than those that have the weight of collective authority, and public categories tend to be more rigid than private ones. This is why it is possible for a priest to uphold the values of celibacy and chastity, and to condemn the practice of homosexuality, while frequenting a gay massage parlor.[7] The existence of numerous married Roman Catholic priests does not of itself alter the church's ruling on celibacy. An entire culture (in this instance the Roman Catholic Church) is unlikely to reorder its view of the world in the face of each and every anomaly that it meets, and will seek alternative strategies for dealing with anomalies as they arise. As Thomas Kuhn noted, when changes do occur, they are often rapid and decisive rather than piecemeal, as the old paradigms give way to new.

Thomas Kuhn (1922–96) argued that scientific development proceeds in distinct stages. There are periods of "normal science" in which accepted *paradigms* (frameworks or theories) appear to provide an adequate basis for explaining the world. When the force of competing theories (or the authority of alternative views) seriously threatens the prevailing orthodoxies, a "scientific revolution" takes place in which paradigms shift and new concepts are explored. Eventually some of these new ideas, which appear to provide a more satisfactory model for the data, will be accepted as dominant paradigms.[8] The same process can be observed more generally in social life, and provides a model of the way in which anomalous information may be resisted, and then incorporated into new or existing symbolic categories.

Dealing with anomalies

Mary Douglas (1976, pp. 39–40) lists five "negative" strategies for dealing with ambiguous or anomalous events. Although these are not exhaustive, many public reactions can be seen to fall into one of these (overlapping) categories.

1 *The anomaly can be redefined.* The birth of a handicapped child may seem to threaten the dividing line between human and non-human animals. The Nuer of the Southern Sudan deal with a "monstrous birth" by redefining the child as a hippopotamus, accidentally born to human parents.[9] With this reclassification in place, the baby is gently laid in the water, where a young hippopotamus belongs.

2 *Elimination of the anomaly through physical control.* Among the Ibo of Nigeria it is held that all human births should be singletons. The birth of twins threatens this social classification. In the past twins were left in the bush to die, and the mother was expelled from the village. Douglas also cites the example of cocks that crow in the night in a society in which cocks are defined as birds that crow at dawn. If a night-crowing cock has its neck wrung, the anomaly simply disappears.

3 *Avoidance of the anomalous.* There may be taboos or rules prohibiting contact with an anomalous person or thing, thus reinforcing the definition of the approved and normal. Michel Foucault, for example, in his work *Madness and Civilization* (first published in 1964) traced the Western use of mental institutions to hide from view all those considered deviant. Well into the twentieth century the mothers of illegitimate children and orphans were consigned to Victorian psychiatric hospitals, designed and located so as to remove from public view those who did not fit predetermined categories (in this case a particular model of "the family"). In the hieratic code of the *Book of Leviticus* the Hebrews were enjoined to avoid certain foods. Crawling things were regarded as an "abomination." They did not fit into the categories of edible game, fowl or fish.[10]

4   *Anomalous events or individuals may be labeled dangerous.* Deviant individuals or groups may find themselves stigmatized, and in some instances actively persecuted. In recent years families who openly declare themselves to be followers of the Craft (witches) have provoked fear and hostility in Western societies, and have lived with the realistic fear that the authorities will remove their children from them. Charges of child abuse and Satanism have been leveled at the Craft since the late Middle Ages, and are still used to control the behavior of practitioners of a little-understood minority faith.[11]

5   *Anomalies can be elevated through ritual.* Ritualization is one way of coming to terms with ambiguous symbols. If death, for instance, which contravenes all our most basic taboos and reminds us of our human frailty, is drawn into ritual, it can be seen as part of a greater scheme of things, and help give meaning to life. If death cannot be avoided, we can, at least, through ritualization, become reconciled to our mortality, by suggesting that death is but a new form of existence in another realm, or that it is a fitting end to a life which has meaning in and of itself. Alternatively, mortuary rituals may simply banish the dead so as to protect the living, and thus preserve human societies from their malign influences.

One could add a sixth category. Anomalies or ambiguities may be a source of amusement or ridicule (Lincoln, 1989, p. 165). Humor is often based on the sense of the absurd, that which does not fit, whether it is dealt with kindly or cruelly. Finally, without exhausting the possibilities, anomalies may be aestheticized, turned into objects of art or reverence.

The positive reaction to anomalous events, ideas, or people, indicated by Douglas, involves a redrawing of the classificatory boundaries in order to incorporate the anomaly. This is a process which occurs continually, either publicly through contestation, or quietly and without controversy. The process may be gradual or sudden, backed by force of law, or following a shift in public opinion. The ordination of women as priests within the Anglican Communion can be seen as one example of a boundary that is being redrawn, largely in response to changes in society at large. In many parts of the world the association between holding public office and masculinity has been weakened. The idea of a woman doctor, police officer, or soldier is not the anomaly that it might have been even fifty years ago, and the churches too are responding to this reclassification of gender roles.

Bruce Lincoln makes the useful distinction between an anomaly consisting of "any entity that defies the rules of an operative taxonomy" and an anomaly "the existence of which an operative taxonomy is incapable of acknowledging." In the former case the taxonomy or classificatory system is regarded as normative, whereas in the second instance it is the anomaly which is regarded as legitimate, "the taxonomy, inadequate, distorting, and exclusionary" (Lincoln, 1989, p. 165).

> Under the terms of both definitions, however, it is possible to see how an anomaly may both pose a danger to and be exposed to danger from the taxonomic order in which it is anomalous, just as deviants are considered outlaws when the legitimacy of legal systems is affirmed, but rebels when such systems are judged illegitimate. (Lincoln, 1989, p. 165)

In conclusion, Douglas contests Durkheim's distinction between the sacred and the profane. Categories of pollution and purity cannot be neatly divided between the two. They occur together, and in opposition to one another. They are not separate types of experience concerned on the one hand with the metaphysical realm of religion, and on the other hand with the mundanity of everyday life. Both the sacred and the profane are part of the same ordering system.

> Uncleanness or dirt is that which must not be included if a pattern is to be maintained. To recognise this is the first step towards insight into pollution. It involves us in no clear-cut distinction between sacred and secular. . . . Furthermore it involves no special distinction between primitives and moderns: we are all subject to the same rules. (Douglas, 1976, p. 40)

Symbolic bodies and atomic bombs

In *Stealing Fire: the Atomic Bomb as Symbolic Body*, Peter Reynolds extends Douglas's work on the links between the individual body and cultural forms, arguing that technology can be defined as "landscape projection of the symbolic body" or as "the artifacts and physical techniques that implement these projections" (Reynolds, 1991, p. 129). Reynolds uses the notion of the symbolic body in order to look at the relationship between physics and biology, and at the ways in which both disciplines reflect wider social, political, and cosmological concerns.

> Physics and biology play complementary but hierarchically differentiated roles within the symbolic body. Physics provides the ultimate mechanistic model of the universe, whereas biology brings the organic world into conformity with the assumptions of physics by demonstrating that the soft, wet, interdependent web of organic processes "is really" a hard, dry, crystalline, structure explicable by energy transactions. Conversely, to the extent that biology is successful in reducing life to matter, so physics must elevate matter to life. Biology and

physics are complementary processes of mutilation and prosthesis, joined by a mutual agenda of transforming life on earth into images of celestial fire under the control of a male apparatus. Nowhere is this imagery better exemplified than in the Manhattan Project – the making of the first atomic bomb. (Reynolds, 1991, p. 135)

Although this is not the place to rehearse Reynolds's carefully argued case, it is worth noting the explicit link he detects between the Manhattan Project and the mythology of its creators. In 1942, many of the United States' top nuclear physicists disappeared from their universities and laboratories, to be isolated on a remote mesa in New Mexico. The timing and siting of the project, the spatial arrangements of the base, the form and above all the language that informed the science, all revealed an unconscious drive to create a perfect male body: hard, phallic, projected toward the skies – and destructive.

> The anthropological hypothesis is that the detailed architecture of the atomic bomb reflects the mythology and social organization of the society that built it; and the dominant myth is the creation of a purified male body, separated by intellectual brilliance from an inferior and polluting nature conceptualized as female. (Reynolds, 1991, p. 136)

Reynolds describes the Manhattan Project as "a cult of male solidarity" (women and children were kept well away from the base), with a rationale which was teleological rather than technological, its product "a ritual object that defined the major categories of the post war symbolic body" (Reynolds, 1991, p. 138). It is well known that the scientists working on the atomic bomb used the language of conception and birth. The first successful hydrogen bomb had been given the name "Mike," and the message to headquarters in Los Alamos from the scientist who observed its detonation was famously, "It's a boy" (Reynolds, 1991, p. 145).[12]

The connections between politics, literature, myth, ritual, and science are not usually obvious to us. It is part of the contemporary Western worldview that these are discrete areas of activity, each with its own rules and values. Reynolds, however, demonstrates the interconnections between these fields as they converge in the Manhattan Project. Leo Szilard, one of the initiators of the Manhattan Project, admitted that the idea for a nuclear chain reaction based on the fissioning of uranium by neutrons came to him after reading *The World Set Free*, a work of fiction by H. G. Wells first published in 1914, which describes (in highly sexualized language) the transformation of uranium into a manmade element and the development and dropping of atomic bombs (Reynolds, 1991, pp. 144–55).

Thus, the concept of the atomic bomb, far from developing fortuitously from discoveries in pure science, *preceded* most research in atomic physics, and its potential political implications drove the scientific agenda. Moreover, in the initial vision of the atomic bomb, it is no ordinary weapon but a vehicle for social transformation and universal peace. In short, the atomic bomb, from the first glimmering of its possibility, was seen as intrinsically eschatological, which is why hundreds of physicists, some of them self-proclaimed pacifists, could so easily be persuaded to put aside their indifference to politics and fight the war to end all wars.... Science and science fiction are two aspects of the same process of mythic implementation. In the terminology of anthropology, science fiction creates the myth and science does the ritual. (Reynolds, 1991, p. 145)

Training the Body and Social Control

Well publicized concerns over "brainwashing" techniques, said to be used by "cults" in order to keep their members, point to a connection between the body and religious adherence. Converts are supposedly deprived of sleep and privacy, and subjected to strong group pressures that can alter their belief systems and personalities. While the whole concept of brainwashing has been challenged,[13] the Christian groups who most frequently make such accusations recognize, from their own practices, that the body, mind, and emotions are intimately connected. Modification of beliefs and modification of behavior usually go hand in hand. This section starts, therefore, with discussion of a seminal article by Marcel Mauss on the training of the body. The link between the training of the body and conscious social control by those in power is then illustrated through an example given by Judith Okely of her girls' boarding school in the 1950s.

Techniques of the body

Marcel Mauss (1872–1950) was a student and nephew of Durkheim. His writing on gift exchange has influenced later structuralist thinking, particularly that of Claude Lévi-Strauss.[14] Mauss's study of "*techniques of the body*" and the concept of *habitus* is reflected in the later writings of Pierre Bourdieu and Michel Foucault. In "techniques of the body" Mauss describes the ways in which the body is trained. As Mauss put it, "In every society, everyone knows and has to know and learn what he has to do in all conditions" (Mauss, 1979, p. 120).[15]

Mauss became acutely aware, through his experiences as a soldier in the First World War (1914–18), that what we think of as purely biological or

physiological skills have in fact to be learnt. One example Mauss gives
concerns the technique of digging. English troops were unable to dig with
French spades, and every time a French division was relieved by an English
division, or vice versa, 8,000 spades had to be changed (Mauss, 1979, p. 99).
In another example, Mauss describes the inconvenience of having unlearnt a
bodily technique, in this case squatting:

> The child normally squats. We no longer know how to. I believe that this is an
> absurdity and an inferiority of our races, civilizations, societies. An example:
> I lived at the front with Australians (whites). They had one considerable
> advantage over me. When we made a stop in mud or water, they could sit
> down on their heels to rest, and the "*flotte*" as it was called, stayed below their
> heels. I was forced to stay standing up in my boots with my whole foot in the
> water. The squatting position is, in my opinion, an interesting one that could be
> preserved in a child. It is a very stupid mistake to take it away from him. All
> mankind, excepting our own societies, has so preserved it. (Mauss, 1979, p. 107)

Mauss describes sex differences (women are said to make a fist with the
thumb inside the fingers, men with the thumb on the outside), as well as
age and cultural differences, in physical competence. In some instances we
learn to control our bodies in order to conform to an accepted notion of
manners. As Mauss noted:

> there are polite and impolite *positions for the hands* at rest. Thus you can be
> certain that if a child at table keeps his elbows in when he is not eating, he is
> English. A young Frenchman has no idea how to sit up straight; his elbows stick
> out sideways; he puts them on the table, and so on. (Mauss, 1979, p. 100)

These learned techniques, including such basic activities as running, swim-
ming, or walking, can change within a person's lifetime. Although it may be
difficult to unlearn techniques that we have practiced unconsciously over
many years, the process is certainly one of change rather than stasis, and has
to do as much with society as with biology. Mauss's preferred term for such
learnt techniques is *habitus*.

> Hence I have had this notion of the social nature of the "*habitus*" for many
> years. Please note that I use the Latin word – it should be understood in France –
> *habitus*. The word translates infinitely better than "*habitude*" (habit or custom),
> the "*exis*," the "acquired ability" and "faculty" of Aristotle (who was a psych-
> ologist). It does not designate those metaphysical *habitudes*, that mysterious
> "memory," the subjects of volumes or short and famous theses. These "habits"
> do not vary just with individuals and their imitations; they vary especially
> between societies, educations, proprieties and fashions, prestiges. In them we

should see the techniques at work of collective and individual practical reason rather than, in the ordinary way, merely the soul and its repetitive faculties. (Mauss, 1979, p. 101)

Mauss explains the relationship between the social, psychological, and biological elements of *habitus* in the following way. "The child, the adult, imitates actions which have succeeded and which he has seen successfully performed by people in whom he has confidence and who have authority over him" (Mauss, 1979, p. 101). The techniques the child imitates may be biological (learning to eat) but the fact of imitation immediately brings the social aspect to the fore. Children must eat to survive, but whether they eat with their fingers, with chopsticks, or with a knife and fork is a reflection of social values inscribed on the body. The child may choose to imitate certain individuals whom he or she admires, or may be forced to perform certain actions in a particular way. One individual may learn to perform a task well while another does it badly. There will be both psychological and biological factors at play here. The small boy who decides to imitate his sporting hero and become a footballer or baseball player, for example, is reflecting the social status given to successful athletes in his society. There will be individual psychological and social factors which lead one child to persevere and another to give up competing (alternative interests may intervene and the level of encouragement a child receives from parents and peers may be crucial), as well as different biological capabilities. A left-handed baseball pitcher forced to pitch with the right hand may never become proficient. Someone who cannot see the ball will never make a professional player, and so on. These three elements (the social, psychological, and biological) are "indissolubly mixed together," and from this perspective many of the *nature/nurture* debates of the past three decades seem to have missed the point. Mauss points to a more fruitful line of inquiry. Instead of asking whether genetics or upbringing are responsible for behavior, Mauss looks at the ways in which social meanings are inscribed on the physical body, and at the role of individual choice (*agency*) and social structure (*power*) in limiting or enabling individual and collective actions.

For Mauss the body is defined both as a "technique without an instrument" and as our "first and most natural instrument." A technique is defined as "an action which is *effective* and *traditional*." This is true of all actions, whether magical, symbolic, or religious. What differentiates techniques of the body from religious, symbolic, or juridical acts is that they are "felt by the author as *actions of a mechanical, physical or physico-chemical order* and that they are pursued with that aim in view" (Mauss, 1979, p. 104). That is, they appear to the individual both natural and inevitable. Mauss, however, was aware that while they may appear to be unrelated, religious sensibilities and physical training can never be completely separated. Breathing techniques, for instance, figure in religious training in China and India. Mauss concluded his essay with an assertion of the interrelationship between the body and religion: "I believe precisely that at the bottom of all our mystical states there are body techniques which we have not studied, but which were studied fully in China and India, even in very remote periods" (Mauss, 1979, p. 122). This interesting suggestion is developed by Michael Saso in his article "The Taoist body and cosmic prayer." Saso states that "The use of the entire body, mind, heart, and belly, as a single unit in meditation is a unique phenomenon found in Taoist and Tantric Buddhist practice." Although Taoism (pronounced "Daoism") and Tantra use a different vocabulary, Saso goes on to explain that:

> Taoist ritual contemplation and Buddhist Tantric practice define prayer as the simultaneous use of mind, mouth, and body for encountering the absolute . . . or the other-shore. . . . In this meditative process, the mind is used to contemplate the sacred image, the mouth is used to chant sacred phrases that make the image one with the meditator, and the body is used to seal the union through physical dance steps or hand dance, called mudra. . . . These three locations in the Taoist and the Tantric Buddhist body are focus points for a kind of prayer that visualizes the human body and the outer cosmos to be related, that is, to be analogously one in their meditative and orderly physical cycle of activity. (Saso, 1998, p. 231)

One could make interesting comparisons between the bodily/cosmic links in Taoist and Tantric traditions and in shamanic practices, which arguably have an alternative but equally integrated understanding of the relationship of the physical and cosmic realms (see chapter 7).

> The French anthropologist **Pierre Bourdieu** developed Mauss's notion of *habitus* by looking in detail at the ways in which we orient ourselves in social space. We each learn a particular set of tastes, preferences, habits, and skills according to our status (age, sex, class, and so on). Moving from one social and economic class, or occupational group, just as much as moving from one country or culture to another, involves learning (or refusing or failing to learn) a new set of techniques which constitute that particular *habitus*.[16]

Schooling the body

One particularly clear example of the "techniques of the body" is the *habitus* of a girls' private boarding school, described by the English anthropologist Judith Okely (1978).

> **Erving Goffman** caused some controversy by his comparison of boarding schools, monasteries, and hospitals with military, mental, and penal establishments – all referred to as "total institutions." "A total institution may be defined as a place of residence and work where a large number of like-situated individuals, cut off from the wider society for an appreciable period of time, together lead an enclosed, formally administered round of life" (Goffman, 1984a, p. 11).

Okely's militaristic boarding school in the 1950s fits Goffman's description of a total institution very well. The school had few academic pretensions, and concentrated on inculcating wider social messages concerning class and gender. In a section entitled "The body: subjugated and unsexed," Okely describes the way in which the school authorities utilized the girls' carriage and demeanor to impress their control over the girls' minds and bodies. The ideal was to acquire movements that would allow one to combine "the longed-for anonymity, as well as conspicuous selection as a team member" (Okely, 1978, p. 128). As Mauss had pointed out, even such supposedly physiological capacities as walking and running are in fact learnt, and have a strong social element.

> Within our school there could be no "natural" movement which might contradict what the authorities considered correct. "Bad" ways we had learnt elsewhere had to be changed. We did not merely unconsciously imitate movements and gestures, we were consciously made to sit, stand and move in uniform ways. We were drilled and schooled, not by those in whom we had confidence, but by those who had power over us. Our flesh unscarred, yet our gestures bore their marks. Even when outside the classroom or off the games field, we were to sit, stand and walk erect, chin up, back straight, shoulders well back. At table when not eating, our hands were to rest in our laps. During the afternoon rest period matrons ordered us not to lie on our backs with knees bent. The games mistresses watched girls at meals, at roll-call and in chapel, and would award good and bad "deportment marks," recorded on a chart, and with house cups. If you were consistently upright you won a red felt badge, embroidered with the word "Deportment." This, sewn on your tunic, was a sign of both achievement and defeat. Our minds and understanding of the world were to reflect our custodians. With no private space, we could not even hide in our bodies which also had to move in unison with their thoughts. (Okely, 1978, pp. 128–9)

Okely reflects on the way in which our bodies betray an inner attitude, and the effort required to make them conform. As Mauss observed in relation to mystical states, the external and internal worlds are closely related and there are probably limits to the extent that we can "lie" with our bodies.

> The authorities observed accurately the language of the body. However much a girl might say the right things, do and act within the rules, and however in order her uniform may be, her general carriage, her minutest gesture could betray a lack of conviction, a failure in conversion. I remember (after yet another term's anxious waiting for promotion) being called to the headmistress who said that I needed to improve my "attitude" before I could be made a sergeant. I was baffled because I thought I had successfully concealed my unorthodoxy. I had said and done what appeared to me to be in order. But they must have seen through me, just by the way my body spoke. It had also to be tempered. I eventually won my deportment badge, and then soared from sergeant, to sub-prefect. But my conformity over-reached itself; the games mistress took me aside and said I was now sitting and walking too stiffly, too rigidly. I was becoming conspicuous again. (Okely, 1978, p. 129)

The school authorities were well aware that the body was a symbol and cipher for the social values they wished to inscribe. With careful training and the ever-present gaze of authority, pupils learnt to conform to the thought patterns and movements of the "total institution," the boarding school.

In *Outline of a Theory of Practice*, Bourdieu (1977, p. 94) writes of the body as a "memory" in which a whole cosmology and ethic are placed beyond the grasp of consciousness and deliberate transformation. Okely, citing this passage, gives the example of a former schoolmate who failed to become an opera singer, blaming her schooling for so restricting her deportment that she could never learn to breathe deeply enough (Okely, 1978, pp. 129–30).

In *Discipline and Punish* (1991), Michel Foucault describes the architectural innovation, the *Panopticon*, recommended by Jeremy Bentham (1748–1832). The plan was based on a circular building with a central tower. Every person within the institution would be isolated in a small cell, invisible to one another, but visible to a single central observer (the term "panopticon" conjures up the idea of the all-seeing eye of God). This design was adopted for prisons, but Bentham envisaged the same model applying to schools, hospitals, and indeed any institution that wished to control its inmates. The notion of control via the gaze, the constant surveillance of people by those in authority, is still popular today, whether in an army camp, a boarding school, or a shopping mall via close-circuit television.

Personal and Cultural Symbols

A personal symbol can be defined as a symbol that is (1) optional for the individual. The imperative to adopt a particular personal symbol springs from psychological needs rather than obligatory social conformity. Body piercing in contemporary Western societies is optional, whereas circumcision for an Orthodox Jew, or the infibulation of women in parts of Africa, do not depend upon an individual's free choice. (2) A personal symbol is recognized by the culture of the person concerned as meaningful, rational, objective and normal. An Indian *saddhu* (ascetic) who wanders around naked with unkempt hair, perhaps covered in ash, may be considered holy by Hindus, whereas a man acting similarly in the UK or the USA would probably be arrested and confined to a mental institution. (3) Personal symbols are psychologically relevant to the individual, with the suggestion that if he or she does not express inner drives symbolically, giving objective reality to a state of mind, the individual would suffer psychologically. Such personal symbols are rather different from those that are ritualized and conventional for certain occasions. Wearing black at a funeral may express grief and suit the bereaved's frame of mind, but equally may signify conformity to cultural norms rather than a personal emotion.[17]

Medusa's hair

In Classical Greek mythology, Medusa was one of the three Gorgons (female monsters), with snakes for hair, whose terrifying appearance turned anyone who looked at them to stone. In his book *Medusa's Hair* (1984) the Sri Lankan anthropologist Gananath Obeyesekere, using the example of the matted snake-like hair of female ascetics in Sri Lanka, takes issue with an article by Edmund Leach (1958). Leach argues that public symbols have no emotional force for the individual, whereas private symbols, arising from the unconscious, lack wider cultural significance. Obeyesekere challenges this assumption. There is no intrinsic reason why public cultural symbols might not also carry a deep emotional force, and why they should not arise from individual unconscious motivations. The position Obeyesekere is attacking is not as rigorously defended as might be construed from reading *Medusa's Hair*, nevertheless, the strengths of a psychological approach to the anthropology of religion are amply demonstrated in Obeyesekere's work.

Medusa's Hair is based on case studies of six women, described by Obeyesekere as "religious virtuosos," who attended rituals at the great multifaith pilgrimage center of Kataragama in southern Sri Lanka in the 1970s. Obeyesekere made a point of getting to know his informants well. The personal life history, filtered through the selective memories of the individual, was crucial in reaching an understanding of the personal significance of the symbols employed by the ascetic – in particular her long matted locks.

Obeyesekere identifies three levels in the symbolic analysis of matted hair. First, we have the origin and genesis of the symbol. Second, there is the personal meaning of the symbol, whether for the individual or the group; third, the sociocultural message or meaning of the symbol. Psychological interpretations are particularly relevant at the first level of analysis – the genesis of the symbol.

> It can demonstrate that a certain class of experiences are so painful, complicated, and out of the reach of conscious awareness that the individual must express them in indirect representations and symbol formation. In the case of matted hair the symbol is a public one, but it is *recreated* each time by individuals. Moreover, the symbol would cease to exist (except in texts and nonliving icons) if individuals did not create it each time on the anvil of their personal anguish. (Obeyesekere, 1984, p. 33)

Obeyesekere noted three common elements in the lives of his informants connected with the genesis of their matted locks. First was a loss of an emotional-sexual relationship with her husband and rejection of the husband's penis. Second was an intensified, idealized relationship with a divine "alter" (glossed in Freudian terms as "an image of both husband and father"). This love was demonstrated in "orgasmic" "shaking from within" or divine ecstasy. Third, in each case the god's gift for having renounced the human spouse (*eros*) for the divine lover (*agape*) was matted locks. In yogic and tantric practices the vital (divine) energy of the body (*sakti*) is represented as *kundalini* or serpent power. This resides at the lowest *chakra* or energy point on the body, but is aroused through the practice of yoga. The serpentlike hair can be seen as a manifestation of sexual *kundalini* power as it rises through the body, although in the case of Obeyesekere's informants it is through possession trance, rather than yogic practice, that "the god infuses and suffuses the body of the priestess" (Obeyesekere, 1984, p. 34). The number of locks given to a woman was related to a particular deity, each of whom is symbolized as having a corresponding number of locks.

Obeyesekere seeks to make explicit the sexual-symbolic significance of the matted, serpentine locks, not at an abstract level, but as related to the life experiences and interpretations of his informants.

> If the hair is the sublimated penis emerging from the head, what kind of penis is it? Clearly it is no longer the husband's but the god's. But the relationship with the god is of a different order: eroticism is sublimated, idealized, and indirectly expressed. Gods, those idealized beings, cannot have penes like yours or mine; thus the matted hair is no ordinary penis, his *sakti*, the source of life and vitality.

Hence on another level of meaning it is the life force itself, and its loss . . . heralds the death of its bearer. Thus the hair emerges initially as a symptom . . . progressively it is transformed into a symbol. (Obeyesekere, 1984, p. 34)

The public meaning of the symbol relates to, but is not the same as, its genesis and personal meaning. Obeyesekere found that practically everyone he spoke to (other than the women themselves) regarded the matted hair with fear and revulsion (a reaction he himself recorded on first witnessing them). They were also convinced that the matted locks contained fleshy growths, a view not shared by the ascetics. Obeyesekere links the disgust and revulsion with which the matted hair is regarded to the fact that it is a particular type of symbol: "It is manipulatory, that is, *used* by individuals. It is like other ritual symbols that are manipulated by the worshipper, but quite unlike a symbol that exists in a myth or story" (Obeyesekere, 1984, p. 36). The symbol of matted hair is, therefore, personal and voluntary, but also ordered and predictable. "That the symbol is related to the life experience of the ascetic does not mean that it is a private symbol: it only means that we have to reject the conventional wisdom that there is a radical hiatus between custom and emotion" (Obeyesekere, 1984, p. 37).

Conclusion

Richard Shweder (1996, p. 340) points out that Obeyesekere is not talking about a particular type of symbol, but a type of expressive symbolic performance in which inner and outer states are closely related to one another. The examples we have looked at do seem to indicate that while there is a random, arbitrary element in body symbolism, cultures also take strong hints from biological and psychological cues. Hertz first noted the consistency between right- and left-handedness and symbolic categories, and Reynolds and others have pointed to the frequently drawn analogy between nuclear weapons and the male sex organ. Obeyesekere draws on Western psychoanalysis in his explication of the phallic snake-like locks of female ascetics. We need to remain sensitive to the type of symbol we are dealing with, whether it is personal or collective, individually motivated or obligatory, whether or not it is ritualized, and whether it is passively received or actively performed. The degree to which symbols may be regarded as arbitrary or contingent is still widely debated within anthropology and the body, biologically given but trained and manipulable, is an ideal focus for trying to understand the nature and role of symbols in human societies.

Notes

1 See Malinowski's description of the Kula ring in *Argonauts of the Western Pacific*, first published in 1922.

2 There are two poles of interpretation in the study of symbols, although few authors would support an extreme position at either end of the spectrum. On the one hand we have the "doctrine of conventionalism," which states that the link between a symbol and what it symbolizes is entirely arbitrary and depends upon social agreement. This is usually argued for language (with the exception of "mama" and "papa"). Whether one calls a particular animal a "dog," "*Hund*," or "*chien*," or by any other term, depends entirely on the understood usage in the language concerned. At the opposite pole we would assume that there is some intrinsic genetic or psychological mechanism that generates appropriate symbols that have a particular emotional resonance. Carl Jung's notion of archetypes as well as Freudian psychology would be at this end of the spectrum (a snake – or a cigar – represents a penis, a cauldron a vagina, and so on). See Shweder (1996, pp. 332ff).

3 Merleau-Ponty (1962, 1964). The term "Cartesian" refers to the ideas and writings of the French philosopher René Descartes (1596–1650).

4 See, for instance, one of Douglas's earliest published works, *The Lele of Kasai* (1963), a conventional fieldwork monograph, and for one of her more recent studies on the Bible, *In the Wilderness: the Doctrine of Defilement in the Book of Numbers* (1993). Douglas has also demonstrated a longterm interest in institutions. See, for instance, *How Institutions Think* (1986).

5 Gandhi renamed the Untouchables *Harijans*, from *Hari*, a name for Lord Vishnu, and *jana*, a person. A classic anthropological description of the Hindu caste system is Louis Dumont's *Homo Hierarchicus*, first published in 1966. For a more recent scholarly work on caste see Brian Smith (1994).

6 An interesting attempt to approach a similar theme from a more sociological perspective is *Stigma: Notes on the Management of Spoiled Identity* (first published in 1963), in which Erving Goffman identifies three broad categories of stigma. First, there are "abominations of the body," consisting of various types of physical deformity. Second, there are the many attributes which can be classed as "blemishes of individual character." Finally, there is the "tribal stigma of race, nation, and religion" (Goffman, 1984b, p. 14).

7 As was widely reported from Dublin (Ireland) recently – when a priest collapsed in a gay massage parlor, it transpired that there were other priests on hand to administer the last rites!

8 Thomas S. Kuhn (1962). The word "paradigm" comes from the Greek *para*, "beside," "beyond," and *deiknynai*, "to show." As conceptual frameworks, paradigms provide basic operational assumptions for scientific work (Newtonian gravity, Einsteinian relativity, and so on), as well as the cultural and value systems of a society. Most dominant paradigms are conservative without being

static, and criticisms of them often lead to their being overturned by new and more convincing paradigms. When one dominant paradigm gives way to another, this is known as a "paradigm shift." The dynamic of social, as opposed to scientific, change has been documented by (among others) Alain Touraine (b. 1929), who emphasizes the importance of social action and social movements in changing social institutions and cultural forms, i.e. in giving birth to new paradigms (Touraine, 1977).

9   See Evans-Pritchard (1956, p. 84).
10 See *Purity and Danger*, chapter 3, "The abominations of Leviticus."
11 See Adler (1986) for a comprehensive account of contemporary Paganism in the United States.
12 The novelist Martin Amis speaks of "a resilient theme of infantilism" throughout the nuclear project, which is reflected in such comments as "it's a boy" and the naming of the first bomb dropped over Japan as "Little Boy" (Amis, 1987, p. 10). (My thanks to Gavin Flood for this reference.)
13 See Barker (1989).
14 See Mauss (1970) and Lévi-Strauss (1987).
15 *Habitus* is also a major theme in the writings of Thomas Aquinas. See, for instance, Thomas Aquinas's *Summa Theologica II Prima Secundae*. Questions 49–54 "Treatise on Habits" "*De habitibus in gernerali, quad eorum substantiam*" (pp. 304 –38), Biblioteca de Autores Cristianos, La Editorial Catolica, Madrid, 1962. English translation, Anton C. Pegis, *Basic Writings of Saint Thomas Aquinas, volume* 2. New York: Random House, 1945, pp. 366–411.
16 These ideas were first developed in *Outline of a Theory of Practice* (1977) and *The Logic of Practice* (1995), especially chapter 4, "Belief and the Body," although they also inform much of Bourdieu's other work. A discussion of the concept of *habitus* in the works of Mauss and Bourdieu, as well as Mauss's influence on Mary Douglas, is found in Strathern (1999, pp. 25–39).
17 See Shweder (1996, p. 341), from whom these categories (but not the examples) are drawn. Shweder relates his discussion directly to hair, and Obeyesekere's work.

References and Further Reading

Adler, Margot (1986) *Drawing Down the Moon: Witches, Druids, Goddess Worshippers, and Other Pagans in America Today*. New York and London: Penguin Arkana.
Amis, Martin (1987) *Einstein's Monsters*. London: Jonathan Cape.
Barker, Eileen (1989) *New Religious Movements: a Practical Introduction*. London: HMSO Publications.
Becker, Anne E. (1995) *Body, Self and Society: the View from Fiji*. Philadelphia: University of Pennsylvania Press.
Bourdieu, Pierre (1977) *Outline of a Theory of Practice*, translated by Richard Nice. Cambridge: Cambridge University Press (first published in 1972).

Bourdieu, Pierre (1995) *The Logic of Practice*, translated by Richard Nice. Cambridge and Oxford: Polity Press in association with Blackwell Publishers (first published in 1980).

Coakley, Sarah (ed.) (1998) *Religion and the Body*. Cambridge: Cambridge University Press.

Douglas, Mary (1963) *The Lele of Kasai*. London: International African Institute.

Douglas, Mary (1975) *Implicit Meanings*. London: Routledge.

Douglas, Mary (1976) *Purity and Danger: an Analysis of Concepts of Pollution and Taboo*. London and Henley: Routledge and Kegan Paul (first published in 1966).

Douglas, Mary (1986) *How Institutions Think*. Syracuse, NY: Syracuse University Press.

Douglas, Mary (1993) *In the Wilderness: the Doctrine of Defilement in the Book of Numbers*. Sheffield: Sheffield Academic Press.

Dumont, Louis (1970) *Homo Hierarchicus: the Caste System and its Implications*. London: Weidenfeld & Nicolson (first published in 1966).

Evans-Pritchard, E. E. (1956) *Nuer Religion*. Oxford: Clarendon Press.

Evans-Pritchard, E. E. (1981) *A History of Anthropological Thought*. London: Faber & Faber.

Feher, Michel (ed.) (1989/1990) *Fragments for a History of the Human Body*. Three volumes. New York: MIT Press.

Firth, Raymond (1973) *Symbols: Public and Private*. London: George Allen & Unwin.

Foucault, Michel (1990) *Madness and Civilization: a History of Insanity in the Age of Reason*. London: Routledge (first published in 1964).

Foucault, Michel (1991) *Discipline and Punish: the Birth of the Prison*. Harmondsworth: Penguin (first published in 1975).

Goffman, Erving (1984) *Asylums: Essays on the Social Situation of Mental Patients and other Inmates*. Harmondsworth and New York: Penguin (first published in 1961).

Goffman, Erving 1984 *Stigma: Notes on the Management of Spoiled Identity*. Harmondsworth and New York: Penguin (first published in 1963).

Gusterson, Hugh (1998) *Nuclear Rites: a Weapons Laboratory at the End of the Cold War*. Berkeley: University of California Press.

Hallpike, C. R. (1979) Social hair. In W. A. Lessa and E. Z. Vogt (eds), *Reader in Comparative Religion: an Anthropological Approach*, 4th edn. New York: HarperCollins, pp. 99–105.

Haraway, Donna J. (1991) *Simians, Cyborgs, and Women: the Reinvention of Nature*. London: Free Association Books.

Hertz, Robert (1973) The pre-eminence of the right hand: a study of religious polarity. In Rodney Needham (ed.), *Right and Left: Essays on Dual Symbolic Classification*, translated by R. Needham. Chicago and London: University of Chicago Press, pp. 3–31 (first published in 1909).

Kuhn, Thomas S. (1962) *The Structure of Scientific Revolutions*. Chicago: University of Chicago Press.

Leach, Edmund (1958) Magical hair. *Journal of the Royal Anthropological Institute*, 88, 147–64.

Lévi-Strauss, Claude (1987) *Introduction to the Work of Marcel Mauss*. London: Routledge & Kegan Paul (first published in 1950).

Lincoln, Bruce (1989) *Discourse and the Deconstruction of Society: Comparative Studies of Myth, Ritual, and Classification*. New York and Oxford: Oxford University Press.

Littlewood, Roland (1993) *Pathology and Identity: the Work of Mother Earth in Trinidad*. Cambridge: Cambridge University Press.

Malinowski, B. (1978) *Argonauts of the Western Pacific*. London: Routledge and Kegan Paul (first published in 1922).

Mauss, Marcel (1970) *The Gift: Forms and Functions of Exchange in Archaic Societies*, translated by Ian Cunnison. London: Cohen & West (first published in 1925).

Mauss, Marcel (1979) Body techniques. In *Sociology and Psychology. Essays by Marcel Mauss*, translated by Ben Brewster. London and Boston: Routledge and Kegan Paul, pp. 95–123 (first published in 1935).

Merleau-Ponty, Maurice (1962) *Phenomenology of Perception*, translated by Colin Smith. London: Routledge (first published in 1945).

Merleau-Ponty, Maurice (1964) *The Primacy of Perception*, edited by James M. Edie. Evanston, IL: Northwestern University Press.

Needham, Rodney (1972) *Belief, Language and Experience*. Oxford: Blackwell.

Needham, Rodney (ed.) (1973) *Right and Left: Essays on Dual Symbolic Classification*. Chicago and London: University of Chicago Press.

Obeyesekere, Gananath (1984) *Medusa's Hair: an Essay on Personal Symbols and Religious Experience*. Chicago: Chicago University Press.

Okely, Judith (1978) Privileged, schooled and finished: boarding education for girls. In Shirley Ardener (ed.), *Defining Females*. London: Croom Helm, in association with the Oxford University Women's Studies Committee, pp. 109–39.

Ortner, Sherry B. (1979) On key symbols. In W. A. Lessa and E. Z. Vogt (eds), *Reader in Comparative Religion: an Anthropological Approach*, 4th edn. New York: Harper-Collins, pp. 92–8.

Reynolds, Peter C. (1991) *Stealing Fire: the Atomic Bomb as Symbolic Body*. Palo Alto, CA: Iconic Anthropology Press.

Saso, Michael (1998) The Taoist body and cosmic prayer. In Sarah Coakley (ed.), *Religion and the Body*. Cambridge: Cambridge University Press, pp. 231–47.

Shweder, Richard A. (1996) *Thinking through Cultures: Expeditions in Cultural Psychology*. Cambridge, MA, and London: Harvard University Press.

Smith, Brian K. (1994) *Classifying the Universe: the Ancient Indian Varna System and the Origins of Caste*. New York: Oxford University Press.

Strathern, Andrew J. (1999) *Body Thoughts*. Ann Arbor: University of Michigan Press.

Touraine, Alain (1977) *The Self-production of Society*, translated by Derek Coltman. Chicago: University of Chicago Press (first published in 1973).

van der Geest, Sjaak (1998) Akan shit: getting rid of dirt in Ghana. *Anthropology Today*, 14(3), 8–12.

Wells, Herbert George (1914) *The World Set Free: a Story of Mankind*. London: Macmillan.

Chapter 3

Maintaining and Transforming Boundaries: the Politics of Religious Identity

Introduction

In this chapter we continue to look at symbolic systems and at the relationship between the body and society. The focus is on the ways in which identities are formed and maintained through the use of symbols, in particular symbols that draw upon the body, whether in its biological functions, such as eating, or through clothing. The chapter is divided into three main parts. After looking in general terms at the question of identity, we consider *ritual purity and social boundaries*, drawing once again upon the work of Mary Douglas and on Judith Okely's work on Gypsies. Traveler-Gypsies in England provide an example of the maintenance of a Gypsy identity separate from that of the dominant house-dwelling society through the use of purity rules. The second part of the chapter, on *negotiating identities*, considers ways in which we are active agents in the creation of our identity. Discourses surrounding clothing provide an arena for the negotiation of who and what we are. The primary example is Jean Comaroff's analysis of the uniforms of Zionist Christians among the Tshidi in South Africa. The final part, on *contesting boundaries*, uses historical studies of medieval and early modern Europe to examine the use of the body to challenge existing hegemonic structures. On the one hand we look at medieval women ascetics, who often mutilated or starved their bodies in the pursuit of holiness. By way of contrast, the carnival presents a wholly positive view of the body, open and unstructured, which can undermine the closed and controlled hierarchies of power. What all these examples have in common is the symbolic use of the body to maintain, contest, and negotiate social boundaries.

A question of identity

Who are you? This is a deceptively simple question. You may respond by giving your name, or a version of it. Perhaps you will mention an occupation or nationality. It might seem appropriate to qualify your answer with adjectives describing your gender, sexuality, color, language, or religion. The form of your answer will undoubtedly depend on the context. This will include your relationship to the questioner and his or her prior level of knowledge, what you know of his or her motive in asking the question, your ability to read the situation, and so on. But who is the real you? One might respond by pointing to the physical person who changes and grows older, but who maintains a sense of self through the operation of memory and the maintenance of relationships. Another, equally valid, answer might be that there is no "real me," as my identity is continually being constructed through the experience of living in and interacting with the world. A Christian, Jew, or Muslim may wish to assert that he or she is a unique pre-existent being, made in the image of God, with an immortal soul. These ideas are not necessarily contradictory, they merely approach the same question from different angles.

Whoever we are, we do not exist as isolated individuals, but belong to a hierarchy of social groups. We might simultaneously be members of a household, a family, a town or village, a parish, and a political constituency. Many people are in possession of a passport that gives them claims to statehood. We belong to linguistic and ethnic or cultural groups, or may identify strongly with a religious, occupational, or lifestyle community. Each group will have certain membership rules. Some groups may be relatively open and easy to join, others will try hard to maintain their exclusivity. Whether we are talking about a golf club, a church, a profession, or an ethnic and linguistic group, there will be boundaries that define who is in and who is out. By examining boundaries, anthropologists try to understand the rules, often unstated, that determine the characteristics of a particular collective. When British women cricketers initially sought to join the MCC (Marylebone Cricket Club), the regulation stating that members must be male was quickly invoked. Gender was revealed as a crucial boundary marker in determining who could belong to this exclusive group. If you want to be recognized as a member of the loose-knit New Age Traveler community in Britain it helps to wear dreadlocks and to drive a battered van or own a horse and trailer. To become a Muslim one must, with faith and in front of witnesses, make the declaration that there is one God, Allah, and that Muhammad is his Prophet. Identities are, however, seldom simple. They are often contested and the rules of membership change. A frequently debated topic in Wales is what constitutes Welshness. Is it enough to be born in Wales? Or do you have to speak Welsh? Is a London-Welsh man or woman "really" Welsh? Can someone who has learnt the language ever become Welsh? These are not questions with a right or a wrong answer. They are identity boundaries that are fought over, using language and geography as salient markers.[1]

We are not consciously aware of a particular identity unless we come up against another group who are different. If everyone in the world were black, skin color would not be an issue. Black would just be the color of skin, full stop. In a monoglot society the choice of which language to speak does not arise. Identity is defined by the other. It is not an absolute, but a category within a system of values. In many languages there is a word that translates as "one of us," "kin," or "countryman/woman." When nineteenth-century missionaries and travelers asked people they encountered "Who are you?" they were usually answered with some equivalent of "the human beings" or "the speakers of x or y language," and in many cases this became the name of the "tribe" in colonial and post-colonial societies. When, on the other hand, the same Europeans asked, "And who are they, the people over the hill?" the answer often translated as "the non-humans," "the people who eat people," "those who are not kin." These names too became fixed in history. In Welsh, people refer to themselves as the *cymru*, "the kin." The Anglo-Saxons, however, referred to them as the "Welsh," meaning "Romanized Celts" (i.e. foreigners).[2]

Ritual Purity and Social Boundaries

The boundaries marking one group off from another may be physical. The Berlin Wall and Iron Curtain separated the citizens of communist Eastern Europe from the democratic states of the West. Prisons and military establishments erect barriers that are heavily guarded. Boundaries can also be conceptual, expressed in ideas, rituals and belief systems. In chapter 7 of *Purity and Danger* (1966), entitled "External Boundaries," Mary Douglas shows how the physical body can act as a symbol of group identity. The boundaries of the human body are a metaphor for the boundaries of the group. There is no single way in which societies utilize the human body in order to symbolize society, although the left–right polarity described in chapter 2 comes close to a universal symbolic system. In some societies, for instance, menstrual pollution is feared and there are elaborate rules dealing with menstruation. In other societies menstruation is virtually ignored and has little symbolic significance. One society may be preoccupied with death and its ritual avoidance, while another pays little attention to it. There is,

however, according to Douglas, an appositeness about the relationship between body symbolism, pollution beliefs, and the nature of a particular
society. Concern over the body's physical boundaries indicates anxiety over
social boundaries. If a group or society tries to control the physical body it is
almost certainly attempting to control and define group purity and identity.
In a study of the Israelite purity rules in the *Book of Leviticus*, the priestly code
of the *Pentateuch* (the first five books of the Hebrew Bible which constitute
the Torah), Douglas writes:

> The Israelites were always in their history a hard-pressed minority. In their
> beliefs all the bodily issues were polluting, blood, pus, excreta, semen etc. The
> threatened boundaries of their body politic would be well mirrored in their care
> for the integrity, unity and purity of the physical body. (Douglas, 1966, p. 121)[3]

A function of Hebrew and contemporary Orthodox Jewish food taboos is
to separate the community from its gentile neighbors. Any group concerned
to protect its ethnic/group identity is likely to place limits on commensality
with outsiders. Douglas also illustrates her thesis with the example of the
Havik Brahmins in India (see chapter 2), whose concern to maintain inviol-
able their caste boundary leads to excessive concern with physical pollution
and purity. In *Natural Symbols* (1973) Mary Douglas writes about the ways in
which Irish immigrants to England exaggerate food regulations, such as
abstention from meat on a Friday, as a marker of Roman Catholic identity.
The conservatism of expatriate British colonialists in matters of food, dress,
and daily rituals was also notorious, and marked a clear separation between
Europeans and "natives."

The Traveler-Gypsies

Judith Okely carried out her doctoral fieldwork among Traveler-Gypsies in
Hertfordshire (England) in the late 1970s. The concern of the Gypsies with
the boundaries of the physical body was matched by their efforts to maintain
a distinct identity, to separate themselves from the house-dwelling society
that constantly attempts to absorb them. Okely rightly points out that "The
Gypsies' beliefs cannot be seen independently of those of the larger society,
mainly because they create and express symbolic boundaries between the
minority and majority" (Okely, 1983, p. 78). The English Gypsies make a
distinction between the inner and outer body, which can be seen to symbolize the boundary separating the Gypsy from the non-Gypsy (*Gorgio*).[4] The
"inner self" and "true Gypsy" identity are associated with the inner body and
are mirrored in the immaculate inside of a trailer (caravan), or the orderly

inner circle of a camp site, which is kept clean and ritually pure. The "outer self" is compromised through contact with *Gorgios* and is polluted or *mochadi*. Contact between the inner and outer body, the inside and outside of a trailer, and the inner circle and outer edge of a camp site are closely controlled. Waste and rubbish are thrown to the outside of the trailer and camp site – areas already defined as *mochadi*.

Okely points to the many areas of potential misunderstanding between Gypsy and *Gorgio*. The *Gorgio* sees the outside of a Gypsy camp and the trickster aspect of the Gypsy, and regards them as a "dirty" people. The Gypsy sees the *Gorgio* as polluted and polluting (*mochadi*), and tries to protect the inner self from the dangers of *Gorgio* society. "The Gypsies' beliefs not only classify the *Gorgio* as polluting, but also offer the means to retain an inner purity. If certain observances are maintained, the Gypsies can enter *Gorgio* territory unscathed.... All roles, whether trickster, exotic or victim, carry the risk of self-degradation and a dangerous sense of unreality, unless the 'inner self' is protected intact, and unless the actor can distinguish between the self and the part" (Okely, 1983, p. 77).

As an ethnic group the Gypsies are constantly threatened – by well-meaning *Gorgio* attempts to integrate and settle them, as well as by economic and legal harassment. Gypsy concerns with boundaries and issues of purity confirm Douglas's hypothesis that vulnerable groups will "police" the boundaries of the body as well as social boundaries. "The outer body or public self is a protective covering for the inside which must be kept pure and inviolate. The inner body symbolizes the secret ethnic self, sustained individually and reaffirmed by the solidarity of the Gypsy group" (Okely, 1983, p. 80).

There is often a clash between *Gorgio* and Gypsy notions of cleanliness, as Okely illustrates. The *Oxford Journal* for March 8, 1974, ran the headline "Squalor," followed by this account:

> Disillusioned warden quits council caravan park to run Isle of Skye youth hostel. The wife of the warden said of the Travellers: "They are filthy, I just cannot understand how they can live like that.... They seem to want to live in squalor.... We set out with such high ideals and now we are completely disillusioned. They don't want to be helped. (Quoted in Okely, 1983, p. 79)

The story continued with a description of the site:

> The outhouses which have lavatories, washing facilities and a room for sleeping were filthy... old clothing, human excreta and dirt were everywhere. Every window of the outhouses had been smashed. The park was littered with wrecked cars and old rags. The scene was one of utter desolation apart from the three caravans parked on the site. (Quoted in Okely, 1983, p. 79)

Okely makes the following observations on the *Oxford Journal* story:

> The last reference to the caravans, apparently devoid of squalor, unwittingly indicates the main focus for the Travellers' sense of order and cleanliness. The installation of modern plumbing and other facilities on official sites for Gypsies did not always appear to be reducing the conflict over hygiene. The council provision was adjusted to the value system of Gorgio housedwellers. The under- lying intention was to change and convert the Gypsy tenants, for ultimate assimilation. But so long as the Gypsies retain their ethnic and economic inde- pendence, their differing ideas of cleanliness will survive. It is pointless to expect change by operating only at the level of the symbolic. (Okely, 1983, p. 79)

In other words, symbols can be potent and acquire particular meanings when they are supported by political, economic, and social relationships. They serve a purpose and are not merely an end in themselves. As long as the Gypsies maintain a viable economic role at the margins of the existing commercial structure they are likely to generate and maintain a symbolic system that reinforces their separation from *Gorgio* society.

Okely explains in some detail the ways in which the inner/outer distinc- tion is made in practice, throwing light on the contested boundary between *Gorgio* and Gypsy notions of hygiene.

> The Gorgio is condemned as *mochadi* by definition since he or she is not Gypsy. This is confirmed by the Gorgio's failure to distinguish between the inner and outer body. Gorgios design and use kitchen sinks for multiple purposes. This is proven by the Gorgio's habit of placing hand soap or even tooth brushes near the kitchen sink. Hand soap must be kept away from the sink and crockery. One day the Gypsy children offered to clean up my trailer. Among other things I noticed was that they had hidden my hand soap in a cupboard and wrapped it up in several layers of tissue paper. (Okely, 1983, p. 82)

Soap is seen as potential dirt, rather than cleanliness, if kept near the place where utensils are washed. The logic behind this symbolic system is explained in the following passage:

> the outer body (or skin) with its discarded scales, accumulated dirt, by-products of hair and waste such as faeces are all potentially polluting if recycled through the inner body. By contrast, anything taken into the inner body via the mouth must be ritually clean. Attention is directed not only towards food, but also vessels and cutlery which are placed between the lips; the entry to the inner body. Chipped and cracked crockery must be jettisoned. The outer body must be kept separate from the inner – a person's shadow can pollute food. (Okely, 1983, p. 80)

Gypsies take great care to distinguish between vessels used for washing crockery and cutlery, associated with food consumption and therefore the inner body, and those used for washing the outer body and clothes. Ideally, each trailer will have at least two bowls, one for crockery and tea towels and one for personal washing and laundry. When a *Gorgio* health visitor poured disinfectant into the first bowl within reach in order to wash a wound on a man's foot the Gypsies were horrified. The bowl had to be discarded as permanently *mochadi*. In another incident described by Okely, Gypsies eating in a cafe were unsure as to how the cutlery had been washed, so ate with their fingers. To the watching *Gorgio* this was a sign of Gypsy uncouthness and served to reinforce notions of uncivilized Gypsy behavior. To the Gypsies, however, it is *Gorgio* habits, such as washing cutlery and hands in the same bowl or sink, which are disgusting and polluting. Okely describes the tea towel washed and hanging on its own, apart from clothes, as a powerful symbol of separation from the values of *Gorgio* society, a "flag of ethnic purity" (Okely, 1983, p. 81).

Negotiating Identities

The boundary between Gypsies and *Gorgios* may seem fixed and strictly "policed" by a symbolic system that clearly separates insiders from outsiders. In practice, however, both identities and the semantics that maintain them are fluid. *Gorgios* may marry into Gypsy society, learn how to think and act, and as long as they follow the purity rules they will be accepted. While an Untouchable can never become a Brahmin, there is nonetheless a process of development and symbolic adaptation within each caste. In some instances symbolic systems and identities are more obviously being negotiated and defined. One example of this dynamic process is illustrated by Zionist Christians among the Tshidi Barolong of the Mafeking District of South Africa. Jean Comaroff argues that Zionism for the Tshidi is not a marginal religious activity, but a powerful vehicle of resistance that enables adherents to forge an alternative identity capable of transcending the diremption (the disjunctions and ambiguities) of their everyday lives.

Max Weber (1864–1920), a German historian and social scientist, is recognized as one of the foremost intellectual figures of the twentieth century. Weber argued that the value system of scholars or observers influences what they choose to study and how they undertake their investigations. Whereas Karl Marx (1818–83) emphasized the historical and material conditions that structure society, Weber stressed the importance of *Verstehen*, the understanding of what motivates human beings. The materialist base of society (its political and economic structures) is not necessarily, as Marx held, prior to religion. In *The Protestant Ethic and the Spirit of Capitalism* (originally published in 1920), Weber demonstrated the way in which Calvinist Protestantism, with its ethics of individualism, hard work, self-control, and obedience to authority, laid the foundation for the development of capitalism, as the feudal world of the Middle Ages started to break down. Religion is not therefore merely a reflection of society, or a superstructure built upon the framework of materialist conditions. Religion, human motivations, and individual agency exist in a dialectical relationship with social structure.

Wilhelm Friedrich Hegel (1770–1831) developed the notion of *dialectic*. For Hegel totalities are composed of particular sets of objects in dynamic relation with one another. In order to describe society we should not study events or people and the relations between them as fixed, static objects, but as part of a process that has directionality and potentiality. There is often a conflict involved in these relations, and events frequently occur as a reaction to existing forces, leading to a pendulum swing effect. History is not an inevitable teleological process leading inexorably to a particular end, but a dialectic between oppositional systems that give rise to a kaleidoscope of possible outcomes.

Karl Marx viewed history as a conflict between opposing forces, referred to as *thesis* and *antithesis*. The outcome of a struggle between the two leads to a new *synthesis*, known as *dialectical materalism*. Marx viewed the history of the modern period as characterized by class struggle between the proletariat, who sold their labor, and capitalists, who owned the means of production.

Jean Comaroff (1985) examines the dialectic between "traditional" pre-colonial Tshidi values and the post-colonial world of modern South Africa in which the Tshidi are a marginalized group, part agricultural peasants and part urbanized proletariat.

Zionist Christianity grew out of late nineteenth-century urban American counterculture and posed a challenge to orthodox Protestantism. The Christian Catholic Apostolic Church in Zion (CCACZ) was founded in Chicago in 1896, and was introduced to South Africa in 1904. In the USA the CCACZ drew most of its membership from impoverished urban communities in the industrial Midwest, where it challenged, through the use of religious symbols, the marginalization of its members from the mainstream American economic dream and from orthodox Protestant denominations. This challenge found an echo among poor black workers in South Africa.

Comaroff argues that the Zionist churches draw on both indigenous and modern capitalist symbols, and by reshaping them challenge existing value systems. Zionism provides the Tshidi with an identity and reconfigures the symbolic order so as to resolve some of the tensions within their material conditions.

> The Zionist church provided indigenous workers with an order of symbols, concepts, and practical forms that promised novel resolutions to the problems of living between the impoverished worlds of rural subsistence and wage labor. In this process, the incoming movement was itself considerably transformed. But its initial appeal lay in the resonance of its cultural categories with the historical experience of such peripheralized peoples as the Tshidi. (Comaroff, 1985, p. 177)

In South African Zionist churches, evangelical Christianity interacted with indigenous cultures in such a way that they "opened up a general discourse about estrangement and reclamation, domination and resistance" that "stretched far beyond the domain of ritual itself, penetrating acutely into the experiential fabric of everyday life" (Comaroff, 1985, p. 11). The body is regarded as a mediator between personal experience and the social and material world. The social divisions and tensions felt by the Tshidi are conceptualized in a divided and ailing body. Bodily healing can therefore represent individual health, restored social relations, and improved material conditions, and ritual is one central mechanism through which the healing of the physical and social body is accomplished.

> The rituals of Zion are a *bricolage* whose signs appropriate the power both of colonialism and of an objectified Tshidi "tradition," welding them into a transcendent synthesis; an integrated order of symbols and practices that seeks to reverse estrangement, to reconstitute the divided self. (Comaroff, 1985, p. 12)

Bricolage is a term used by Claude Lévi-Strauss (1908–) in his discussion of myth in *The Savage Mind* (1976, pp. 16ff). The *bricoleur* is a craftsman or Jack of all trades, who uses whatever is to hand to complete a particular task. Lévi-Strauss likens mythical thought to the work of the *bricoleur*, in that it "expresses itself by means of a heterogeneous repertoire which, even if extensive, is nevertheless limited" (Lévi-Strauss, 1976, p. 17). The term *bricolage* has been widely adopted within anthropology to refer to the creation of symbolic structures from a variety of culturally available symbols.

The politics of dress

The clothes people wear are one way of expressing identity. Outer clothes are visible and therefore carry public messages. Teenagers growing up in Western societies may use "outrageous" fashions to mark a move from parental control to independence, although the power to shock is limited in a mass culture which endlessly reproduces the images of mass consumption.[5] Jeans, or high-heeled shoes, mini or maxi skirts, or whatever the prevailing fashions might dictate, can soon resemble a uniform. Clothes can become a battleground, not just between parents and children, but also between teachers and pupils, or indeed anyone in authority and those over whom he or she seeks to exercise that authority. Judith Okely records that in her boarding school the uniform changed in time with prevailing fashions, but in the opposite direction. When long full skirts were in vogue, the school dress, designed to disguise any feminine curves, had to be three inches above the knee when kneeling (Okely, 1978, p. 131). At the end of their school career girls would destroy the hated uniforms, sometimes hurling items into the sea.[6]

The Christian churches have often used clothes as boundary markers to separate members from those outside their fellowship. Tabitha Kanogo describes the transformation of mission girls in Church Missionary Society (CMS) schools in early twentieth-century Kenya.

> The most noticeable and immediate changes in the lives of mission girls were external. As a first step towards the "cleansing" of their wards, the girls were stripped of their traditional attire and jewelry. These were replaced with mission uniforms. Among the Kikuyu, those who had had their ear-lobes pierced and subsequently enlarged for decoration had them sewn-up in keeping with the prevailing spirit of Christian modesty. In their checked uniforms, the Thogoto CMS girls stood apart from their peers in the villages. They were cleaned-up, and all ochre and other decorations removed. Subsequent catechumens attested to the attraction of those uniforms and the "cleaned-up" image of new recruits. (Kanogo, 1993, p. 169)

Among Tshidi Zionists uniforms are also important. In the *semantic system* of dress (the meanings given to various items) both pre-colonial customs and the dress codes imposed by the missions are significant points of reference. "The power of uniforms in Tshidi perception was both expressive and pragmatic, for the uniform instantiated the ritual practice it represented" (Comaroff, 1985, p. 220). The clothes worn for ritual were not just a means of demarcating group boundaries, however. They were attributed a semi-magical quality. A Methodist minister in Mafeking in the 1960s remarked, "Our Methodist women say that if they break church law while wearing the uniform they might be strangled by it" (Comaroff, 1985, p. 270).

Comaroff unpacks the rich symbolism of the Zionist dress code. While there were small variations between different Zionist churches, the greatest contrast was with the uniforms of the mission churches and with everyday work clothes. Most strikingly, Zionist men wear white skirts, the effect of which is to "blur the stark Western contrast between male severity and female opulence" (Comaroff, 1985, p. 270). As migrant workers the men are separated from their families and communities, and find themselves at the bottom of the social pile. By wearing clothes that contrast sharply with those they must wear for work, Comaroff claims, the men are seeking "to return to a world in which producer is not severed from consumer, or use from exchange, and where direct and controllable social relations replace commoditized transactions" (Comaroff, 1985, p. 221).

> More generally, the Zionist's outward appearance is crowded with signs that speak to a particular relationship between bodies personal and social. The sparkling robes and flowing hair of the men, and the Victorian tunics of the women, are conspicuously set off from the mass-produced, often threadbare clothing worn by the majority of rural Tshidi. The Zionist might also trudge on the dusty roads of the stad, or on the bustling streets of the modern town; but he is visible of neither place. The colors and contours of his appearance make reference to images of distant times and contexts; his style communicates his "otherness," a fact which all Tshidi perceive. He personifies the distant biblical world of Victorian mission illustrations, which still line the walls of many Tshidi homes, conveying a general message both of disillusion and passionate intention – a message at once of deconstruction and recreation. (Comaroff, 1985, p. 221)

Although it might be argued that Zionism does little to transform the material conditions of people's lives, Comaroff sees the integrative and creative use of colonial and traditional symbols in ritual practice as genuinely transformative. They can be interpreted as a way of reclaiming power and resisting structures of inequality.

> On the dynamic ground of the Zionist robe, the insignia of Western and indigenous ritual, of colonial and precolonial orders, are unified and subsumed in a transcendent identity. The power relations of the established world are inverted and imprinted on the body of a community reborn. (Comaroff, 1985, p. 228)

Contesting Boundaries

In this final section we will look at two examples of ways in which the boundaries of the physical body are used to make political statements. Mikhail Bakhtin's study of the medieval and Renaissance carnival in the works of the French writer Rabelais is a celebration of the body and its openness to life. The egalitarianism of the carnival and its focus on the body at its most basic was a challenge to the rigidly hierarchical social structures of the time. The carnival "grotesque" body stands in stark contrast to the emaciated controlled bodies of holy women who starved themselves in pursuit of sanctity. Medieval women ascetics were, however, also engaged in a struggle. Control over consumption is linked to a sense of autonomy and independence. An obsession with physical boundaries (eating and fasting) was at the same time a mechanism for denying female biology (menstruation and motherhood), and the roles assigned to women in a patriarchal society.[7]

Imitating Christ – medieval women's asceticism

The twelfth and thirteenth centuries were a time of change and innovation in Western Europe. Universities, towns, and the craft guilds began to develop from a previously agrarian society. There were new religious impulses, in both the monastic and itinerant life. The Cistercians revived the Rule of Saint Benedict, while the Cluniac Benedictines founded vast monastic settlements. Both Saint Francis of Assisi (1181–1226) and St Dominic (1170–1221) formed mendicant orders, while the evangelical preacher Norbert of Xanten (c.1085–1134) established the Premonstratensian canons and canonesses. Women's roles in these new orders were, however, far more restricted than men's. Women could not be ordained to the priesthood and a mendicant life was considered unseemly. While Dominican and Franciscan friars and Premonstratensian canons might wander from place to place to preach, beg, and give witness to their faith, the women who were accepted into these communities were cloistered. Civil authority was also largely in male hands. The powerful abbesses and female landholders of earlier times had disappeared. Women's independent commercial activities were circumscribed and the guilds acted as protectionist trades unions, which led to the exclusion of women, denying them access to many crafts that they had previously practiced. In some parts of Europe, particularly the Low Countries, communities of women known as *beguines* developed. They were dedicated to a life of prayer and service, taking temporary vows of celibacy. Beguines succeeded in avoiding the control of both husband and conventual claustration.[8]

The very different life trajectories of men and women led to different choices of symbols in the search for holiness. The example of the wealthy young Francis stripping off his finery in front of his father and assembled dignitaries, and embracing a life of poverty, is characteristic of the heroic male model. Men could make dramatic gestures that reflected real choices in their lives. Women had less control over their lives, and in place of sudden conversions and role reversals used their ordinary experiences of powerlessness, service, sexuality, disease, and nurturing as symbols that could contain their desires, passions, and aspirations.[9]

Holiness for women was often equated with extraordinary feats of self-denial. If women's bodies and sexuality were impure (a distinct and deeply rooted topos in the Western church), control of sexuality and other physical needs, particularly food, sleep, and warmth, were seen as a means of achieving sanctity. As Obeyesekere noted in the case of Sri Lankan women ascetics, publicly recognized significations do not reduce the importance of the psychological, emotional impact of bodily symbols employed by women (see chapter 2). Male clerics who observed the austerities of medieval holy women were simultaneously attracted and repelled. They often encouraged mortifications and wondered at paranormal feats, while distancing themselves from the extremes to which some women went in their search for holiness. The twelfth-century beguine, Marie of Oignies, was probably one of the first stigmatics – physically displaying marks in imitation of Jesus' crucifixion on her own body. She had been married young, but took a vow of chastity and devoted herself to good works. She was filled with a horror of physical pleasure, and, as her chronicler Jacques of Vitry records:

> began to afflict herself and she found no rest in spirit, until, by means of extraordinary bodily chastisement, she had made up for all the pleasures she had experienced in the past. In vehemence of spirit, almost as if she were inebriated, she began to loathe her body when she compared it to the sweetness of the Paschal Lamb and, with a knife, in error she cut out a large piece of her flesh which, from embarrassment, she buried in the earth. (Petroff, 1986, p. 7)[10]

What de Vitry does not note, in his haste to condemn her self-mutilation, is that Marie of Oignies, in cutting off a piece of her own flesh, could have been unconsciously performing a "eucharistic" act. She was giving of her body in a very literal sense, just as Christ did in the Last Supper and does anew at every celebration of the Eucharist. If women could not give birth to Christ through the Word, by preaching, or through the Eucharist, by celebrating Mass, they could imitate him in his suffering, and live in hope of union with him on earth in the expectation of sharing his bodily resurrection in the world to come.

The use of food and renunciation of food as a symbol of holiness has been documented by Rudolf Bell (1985) and Caroline Walker Bynum (1987b). Bynum, for instance, notes that at one level both eucharistic and mystical union can be seen as reversals of normal cultural roles for women. "Woman's jubilant, vision-inducing, intoxicated eating of God was the opposite of the ordinary female acts of food preparation and of bearing and nursing children" (Bynum, 1987b, p. 289). A symbol as complex as the body is, however, capable of multivalent readings, and at a deeper level:

> in the mass and in mystical ecstasy women became a fuller version of the food and flesh they were assumed by their culture to be. In union with the dying Christ, woman became a fully fleshly and feeding self – at one with the generative suffering of God. Woman's eating, fasting, and feeding others were synonymous acts, because in all three the woman, by suffering, fused with a cosmic suffering that really redeemed the world. And these three synonymous acts and symbols were not finally symbolic reversals but, rather, a transfiguring and becoming of what the female symbolized: the fleshly, the nurturing, the suffering, the human. (Bynum, 1987b, p. 289)

Rudolf Bell's book *Holy Anorexia* draws on the experience of women officially recognized as saints, blesseds, venerables, or servants of God who lived in the Italian peninsula between 1200 and the present. Of the 261 individuals so designated, the historical records of about a third are too meager to be taken into account. Of the remaining 170 or so women, more than half displayed signs of anorexia. They included such well-known figures as Catherine of Sienna and Mary Magdalen de' Pazzi. Women who "were heroic models and protectors for the believers who flocked to their tombs, fought for possession of their relics, and listened in awe as preachers spread word of their holy behavior" (Bell, 1985, p. x). In a fascinating comparison between Bell's "holy anorectics" and sufferers of anorexia nervosa today, William N. Davis, a clinical psychologist, makes the point in the epilogue to *Holy Anorexia* that holiness and thinness substitute for one another.

> Holy anorectics detested their bodily desires and were terrified at the possibility of their unbidden appearance. In order to be holy it was necessary to have no needs, be they sexual, narcissistic, or nutritional. The sine qua non for holiness was purity, and so attractive men, or opportunities to be selfish, or food had to be obsessively avoided. It is here that there is an explicit connection between holiness and starvation. The avoidance of food is part of the path to saintliness. Modern-day anorectics are just as suspicious of their bodies, and just as frightened that they will suddenly be betrayed by their bodily needs. Food and the desire to eat are paramount, but all primary anorectics are also repulsed by

sexuality and disgusted by selfishness. The notion of bodily purity and cleanliness is just as significant for them as it was for holy anorectics. Thinness means the absence of desire just as surely as it means emaciation. (Davis, 1985, pp. 182–3)

A fixation on diet and therefore on the body gives some women a far greater sense of connection with themselves than is possible by means of ordinary human relationships. The holy anorexic, in rejecting food, achieved both inner connection and connection with God, just as the Sri Lankan ascetics rejected human lovers and accepted their matted locks as manifestations of union with their chosen deity. That there is an intricate relationship between the unconscious choice of symbols (hair or fasting) and public meanings is demonstrated by the fact that cases of holy anorexia declined as excessive fasting became gradually detached from notions of holiness. It might be supposed that anorexia nervosa will also diminish if thinness ceases to be regarded as a feminine ideal (Davis, 1985, p. 190). Neither snake hair nor anorexia are inevitable choices for women; they occur when personal psychological and emotional yearnings coincide with established and commonly understood cultural symbols. In both instances the holy women could be interpreted as manipulating private and public symbols so as to contest the boundaries of gender and conventional female roles. These private rebellions are one way in which women can construct an identity that transcends the roles of daughter, wife, and mother, making them central actors in the drama of their lives.

The grotesque body

The work of literary theorist and philosopher Mikhail Bakhtin is important to us here for several reasons. In *Rabelais and His World* (1984), his study of medieval and Renaissance humor and the world of the carnival, Bakhtin reveals the body as an experience and symbol of creative ambiguity, quite at odds with the official views illustrated above by examples of holy women's biophobia, and far removed from contemporary Western notions of humour. In stressing the *liminal* aspects of carnival, with its potential for change and transformation, Bakhtin challenges the view that role reversals merely strengthen the status quo. This theme is explored further in chapter 6, looking at the work of Arnold van Gennep and Victor Turner. Bakhtin also alerts the reader to the dangers of reading other cultures (other historical periods) through the lens of our own. In one sense this is of course inevitable (we cannot become the other). Because we all have bodies we can make the mistake of assuming that our particular experience of embodiment is universal, whereas our bodies both connect us with others and separate us – formed by our genes and by individual and collective cultural experiences.

Mikhail Bakhtin (1895–1975) was a Russian intellectual whose work, particularly in the field of literary theory, is becoming increasingly influential in both Russia and the West. Bakhtin's study of the carnival in the writings of the French novelist Rabelais (1494–1553) is a powerful political comment on Stalinist Russia. When Bakhtin wrote *Rabelais and His World* (1934–5) the Communist Academy was attempting to assert control over the form and content of Russian literature. In the image of the medieval and Renaissance carnival, as described by Rabelais, Bakhtin detected a radical critique of authoritarian structures, typified by the "grotesque" body, at once earthy, transcendent, and universal.

In order to appreciate the place of carnivals in medieval and Renaissance society we need to realize that they played a dominant role in people's lives (perhaps television would be the closest parallel today in terms of its influence). In large medieval cities as much as three months a year was devoted to carnival-type activities. Carnivals represented "the people" and provided space for unofficial forms of humor. They were not, however, the preserve of the urban and rural masses – clergy and other elites were also drawn into them.[11] A key element of the carnival, as explored by Bakhtin, is festive laughter, which has three main characteristics: (a) it is the laughter of all the people; (b) it is universal – encompassing all participants in its scope; and (c) it is ambivalent (Bakhtin, 1984, pp. 11–13). An important aspect of carnival humor is its attitude to the body, based on a very different aesthetic to the official world of institutions and hierarchies and to contemporary Western humor. Bakhtin called this concept "grotesque realism," the chief characteristics of which were as follows:

> In grotesque realism ... the bodily element is deeply positive. It is presented not in a private, egotistic form, severed from other spheres of life, but as something universal, representing all the people. As such it is opposed to severance from the material and bodily roots of the world; it makes no pretense to renunciation of the earthy, or independence of the earth and the body. We repeat: the body and bodily life have here a cosmic and at the same time an all-people's character; this is not the body and its physiology in the modern sense of these words, because it is not individualized. The material bodily principle is contained not in the biological individual, not in the bourgeois ego, but in the people, a people who are continually growing and renewed. This is why all that is bodily becomes grandiose, exaggerated, immeasurable.
>
> This exaggeration has a positive, assertive character. The leading themes of these images of bodily life are fertility, growth, and a brimming-over

abundance . . . the material bodily principle is a triumphant, festive principle, it is a "banquet for all the world." (Bakhtin, 1984, p. 19)

In grotesque realism the body is not a discrete unit, experienced as separate from the rest of the world, nor is it merely a vehicle for the soul. Bakhtin understood that the image of the body expressed in carnival incorporates a whole cosmology – a radically different image of society from that of the hegemonic institutions of the day.

> The unfinished and open body (dying, bringing forth and being born) is not separated from the world by clearly defined boundaries; it is blended with the world, with animals, with objects. It is cosmic, it represents the entire material bodily world in all its elements. It is an incarnation of this world as the absolute lower stratum, as the swallowing up and generating principle, as the bodily grave and bosom, as a field which has been sown and in which new shoots are preparing to sprout. (Bakhtin, 1984, pp. 26–7)

The image of the open body corresponds to the universality of the carnival experience. It destroyed social hierarchy with its pomp and rank, and through humor also dethroned spiritual hierarchies, which placed the spirit above the earth and the material world. With its popular depictions of simultaneous birth and death, the grotesque body succeeds in transcending time. It is the cosmic tree that links the individual to the universal, heaven to earth, and encapsulates past, present, and future.

Conclusion

In this chapter we have continued to look at the body as a symbol and as an instrument that mediates between self and society. Nancy Scheper-Hughes and Margaret Lock (1987) have developed the notion of the "mindful body" in an attempt to go beyond studies that focus on either individual psycho-biology or linguistic and cultural factors. They claim that we need to examine three levels or facets of the body, and to explore the links between them. We experience our bodies first on an individual level, as an intricate part of ourselves, defining who we are. Second, our bodies are socially constructed, used symbolically, and subject to cultural modification. Finally, we have the body politic, the control of bodies on both an individual and a collective level.[12] When examining the formation of religious identity all three levels of body experience need to be considered. As the mindful body is not a static concept, this involves taking account of historical changes, individual agency, and the positioning of the body in terms of hegemonic and alternative discourses.

Notes

1 See Bowie and Davies (1992) and Bowie (1993) for an analysis of Welsh language and identity issues.
2 For a brief discussion of the terminology of Welsh and Celtic identities see Davies and Bowie (1995).
3 See Jacobs (1998) for a description of the body in Jewish worship.
4 This is in contrast to the Californian Rom studied by Anne Sutherland (1975), who make a greater distinction between the upper and lower parts of the body than the inner/outer dichotomy.
5 See Baudrillard (1975).
6 Malcolm Young (1994) has written in a similar vein concerning police uniforms, which serve to differentiate women police officers both from their male colleagues and from other women.
7 For interesting discussions of the body in Western Catholicism and Protestantism see Louth (1998) and Tripp (1998).
8 See Bowie (1989).
9 See Bowie (1989, p. 33) and Bynum (1987a, pp. 121–39).
10 Jacques of Vitry's "*Life*" of Marie of Oignies. See Bowie (1989, pp. 29–30).
11 One of the weaknesses of Bakhtin's brilliant exposition, with its sensitivity to elite and popular cultures, is his failure to pay sufficient attention to gender. The experiences described may well apply disproportionately to men.
12 See Asad (1998, p. 45).

References and Further Reading

Asad, Talal (1998) Remarks on the anthropology of the body. In Sarah Coakely (ed.), *Religion and the Body*. Cambridge: Cambridge University Press, pp. 42–52.
Bakhtin, Mikhail (1984) *Rabelais and His World*, translated by Hélène Iswolsky. Bloomington: Indiana University Press (first published in 1965).
Baudrillard, Jean (1975) *The Mirror of Production*. St Louis: Telos Press.
Bell, Rudolph M. (1985) *Holy Anorexia*. Chicago and London: University of Chicago Press.
Belton, Brian A. (2004) *Questioning Gypsy Identity: Ethnic Narratives in Britain and America*. Oxford: AltaMira Press.
Bowie, Fiona (1989) *Beguine Spirituality: an Anthology*. London: SPCK. Published in the USA in 1990 as *Beguine Spirituality: Mystical Writings of Mechthild of Magdeburg, Beatrice of Nazareth, and Hadewijch of Brabant*. New York: Crossroad.

Bowie, Fiona and Oliver Davies (eds) (1992) *Discovering Welshness*. Llandysul: Gwasg Gomer.

Bowie, Fiona (1993) Wales from within: conflicting interpretations of Welsh identity. In Sharon Macdonald (ed.), *Inside European Identities: Ethnography in Western Europe*. Providence, RI, and Oxford: Berg, pp. 167–93.

Bynum, Caroline Walker (1987a) Religious women in the later Middle Ages. In J. Raitt (ed.), *Christian Spirituality in the High Middle Ages and Reformation*. London: Routledge, pp. 121–39.

Bynum, Caroline Walker (1987b) *Holy Feast and Holy Fast: the Religious Significance of Food to Medieval Women*. Berkeley, Los Angeles and London: University of California Press.

Cohen, Anthony P. (ed.) (1986) *Symbolising Boundaries: Identity and Diversity in British Cultures*. Manchester: Manchester University Press.

Comaroff, Jean (1985) *Body of Power, Spirit of Resistance: the Culture and History of a South African People*. Chicago and London: University of Chicago Press.

Davies, Oliver and Bowie, Fiona (eds) (1995) *Celtic Christian Spirituality: an Anthology of Medieval and Modern Sources*. London: SPCK. Published in the USA as *Celtic Spirituality: an Anthology*. New York: Crossroad.

Davis, William N. (1985) Epilogue. In Rudolf Bell, *Holy Anorexia*. Chicago and London: Chicago University Press.

Douglas, Mary (1966) *Purity and Danger*. London: Routledge and Kegan Paul.

Douglas, Mary (1973) *Natural Symbols*. Harmondsworth: Penguin.

Jacobs, Louis (1998) The body in Jewish worship. Three rivals examined. In Sarah Coakely (ed.), *Religion and the Body*. Cambridge: Cambridge University Press, pp. 71–89.

Kanogo, Tabitha (1993) Mission impact on women in colonial Kenya. In Fiona Bowie, Deborah Kirkwood, and Shirley Ardener (eds), *Women and Missions: Past and Present. Anthropological and Historical Perceptions*. Providence, RI, and Oxford: Berg, pp. 165–86.

Lévi-Strauss, Claude (1976) *The Savage Mind*, translated by Rodney Needham. London: Weidenfeld and Nicolson (first published in 1962).

Lincoln, Bruce (1992) *Discourse and the Construction of Society*. Oxford: Oxford University Press.

Louth, Andrew (1998) The body in Western Catholic Christianity. In Sarah Coakely (ed.), *Religion and the Body*. Cambridge: Cambridge University Press, pp. 111–30.

Okely, Judith (1978) Privileged, schooled and finished: boarding education for girls. In Shirley Ardener (ed.), *Defining Females*. London: Croom Helm, in association with the Oxford University Women's Studies Committee, pp. 109–39.

Okely, Judith (1983) *The Traveller-Gypsies*. Cambridge: Cambridge University Press.

Okely, Judith (1994) Ethnic identity and place of origin: the Traveller Gypsies in Great Britain. In Hans Vermeulen and Jeremy Boissevain (eds), *Ethnic Challenge: the Politics of Ethnicity in Europe*. Gottingen: Edition Herodot, pp. 50–65.

Petroff, E. A. (ed.) (1986) *Medieval Women's Visionary Literature*. Oxford: Oxford University Press.

Scheper-Hughes, Nancy and Lock, Margaret M. (1987) The mindful body: a prolegomena to future work in medical anthropology. *Medical Anthropology Quarterly*, new series, 1(1), 6–41.

Sutherland, Anne (1975) *Gypsies: the Hidden Americans*. London: Tavistock.

Tripp, David (1998) The image of the body in the formative phases of the Protestant Reformation. In Sarah Coakely (ed.), *Religion and the Body*. Cambridge: Cambridge University Press, pp. 131–52.

Weber, Max (1958) *The Protestant Ethic and the Spirit of Capitalism*, translated by Talcott Parsons. New York: Scribner's (first published in 1920).

Young, Malcolm (1994) The symbolism of uniform: female marginality in police society. Paper delivered to the Third ENP Conference, Brussels, November.

Chapter 4

Sex, Gender, and the Sacred

Introduction

The "myth of equality" in Western societies disguises the extent to which sex and gender remain key organizing social principles. When men and women compare experiences, however, or when confronted with statistical information, it becomes clear that whether we are born male or female profoundly affects the choices, opportunities, and view of the world we will have throughout life. In most small-scale societies gender is even more obviously a key determinant in social processes and structures, although to differing degrees. In Bali in Indonesia there is relatively little sexual differentiation between men and women. Both dress in a similar fashion, undertake similar tasks, and, where there is role differentiation, can often substitute for one another. Significantly, there is also considerable gender equality expressed in Balinese mythology, and similar access to resources in this rice-based culture. Some hunter-gatherer societies, including the Mbuti Pygmies of Central Africa and the Kung Bushmen of South West Africa, have a much greater degree of sex role specialization than the Balinese, but also display minimal differentiation in terms of economic control, symbolic and religious authority, and childcare. In other societies, such as the Fulani of Africa's Western Sahel, men and women are very strictly segregated. Islam may have intensified male control of women by further subduing female religious cults. Fulani women are confined to the private sphere, and if they do appear in public are fully veiled. Occupations are quite separate, with little or no overlap between male and female roles.[1]

In this chapter we will look at some of the ways in which sexuality and gender issues have been studied in the anthropology of religion, and give some examples of studies in which gender or sexuality have been a primary focus of ethnographic or theoretical interest. One could argue that framing the discussion above in terms of "equality" has more to do with the agenda of "second wave" feminism in the West than with any indigenous understanding of social organization in other parts of the world. This problematic alerts us to the central question of *translation* within anthropology. No account of another society is value-free or objective. Any ethnography or theory arising from it reflects the agenda of the observer and the quality of his or her access to other ways of thinking and being, filtered through his or her prior experience, life history, and conscious and unconscious intention (see chapter 1).[2]

Some key terms

Sex: a biological category, *man* or *woman*.

Gender: a social category, *male* or *female*.

Sex role: behavior and occupations defined as *masculine* or *feminine*, seen as appropriate to a particular gender.

Sexuality: the social and biological expression, organization, and orientation of desire. This includes, but is not limited to, reproduction.

Cultural construction: the social/cultural rather than biological formation of categories such as gender.

Biological determinism: the attempt to explain higher level behavior by reference to biology.

Emic: an insider or native perspective as opposed to an **etic** or external view. The terms were coined by Kenneth Pike (1954) from the analogous linguistic terms "phon*emic*" and "phon*etic*."

Hegemony: the domination of one elite or class over another (Greek *hegemon*, "leader").

As we saw in chapter 1, an anthropological account is written for a particular audience. There may be a translation from one language to another, but also from one symbolic system to another one that may be very alien to it. The ethnographer must try to find points of contact between two societies in order to communicate. The resulting text will be a unique record of a particular three-way encounter between the people studied, the anthropologist, and the intended audience.[3] All studies of other cultures reflect their times. One consequence of this has been the almost total absence of women's voices and experience in the anthropological record. Much anthropology by women scholars from the 1970s onwards represents an effort to redress this balance. The first part of this chapter, "Looking at Women," traces some of the significant steps in social anthropology's attempt to restore women's voices in the ethnographic record. The work of Edwin and Shirley Ardener is discussed in this context. The second part of the chapter, "Reflexivity and Gender," draws on Pat

Caplan's discussion of gender in relation to fieldwork practice. In the final part of the chapter, "Gendered Studies," we look at some theoretical and ethnographic writing in which gender and sexuality are central to the analysis. The related question of women's association with nature and men with culture, and the links between gender, mythology, and the environment are debated in chapter 5. Sexuality and ritual have been long-standing interests in the anthropology of religion, reflected in particular in the increasingly rich ethnographic record concerned with male and female initiation rites in various parts of the world. Although equally relevant here, some of these texts appear instead among the readings for chapter 6 in the context of rites of passage. There are numerous anthropological works focusing on links between feminism, sexuality, religion, ethnography, and gender, and I can attempt to do little more than direct readers to a sample of some of the available literature in the reading list at the end of this chapter.

Looking at Women

Women were never absent from the ethnographic record, but their lives were filtered through and interpreted by men. The devaluation of women in Western cultures and an empirical bias toward the study of structures and institutions meant that women were considered less important than men as informants. Ethnographers who speak mainly or only to men will often find that a similar bias exists in the host culture. In this way women and women's representations of the world are doubly marginalized.

Sir Edward Evan Evans-Pritchard (1902–73), Professor of Social Anthropology in Oxford from 1946 to 1970, is associated with the structural-functionalist school of British social anthropology. Most of his fieldwork was conducted in colonial Africa, most notably among the *Nuer* and *Azande* of the Southern Sudan. In his study *Witchcraft, Magic and Oracles among the Azande* (1937), Evans-Pritchard demonstrated not just the function of Zande witchcraft but above all its logic. In 1974 his posthumous *Man and Woman among the Azande* was published. This was a very different sort of book, in which the voices of informants were recorded with minimal interpretation. Although the focus on gender, sex, and the emic (insider) perspective reflects new interests within anthropology, the preface makes clear that Evans-Pritchard's data consisted of men talking *about* women: "When in Zandeland I perhaps felt on the whole on the side of the men rather than the women, though I knew that the women suffered discriminations. . . . I ought to add that all the texts in this collection were taken down from men, who naturally had a bias in their own favour" (Evans-Pritchard, 1974, p. 10). Evans-Pritchard might have added that the texts were also taken down *by* men. It is impossible to avoid the sense of the male interlocutor looking at and talking about the female of the species.

Women as a muted group

The rise of the women's movement in the 1960s and 1970s prompted a reassessment of the treatment of women in anthropology. Edwin Ardener (1927–87), in a paper first delivered in 1968, suggested that women had been given insufficient attention in anthropology.

> At the level of "observation" in fieldwork, the behaviour of women has, of course, like that of men, been exhaustively plotted: their marriages, their economic activity, their rites, and the rest. When we come to that second or "meta" level of fieldwork, the vast body of debate, discussion, question and answer, that social anthropologists really depend upon to give conviction to their interpretations, there is a real imbalance. We are, for practical purposes, in a male world. The study of women is on a level little higher than the study of ducks and fowls they commonly own – a mere bird-watching indeed. (Ardener, 1975, pp. 1–2)

Several reasons for this failure are advanced. First, the kinds of question the ethnographer (male or female) asks are structured so as to construct the kind of model of society that male informants are most likely to provide. Inspired by Mauss's study of gift exchange, Lévi-Strauss developed a model based on the circulation of women, in which women were seen as "items of exchange inexplicably and inappropriately giving tongue" (Ardener, 1975, p. 2). It was another generation before anthropologists started to systematically explore marriage in "closed" or "elementary" systems from the perspective of the women themselves. The second problem was of a more technical nature. An ethnographer unfamiliar with the language of the host society is more likely to find interpreters and informants who can bridge the language gap among men, due to their greater mobility, access to education, and political domin- ance. One might add that men, in most societies, also have more leisure time than women. The ethnographer who wishes to talk to women must be prepared to accompany female informants to the fields and to collect water; to sit in the kitchen and help with cooking and childcare duties. The luxury of whiling away the afternoon talking to cronies or to anthropologists is usually a male preserve.

"The fact is that no one could come back from an ethnographic study of 'the x,' having talked only *to* women, and *about* men, without professional comment and some self-doubt. The reverse can and does happen constantly" (Ardener, 1975, p. 3).

Ardener insists, however, that the problem is symbolic rather than technical – it is about ways of looking at the world and of understanding our place within it. Women have a view of the world, but "will not necessarily provide a model for society as a unit that will contain both men and themselves. They may indeed provide a model in which women and nature are outside men and society" (Ardener, 1975, p. 3). If women's models are less accessible discursively, they may be revealed through ritual, dance, art, myth, or less analytical speech registers. The example Edwin Ardener uses to illustrate his argument is drawn from the Bakweri of South West Cameroon. In his analysis of the Bakweri women's mermaid cult, for example, Ardener shows not only how the rituals are *polysemic* (i.e. carry different levels of meaning), but how they can "mean" different things to men and to women. For men the rites fit a girl for marriage by "rescuing" her from the wild, from nature (defined as the area outside the village where women farm). Nonetheless, married women continue to farm outside the village fence in the men's "wild." The boundary of their world is drawn so that they live partly in the male arena of the village and partly in the bush, beyond the experience and control of men (Ardener, 1975, pp. 12–13). While the bush is perceived as the realm of untamed nature by men, it is part of the domestic world of female subsistence farming.

Ardener's discussion is phrased in terms of his fieldwork experience in Nigeria and Cameroon, but the force of the argument does not depend on a cultural or linguistic discrepancy between fieldworker and informants. The term *muted group* is used to describe the relationship between all dominant and subordinate models of communication. Charlotte Hardman used the term "muted" to refer to modes of speech, but it has become popular within anthropology in a much wider sociological sense. All societies have some groups that to a greater or lesser extent control the ways in which language is used and formed, the acquisition of knowledge and its dissemination, and what is defined as "normal" or acceptable. In the Western world this elite is predominantly male, middle-class, white, and nominally Christian (or in some contexts Jewish). Members of this elite represent a range of institutions, such as local and national government, education, business, and the church. Although women, people from religious or ethnic minorities, the poor, or others on the fringes of society may be co-opted into these elites, they have a limited ability to change the dominant ethos, prevailing models of society, or forms of communication. If men, or certain groups of men, construct the language and models of a society, communication is restricted for women and other so-called "muted" groups. Most Christian churches (and other religious groups), for example, reflect the views of heterosexual men (even if they contain practicing homosexuals in positions of influence). It is very difficult for homosexual men and lesbian women Christians to communicate their experience to those in power, or to change the thought patterns, forms of scriptural interpretation, language, and ritual that maintain a heterosexist view of "normality" and morality. Their experiences of the world, their models, are "muted" in relation to the hegemonic voices of those in power. Children, similarly, are relatively inarticulate ("muted") in relation to adults, not merely because they are still developing linguistic skills, but because adults are in control. Grown-ups forget what the world looks like through the eyes of a child. To understand what children's models of the world are like one would need not only to speak to them, but also to interpret their games, their songs, the articulation of fantasy and imagination, their art, and their dreams.

The concept of a "muted group" has been useful in directing the attention of anthropologists to non-linguistic forms of expression, pointing out the limitations of abstract philosophical models as total descriptions of a society. It has also served to remind the ethnographer that societies are not hetero-geneous. They are made up of individuals and groups with different experiences and interpretations. Any abstract or generalized description is therefore inevitably partial. This does not mean that the anthropologist should shy away from the task of imposing order or meaning on material, or avoid all attempts at generalization. He or she should, however, be aware of their limitations and accept them for the (useful) fiction that they are.

Men and women in the field

The extent to which the gender and ideological presuppositions of the ethnographer affect the analysis of another society is graphically illustrated in an article comparing the findings of male and female anthropologists looking at Australian Aboriginal women (Rohrich-Leavitt et al., 1975). Male anthropologists have tended to present these societies as male-dominated, with women in a "subordinate, degraded status" (Rohrich-Leavitt et al., 1975, p. 112). C. W. M. Hart, who studied the Tiwi of North Australia, for instance, apparently "focused on the genealogical system and deliberately ignored their mythology and subsistence techniques because they "bored" him" (Rohrich-Leavitt et al., 1975, p. 113). A very different picture of the Tiwi emerges from Jane Goodale's *Tiwi Wives*, in which women's central economic role is acknowledged. It is also argued that "the full force of the Judeo-Christian theme of female uncleanliness is projected on the aboriginal women by male anthropologists" (Rohrich-Leavitt et al., 1975, p. 117). W. Lloyd Warner's analysis of male and female purity among the Murngin is contrasted with the work of Phyllis Kaberry. Warner, for instance, argued that "masculinity is inextricably interwoven with ritual cleanliness, and femininity is equally entwined with the concept of uncleanliness, the former being the sacred principle and the latter the profane" (Warner, 1937, p. 394).[4] According to Kaberry, menstrual blood was "endowed with powerful magical properties and associated with taboos" (Kaberry, 1939, p. 394) and, because of its potential to harm men, menstruating women would avoid male contact. Neither men nor women, however, thought of menstruation or women as "dirty" or "unclean." There was not even a term that implied ritual uncleanliness. Far from being excluded from the religious sphere because they were excluded from male ceremonies, women had their own secret ceremonies which men were forbidden to see or participate in.

The article concludes its comparison of male and female analyses of Aboriginal women with a plea for a greater awareness of gender in anthropological studies.

> The basic inference to be drawn from the differences between male and female ethnographies is that many Western male anthropologists are unwilling or unable to expunge their ethnocentricism, of which the predominant elements are androcentricism and sexism. Androcentricism and sexism lead to the misinterpretation and distortion of the status and roles of women in non-Western cultures. But if the status and roles of women are misinterpreted and distorted, so inevitably must be those of men. Since the relationships of women and men interlock, the distortion of roles of men and women leads to a distortion of the total social system. (Rohrich-Leavitt et al., 1975, p. 124)

Whereas the male anthropologists discussed tended to apply only etic (external) models to the people they studied, the female ethnographers combined emic and etic perspectives to give a more "holistic, accurate, and objective" view of their subject. Women are also, however, no less than their male colleagues, influenced by their personal histories and social context. The move toward a more reflexive attitude to both fieldworker and subject has sought to make these personal constraints explicit.

Reflexivity and Gender

Reflexive anthropology undermines the "fly on the wall" approach to "scientific" observation, in which the ethnographer might imagine him or herself as a neutral observer of empirical facts. The cultural assumptions, language, experience, and intentions of the anthropologist will inevitably direct and delimit what he or she sees and understands in another culture (and in his or her own). The society being studied is also made up of individuals, each with his or her own story and perspective, and cannot be reduced to a homogeneous "other."

> **Reflexivity** in anthropology refers to the examination of the ethnographic encounter as a dialogue between individuals and cultures, and its attempt to understand the limitations these subjectivities impose.[5]

A reflexive re-examination of field material in the light of this postmodernist challenge has been evident in the work of many anthropologists, particularly women. As Helen Callaway put it, some feminist anthropologists have adopted "a dialogical methodology which rejects the division between subject and object, places the self within the field of investigation, evaluates positionality and power relations, and creates an intersubjective matrix for knowledge" (Callaway, 1992, p. 44).

Learning gender

Pat Caplan is a British anthropologist who has written about the impact of gender awareness on the direction and interpretation of her fieldwork material.[6] From 1965 to 1967 Caplan carried out fieldwork on Mafia Island in Tanzania, looking at the system of land tenure. At the time she was in her twenties, single and childless, as well as white and well educated. Of that first visit to Mafia, Caplan wrote:

> I saw the villagers, and especially the women, as "other." Women like them, constantly pregnant or lactating, illiterate, and subject to rules of sexual segregation, were what I, determined to prove myself as good as a man, was not. I did not wish to identify myself as that kind of a woman either in the field setting or at home. I was determined to have a career, not to be just another woman who would disappear into a world of marriage and babies. (Caplan, 1993, p. 178)

Accordingly, Caplan focused her attention on male informants, on the assumption that they would be more important than the women, and tried to position herself as an "honorary male" in order to gain access to spaces and events normally reserved for men. As a graduate student, Caplan's awareness of the implications of her gender were focused on the tension in her private life between wishing to pursue an academic career and wanting to marry and have a family. But as the strains implicit in maintaining these two positions increased, so did her feminist awareness. Caplan increasingly came to see the women on Mafia in a different light. Compared to women in Britain they appeared articulate, important in ritual, and sexually autonomous.

> Reviewing the material on Mafia, it seemed as if women there had in many respects a better deal than women in the west: they controlled their sexuality and property *and* they were productive workers. I came to see them as different from their men, but not necessarily subordinate, and different from women in the west, but not necessarily worse off. (Caplan, 1993, p. 179)

By the time of her second trip to Mafia in 1976, Caplan was familiar with the feminist critiques of mainstream anthropology, with its male bias and marginalization of women. She had also matured, and was a wife and mother. The struggle to maintain a professional status was of no concern to the people of Mafia, some of whom greeted her with: "Before you were just a young girl; now you're grown up and we can talk to you properly" (Caplan, 1993, p. 174). By making a conscious effort to talk to women and to re-evaluate their role in society, Caplan became aware of some dimensions to their lives she had missed nine years previously.

> Although I had realised from the data that I gathered on the first trip that women had important productive roles, this time I was able to see the signifi-cance of female links, especially between mothers *and* daughters, which not only enabled women to be mothers and workers, but also facilitated their remarriages after divorce, since children were usually taken to be fostered by their grandmothers. (Caplan, 1993, p. 174)

The purpose of this visit was to shoot some documentary footage for the BBC TV series *Face Values*. Caplan was aware that she "specifically wanted to show a western audience that things could be different for women, that there was nothing 'natural' or inevitable about the way they were in the west" (Caplan, 1993, p. 179).

A third visit in 1985 was to research the topic of food, health, and fertility. The data collected included statistical material on health and survival rates of male and female children, which revealed some worrying trends. It was evident that a higher proportion of female babies and toddlers failed to thrive than their male counterparts, and two main factors seemed to account for this. One was that although women were happy to have both male and female children, most men expressed a preference for boys. Men also wanted more children than women. A woman who gave birth to a girl was more likely to get pregnant again quickly, thus endangering both the mother's and daughter's health. Men and women eat separately, children eating with the parent of the same sex. When food was short women gave their husbands (and therefore sons) better food than they kept for themselves (and their daughters).

> In short, then, it became clear to me that talking to women was not always sufficient – women, especially young women who had been to school, did know what kinds of food were good for small children, but they did not control the purse strings. Women usually had clear ideas about the number of children they wanted and the mixture of the sexes, whereas men wanted unlimited numbers and had a strong preference for boys. It seems possible, then, that there is a correlation between these factors and the skewed morbidity and mortality rates of small children. (Caplan, 1993, p. 178)

Caplan was also far more aware than on her previous visit of the women's heavy workload and lack of leisure. As in so much of Africa and elsewhere in the world, women did most of the manual labor, while subject to frequent pregnancies and eating insufficient food. It was no wonder that most women suffered from anemia and had higher morbidity rates than men. Again, Caplan relates her ability to "see" the life of Mafia to her own circumstances, both intellectual and personal, at home.

> By 1985 feminist anthropology had also abandoned a rather simplistic, neo-Engelian assumption that if women did productive work, their status must necessarily be higher than if they did not. Indeed, for women to work productively may mean that they are grossly overburdened. But another reason why I was perhaps able to see this more clearly was my own life circumstances. I had come to realise that the double shift is not necessarily a bed of roses, and that even with a supportive partner and perhaps paid help, it comes with a high price tag. Energies are limited, time is always too little. With this new awareness, as I looked on my third trip at the work-load and fertility rates on Mafia, I could see more clearly than before overburdened women having too many pregnancies, losing too many babies, not eating enough and suffering a high level of morbidity. (Caplan, 1993, pp. 179–80)

In conclusion, Caplan summarizes this reflexive understanding in anthropology as follows: "I have become aware that being an ethnographer means studying the self as well as the other. In this way, the self becomes "othered," an object of study, while at the same time, the other, because of familiarity, and a different approach to fieldwork, becomes part of the self" (Caplan, 1993, p. 180).

Gendered Studies

In this final section we look at some studies which have made sex, gender, and the position of women central to their analysis. This theme is picked up again in chapter 5, in a discussion of women's relationship to nature, culture, and mythology. As Margaret Mead (1966, 1975a, b) and Malinowski (1929) demonstrated most eloquently, sexuality, morality and ethics, notions of pollution and taboo – or their absence – and sex roles are cultural variables. There is no biological fact that is not worked over and interpreted via a society and its ideological lens.

Pioneer fieldworkers

An awareness of the importance of sexuality in social life is not new. The American anthropologist Margaret Mead spent most of her long career looking at family patterns, particularly the ordinary lives of women and children. Malinowski was also a pioneer in this area with his 1929 publication *The Sexual Life of Savages*.

Bronislaw Malinowski (1884–1942) was born in Poland, but spent most of his career at the London School of Economics, being made a professor there in 1927. At the outbreak of the First World War in 1914 Malinowski was in Australia, where he was regarded as an "enemy alien." As an alternative to internment Malinowski was permitted to carry out fieldwork in the Trobriand Islands off Papua New Guinea. The first of several Trobriand ethnographies was *Argonauts of the Western Pacific: an Account of Native Enterprise and Adventure in the Archipelagoes of Melanesian New Guinea* (originally published in 1922), which looked at the *kula* cycle of exchange. The second book, entitled *The Sexual Life of Savages in North-Western Melanesia: an Ethnographic Account of Courtship, Marriage and Family Life among the Natives of the Trobriand Islands, British New Guinea* (1929), contained a preface by an exponent of the new science of "sexology," Havelock Ellis, and sought to move away from the prudery or credulity of earlier accounts of so-called "primitive" peoples. Malinowski's approach was sociological, owing much to Durkheim and Mauss, and psychological, expressing an interest in individual motivations as well as in the functioning of society as a whole.[7] Malinowski's descriptions of the ethnographic method and the account of his idealized relationship with the Trobrianders underwent a radical reassessment with the controversial publication of his fieldwork diaries in 1967.

Margaret Mead (1901–78) was a pupil of one of the founding fathers of American anthropology, Franz Boas (1858–1942). Boas's contribution to social anthropology included an emphasis on the individual, unique aspects of a given culture. Boas was a relativist at a time in which grand comparative theories were the order of the day, and in that sense anticipated an important trend in twentieth-century social anthropology. Mead carried out fieldwork in many parts of the Pacific, but her interest was mainly comparative. She was more explicitly aware than most of the interests of her audience at home, and sought to draw parallels between the cultures of the South Seas and contemporary America. From the start Mead decided to focus on women and children. Whereas in Britain women anthropologists looking at women were readily marginalized, Margaret Mead became an American culture hero. Her first fieldtrip to Samoa in 1925 resulted in the phenomenally successful *Coming of Age in Samoa* (first published in 1928) which sought to compare the relaxed attitudes to sexuality of the Samoans with the more puritanical and restrictive code of the United States. In this and subsequent works Mead stressed that biology does not dictate one's destiny, and that sex roles depend on cultural and not "natural" choices. Mead too had her detractors. Derek Freeman (1983, 1999) undertook a restudy of her Samoan material that provoked a storm of controversy. Mead had found what she wanted to find, and had the wool pulled over her eyes, Freeman claimed. As the dust settled most anthropologists accepted that even the best ethnographic monograph tells you as much about the ethnographer as it does about the society it purports to describe.

Sex and the sacred

A symbolic approach to religion and sexuality is taken by Kirsten Hastrup in her article "The semantics of biology: virginity" (1978). Rather than dismissing the role of biology in people's lives (particularly those of women), Hastrup wishes to reinstate it, but as a social rather than a biological "fact." As we saw in chapter 2, in Robert Hertz's study of the right and left hands, "natural" differences are used by all societies as classificatory markers. In this instance, Hastrup is interested in the ways in which the female body becomes a model for understanding the relationship between the social and the sacred. The task Hastrup sets herself is to:

> analyse how socially significant distinctions are mapped onto basic biological differences, and vice versa. In any social context we must study "what difference the difference makes," since this will yield information about the social and ideological organisation of the society in question.... In short, I shall enquire into the "semantics of biology." (Hastrup, 1978, p. 49)

> **Semantics** is a term borrowed from linguistics. It refers to the *meaning* rather than the *form* or *structure* of an utterance.

Hastrup is particularly interested in the *meaning* of virginity. It cannot be understood simply in physiological terms. It means something very different to men and to women. The significance of virginity will vary at the ages of ten, twenty, or sixty. There is often a contrast between a *matrilineal* or *patrilineal* system – with the former placing less emphasis on paternity and consequently having a more relaxed attitude toward female sexuality. One consequence of this is that pre-marital virginity will be less prized in a matrilineal than in a patrilineal society in which knowledge of paternity is regarded as crucial. The circumstances in which virginity is lost, whether voluntary or forced, will also affect its meaning.

> The significance of virginity cannot be understood all by itself. As a biological fact, yes, but not as a social fact, a fact that enters into the lives of young women as a demand or as a virtue. We have to know the meaning of virginity in relation to a larger social whole, and in relation to the evaluations attached to different stages of a woman's life. (Hastrup, 1978, p. 50)

For a young girl in some Arab societies or in the Northern Sudan, for instance, to lose one's virginity before marriage can bring shame to the family and even death at the hands of one's brothers. If, on the other hand, you are a girl at an American high school, virginity may be seen as a sign of failure – of not being sufficiently attractive to members of the opposite sex (or of being a lesbian). Virginity is something to lose as soon as decently possible by "falling in love," rather than by just sleeping around.

The meanings of virginity therefore depend upon its relations to other categories. Linguists talk about a *semantic field*, a series of meanings that provide a context for a particular statement. In the case of virginity the semantic field is "female sexuality," which in turn takes its meaning from the wider field of human sexuality and from its relation to society at large. Drawing on Mary Douglas's work, Hastrup points to the importance of the conceptual boundaries drawn in all societies between the categories "man" and "woman." These boundaries are not drawn in the same place in all societies, as numerous studies testify, but it is certainly the case that "Social intercourse, as well as sexual intercourse, somehow requires that the inter-acting parties know to which sexual category 'the other' belongs" (Hastrup, 1978, p. 52). Women's bodies and female sexuality are a prime symbol for female identity.

Virgin	Mother	Crone
sexual potentiality	sexual fertility	desexualized
ambiguous	unambiguous	possible ambiguity (wise woman or witch

          ↑   ↑

     sexual intercourse   menopause

Figure 4.1 Diagrammatic representation of a threefold division of a woman's life.

The course of a woman's life is often conceptually divided into three stages: the unspecified virgin, the sexually specified childbearing woman, and the unspecified post-menopausal woman. This threefold division is reflected in the image of the triple goddess as virgin or maid, mother, and crone, and we can express this diagrammatically in the form shown in figure 4.1.[8] These are clearly conceptual rather than biological categories, although they take their cue from biology. Among the Ashanti of Ghana the division between virgin and mother is not marked by sexual intercourse, marriage, or childbearing, but by female circumcision. An uncircumcised girl who has a child can never be a "mother," whereas all circumcised girls, whether or not they have children, are referred to as mothers. Men's bodies are not used to mark divisions in the same way. A man is "generalized" and male identity is not tied up with biology or sexual status in quite the same manner. As Hastrup remarks of women,

> They can be used as social markers because they are marked by nature in a way that invites the use of these bodies in other than just sexual ways. Men are just men, all the time. Being the generalised sex, their identification is not tied up with their sexual states to the same extent that it is for women. (Hastrup, 1978, p. 60)

Shirley Ardener (1978) notes that virgins are often marked as a kind of "third sex," a category usually unmarked for men. In the West, where virginity has been highly valued by the Roman Catholic Church, women who extend the period of virginity throughout their lives may be attributed special powers. Nuns, for instance, may be seen in some respects as a third sex, and be permitted to perform some functions normally reserved for male priests or deacons, such as reading the Gospel during Mass or distributing the sacraments. Queen Elizabeth I of England and the French Joan of Arc were both powerful women who operated in a male sphere, whose reputed virginity was part of their power and mystique.

The idea of anomalous births is explored by Hastrup, and we can see that the status accorded both child and mother depends upon which category they are straddling or transgressing. Wherever you have a virgin birth story, which is fairly common in the world's mythologies, both mother and child (usually but not always a son) become immortalized. The Virgin Mary and Jesus in the Christian tradition is one of the most prominent examples of a virgin birth. Medieval theologians held that Mary, like the mother of the Buddha, gave birth not vaginally but through her side, emphasizing more strongly the miraculous nature of the delivery. A birth in the third stage of life, to a post-menopausal woman, is also anomalous, but is often regarded positively. The mother is, however, unlikely to be divinized. She has been sexually active, unlike the virgin mother, and is thereby disqualified. She is often presented as barren as well as old – again emphasizing the miraculous or anomalous nature of the birth. Her son may well be regarded not as a deity (as his mother was not a virgin) but at least as a culture hero. There are numerous instances of such births in the Hebrew Bible, including Sarah and Isaac and Hannah and Samuel. In the Christian New Testament we are told that Elizabeth was already old when she gave birth to John the Baptist (Jesus' cousin).

In the middle stage of life it is barrenness rather than birth that is anomalous. There is usually a stigma attached to the childless married woman. Among the Bangwa in Cameroon an unmarried post-pubertal woman is also likely to be pitied if childless, and an illegitimate child is preferred to the stigma of barrenness. A childless wife may be mistreated, and can find herself the victim of witchcraft accusations. In many societies a young widow is considered anomalous, as she is still fertile but not reproducing. In India young Hindu girls are traditionally married to much older men, and widows are not permitted to remarry. The plight of young widows is grim, as they are both feared and badly treated. The Hindu ideal of *sati*, in which the widow immolates herself on her husband's funeral pyre, is now illegal, but pressures on widows to "remove the anomaly" in this way by committing suicide continue.[9] We can therefore extend the diagrammatic representation as in figure 4.2.

Women's bodies are more apt than men's bodies for making social and conceptual statements because of the biological specificity of the female experience of virginity, sexual intercourse, fertility, childbearing, and menopause. The variety of ways in which this can be done is, however, as diverse as the human imagination. The following case study on the politics of

Virgin	Mother	Crone
birth anomalous	barrenness anomalous	birth anomalous
divinized	shamed	blessed
Mary and Jesus	Elizabeth → Hannah →	John the Bapist Samuel

Figure 4.2 Extension of the representation of the threefold division of a woman's life.

birth in the northern Sudan illustrates the interplay of politics, religion, and culture in dealing with pregnancy. Janice Boddy, like Margaret Mead, adopts a comparative approach, alternating between a description of birth practices in the Sudan and in Canada, in order to reflect on the impact of medicalization and the limits of personal autonomy in the experience of giving birth.

Birth and death in the Sudan

"Amal was pregnant and understandably apprehensive. She had been ill with malaria, anemia, and a bladder infection" (Boddy, 1998, p. 28). In this way we are introduced to an eighteen-year-old Sudanese bride.

> From the moment she knew she was expecting, Amal wore her wedding gold to thwart capricious spirits that might seize her womb and loosen its captive seed. Amal's body had become a protected domestic space, a figurative house wherein mingle the male and female contributions that shape and sustain human life. (Boddy, 1998, p. 29)

In Sudan, however, maternal mortality is high, and while Amal successfully gave birth to a baby girl, Nura, she did not herself survive. Boddy's article moves between narratives of pregnancy and birth in Sudan and Canada, and reflections on these cultures, on the surface so very different from one another. Any quick judgments we may have are dismantled, and the role of individuals, and not just cultural practices, is stressed. In Canada pregnant women can expect to survive pregnancy and to deliver a healthy child. Mortality rates for both mother and child are low and have declined as medical intervention has increased. There is evidence that it is increased nutrition and the elimination of poverty, rather than medicalization and the ready resort to Casarian deliveries, that accounts for this trend. Women may be safer, but may feel angry, out of control, turned into objects of a (male) medical gaze. The reader is not, however, permitted to romanticize the more "natural" customs of Africa. Sudanese Muslims practice female circumcision, which can complicate birth and cause chronic health problems. A midwife is essential to cut a woman open to allow a baby to pass through the sewn vagina. There is no such thing as a "natural" birth.

Under British colonial rule expatriate midwives attempted to improve women's health and safety, for the sake of the women certainly, but also to ensure a labor supply. The supposedly civilizing lessons of the medical authorities did not, however, have quite the effect anticipated. Sudanese midwives, for instance, were encouraged to perform circumcisions that were progressively less severe, in the hope that the practice would gradually die out altogether. It became evident, however, that the interplay of cultural, religious, and political factors that maintained the custom prevented its rapid demise.

> The civilizing of midwifery was intended not only to expand the potential workforce, but also to ameliorate the "degraded" condition of women and effect a rise in their status that would signal "progress" for Sudan as a whole. Yet it also effectively reaffirmed what the *fugara*, village clerics, declaimed: that women are inherently weak and dependent beings, at the mercy of physical processes beyond their ken and control. If anything, adopting a locally tempered biomedical view of their bodies may have fostered in women a sense of powerlessness, even as it boosted midwives' agency and independence. And here lay a paradox for colonial and postcolonial mandates: for it is precisely their dependence and material vulnerability that leads women to ignore the harm that attends female circumcision. Because childbearing in the context of marriage is the socially approved route to social and economic security, and infibulation renders women marriageable, most women of my acquaintance are still loath to risk their daughters' futures and continue to insist the procedure be done. (Boddy, 1998, pp. 40–1)

Boddy was tempted to think that medical intervention could have saved Amal's life, and was well aware of the distress caused to women by circumcision. Cultural determinants that privilege men over women and increasing poverty, rather than merely lack of access to Western medical care and circumcision, are evidently the greatest threat to women and children. As Caplan found on Mafia Island, men expected their wives to produce large families. Women's economic dependence on men means that they are forced, in so far as their reproductive health allows, to comply, despite the inability of parents to feed their children adequately or to ensure their health. The situation Boddy paints for women is grim:

> Moreover, malnutrition compromised immunity, and is therefore linked to the prevalence of illnesses like dysentery, malaria, and hepatitis which add to childbearing risks and for which infibulation may be performed as a childhood cure. It is also responsible for rickets, which causes bone malformation leading to pelvic disproportion during pregnancy and, failing cesarean delivery, death. As Amal's country sinks deeper into poverty with the rest of the developing world, the nutritional status of its womenfolk is increasingly threatened. The economically motivated early marriage of daughters is becoming more common as well, adding precocious pregnancy to the litany of hazards women face. Yet there as elsewhere, technological fixes are offered for problems that are political and economic at heart. (Boddy, 1998, p. 51)

By focusing on actual examples of women's lives, Boddy demonstrates not only the human face of death in the case of Amal, but also the possibility for change. She felt that with a different midwife, someone like Sheffa, Amal could have survived. Sheffa has evolved an alternative synthesis of Western and Sudanese practices to that of Amal's midwife, Miriam. She dresses in Western style jeans and T-shirt, and runs a clean, cheerful clinic with sterile implements and good nutritional information. Sheffa also developed her own compromise between traditional delivery in a standing position holding a rope, and the prone posture with the legs raised beloved of the Europeans who trained Sudanese midwives in earlier decades. Unlike Miriam, Sheffa helps women to deliver in a semi-upright position, supported by relatives, so that gravity can play its role in aiding delivery. Much to Boddy's surprise, Sheffa is also a "strong believer in the power of the spirits." Boddy had assumed that her medical training would have "inclined her to disbelief" (Boddy, 1998, p. 44).

There are no easy answers or explanations in Boddy's analysis. What we do get, however, is an understanding of the complex interplay of individual and social forces, religion, politics, and globalization. One conclusion from the comparison between Canada and Sudan could be that in the Sudan "persons are unthinkable save as members of a social whole, and spirit possession is a conventional event, the body and its parts may be less reified, less readily viewed as objects in themselves" (Boddy, 1998, p. 49). As the example of infibulation demonstrates, this does not make Sudanese birth more "natural," and Sheffa chose to have her baby in a hospital. The medicalization of birth has taken place largely with the consent of women: "an impressive coloniza-tion of consciousness – of selfhood" (Boddy, 1998, p. 49). Its relative absence in the Sudan is due to a lack of resources rather than cultural resistance.

Deconstructing gender

Recent studies have usefully pointed away from the notion that there is a single way of being male or female in any particular society.[10] If there are sexual scripts they are not monosyllabic, but contain numerous different parts for both men and women. People have an element of choice, even if constrained, when making a conscious or unconscious investment in the particular model of masculinity or femininity they will adopt in any particular circumstance. Ideologies of gender may be ranked hierarchically and carry different rewards. To resist dominant models can leave an individual or group vulnerable to persecution or marginalization (see chapter 2). In contemporary Western societies ideologies of male and female antagonism and male and female equality coexist. Discourses of masculinity may construct: the tough, go-getting, successful businessman, heterosexual and promiscuous; the caring "new man," in touch with his feelings, adept at changing nappies, devoted to his wife and family; or the gay, clubbing, sociable (but possibly ill) male, with arty friends and media contacts. These are of course stereotypes, but they indicate the range of masculine scripts that can coexist within a society. Women's choices are more problematic, in that most discourses construct femininity in negative terms relative to masculinity. The career woman, single, with a nanny, or without children, may be seen as "selfish," failing in maternal and wifely duties. The full-time wife and mother, deprived of economic independence, is negatively defined by her lack of a career or public identity – a dependent drudge. The sexually attractive young woman who takes care of her figure and appearance is subject to an implicit objectification and devaluation as an intelligent independent agent (i.e. the dumb blond or bimbo image).

The notion of a hierarchy of gendered subjective identities is itself a Western, postmodernist form of theorization. Although it has the advantage of alerting the fieldworker to the possibility of multiple discourses of gender within other societies, there is also a danger that the deconstruction of gender as a category can do violence to the experience of men and women (biologically defined). While it may be true that masculinity or femininity in Papua New Guinea or elsewhere is relational and attached to behaviors rather than to men or women, it still happens to be women who have the children, and in most cases care for them, who almost invariably do most of the heavy physical work, are more limited in their possibilities for personal autonomy, and are disadvantaged nutritionally in relation to men. Male violence against women, especially when culturally sanctioned, as in the case of female circumcision, wife-beating, or ritualized gang rape, may in effect be excused or downplayed by the decoupling of gender entirely from biological men and women.[11]

Conclusion

Intellectual trends in recent decades have made it increasingly difficult to ignore gender as a practical and interpretative issue (although a few anthropologists still try!). In this chapter I have traced some significant developments in the study of gender and sexuality, but inevitably have done little more than scratch the surface. There is still a relative paucity of information on and by women in the anthropological record. While the move from "filling in the gaps" and critiquing male bias to the study of gender constructs is often presented sequentially, the truth is that they coexist. There are certainly still gaps to be filled and a place for studies with an explicit focus on women. Nor has the feminist voice been so powerful that the necessity of critiquing male bias is redundant. Increasingly, anthropologists study gender rather than women, and whereas formerly the two were often synonymous, gender no longer automatically equates with female, or sex with women's bodies. Recent ethnographic studies have also looked at the construction of masculinity and at sexual relationships between fieldworker and hosts. There remains a danger of ghettoizing gender as a sub-category of women's anthropology, which is one reason for making this topic explicit, and the significance of gender is a theme that runs throughout the chapters of this book.

Notes

1   See Sanday (1981). These themes are explored further in chapter 5.
2   Ingrid Rudie (1993, p. 112) gives the following account of reflexive fieldwork: "The fieldworker's history has been described as a history of passing through personal paradigms which are used to interpret the field, and are changed through this experience. The experience itself is a revelation of contrasts and likenesses, and it is this experience that triggers the selection of what goes into the fieldnotes in the first place. The informants also note the contrasts and likenesses, and start reflecting on their own practice from the same kind of experience.... This suggests that the field dialogue is one in which the distinction between the 'emic' and the 'etic' view is partly dissolved."
3   This is not a new idea, as can be seen from the following passage by one of the earliest proponents of anthropological fieldwork, Bronislaw Malinowski (1929, p. xxv): "The Anthropologist in his observations has to understand the native through his own psychology, and he must form the picture of a foreign culture from the elements of his own and of others practically and theoretically known to him. The whole difficulty and art of field-work consists of starting from those elements which are familiar in the foreign culture and gradually working the

strange and diverse into a comprehensible scheme. In this the learning of a foreign culture is like the learning of a foreign tongue: at first mere assimilation and crude translation, at the end a complete detachment from the original medium and a mastery of the new one. And since an adequate ethnographic description must reproduce in miniature the gradual, lengthy, and painful process of field-work, the references to the familiar, the parallels between Europe and the Trobriands have to serve as starting points."

4   Cited in Rohrich-Leavitt et al. (1975, p. 117).

5   The term "reflexivity" was used by Scholte (1972, p. 435) to counter the bias toward a depersonalized anthropology.

6   See also Caplan (1992), and the films in the *Face Values* series listed in the appendix.

7   This dual focus on both the individual and social institutions is indicated in the Introduction to *The Sexual Life of Savages*: "Sex is not a mere physiological transaction to the primitive South Sea Islander any more than it is to us; it implies love and love-making; it becomes the nucleus of such venerable institutions as marriage and the family; it pervades art and it produces its spells and magic. It dominates in fact almost every aspect of culture. *Sex*, in its widest meaning – and it is thus that I have used it in the title of this book – is rather a sociological and cultural force than a mere bodily relation of two individuals. But the scientific treatment of this subject obviously involves also a keen interest in the biological nucleus. The anthropologist must therefore give a description of the direct approaches between two lovers, as we find them in Oceania, shaped by their traditions, obeying their laws, following the customs of their tribe" (Malinowski, 1929, p. xxiii).

8   See also Shirley Ardener's discussion in the introduction to *Defining Females* (1978), which draws on Mongolian examples of women's lives.

9   See Shweder (1991), who argues that Roop Kanwar, an eighteen-year-old college-educated Rajput woman who immolated herself with her dead husband in 1987, might not have been pushed into this act of "suicide" by her dead husband's family, as many commentators supposed, but that it may have been an act of free will stemming from a particular cultural conception of the metaphysical relationship between the human body and pure existence, human beings and gods. "[I]t is conceivable that Roop Kanwar herself understood and experienced her immolation as an astonishing moment when her body and its senses, profane things, became fully sacred, and hence invulnerable to pain, through an act of sacrifice by a goddess seeking eternal union with her god-man" (Shweder, 1991, pp. 16–17).

10   See Strathern (1987b) and Moore (1994b).

11   Marilyn Strathern (1987b) argued that feminists and anthropologists (who may of course coincide in a single individual) have different agendas. Feminism is engaged in a political battle for female equality, and is essentially antagonistic. Anthropology, on the other hand, seeks to deconstruct the categories that feminism takes for granted and to explicate cultural difference. The two need

not be mutually exclusive. Anthropology and feminism are both capable of recognizing a plurality of perspectives and voices. By accepting that both are products of a Western liberal humanistic discourse, feminist anthropology can seek to re-examine the categories often taken for granted while privileging the experience of women (see Bowie 1998).

References and Further Reading

Abel, Emily K. and Pearson, Marjorie L. (1989) *Across Cultures: the Spectrum of Women's Lives.* New York and London: Gordon and Breach.

Archer, John and Lloyd, Barbara (1988) *Sex and Gender.* Cambridge, New York and Melbourne: Cambridge University Press.

Ardener, Edwin (1975) Belief and the problem of women. And the "problem" revisited. In Shirley Ardener (ed.), *Perceiving Women.* London: J. M. Dent & Sons, pp. 1–28. Reprinted in *Edwin Ardener: the Voice of Prophecy and Other Essays,* edited by Malcolm Chapman. Oxford and Cambridge, MA: Blackwell (1989), pp. 72–85 and 127–33.

Ardener, Shirley (1978) Introduction: the nature of women in society. In Shirley Ardener (ed.), *Defining Females: the Nature of Women in Society.* London: Croom Helm, pp. 9–48.

Boddy, Janice (1998) Remembering Amal: on birth and the British in northern Sudan. In Margaret Lock and Patricia A. Kaufert (eds), *Pragmatic Women and Body Politics.* Cambridge: Cambridge University Press, pp. 28–57.

Bowie, Fiona (1998) Trespassing on sacred domains. A feminist anthropological approach to theology and religious studies. *Journal of Feminist Studies in Religion,* 14(1), 40–62.

Callaway, Helen (1992) Ethnography and experience: gender implications in fieldwork and texts. In Judith Okely and Helen Callaway (eds), *Anthropology and Autobiography.* ASA Monographs 29. London and New York: Routledge, pp. 29–49.

Caplan, Pat (ed.) (1987) *The Cultural Construction of Sexuality.* London and New York: Tavistock.

Caplan, Pat (1992) Engendering knowledge: the politics of ethnography. In Shirley Ardener (ed.), *Persons and Powers of Women in Diverse Cultures.* Providence, RI and Oxford: Berg, pp. 65–88.

Caplan, Pat (1993) Learning gender: fieldwork in a Tanzanian coastal village, 1965–85. In Diane Bell, Pat Caplan and Wazir Jahan Karim (eds), *Gendered Fields: Women, Men and Ethnography.* London and New York: Routledge, pp. 168–81.

Cornwall, Andrea and Lindisfarne, Nancy (eds) (1994) *Dislocating Masculinity: Comparative Ethnographies.* London and New York: Routledge.

Del Valle, Teresa (ed.) (1993) *Gendered Anthropology.* London and New York: Routledge.

Di Leonardo, Micaela (ed.) (1991) *Gender at the Crossroads of Knowledge: Feminist Anthropology in the Postmodern Era.* Berkeley, Los Angeles and Oxford: University of California Press.

Errington, Frederick and Gewertz, Deborah (1989) *Cultural Alternatives and a Feminist Anthropology: an Analysis of Culturally Constructed Gender Interests in Papua New Guinea.* Cambridge, New York, and Melbourne: Cambridge University Press.

Evans-Pritchard, E. E. (1937) *Witchcraft, Oracles and Magic among the Azande.* Oxford: Clarendon Press (abridged version 1976).

Evans-Pritchard, E. E. (1974) *Man and Woman among the Azande.* London: Faber and Faber.

Freeman, Derek (1983) *Margaret Mead and Samoa: the Making and Unmaking of an Anthropological Myth.* Cambridge, MA: Harvard University Press.

Freeman, Derek (1999) *The Fateful Hoaxing of Margaret Mead: a Historical Analysis of Her Samoan Research.* Boulder, CO: Westview Press.

Gilligan, Carol (1982) *In a Different Voice: Psychological Theory and Women's Development.* Cambridge, MA and London: Harvard University Press.

Goodale, Jane C. (1971) *Tiwi Wives.* Seattle: University of Washington Press.

Greenhalgh, Susan (ed.) (1995) *Situating Fertility: Anthropology and Demographic Enquiry.* Cambridge: Cambridge University Press.

Gregor, Thomas (1985) *Anxious Pleasures: the Sexual Lives of an Amazonian People.* Chicago and London: Chicago University Press.

Gunew, Sneja (ed.) (1990) *Feminist Knowledge: Critique and Construct.* London and New York: Routledge.

Gunew, Sneja (ed.) (1991) *A Reader in Feminist Knowledge.* London and New York: Routledge.

Hart, C. W. M. and Pilling, Arnold R. (1960) *The Tiwi of North Australia.* New York and London: Holt, Rinehart and Winston.

Harvey, Penelope and Gow, Peter (eds) (1994) *Sex and Violence: Issues in Representation and Experience.* London: Routledge.

Hastrup, Kirsten (1978) The semantics of biology: virginity. In Shirley Ardener (ed.), *Defining Females: the Nature of Women in Society.* London: Croom Helm, pp. 49–65.

Hughes-Freeland, Felicia and Charles, Nickie (eds) (1996) *Practising Feminism: Identity, Difference, Power.* London: Routledge.

Humm, Maggie (ed.) (1992) *Feminisms: a Reader.* New York and London: Harvester Wheatsheaf.

Humm, Maggie (1995) *The Dictionary of Feminist Theory,* 2nd edn. New York and London: Prentice Hall.

Jackson, Stevi and Scott, Sue (eds) (1996) *Feminism and Sexuality: a Reader.* Edinburgh: Edinburgh University Press.

Jackson, Stevi and Jones, Jackie (eds) (1998) *Contemporary Feminist Theories.* Edinburgh: Edinburgh University Press.

Kaberry, Phyllis M. (1939) *Aboriginal Women: Sacred and Profane.* London: Routledge and Kegan Paul.

Kulick, Don and Willson, Margaret (eds) (1995) *Taboo: Sex, Identity and Erotic Subjectivity in Anthropological Fieldwork.* London and New York: Routledge.

MacCormack, Carol P. (1980) Nature, culture and gender: a critique. In Carol MacCormack and Marilyn Strathern (eds), *Nature, Culture and Gender*. Cambridge, New York, and Melbourne: Cambridge University Press.

Malinowski, Bronislaw (1929) *The Sexual Life of Savages in North-Western Melanesia*. London: G. Routledge and Sons. American edition, New York: Eugenics Publishing Company.

Malinowski, Bronislaw (1978) *Argonauts of the Western Pacific*. London: Routledge and Kegan Paul (first published in 1922).

Malinowski, Bronislaw (1967) *A Diary in the Strict Sense of the Term*. London: Routledge.

Mead, Margaret (1966) *Coming of Age in Samoa*. Harmondsworth: Penguin (first published in 1928).

Mead, Margaret (1975a) *Growing up in New Guinea*. New York: William Morrow (first published in 1930).

Mead, Margaret (1975b) *Male and Female*. New York: William Morrow (first published in 1949).

Miller, Barbara Diane (ed.) (1993) *Sex and Gender Hierarchies*. Cambridge and New York: Cambridge University Press.

Moore, Henrietta L. (1988) *Feminism and Anthropology*. Cambridge: Polity Press.

Moore, Henrietta L. (1994a) *A Passion for Difference: Essays in Anthropology and Gender*. Cambridge: Polity Press.

Moore, Henrietta L. (1994b) The problem of explaining violence in the social sciences. In Penelope Harvey and Peter Gow (eds), *Sex and Violence: Issues in Representation and Experience*. London and New York: Routledge, pp. 138–55.

Ortner, Sherry B. and Whitehead, Harriet (eds) (1986) *Sexual Meanings: the Cultural Construction of Gender and Sexuality*. Cambridge and New York: Cambridge University Press.

Philips, Susan U., Steele, Susan, and Tanz, Christine (eds) (1987) *Language, Gender and Sex in Comparative Perspective*. Cambridge and New York: Cambridge University Press.

Pike, Kenneth L. (1954) Emic and etic standpoints for the description of behaviour. In K. L. Pike, *Language in Relation to a Unified Theory of Structure of Human Behaviour*, part I, preliminary edition. Glendale, IL: Summer Institute of Linguistics, pp. 8–28.

Price, Janet and Shildrick, Margrit (eds) (1999) *Feminist Theory and the Body: a Reader*. Edinburgh: Edinburgh University Press.

Raphael, Melissa (1996) *Theology and Embodiment: the Post-patriarchal Reconstruction of Female Sacrality*. Sheffield: Sheffield Academic Press.

Reiter, Rayna R. (ed.) (1975) *Toward an Anthropology of Women*. New York and London: Monthly Review Press.

Rohrich-Leavitt, Ruby, Sykes, Barbara, and Weatherford, Elizabeth (1975) Aboriginal woman: male and female anthropological perspectives. In Rayna R. Reiter (ed.), *Toward an Anthropology of Women*. New York and London: Monthly Review Press, pp. 110–26.

Rudie, Ingrid (1993) A hall of mirrors: autonomy translated over time in Malaysia. In Diane Bell, Pat Caplan, and Wazir Jahan Karim (eds), *Gendered Fields: Women, Men and Ethnography*. London and New York: Routledge, pp. 103–16.

Sanday, Peggy Reeves (1981) *Female Power and Male Dominance: On the Origins of Sexual Inequality*. Cambridge and New York: Cambridge University Press.

Scholte, B. (1972) Toward a reflexive and critical anthropology. In D. Hymes (ed.), *Reinventing Anthropology*. New York: Pantheon Books (cited in Callaway, 1992, p. 48).

Shildrick, Margrit and Price, Janet (eds) (1998) *Vital Signs: Feminist Reconfigurations of the Bio/Logical Body*. Edinburgh: Edinburgh University Press.

Shostak, Marjorie (1994) *Nisa: the Life and Words of a !Kung Woman*. London: Earthscan.

Shweder, Richard A. (1991) *Thinking through Cultures: Expeditions in Cultural Psychology*. Cambridge, MA and London: Harvard University Press.

Strathern, Marilyn (ed.) (1987a) *Dealing with Inequality: Analysing Gender Relationships in Melanesia and Beyond*. Cambridge and New York: Cambridge University Press.

Strathern, Marilyn (1987b) An awkward relationship: the case of feminism and anthropology. *Signs*, 12(2), 276–92.

Strathern, Marilyn (1990) *The Gender of the Gift: Problems with Women and Problems with Society in Melanesia*. Berkeley, Los Angeles, and London: University of California Press.

Tong, Rosemarie (ed.) (1992) *Feminist Thought: a Comprehensive Introduction*. London: Routledge (first published in 1989 by Westview Press, Boulder, CO).

Warner, W. Lloyd (1937) *A Black Civilization*. New York: Harper and Brothers.

Yanagisako, Sylvia and Delaney, Carol (eds) (1995) *Naturalising Power: Essays in Feminist Cultural Analysis*. New York and London: Routledge.

Chapter 5

Religion, Culture, and Environment

Introduction

As biological and social beings we are all dependent upon our physical and social environment in order to live. We do not, however, experience the world passively. The way we act affects both society and the web of life around us. Our actions are determined by what we think, by our values and belief systems. These in turn are actualized and reinforced by our education, through various aspects of our culture, and by means of ritual activity. This chapter explores this interrelationship of religion, culture, and environment from a number of different angles. The terms themselves are not discrete (separate). Religion is an aspect of culture, and the environment includes both the natural world and human society.

> **Environment:** from the French *environner*, "to turn around." Our surroundings, all that influences the growth of animal and plant life.

In the first part of this chapter we look at the role of *cosmology* and the way in which different cosmological formulations lead to contrasting attitudes to the natural world. We examine the notion of an adaptive versus a maladaptive cosmology, with examples from both the industrialized West and small-scale societies. We then go on to look in more detail at the relationship between *mythology, gender,* and *the environment,* stemming from the work of Peggy Reeves Sanday. In the third section, "Totemism and the Dreamtime," we encounter some of the theoretical discussions on totemism and more recent work on Australian Aboriginal cultures which stress, albeit in different ways, the intimate connection between beliefs, rituals, social organization, cultural artifacts, a sense of history, and connection with the land among native Australian peoples.

Cosmology

> **Cosmology:** a theory or conception of the nature of the universe and its workings, and of the place of human beings and other creatures within that order.
> **Cosmogony:** stories, myths, and theories relating to the origin of the universe, and of human beings.

The philosopher Freya Mathews rejects the views of Marxist and empiricist scholars who see cosmology, together with religion and mythology, as either outmoded or irrelevant because it cannot be verified. Rather than dismiss cosmology, Mathews argues, we need to recognize its fundamental import-ance within all human societies:

> Is there a perennial human need, which cosmology can meet, and which, unmet, may lead to dangerous cultural dislocations? Is cosmology integral to the worldview a culture embodies, where the currency of such a worldview is a prerequisite of social and psychological integrity within that culture? (Math-ews, 1994, p. 11)

The anthropological record indicates that all cultures compose stories to account for the origin and nature of the world, and these stories have, according to Mathews, an important function in orientating human beings within the world.

> [A] cosmology serves to orient a community to its world, in the sense that it defines, for the community in question, the place of humankind in the cosmic scheme of things. Such cosmic orientation tells the members of the community, in the broadest possible terms, who they are and where they stand in relation to the rest of creation. (Mathews, 1994, p. 12)

A community whose cosmology represents the world as hostile to human interests, perhaps inhabited by "malevolent spirits which are nourished on the energies of their human playthings," could indicate a generally pessim-istic view of the world and minimal expectations of a successful interaction with the environment. Conversely, a community with a cosmology that represents the world as hospitable to human interests is likely to have more positive interactions with the environment and perhaps a better chance of happiness. Mathews also suggests that such a community (although admittedly idealized) is likely to operate with more high-minded principles, whereas the former might be expected to develop more ingratiating characteristics (as they spend time and energy propitiating or avoiding malevolent or indifferent forces) (Mathews, 1994, p. 13). Although Mathews is making a philosophical rather than an ethnographic statement, her insistence on the importance of cosmologies and on their relation to other aspects of culture is relevant to anthropology.

> Cosmologies are not of course pulled out of the air to suit the convenience of the communities to which they are attached. They are conditioned by many and various historical, environmental, technological, psychological, and social factors. A flourishing community is likely to evolve a bright, self-affirming cosmology, and a languishing community is likely to see the world in darker shades. But my point here is that cosmology is not a cultural epiphenomenon; once it has taken hold of the communal imagination, it can on the one hand serve the community, tiding it through periods of material adversity, or on the other hand disserve it, undermining its morale even when material conditions improve and permit expansion. A good cosmology, in other words, is good for its adherents, and a bad cosmology predictably has the reverse effect. (Mathews, 1994, p. 13)

While Mathews contends that a "bad cosmology" may be better than no cosmology at all, it is characterized by individuals who are metaphysically adrift and insecure. The main thrust of her work is a demonstration of the inadequacy of a classical Western "atomized" cosmology, which regards people and things as separate rather than interdependent. Peggy Reeves Sanday's cross-cultural study in the next section lends some support to Mathews's assertion that there is a direct, if complex, relationship between cosmology, the environment in which it is located, and social attitudes. Anthropologists, most notably Roy Rappaport, have also advanced arguments similar to those of Mathews, concerning functional and dysfunctional cosmologies and their impact.

Sacred hierarchies and the natural world

In a series of articles in his book *Ecology, Meaning and Religion* (1979), Roy Rappaport develops this notion of adaptive and maladaptive or dysfunctional cosmologies. While acknowledging the difficulties involved in defining an adaptive or a dysfunctional model of the world, Rappaport proposes an "ecological" argument, linked to the concept of hierarchies of knowledge. The problem is framed in terms of the disparity between our images of nature and the actual structure of the ecosystems of which we are a part.

> Nature is seen by humans through a screen of beliefs, knowledge, and purposes, and it is in terms of their images of nature, rather than of the actual structure of nature, that they act. Yet, it is upon nature itself that they do act, and it is nature itself that acts upon them, nurturing or destroying them. (Rappaport, 1979, p. 97)

Cognized model: "a description of a people's knowledge of their environment and of their beliefs concerning it" (Rappaport, 1979, p. 97).
Operational model: a scientific description of an ecosystem.
Reference values: a cultural model of how the world and relationships should operate.
Goal range: the adaptive limits of sustainability for a particular ecosystem.

We all form "cognized models" of the world (Mathews's "cosmologies"), that are more or less close to an "operational model" that might be drawn up by ecologists to describe the functioning of ecosystems. Rappaport argues that it is not important whether the cognized model of a society fits well or badly with an operational model of the same environment, but whether it actually "works" in the sense of sustaining that environment. The "reference values" of a society are the culturally determined notions of how things should be. Problems arise when reference values fall outside the adaptive limits or "goal range" of an ecosystem. Rappaport, like Mathews, has a negative view of most Western cognized models, which have totally unsustainable reference values.

> Economic terms, for instance, are incommensurable with ecological terms, and the state of the "developed" world strongly suggests that the regulation of ecosystems in accordance with economic reference values is likely to result in environmental destruction, just as the regulation of social relations and health care in economic terms may degrade social relations and obstruct medical treatment. (Rappaport, 1979, p. 100)

An "irrational" view of the world as peopled by spirits may be more adaptive than a "scientific" view that sees the world in mechanistic terms. The key, for Rappaport, is the degree of respect engendered by a particular model, and whether it is capable of investing an ecosystem with a significance and value beyond itself. A Western economic model of the world as seen by the IMF, for instance, contrasts strongly with that of the Ituri Pygmies of Central Africa.[1]

> All cognized models encode values, but all do not value the same things equally, and we may inquire into the adaptiveness of different sets of evaluative understandings. A model dominated by, let us say, the postulates of economic rationality would propose that an ecosystem is composed of elements of three general sorts: those that qualify as "resources," those that are neutrally useless, and those that may be regarded as pests, antagonists, or competitors. In contrast, the Ituri Pygmies take the forest encompassing them to be the body of God. These two views of the world obviously suggest radically different ways of living in it. (Rappaport, 1979, p. 101)[2]

Central to Rappaport's argument is the notion of a hierarchy of values. At the bottom of the hierarchy are instrumental values that are highly specific and goal-oriented. How to build a house or earn a living would come into this category. At the other end of the continuum there are ultimate values that are intentionally vague and abstract. These include notions such as liberty, freedom, and happiness. The loosely defined nature of ultimate values is central to their adaptive value. Because propositions about God, for instance, are typically devoid of material terms and do not in themselves specify any particular type of social arrangement or institution, they can "sanctify changing social arrangements while they themselves, remaining unchanged, provide continuity and meaning through those changes" (Rappaport, 1979, p. 155). This hierarchy is more easily maintained in small-scale societies of

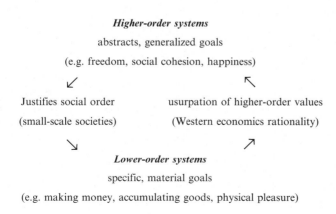

Figure 5.1   Rappaport's hierarchy of values.

limited complexity. In a global system, lower-order goals, such as the building of cars by multinational companies, can achieve enormous power and become selfsustaining with little or no reference to any higher good. Rappaport even refers to the "degradation" of sanctity. As "the material goals of lower-order systems usurp the places properly belonging to values of greater generality, they may lay claim to their sanctity" (Rappaport, 1979, p. 165). Lower-order goals may also become conflated with those of a more abstract nature. The pursuit of "happiness," for instance, loses the sense of "felicity" and is equated with the pursuit of pleasure and accumulation of material goods. "Liberty becomes little more than the right to serve oneself. Materialism and selfishness become honored as highest ideals" (Rappaport, 1979, p. 165), all with equally disastrous results for the ecosystem.[3]

The Kogi of Colombia

The ethnographic and historical record can quickly disabuse the romantic of any tendency to view non-Western peoples as the repository of all ecological wisdom. The early Polynesian settlers in New Zealand, for instance, deforested vast tracts of land within the early years of settlement. At the same time, it is also the case that small-scale societies in various parts of the world have achieved a high degree of sustainability, living in harsh as well as fertile regions. Entry into the global economy and its demands can, however, have profoundly unsettling effects upon ecosystems, societies, and the cosmologies that underpin them. One example of an adaptive cosmology that has been relatively successful in resisting overexploitation of the physical environment is that of the Kogi of the Sierra Nevada de Santa Marta in the north of Colombia, Central America. The Spanish conquistadors first landed on the Colombian coast at Santa Marta in 1514, and met representatives of the Tairona culture. For a century or so there was a period of relatively peaceful coexistence, during which the Taironas were forced to provide labor, food, and gold for the Spanish. Eventually, however, the Spanish turned on the native peoples and tried to kill them, on the pretext that the men were homosexual. Those who could fled into the higher reaches of the Sierra Nevada, a northern outcrop of the Andean mountain chain, which rises from sea level to snow-capped peaks. The Kogi are one of three groups descended from the Tairona. They have maintained a high degree of cultural autonomy, partly due to the protection afforded by the terrain, but also because of the level of control exerted by the priestly caste (male and female), known as *mamas* (Ereira, 1992).

The Kogi have been described as the most complete pre-Columbian civilization. This does not mean that they have not changed. But what is

Figure 5.2 Ramon Gil and Juancho: Kogi priests (*mamas*) from the Sierra Nevada de Santa Marta in Colombia.
© Felicity Nock, courtesy of Hutchison Picture Library.

remarkable is the degree to which the Kogi have sustained the internal coherence of their culture and managed to direct that change. Alan Ereira, a historian and documentary film-maker who has both filmed and written about the Kogi, claims that:

> Faced by the threat of complete destruction, they were forced to decide what was really central to them, what it would mean to survive. The survival of a culture is not the same as survival of individuals: it is the survival not of the body but of the mind. And the emphasis of Kogi society became, and remains, an emphasis on the life of the mind. (Ereira, 1992, pp. 8–9)

The Sierra Nevada can be regarded as an ecological microcosm of the planet in the sense that the whole range of climatic zones, from tropical rain forest, to savannah and glacial peaks – with their associated flora and fauna – are represented at different altitudes. The Kogi see themselves as the "Elder Brother," charged with protecting the heart of the world. Europeans are the "Younger Brother," technologically gifted but destructive. The care for the "heart of the world" consists of a cycle of exchange of goods between different levels of the system. There is the economic exchange of goods between different zones, and a crucial system of offerings, from the mountains

Figure 5.3 A Kogi mother and children.
© Felicity Nock, courtesy of Hutchison Picture Library.

to the sea, that imitates the water cycle on which all life depends. The *mamas* train for nine or more years in virtual seclusion in order to prepare themselves to live in both this world and *aluna*, a parallel ethereal realm which mirrors the physical world. Exchanges are made simultaneously in *aluna* and on earth in order to maintain fertility and the cycles of existence. The earth is sacred, it is the Great Mother, whose menstrual blood is gold, the secret life-blood of the earth. While Kogi gold, once central to ritual and to the orientation of sacred space, is now either displayed in the metropolitan museums of the world or long since melted down into Spanish bullion, the integrative cosmology of the Kogi persists. The men's ceremonial house, the *nuhue*, for example, is a model of the cosmos, with its circular frame mirroring the worlds above (and below) the earth, and its four fires representing the four corners of the physical world. The central axis from which the *nuhue* is suspended symbolizes the spindle on which the Mother spun the world, while the men's hammocks suspend them between worlds.

The *mamas* dictate what can be adopted from the outside world and what is to be rejected. Christian missionaries are allowed to build chapels, but they have no Kogi converts. While men have adopted trousers, both men and women continue to dress in the homespun white cloth that connects them to the Great Mother and to the earth. Some Kogi have been instructed to learn

Spanish in order to press the Kogi's case for their traditional lands to be restored to them, but they remain an oral society. Kogi cosmology convinces them that they have a vital role to play in saving the world from the ecological destruction caused by global warming, which they see clearly reflected in the disappearing snow on the mountain peaks of the Sierra Nevada. Their offerings are combined with an exhortation to the Younger Brother to stop extracting minerals from the earth, which tear at the body of the Mother and make her sick. "Younger Brother thinks 'Yes! Here I am! I know much about the universe!' But this knowing is learning to destroy the world, to destroy everything, all humanity" (Ereira, 1992, p. 225).[4]

Western interest in "indigenous" cosmologies that are perceived as more sustainable than those of the industrialized world has taken several forms, affecting both the Green Movement and contemporary earth-based religions (usually covered by the blanket term "Paganism"). The reading list at the end of this chapter gives a few examples from the rapidly growing literature in this field. We will now look briefly at some examples of a Western ecological cosmology and ethics being created by contemporary Pagans.

An ecological ethical cosmology

Contemporary Paganism is a twentieth-century creation (although many groups claim continuity with the past), offering a response to dominant Western cognized models. A modern scientific cosmology fails to offer an integrated model of the world that incorporates and values both human beings and the ecosystem, and which feels at ease with the natural processes of life and death. Graham Harvey states that:

> Pagan cosmology re-enchants the world. Pagans talk about deities and faeries not because they "believe" in them but because they take seriously the intimation of many cultures that the world is inhabited not only by animals, vegetables and minerals but also by less commonly seen people. The world is an exciting and sacred place to live. (Harvey, 1997, p. 174)

Developing Pagan cosmologies are based on this notion of a sacred universe in which human beings are decentered from the destructive role of masters and manipulators of the rest of creation. Pagans do not fit neatly into categories such as polytheist, pantheist, animist, monist, or monotheist – partly because the term Paganism encompasses a wide range of beliefs, but also because beliefs are often fluid and contextual. Pagans are trying to express the sacrality of living things and their interconnections, rather than formulating dogma.

A contemporary myth might suggest that deities evolved along with all other life on the planet and are equally threatened by the ecological devastation many humans fear and deplore. Polytheists do not deny the underlying unity of life, or the singularity of the planet which itself can be seen as a (or the) goddess or, more rarely, the God. Polytheism is not fundamentally a question of numbers of deities or their distance from non-divine life. It is, rather, a concern with the many and varied relationships between living things. It is an affirmation of the importance, beauty and absorbing engagement with ordinary everyday life. It allows both presence and absence, approach and distance, privacy, intimacy and mystery, companionship and detachment. (Harvey, 1997, p. 176)

The Green Movement (many of whose activists describe themselves as Pagans) has enthusiastically embraced the "Gaia hypothesis," put forward by the ex-NASA freelance physicist James Lovelock. Lovelock (1979, 1988) used the name of the Greek earth goddess (Gaia) to describe his scientific model of the planet as a single "organic" system, seen as analogous to a human body rather than as a series of atomized, unrelated elements. While there is increasing evidence from a variety of scientific perspectives that the planet earth is a self-regulating mechanism, Lovelock never intended his model to acquire the religious or quasi-mystical overtones in which it is often interpreted (aided by his, perhaps unfortunate, choice of terminology). A biologist, Rupert Sheldrake, has also propounded a "green" view of the world, but in more overtly religious language than Lovelock.

The old dream of progressive humanism is fading fast. There are still those who dream of the conquest of the biosphere by the technosphere, the human control of biological evolution through genetic engineering, and so on. But attitudes are changing around, and within, many of us: there is a shift from humanism to animism, from an intensely mancentred view to a view of a living world. We are not somehow superior to Gaia; we live within her and depend on her life. (Sheldrake, 1994, p. 174)[5]

Wicca and the goddess

One of the best-known proponents of a contemporary earth-based spirituality is Starhawk, an ecofeminist and witch. Her book of "rituals, invocations, exercises and magic," *The Spiral Dance*, has become something of a classic. The following description of the Goddess has parallels with the Kogi cosmogonic myth in which the Great Mother creates the universe out of her own body.[6]

The Goddess is first of all earth, the dark, nurturing mother who brings forth all life. She is the power of fertility and generation; the womb, and also the receptive tomb, the power of death. All proceeds from Her; all returns to Her. As earth, She is also plant life; trees, herbs and grains that sustain life. She is the body, and the body is sacred. Womb, breast, belly, mouth, vagina, penis, bone, and blood – no part of the body is unclean, no aspect of the life processes is stained by any concept of sin. Birth, death, and decay are equally sacred parts of the cycle. Whether we are eating, sleeping, making love, or eliminating body wastes, we are manifesting the Goddess. (Starhawk, 1989, p. 92)

It is no accident that interest in the Goddess, ecology, and the women's movement go hand in hand. There is a close relationship between myths, rituals, the environment, and gender roles. We are not talking about simple causal links – a myth, for instance, does not give rise to a particular social structure. Myths and rituals can be seen both as a partial reflection of ecological and social realities and as a justification for them. When Starhawk creates rituals which honor the earth and the Goddess she is drawing on late twentieth-century American culture, feminism, and the green movement. She is also empowering women and men who recognize their own desires and intuitions in her writing to identify themselves as Wiccans (followers of the Craft) in a society that has traditionally been hostile to witchcraft. The myths open up visions of what could be, and the rituals enable people to "become witches," through performance.

Mythology, Gender, and the Environment

The way in which subjects are studied in academia tends to split off and isolate different facets of existence. Anthropology is a holistic discipline that seeks to understand human behavior and the influences on it from a number of different angles. The anthropology of religion does not focus on beliefs and ritual alone, but tries to contextualize religious behavior within a broad social framework, and to expose the links between religion and other aspects of the social and natural world. There is a fruitful tension within anthropology between the search for general explanations and theories and detailed descriptions of particular peoples and practices. With the decline of the grand unifying theories of social evolutionism and Marxism, much of the drive toward general theory has come from the women's movement. In the 1970s feminist anthropologists started to ask questions concerning the role of women in different societies, with the aim of discovering any underlying principles that could account for similarities and differences in women's experience. (As we have already seen, Margaret Mead and others had undertaken similar projects a generation earlier.) One anthropologist who has pursued the search for general theories is Peggy Reeves Sanday. As Sanday herself states, general statements need to be tested against specific ethnographic examples. While it is easy to find exceptions to any overarching explanation, this does not necessarily invalidate the attempt. As so few anthropologists are currently prepared to risk making generalized statements, it is worth discussing Sanday's arguments concerning mythology, gender, and the environment in some detail.

Female power and male dominance

In her book *Female Power and Male Dominance: On the Origins of Sexual Inequality* (1981),[7] Sanday studied data from the "Standard cross-cultural sample" (Murdoch and White, 1969) in order to look at the cultural context of sex-role configurations. Of the 186 societies, contemporary and historical, listed in the sample, 156 yielded sufficient data for comparison. The comparative survey revealed that symbolism plays a key role in channeling secular power. Sacred symbols are not an epiphenomenon of secular power roles, but are of primary importance. In fact, secular power roles derive from ancient concepts of sacred power. Following Ruth Benedict (1971), Sanday assumes that each culture selects or chooses its ways of doing and being from a "great arc" of behavioral possibilities. The environment or physical constraints provide hints, which institutions then elaborate. Margaret Mead (1963) argued that cultures have an ideal or standardized temperamental type that is selected for. Individuals who conform to the cultural ideals of their society will be more successful, so that while there will always be a range of temperaments, social selection emphasizes and encourages some traits at the expense of others. Clifford Geertz (1993, pp. 216–18) also argues that cultures set up *symbolic templates* or blueprints that define the limits of behavior and guide it along predictable paths. Sanday uses the term *sex-role plan* to describe the symbolic templates that "help men and women orient themselves as male and female to each other, to the world around them, and to the growing boys and girls whose behavior they must shape to a commonly accepted mold" (Sanday, 1981, p. 3). Sex-role plans also solve basic human puzzles, such as how and why the differences between the sexes came about and how men and women should relate to one another and to their environment. Having examined the cross-cultural data, Sanday concluded that *male dominance is not an inherent quality in human sex-role plans*, as many feminist writers of the 1970s had assumed, but a response to particular environmental pressures (whether social or physical).

In a seminal, widely quoted article, "Is female to male as nature is to culture?" (1974), Sherry Ortner argued that a defining characteristic of human societies is that they are engaged in a process of generating and sustaining systems of meaning that enable them to transcend the most basic, natural limits of existence. Rituals, for instance, are a way of manipulating and regulating the relationship between natural forces and human life. Culture is seen as something that works on and transforms nature, and in that sense is superior to it. *Women*, according to Ortner, are seen as *closer to nature* than men. While both women and men are active participants in the processes of culture, women are viewed as being more rooted in or as having more direct contact with nature. This is because a woman's *physiology*, with its role in childbearing, and the social consequences arising from this, mean that she spends more of her life engaged in natural processes than is true for men and for a male physiology.

The argument goes that if culture is seen as superior to nature, it is a small step to viewing men as superior to women. Women's participation in culture is evidenced by their acceptance of this symbolic hierarchy. The constraints of mothering, and the continuity between infant and adult roles for women, mean that *psychologically* women have a more intimate form of relating, and are less interested than men in hierarchical and role-based distinctions. This can be seen simultaneously as a more natural "lower" form of relating, and as a morally superior "higher" position – as either ignoring or transcending social categories. *Feminine symbols* also demonstrate this polarized ambiguity. They can be exalted (goddesses, dispensers of justice, and occupants of the moral high ground) or debased (witches, dispensers of the evil eye, castrating mothers). In either case the symbolic woman is "rarely within the normal range of human possibilities" (Ortner, 1974, p. 86).

Sanday contests Ortner's claim that because men are associated with culture, and it is culture's job to control nature, men are universally regarded as having the right to control women. Sanday does, however, point to the "permeability between the categories of female and nature" in some societies, but not all. She refers to such societies as having an *inner orientation*.

> In societies where the forces of nature are sacralized . . . there is a reciprocal flow between the power of nature and the power inherent in women. The control and manipulation of these forces is left to women and to sacred natural symbols; men are largely extraneous to this domain and must be careful lest they antagonize earthly representatives of nature's power (namely women). (Sanday, 1981, p. 5)

Similarly, men are not unequivocally aligned with "culture" (defined as the transcendence of the natural givens of existence by means of systems of thought and technology). Men are part of nature, not only in their physicality but also in their need or desire to kill. "Men hunt animals, seek to kill other human beings, make weapons for these activities, and pursue power that is *out there*" (Sanday, 1981, p. 5). These more exterior life-taking activities of men are referred to as an *outer orientation*. Societies vary in the extent to which they value an inner or outer orientation, the powers of women, and respect for reproduction, versus the role of men and their more destructive externalized power. This is not a dichotomy between nature and culture, terms that are in fact hard to define and arguably have no cross-cultural reference.[8] Sanday conceptualizes the differences between the sexes as follows:

> Looking as an outsider at males and females in the simpler societies of the world – that is, in societies unencumbered by complex literate traditions – one is struck with the degree to which the sexes conform to a rather basic conceptual symmetry, which is grounded in primary sex differences. Women give birth and grow children; men kill and make weapons. Men display their kills (be it an animal, a human head, or a scalp) with the same pride that women hold up the newly born. If birth and death are among the necessities of existence, then men and women contribute equally but in quite different ways to the continuance of life, and hence of culture . . . all other things being equal, the power to give life is as highly valued as the power to take it away. The questions at issue are: (1) Why do some societies develop a symmetric as opposed to an asymmetric valuation of these two powers? and (2) How does a symmetric or an asymmetric valuation affect the secular power of men and women? (Sanday, 1981, pp. 5–6)

The variations in sex-role plans found in different societies show that they are cultural constructions rather than genetic (even if, as Margaret Mead proposed, there is an element of selection). Historical and political factors, as well as the environment in which people live, will affect the ways in which they interact. Sex-role plans will in turn change the social and natural environment. Sanday identifies four basic templates relating to the sexes, which can be represented as in figure 5.4.

These four types can be combined in various ways. Among the Mbuti of the Ituri forest in Central Africa, for example, the sexes are merged and decision-making powers shared. Among the Iroquois confederacy of North

Sexes segregated	Sexes merged
decision-making powers vested in one sex	decision-making powers shared

Figure 5.4 Sanday's four basic templates relating to the sexes.

America, on the other hand, sexual differentiation was extreme, while decision-making was still shared between the sexes. In both these societies the sex-role scripts give women both secular and religious power. Their cosmologies and rituals display a generally positive attitude to the world and the place of humans within it. In societies in which decision-making is shared, female or paired deities are given prominence. In societies in which males dominate and women are relegated to a subordinate role in both sacred and secular domains, there is an emphasis on a male godhead. The sexes are also invariably segregated, as among the Hausa of Northern Nigeria or Yanomamo of Venezuela and Brazil.

In seeking to answer the question of why a society should develop one type of sex-role plan rather than another, Sanday regards the environment as a crucial variable.

> In societies dependent on animals, women are rarely depicted as the ultimate source of creative power. The latter is usually attributed either to an animal deity or to a supreme being. When large game are hunted, regardless of the contribution of meat to the overall diet, males engage in an activity whose outcome is unpredictable and entails danger. Whether or not men spend part or most of their time in hunting activities is not as important as the psychological energy expended in this effort. This energy is not directed inwardly toward nurturing children or family but toward acquiring and using powers beyond man's dominance. The major source of power is perceived as residing in a supreme being who resides in the sky or in animals. (Sanday, 1981, pp. 65–6)

In fact, any environmental tension, whether created by food scarcity, climatic unpredictability, warfare, or political uncertainty, tends to move a society in the direction of an outer orientation, male dominance, and androcentric mythology. Sanday suggests that there is transference of anxiety from the external world, which is beyond control, to women, who may be taken as symbolic representatives of the natural world. A lack of environmental security therefore correlates with control of women and male domination. If, on the other hand, the world is experienced as benign, an inner orientation develops in which both the environment and women are seen as partners, rather than as sources of danger to men and to society as a whole. If women acquiesce in cultural definitions of female danger and inferiority, they do not necessarily do so passively, or without the necessity for physical sanctions. Joan Bamberger states that, among the Tukuna of Brazil,

> women are excluded from participation in important social and religious events because all females fall short of perfection as defined by the Sun Father and his

earthly protagonist, Jurupari. Sexual differences, defined by and legislated in myth, are demonstrated in ceremony. To preserve these sexual distinctions in social life, supernatural sanctions are invoked. (Bamberger, 1974, p. 275)

Among the Kayapó and Mundurucú of the Amazon basin women who step out of line are punished by ritual humiliations, gang rape, and forced intercourse for young girls (Bamberger, 1974, p. 278). A Tukuna myth tells the story of a young girl who spied on the sacred flutes (which men are said to have stolen from their original female owners), who was killed, quartered, and eaten, with both her mother and sister summoned to the feast. Bamberger concludes that whether or not women believe the myths that record the overthrow of female power and women's subsequent subordination, "the penalties brought to bear on women and children for infractions of the ceremonial injunctions seem to be real enough" (Bamberger, 1974, p. 275).

> To summarize, male dominance and female power are consequences of the way in which peoples come to terms with their historical and natural environments and develop their separate identities. Male and female power roles are cast when peoples forge their sense of peoplehood. A sense of peoplehood implies a shared code that guides behavior, including the behavior of the sexes, not only in relation to each other but also in relation to valued resources and to the supernatural. Power is accorded to whichever sex is thought to embody or to be in touch with the forces upon which people depend for their perceived needs. Conceiving power in this way, one can say that in some societies women have more power, or men have more, or both sexes have an approximately equal amount. (Sanday, 1981, p. 11)

Sanday's attempt to draw general conclusions as to the relationship between gender, religion, and the environment is quite unusual and rather courageous. After all, negative cases that appear to contradict the pattern, or societies which defy the classifications used, are not difficult to find. Nevertheless, the attempt is useful and Sanday's hypothesis broadly convincing. There certainly are numerous ethnographies in which it is possible to trace the configurations predicted by Sanday's model. I will give just one example, Maria Lepowsky's description of Vanatinai, a small island off Papua New Guinea.

Gender in an egalitarian society

According to Maria Lepowsky, Vanatinai society is sexually egalitarian. "There is no ethic of male dominance, the roles and activities of women and men overlap considerably, and the actions of both sexes are considered equally valuable" (Lepowsky, 1990, p. 171). Both women and men have access to economic and ritual spheres of activity and share in the power that accompanies the control of these resources. Unusually for Papua New Guinea, there are no men's houses, and the village leader or "giver" can be male or female. Vanatinai men and women at equivalent stages of the life cycle have similar levels of autonomy, influence, and access to prestige and wealth. Lepowsky says of Vanatinai: "Its gender ideology stresses that both women and men should strive to be strong, wise, and generous, and the highly valued quality of generosity is explicitly modeled after parental nurture. Women are not viewed as polluting or dangerous to themselves or others in their persons, bodily fluids, or sexuality" (Lepowsky, 1990, p. 174).

If Sanday's model has any predictive value we should find that the Vanatinai environment is stable and unthreatening, offering sufficient physical security and food for people to live comfortably. We would also expect to find cosmogonic myths with female deities and positive mythological roles for women. Vanatinai has a low population density (four persons per square mile), unlike the neighboring Trobriand Islands. This means that everyone has enough space to garden, hunt, fish, and make sago without competition for resources. As there are few ascribed statuses (i.e. rank by virtue of birth or title), both men and women can achieve status through their own efforts by competing in the cycles of exchange which bring prestige (similar to the *Kula* ring described by Malinowski in the Trobriands). Lepowsky also suggests that a low population density reduces conflict and fosters an ethic of respect. Not only are people not fighting for scarce resources, but also if they fall out with a neighbor they can simply move away. There is an ideology of individual autonomy in which people have considerable latitude to do things their own way. Supernatural sanctions are similarly individualistic, and misfortune may be attributed to the violation of a *taboo* attached to a particular place by its guardian spirit (Lepowsky, 1990, p. 179). The people of Vanatinai also display another characteristic of egalitarian societies – a lack of differentiation between "domestic" and "public" spheres.[9] Vanatinai is a face-to-face society where most people are related by ties of kinship and affinity (through marriage), and in which the household is the central institution. Women can own and inherit land, live with their own kin after marriage, and control and dispose of culturally valuable resources (Lepowski, 1990, p. 180).

Taboo (tapu): "sacred," both powerful and dangerous. From a Polynesian word *tapu* or *tafoo*. Usually associated with the avoidance of certain places, objects, or people. The term has been extended to refer to the avoidance of *totemic* animals or plants, or prohibitions on marrying certain classes of kin.

It is clear, then, that the people of Vanatinai generally experience the physical and social environment as hospitable. What then of Vanatinai mythology? The creator spirit, Rodyo, is depicted as male, sometimes taking the form of a snake, and lives on Vanatinai's highest peak with his two wives and the spirits of the island's dead. However, according to Lepowsky,

> The Vanatinai creation myth is culturally unelaborated, contains few details, and is rarely recounted by the islanders and not, apparently, because it is a particularly sacred myth. When it is told, the narrator usually launches immediately afterward into the story of Alagh, a supernatural who left Rodyo's community taking with him all the valuable goods that now belong to Europeans. Often narrated alone, this "cargoistic" explanatory myth is obviously more compelling to present-day islanders than the story of Rodyo's creation of the world. (Lepowsky, 1990, p. 197)

More culturally significant and frequently recounted is the myth of the inauguration of exchange relationships, in which "a female being teaches another female the peaceful exchange with off-islanders of surplus food for ceremonial valuables" (Lepowsky, 1990, p. 200). The wise woman is apparently a common element in Vanatinai myths, which include the story of Emuga, a female deity (from *mumuga*, "custom") who is the first being associated with the secret of fire and cooking. Vanatinai myths, therefore, provide a "charter" validating women's right to engage in exchange and learn the magic associated with it, to own goods and to dispose of them. Through both exchange and cooking, women are clearly associated with "culture." Sanday's hypothesis would appear to hold for Vanatinai, although cosmogonic myths, on which Sanday concentrated, are not necessarily those that are most culturally relevant.

Totemism and the Dreamtime

One of the ways in which the relationship between religion, culture, and environment has been studied is via the concept of *totemism*. It is a term that, like witchcraft (see chapter 8), has gained wide currency in anthropology. Totemism has been invoked to explain the way in which early (ancestral) and "primitive" societies ordered human relations and oriented themselves to the natural world. Although the word *totem* is of North American origin, many of the early theoretical studies of totemism took Australian Aboriginal societies as their model. Despite having occupied many leading anthropologists for the best part of a century, totemism as a concept is now seldom discussed, and by many is dismissed altogether. The association of totemic systems with early or "primitive" societies has been unfortunate, leading to views of Australian Aboriginal beliefs as representative of prehistoric types of cosmology. While Australian Aboriginal cultures may have maintained greater continuity over time than Western cultures, there is no evidence that they are in any sense "ancestral" to non-Australian peoples, or that their belief systems were once universal. These views imply that simpler societies are ahistorical and static, which is very different from claiming that they are both adaptable and conservative.[10]

Totem: an Ojibwa word (from the Algonquin people of Canada). The expression *ototeman* can be translated as "He is a relative of mine." A relative was a member of the same exogamic group or clan (i.e. people classed as unmarriageable kin). Each clan was named after an animal species or totem (Morris, 1987, p. 270). Among Australian Aboriginal peoples totems can also include natural features, such as rocks, rainbows, or thunder.

Totemism: the term became widely used to refer to "any situation in which a special relationship was thought to exist between a social group and one or more classes of material objects, specifically animals and plants" (Morris, 1987, p. 270), or, one might add, other natural phenomena.

Totemic principle: Durkheim proposed that totemism was an original, universal form of religious expression, a means of uniting notions of divinity with those of society. A totem is an outward and visible form both of the totemic principle or god, and of a particular clan. "So if it is at once the symbol of the god and of society, is that not because the god and the society are only one?... The god of the clan, the totemic principle, can therefore be nothing else than the clan itself, personified and represented to the imaginations under the visible form of the animal or vegetable which serves as totem" (Durkheim, 1976, p. 206).

Totemism as an early form of religion

Nineteenth- and early twentieth-century anthropology was driven by a desire for explanations and origins (see chapter 1). Totemism, along with shamanism (see chapter 7), was one candidate for an original and universal form of religion. John McLennan (1865, 1869–70), W. Robertson Smith (1889), Sir James Frazer (1903), and Émile Durkheim (1976) all regarded totemism as the earliest form of religion. They shared an evolutionary perspective that assumed a progression from an early (animistic) to a modern Western (monotheistic) religious expression, and looked for their data to the most "primitive" (and therefore most like prehistoric human) societies. For McLennan, totemism derived from the worship of plants and animals ("fetishism"), in association with an exogamous clan structure and unilineal descent groups.

Exogamy: marriage outside one's group or clan.
Endogamy: marriage within one's group or clan.
Unilineal descent: kinship traced through either the male (*patrilineal*) or female (*matrilineal*) line (but not both).

Robertson Smith, an expert on Semitic religions, based his observations on the matrilineal clans of Arabia, each of which had a species of animal as a sacred totem. This totem represented the clan, and the sacrifice of the totemic animal was interpreted by Robertson Smith as a form of communion – a way of entering into relationship with the divine (Morris, 1987, pp. 112–13). It is hard to escape the conclusion that Robertson Smith's theories owed much to his own Christian Presbyterian upbringing. Jewish and Christian traditions do indeed emphasize the sacrificial meal, and in Christianity the notion of communion succeeds the Jewish tradition of atonement and propitiation (although these elements are not absent in Christianity). While Robertson Smith's arguments may seem plausible for Semitic peoples (monotheistic Jews and Arabs), the idea of totemic sacrifice as a primary and universal religious act does not find cross-cultural support. Where Robertson Smith was influential was in his insistence that rituals were prior to and more important than beliefs, and were of primary importance in creating and sustaining social bonds (Morris, 1987, p. 113).

Durkheim, in his monumental work *The Elementary Forms of the Religious Life* (1912, English translation 1915), held that religious beliefs everywhere depended on a primary classification of phenomena, real and ideal, into two categories, the *sacred* and the *profane*.

> This division of the world into two domains, the one containing all that is sacred, the other all that is profane, is the distinctive trait of religious thought; the beliefs, myths, dogmas and legends are either representations or systems of representations which express the nature of sacred things, the virtues and powers which are attributed to them, or their relations with each other and with profane things. But by sacred things one must not understand simply those personal beings which are called gods or spirits; a rock, a tree, a spring, a pebble, a piece of wood, a house, in a word, anything can be sacred. A rite can have this

character; in fact, the rite does not exist which does not have it to a certain degree.... [Sacred things] are naturally considered superior in dignity and power to profane things, and particularly to man, when he is only a man and has nothing sacred about him. (Durkheim, 1976, p. 37)

Many anthropologists have pointed out that it is not always possible to distinguish in practice between the sacred and the profane, and this idea, so central to Durkheim's work, has by and large been discarded, at least as a monolithic organizing principle. For Durkheim, however, who based his ideas on Australian Aboriginal examples, totems were signs (he referred to them as "flags") that linked the clan to the environment and to the sacred. In the "Dreamtime" ancestors walked the land, leaving evidence of their journeys in the physical features of the landscape. Rituals performed by initiated male elders at sacred totemic sites linked clans with the past and reinforced group identity and solidarity. Durkheim concluded that totemism was "a whole complex of belief and rituals that involved a ritual attitude toward nature, and a cosmology that expressed the idea that humans and nature form part of a spiritual totality" (Morris, 1987, p. 118). The sacred was real, but its origins lay in the social group. When worshipping a totemic animal, the clan was affirming and worshipping itself via the visible totemic symbol.

Radcliffe-Brown (1952) was influenced by both Durkheim and Robertson Smith. He affirmed both the social nature of religion and the importance of rituals, which have the task of regulating, maintaining, and transmitting the social mores on which a society depends. Radcliffe-Brown's emphasis, also using Australian source material, was on the social and symbolic value of the totemic animal or object to a particular group, arguing that: "Any object or event which has important effects upon the well-being (material or spiritual) of a society, or anything which stands for or represents any such object or event, tends to become an object of the ritual attitude" (Radcliffe-Brown, 1952, p. 129). For Radcliffe-Brown, however, totemism was not a universal form of religion but a specific specialization in societies characterized by a clan structure. It is just one way among many of relating to the environment and natural world.

Totemism as a mode of thought

In his book *Totemism* (1973), Lévi-Strauss sought to demolish earlier theories, declaring that totemism should not be regarded as an aspect of religion at all. Lévi-Strauss eschewed the functionalist explanation that animals are "good to eat," declaring instead that totems are chosen because they are "good to think." What matters is not some correspondence between a clan and a particular animal or totemic feature, but the structural relation be-tween totemic creatures which are used to think about and express relations between social groups. As a term, "totemism" rests on the conjunction of three elements, which Lévi-Strauss regarded as being artificially associated with one another. There is the organization of society into clans, the attri-bution of the names of natural species or phenomena to specific clans (such as the bear, eagle, or rainbow clan), and, finally, the maintenance of a ritual relationship between a clan and its totemic emblem. These three elements can and do occur independently of one another. Totemism should not, therefore, according to Lévi-Strauss, be regarded as a religious institution, and certainly not as the earliest form of religion. It is a classificatory device that serves to regulate human groups and their relationships with the natural world. Lévi-Strauss concludes his essay with the claim that "there is nothing archaic or remote about it [totemism]. Its image is projected, not received; it does not derive its substance from without. If the illusion contains a particle of truth, this is not outside but within us" (Lévi-Strauss, 1973, p. 177).

Having dismissed the concept of totemism, Lévi-Strauss returned to the theme at great length in *The Savage Mind* (like *Totemism* originally published in 1962). It is, however, the structure and function of totemic classifications that interest Lévi-Strauss. He gives, for instance, an example of a mytho-geographical system in the Sudan that linked the whole Niger valley, crossing the territorial boundaries of numerous cultural and linguistic groups. People were therefore related in both time (*metaphorically*) and space (*synchronic-ally*), thus overcoming the tendency of small-scale societies to "treat the limits of their tribal group as the frontiers of humanity." Totemism can therefore promote a broader and more inclusive view of humanity. "Totemic classifications make it possible both to define the status of persons within a group and to expand the group beyond its traditional confines" (Lévi-Strauss, 1976, p. 166).

The Dreamtime

Arguably some of the most explicitly environmental cosmologies in the world are to be found among the Aboriginal peoples of Australia (i.e. cosmologies in which the interdependence of human life and the ecosystems that sustain them are made conscious and are embodied at the level of myth, ritual, language, and lifestyle). For all Aboriginal groups in Australia the land is at the center of a mythical order that regulates the relations of people with one another and with the physical environment. The land, through the concept of *Dreaming*, connects Aboriginal peoples both to local ecological systems and to the past, providing a durable but flexible mechanism for dealing with change and with the vicissitudes of life and death. According to Veronica Strang, the Aboriginal cosmos is also "non-human centred and non-hierarchical – all parts of the natural and supernatural world are equal, contain moral agency and are sentient" (Strang, 1997, p. 238). Although most Aboriginal societies were formerly depicted as patriarchal (with male elders wielding considerable authority), Strang points out that men and women can both become "elders," own land, and have ritual responsibilities, and that "The symbolic universe is also balanced in terms of gender, with male and female creative forces" (Strang, 1997, p. 238). Strang goes on to explain that "Aboriginal cosmology is both practical and spiritual – there is no division between sacred and secular or between spiritual beliefs and the laws governing everyday life – the cosmology is The Law, entering every aspect of human existence" (Strang, 1997, p. 238).

The Dreamtime is understood as the period of creation "long ago," in which ancestral beings emerged from a featureless landscape. The "story places" are where ancestral beings emerged, acted, or reintegrated themselves with the landscape, while the "story lines" (or "song lines") tell of the ancestors' journeys across the land. All living creatures and natural phenomena are imbued with ancestral spiritual power, and are linked via these story places and lines, where the interaction of the ancestral beings with the land transformed them into rocks, birds, trees, waterholes, and so on. These ancestral figures then become "totems" of individual clans, which have particular obligations and ritualized relationships between them. The story lines traverse linguistic boundaries, forming a network of relations between different Aboriginal groups. They are also dynamic. Like all myths, story lines are capable of developing and of sustaining the connections between people and the land. The "long ago" of the Dreamtime is also immanent. Human spiritual existence is seen to reflect that of ancestral beings, emerging and returning to a particular location, which is identified as their spirit home.

Veronica Strang likens the stories of the Dreamtime to the psychophysical development of human beings. "Thus the stories describe a sequence of emergence, differentiation, categorisation, transformation and reintegration. This provides a striking metaphor of human cognitive development – the epigenetic development of the individual achieved through a process of externalisation, objectification and reintegration" (Strang, 1997, p. 241). The landscape is also described as a conscious, sentient being that co-creates, nurtures, and responds to the actions and emotions of human beings. Johnny Clarke, one of Strang's informants, told her that "If the young people don't come back to this country, the country will feel that, . . . so this country will just sort of die away" (Strang, 1997, p. 253).[11] The landscape can also be dangerous – punishing those who ignore taboos or who fail to respect

Figure 5.5   Ancient Aboriginal rock art from Laura, Northern Queensland (Australia).
© Veronica Strang.

traditional associations between particular clans and their territory. Strangers must be introduced to the ancestral beings if they are to pass unharmed. This view of the land is contrasted with that of the white Australian cattle ranchers, for whom commercial productivity, using the land for what it can yield, is prioritized. Countryside that simply supports its Aboriginal population in a sustainable way, or which is turned into national parks, is viewed as wasted (Strang, 1997, pp. 263ff).[12]

Despite the influence of Christianity and Western educational systems, Aboriginal conceptions of the Dreamtime have proved resilient. With a global trend toward environmental protection, and increased legal enforcement of Aboriginal land rights, there is increasing respect for "indigenous" cosmologies, in Australia as elsewhere in the world. Strang sums up the Aboriginal view of social, spiritual, and environmental relations in the following way:

> Aboriginal Law therefore provides for every aspect of life, setting out foundational beliefs and values that continue to provide the basis for social and environmental relations in the community today. The Law, within the land, is the source of all life, creating, identifying and binding people socially and spiritually. It defines who owns and has rights to which country, and who must marry whom. The land is both father and mother: it is alive, listening, watching, nurturing, disciplining and balancing human and natural resources. Humans share with the ancestral beings a responsibility for maintaining the land and their relationship with it, and their well-being depends on that of the land. Thus the Law constructs a relationship with the land that is complex, qualitative and deeply affective. (Strang, 1997, p. 261)

Conclusion

In this chapter we have looked at various types of cosmology in both Western and small-scale societies from the perspective of their relationship with the environment. The environment has both social and physical aspects, and the actions of individual humans and social groups both shape and are shaped by their interactions with their surroundings. Several of the scholars we have looked at in this chapter argued that Western cosmologies are predominantly destructive and unsustainable, treating ecosystems as endlessly expendable and exploitable. Western societies are often contrasted with those with cosmologies that encourage sustainable (adaptive) economic and environmental practices, exemplified by the Kogi of Colombia and the Aboriginal peoples of Australia, together with contemporary Western Pagan traditions.

A second strand has been the ways in which social structures, and in particular sex-role patterns, develop in different environmental contexts, and the influence of mythology as a charter for society. Sanday distinguished between "inner-oriented" societies, which have positive cosmologies, in relation to both women and the environment, and "outer-oriented" societies, which view both the environment and women as potentially dangerous and in need of control. Discussions on totemism relate to earlier, longstanding concerns in the anthropology of religion, that seek both to explain religion in terms of origins, and to account for societies which have both exogamous kinship groups and ritual relationships with totem animals or other natural phenomena. Claude Lévi-Strauss turned the study of totemism on its head with his insistence that totemism should not be viewed as a form of religion, but as another example of symbolic classification (see chapters 2 and 3). Rituals, which encode and enforce modes of behavior, socializing people into culturally appropriate ways of being and relating, are seen as central to the expression and maintenance of a cosmology. We will explore the role of ritual in greater detail in the next chapter, in the context of rites of passage in general and female initiation in particular.

Notes

1   One may wish to take issue with Rappaport's romanticization of the Ituri Pygmies and their view of the forest (see Turnbull, 1961), but the general point stands. In *Sick Societies: Challenging the Myth of Primitive Harmony*, Robert Edgerton (1992) puts forward a powerful argument that sick or maladaptive societies can and do occur everywhere. Maladaptation is defined as: "the failure of a population or its culture to survive because of the inadequacy or harmfulness of one or more of its institutions or beliefs"; as sufficient dissatisfaction with social institutions or cultural beliefs to threaten the viability of that society; and, third, as the maintenance of "beliefs or practices that so seriously impair the physical or mental health of its members that they cannot adequately meet their own needs or maintain their social and cultural system" (Edgerton, 1992, p. 45).

2   Feminist theologians are also concerned to develop cosmological values that are more sustainable than those that guide most current Western industrial practices. See, for instance, McFague (1997).

3   See, for example, O'Neil et al.'s (1998) article on the conflict between uranium mining and indigenous peoples in Saskatchewan, Canada, which contrasts the goals of the mining company and national government, and supposed benefits of short-term employment for local men, with the social, health, and environmental problems perceived by the Saskatchewan Aboriginal women.

4   The Tairona Heritage Trust, and the Tairona Heritage Studies Centre, founded to give financial support to the Kogi via their organization *Gonavindua Tairona*, and to provide educational materials and information about the Kogi, are based

at the Department of Anthropology, University of Wales Lampeter, SA48 7ED, Wales, UK. http://www.lamp.ac.uk/tairona/.

5   In almost apocalyptic terms, Sheldrake goes on to claim that: "The recognition that we need to change the way we live is now very common. It is like waking up from a dream. It brings with it a spirit of repentance, seeing in a new way, a change of heart. This conversion is intensified by the sense that the end of an age is at hand" (Sheldrake, 1994, p. 175).

6   See Reichel-Dolmatoff (1987).

7   See also Sanday (1974).

8   Ortner's 1974 article has stimulated a wide range of work seeking to critique or refine her thinking. The debates around "nature" and "culture," and the associ-ated terms "domestic" and "public," are too numerous and complex to do justice to here. See, for instance, MacCormack (1980), Strathern (1990), and Lock and Kaufert (1998, pp. 19–21).

9   Strathern (1990) points out that among the Hagan of Highland Papua New Guinea it is not really possible to delineate a "domestic" or a "public" sphere of action. The desire to distinguish these spheres or "domains" is, according to Strathern, a product of Western thinking, with its own hierarchy of values. She writes: "The idea of domains corresponding to men's and women's worlds is not a dualism that needs be sustained in the Melanesian context. Domaining itself is not simply a male description of the world imposed upon a pre-existing hetero-geneous nature; nor do the values ascribed to the domains simply stand for men's and women's intrinsically opposed perspectives. The very questions about the articulation of domains that were so important to the anthropological-feminist critique turn out to endorse a model of a society that must code its own and not other people's gender constructs. . . . Domaining is better taken as an activity, the creation/implementation of difference as a social act" (Strathern 1990, p. 96).

10 I am grateful to Veronica Strang for stressing this point.

11 "The land suffers and the ancestral forces are weakened because of the grief associated with the country owners, and the resultant lack of someone to care for that place" (Veronica Strang, personal communication).

12 Strang points out that it is not that the white ranchers are unconcerned about the environment, but that they have a very different relationship with it from Aboriginal peoples (personal communication).

References and Further Reading

Bamberger, Joan (1974) The myth of matriarchy: why men rule in primitive society. In Michelle Zimbalist Rosaldo and Louise Lamphere (eds), *Woman, Culture and Society*. Standford, CA: Stanford University Press, pp. 263–80.

Benedict, Ruth (1971) *Patterns of Culture*. London: Routledge and Kegan Paul (ori-ginally published in 1935).

Bol, Marsha C. (ed.) (1998) *Stars Above, Earth Below: American Indians and Nature*. Carnegie Museum of National History. Niwort, CO and Dublin: Roberts, Rinehart Publisher.

Croll, Elisabeth and Parkin, David (1992) *Bush Base, Forest Farm: Culture, Environment and Development*. London and New York: Routledge.

Crowley, Vivianne (1995) *Phoenix from the Flame: Living as a Pagan in the 21st Century*. London and San Francisco: Thorsons.

Descola, Philippe (1996) *In the Society of Nature: a Native Ecology in Amazonia*. Cambridge and New York: Cambridge University Press.

Dodd, Elizabeth (1997) The Mamas and the Papas: goddess worship, the Kogi Indians and ecofeminism. *National Women's Studies Association*, 9(3), 77–88.

Durkheim, Émile (1976) *The Elementary Forms of the Religious Life*. With an introduction by Robert Nisbet. London: George Allen and Unwin (originally published in 1915).

Edgerton, Robert B. (1992) *Sick Societies: Challenging the Myth of Primitive Harmony*. New York: The Free Press.

Ellen, Roy and Fukui, Katsuyoshi (eds) (1996) *Redefining Nature: Ecology, Culture and Domestication*. Oxford: Berg.

Ereira, Alan (1992) *The Heart of the World*. London: Jonathan Cape.

Frazer, Sir James G. (1887) *Totemism*. Edinburgh: Adams and Charles.

Frazer, Sir James G. (1903) Taboo: totemism. *Encyclopaedia Britannica*, 9th edn. Cited in Morris (1987).

Gardner, Katy and Lewis, David (1996) *Anthropology, Development and the Postmodern Challenge*. London and Chicago: Pluto Press.

Geertz, Clifford (1993) *The Interpretation of Cultures*. London: Fontana (originally published in 1973).

Harrow, Judy (1996) The contemporary neo-Pagan revival. In James R. Lewis (ed.), *Magical Religion and Modern Witchcraft*. Albany: State University of New York Press, pp. 9–24.

Harvey, Graham (1997) *Listening People, Speaking Earth: Contemporary Paganism*. London: Hurst & Co.

Harvey, Graham and Hardman, Charlotte (eds) (1996) *Paganism Today: Wiccans, Druids, the Goddess and Ancient Earth Traditions for the Twenty-first Century*. London and San Francisco: Thorsons.

Hastrup, Kirsten (1978) The semantics of biology: virginity. In Shirley Ardener (ed.), *Defining Females: the Nature of Women in Society*. London: Croom Helm, pp. 49–65.

Lepowsky, Maria (1990) Gender in an egalitarian society: a case study from the Coral Sea. In Peggy Reeves Sanday and Ruth Gallagher Goodenough (eds), *Beyond the Second Sex: New Directions in the Anthropology of Gender*. Philadelphia: University of Pennsylvania Press, pp. 171–223.

Lévi-Strauss, Claude (1973) *Totemism*. With an introduction by Roger Poole. Harmondsworth: Penguin (originally published in 1962).

Lévi-Strauss, Claude (1976) *The Savage Mind*. London: Weidenfeld and Nicolson (originally published in 1962).

Lock, Margaret and Kaufert, Patricia A. (1998) Introduction. In Margaret Lock and Patricia A. Kaufert (eds), *Pragmatic Women and Body Politics*. Cambridge and New York: Cambridge University Press, pp. 1–27.

Lovelock, James (1979) *Gaia: a New Look at Life on Earth*. Oxford: Oxford University Press.

Lovelock, James (1988) *The Ages of Gaia: a Biography of Our Living Earth*. Oxford: Oxford University Press.

MacCormack, Carol P. (1980) Nature, culture and gender: a critique. In Carol MacCormack and Marilyn Strathern (eds), *Nature, Culture and Gender*. Cambridge and New York: Cambridge University Press.

McFague, Sallie 1997: *Super, Natural Christians: How We Should Love Nature*. London: SCM.

MacKinnon, Mary Heather and McIntyre, Moni (eds) (1995) *Readings in Ecology and Feminist Theology*. Kansas City: Sheed and Ward.

McLennan, John F. (1865) *Primitive Marriage*. Edinburgh: Adam and Charles Black.

McLennan, John F. (1869–70) The worship of animals and plants. *Fortnightly Review*, New Series, 4, 407–27, 562–82; 7, 94–216.

Malinowski, Bronislaw (1963) *The Family among the Australian Aborigines*. New York: Schocken (originally published in 1913).

Mathews, Freya (1994) *The Ecological Self*. London: Routledge.

Mead, Margaret (1963) *Sex and Temperament in Three Primitive Societies*. New York: Morrow (originally published in 1935).

Morphy, Howard (1991) *Ancestral Connections: Art and an Aboriginal System of Knowledge*. Chicago and London: University of Chicago Press.

Morris, Brian (1987) *Anthropological Studies of Religion: an Introductory Text*. Cambridge and New York: Cambridge University Press.

Munn, Nancy D. (1986) *Walbiri Iconography: Graphic Representation and Cultural Symbolism in a Central Australian Society*. With a new afterword. Chicago and London: University of Chicago Press.

Murdoch, George P. and White, Douglas R. (1969) Standard cross-cultural sample. *Ethnology*, 8, 329–69.

O'Neil, John D., Elias, Brenda D., and Yassi, Annalee (1998) Situating resistance in fields of resistance: Aboriginal women and environmentalism. In Margaret Lock and Patricia A. Kaufert (eds), *Pragmatic Women and Body Politics*. Cambridge and New York: Cambridge University Press, pp. 260–86.

Ortner, Sherry B. (1974) Is female to male as nature is to culture? In M. Rosaldo and L. Lamphere (eds), *Woman, Culture and Society*. Stanford, CA: Stanford University Press, pp. 67–88.

Patton, Laurie L. and Doniger, Wendy (eds) (1996) *Myth and Method*. Charlottesville and London: University Press of Virginia.

Pearson, Joanne, Roberts, Richard H., and Samuel, Geoffrey (eds) (1998) *Nature Religion Today: Paganism in the Modern World*. Edinburgh: Edinburgh University Press.

Radcliffe-Brown, A. R. (1952) *Structure and Function in Primitive Society*. London: Cohen & West.

Rappaport, Roy A. (1971) *Pigs for Ancestors: Ritual in the Ecology of a New Guinea People*. New Haven, CT and London: Yale University Press.

Rappaport, Roy A. (1979) *Ecology, Meaning, and Religion*. Berkeley, CA: North Atlantic Books.

Reichel-Dolmatoff, G. (1976) Training for the priesthood among the Kogi of Colombia. In Johannes Wilbert (ed.), *Enculturation in Latin America: an Anthology*. Los Angeles: University of California Los Angeles Latin American Studies, volume 37, pp. 265–88.

Reichel-Dolmatoff, G. (1978) The loom of life: a Kogi principle of integration. *Journal of Latin American Lore*, 4/5(1), 5–27.

Reichel-Dolmatoff, G. (1984) Some Kogi models of the beyond. *Journal of Latin American Lore*, 10(1), 63–85.

Reichel-Dolmatoff, G. (1987) The Great Mother and the Kogi universe: a concise overview. *Journal of Latin American Lore*, 13(1), 73–113.

Robertson Smith, W. (1889) *Lectures in the Religion of the Semites*. Edinburgh: Black.

Rosaldo, Michelle Zimbalist (1974) Woman, culture and society: a theoretical overview. In Michelle Zimbalist Rosaldo and Louise Lamphere (eds), *Woman, Culture and Society*. Standford, CA: Stanford University Press, pp. 17–42.

Sanday, Peggy Reeves (1974) Female status in the public domain. In Michelle Zimbalist Rosaldo and Louise Lamphere (eds), *Woman, Culture and Society*. Standford, CA: Stanford University Press, pp. 189–206.

Sanday, Peggy Reeves (1981) *Female Power and Male Dominance*. Cambridge and New York: Cambridge University Press.

Schlegel, Alice (1990) Gender meanings: general and specific. In Peggy Reeves Sanday and Ruth Gallagher Goodenough (eds), *Beyond the Second Sex: New Directions in the Anthropology of Gender*. Philadelphia: University of Pennsylvania Press, pp. 21–42.

Segal, Robert A. (ed.) (1998) *The Myth and Ritual Theory*. Malden, MA and Oxford: Blackwell.

Sheldrake, Rupert (1994) *The Rebirth of Nature: New Science and the Revival of Animism. The Greening of Science and God*. London: Rider.

Starhawk (1989) *The Spiral Dance: a Rebirth of the Ancient Religion of the Great Goddess*. San Francisco: Harper.

Strang, Veronica (1997) *Uncommon Ground: Cultural Landscapes and Environmental Values*. Oxford and New York: Berg.

Strathern, Marilyn (1980) No nature, no culture: the Hagan case. In Carol MacCormack and Marilyn Strathern (eds), *Nature, Culture and Gender*. Cambridge and New York: Cambridge University Press, pp. 174–222.

Strathern, Marilyn (1990) *The Gender of the Gift: Problems with Women and Problems with Society in Melanesia*. Berkeley and Los Angeles: University of California Press.

Tapper, Richard (1994) Animality, humanity, morality, society. In Tim Ingold (ed.), *What is an Animal?* London and New York: Routledge, pp. 47–62.

Turnbull, Colin M. (1961) *The Forest People*. London: Book Club Associates.
Warren, Karen J. (ed.) (1994) *Ecological Feminism*. London and New York: Routledge.
Worsley, Peter (1997) *Knowledges: What Different Peoples Make of the World. Part 1, Green Knowledge: the Living Environment of an Australian Tribe*. London: Profile Books.

Chapter 6

Ritual Theory, Rites of Passage, and Ritual Violence

Introduction

Rituals have many functions, both at the level of the individual and for groups or societies. They can channel and express emotions, guide and reinforce forms of behavior, support or subvert the status quo, bring about change, or restore harmony and balance. Rituals also have a very important role in healing. They may be used to maintain the life forces and fertility of the earth, and to ensure right relationships with the unseen world, whether of spirits, ancestors, deities, or other supernatural forces. The succession of a culture's most deeply held values from one generation to another may be facilitated by means of ritual. Rituals are also intimately connected with violence, destruction, and scapegoating. Above all, they are dramatic. Rituals can be seen as performances, which involve both audience and actors. Ritual is not, however, a universal, cross-cultural phenomenon, but a particular way of looking at and organizing the world that tells us as much about the anthropologist, and his or her frame of reference, as the people and behavior being studied. This does not mean that as a category ritual has no explanatory or interpretative value, but we would do well to beware universal, essentialist interpretations of actions defined by the anthropologist as "ritual." The first section of this chapter, "What is Ritual?," explores this theme, looking at the concept of ritual and its functions, and at some of the significant debates and developments in ritual studies.

As an example of ritual the second section looks at the writings of Arnold van Gennep on *rites of passage*. Van Gennep used the term "rites of passage" (*rites de passage*) for transition rituals, marking a change of status, whether of persons or seasons, collective or individual. Rites of passage are commonly associated with initiation rituals, but the framework developed by van

Gennep was applicable far more widely. He argued that all rites of passage have a threefold structure. The first stage is that of separation from the previous state, place, time, or status. There follows a middle stage, which is neither one thing nor the other, before the final stage of reintegration, but in a transformed condition. This basic pattern can be discerned within almost all rituals, particularly if they mark some type of transition or movement (from winter to spring, from alive to dead, from single to married, from child to adult, and so on).

Arnold van Gennep's ideas on rites of passage have been taken up and developed by Victor Turner. Both Victor Turner and his wife Edith worked among the Ndembu in Central Africa in the 1950s and 1960s, and Victor Turner published numerous books, focusing in particular on Ndembu rituals. Victor Turner looked closely at the middle stage of a rite of passage, borrowing van Gennep's term "liminal" (from the Latin *limen* or "threshold"). He explored the nature of liminality for Ndembu neophytes in an initiation ritual, as well as for other groups, such as pilgrims or university students, who are also regarded as being in a liminal state. Liminality can become extended indefinitely, as for monks and nuns who do not seek to reintegrate into the world they left. Typical of the liminal state, according to Turner, is "communitas," a communal bond that results from the social leveling and shared experience of liminality. Bruce Lincoln, in his study of women's initiation rituals, argues that both van Gennep and Turner drew heavily on male initiation for their model of a rite of passage. He suggests that women's experience does not fit easily into this pattern, and proposes an alternative threefold structure of enclosure, metamorphosis (or magnification), and emergence. Lincoln concurs with Audrey Richards, in seeing female initiation as a primary means by which a society persuades or coerces women to conform to its demands.

The final section of the chapter explores the concept of *ritual violence*, including Freud's psychoanalytic notion of patricide by a "primal horde," and the influential thesis of the intrinsic violence of sacrifice expounded by the French scholar René Girard. Maurice Bloch coined the term "rebounding violence" to describe the processes in a rite of passage. He looks in particular at the way in which the return from liminality to structure, armed with the power gained through communion with the divine or supernatural forces, can be the prelude to actual violence. Even when violence is not a product of a rite of passage, there is, argues Bloch, at the very least the notion of moral conquest. The victory of the supernatural world over the world of nature and human beings is commonly symbolized by the consumption of natural products (food and drink), or the conquest of women or neighbors (through sex or warfare). Victor Turner pointed out that crisis and fear can encourage a sense of communitas, and the use of fear as an aspect of ritual is developed by

Harvey Whitehouse in his study of male initiation rites in Papua New Guinea. The invocation of fear in initiands is a powerful way of inscribing meanings on the body and mind at its most receptive and vulnerable.

What is Ritual?

Definitions

Finding a definition broad enough to include the wide variety of human activities we might wish to describe under the heading "ritual," while still preserving some explanatory value, is not altogether straightforward. Bobby Alexander emphasizes two facets of ritual: performance and transformation.

> *Ritual* defined in the most general and basic terms is a performance, planned or improvised, that effects a transition from everyday life to an alternative context within which the everyday is transformed. (Alexander, 1997, p. 139)

One of the best known definitions of *religious* ritual is that given by Victor Turner, who describes it as:

> prescribed formal behaviour for occasions not given over to technical routine, having reference to beliefs in mystical (or non-empirical) beings or powers regarded as the first and final causes of all effects. (Turner, 1982, p. 79)

This definition is, however, rather static, whereas Turner's own work demonstrates the dynamic nature of religious rituals. An alternative definition is found in Alexander's statement that:

> Traditional religious rituals open up ordinary life to ultimate reality or some transcendent being or force in order to tap its transformative power. (Alexander, 1997, p. 139)

Alexander stresses that all ritual, including religious ritual, is grounded in the everyday, human world.

So many examples of ritual escape from any but the broadest of definitions, however, that anthropologists sometimes fall back on the "I know one when I see one" approach, or, as Talal Asad (1993, p. 55) states (rhetorically and somewhat ironically), "Every ethnographer will probably recognise a ritual when he or she sees one, because ritual is (is it not?) symbolic activity as opposed to the instrumental behavior of everyday life." A fundamental problem in seeking to define a ritual stems from the basic assumption that what we identify as ritual in Western societies (often in a liturgical or ceremonial setting) can be regarded as a cross-cultural category with parallels elsewhere. There is not, however, a single type of activity called "ritual" that is instantly and universally recognizable, but there are certain forms of behavior that fall into the category identified as such by Western observers. If anthropologists manage to agree on what constitutes a ritual, this does not mean that the purpose or function of a ritual is self-evident.

> Single explanations of ritual behaviour, however satisfying to the observer, seem to me to deny the nature of symbolism itself and its use in human society to express the accepted and approved as well as the hidden and denied, the rules of society and the occasional revolt against them, the common interests of the whole community and the conflicting interests of different parts of it. The use of symbols in ritual secures some kind of emotional compromise which satisfies the majority of the individuals who compose a society and which supports its major institutions. (Richards, 1982, p. 169)

Audrey Richards's warning, first published in 1956, not to look for a single or simple explanation of ritual, is well placed, not least because rituals are multifaceted. Rituals commonly involve participants in physical movement or action, passive and active modes of communication (verbal and non-verbal), esoteric and exoteric knowledge, often in the context of heightened emotional states. Reactions to ritual acts cannot be predetermined. Regular attendance at a place of worship, for instance, may reveal a wide range of possible individual responses to a liturgy, from boredom, anger, and frustration to elevation, joy, the intensity of mystical communion, and a sense of unity with fellow worshipers. The individual may inwardly assent to or dissent from the ritual process. Commentators often stress the formulaic aspect of ritual – a ritual is not simply a spontaneous event created by an individual on the spur of the moment. What, however, about the family burial of a pet rabbit? Spontaneous prayers and actions, and accumulation of symbols (a flower, a memorial, a tree planted), may dignify the committal of the deceased animal. Mere routine – the daily repetition of eating, dressing, and so on, is usually distinguished from (religious) ritual, but Quakers stress the "sacrament of the everyday," the sanctity of every small action, and many other Christian traditions also seek to turn all actions into religious acts through conscious intent by directing them or dedicating them to God.

S. J. Tambiah stated that the difference between ritual and nonritual is relative rather than absolute, and suggested the following working definition:

> Ritual is a culturally constructed system of symbolic communication. It is constituted of patterned and ordered sequences of words and acts, often

expressed in multiple media, whose content and arrangement are characterized in varying degree by formality (conventionality), stereotypy (rigidity), condensation (fusion), and redundancy (repetition). (Tambiah, 1979, p. 119)

The notion that ritual is concerned with symbolic communication is relatively recent. The first edition of the *Encyclopaedia Britannica* (1771) defined "ritual" as "a book directing the order and manner to be observed in celebrating religious ceremonies, and performing divine service in a particular church, diocese, order of the like," whereas a "rite" "denotes the particular manner of celebrating divine service, in this or that country" (Asad, 1993, p. 56). Asad points out that for medieval monastics the performance of a rite – that is, following a set of instructions or "ritual" – was itself a Christian discipline, an ascetic practice and virtuous act, comparable to the scribal copying of Gospel manuscripts. The symbolic "meaning" of praying the divine office (the singing of the psalms as laid down in the ritual) or scribal calligraphy was not an issue. The practice itself was what mattered. Not until the eleventh edition of the *Encyclopaedia Britannica*, published in 1910, did modern definitions appear, incorporating the work of Tylor, Lang, Frazer, Robertson-Smith, Hubert, and Mauss. Asad points out that in this entry "ritual is now regarded as a type of routine behavior that symbolizes or expresses something and, as such, relates differentially to individual consciousness and social organization" (Asad, 1993, p. 57).

The idea that ritual symbols must "mean" something is, as we have seen, central to current anthropological interpretations, but not, however, necessarily shared by an anthropologist's informants. As Asad illustrates, the ethnographer can find himself or herself acting as both *analysand* and *analyst* – both identifying ritual symbols and interpreting them. Alfred Gell (1975, p. 211), for instance, in his interpretation of the *ida* ritual among the Umedas of Papua New Guinea, admits that:

> Among my Umeda informants I found none willing to discuss the meaning of their symbols – to discuss their symbols *as* symbols "standing for" some other thing or idea, rather than as concrete things-in-themselves. In fact I found it impossible to even posit the question of meaning in Umeda, since I could not discover any corresponding Umeda word for the English "mean," "stand for," etc. Questions about symbols were taken by Umedas as questions about the *identity* rather than the *meaning* of a symbol: "what is it?" not "what does it mean?" (Cited in Asad, 1993, p. 61)

The lack of an insider (emic) interpretation of ritual symbols does not in itself invalidate the attempt to look for correspondences between ritual action, social structure, myths, beliefs, and so on, but should alert the anthropologist to the possibility that the action itself, rather than any symbolic meaning, may be the point for participants.[1]

There have been many attempts to say what a ritual is and what it does. One version is what Catherine Bell (1997, p. 94) describes as "a pragmatic compromise between completeness and simplicity." Bell identifies six categories of ritual action:

1 Rites of passage of "life crisis" rituals.
2 Calendrical and commemorative rites.
3 Rites of exchange and communion.
4 Rites of affliction.
5 Rites of feasting, fasting and festivals.
6 Political rituals.

Needless to say, these categories overlap in practice, and do not actually take us any further in understanding the purpose, function, mechanics, or efficacy of the ritual process. We can similarly identify three broad theoretical approaches to the study of ritual, which Bell describes as:

> Ritual as the expression of paradigmatic values of death and rebirth; ritual as a mechanism for bringing the individual into the community and establishing a social entity; or ritual as a process for social transformation, for catharsis, for embodying symbolic values, for defining the nature of the real, or for struggling over control of the sign. (Bell, 1997, p. 89)

Ronald Grimes (1982) prefers to identify various ritual "modes," rather than adopt a checklist approach. These modes include ritualization, decorum, ceremony, liturgy, magic, and celebration. The emphasis on each mode will vary from one ritual to another according to its function.[2] These approaches are not necessarily contradictory, and demonstrate both the diverse nature of rituals themselves and the different interests of theoreticians and observers.

Instrumental versus expressive approaches to ritual

The debate between the *intellectualists* who, following Tylor (1871), view religion as a means of explaining the universe, and the *symbolists*, following Durkheim (1976), who see religion as a symbolic language that makes statements about the social order (see chapter 1) has had a significant impact on ritual studies.[3] Representatives of the intellectualist school include the historian of religion Mircea Eliade (1907–86) and anthropologist Robin Horton. Eliade gives priority to myths in explaining cosmogonic events – how the world, gods, and humans came into being. Ritual is a re-enactment of this primal myth, bringing the past continuously into the present (Eliade, 1989, pp. 85ff).[4] Horton adopts a rather different position, but nevertheless one that also sees religion and ritual primarily as explanatory devices. Using examples from the Kalabari of Nigeria and from elsewhere in Africa, Horton compares an "animistic" personalized model of the world with a Western scientific, impersonal model. Both are "true" for their adherents and adequately account for the way things are. Horton criticizes symbolists (specifically John Beattie and Maurice Bloch) for their inability to accept that taking religious beliefs "literally and seriously as means of explanation, prediction and control of the world" (Horton, 1994, p. 361) can account for the power of a ritual to move and transform its participants.

Horton clearly regards the symbolist approach as unnecessarily reduction-ist, denying the reality and therefore the power of rituals. The symbolist approach assumes that the form a ritual takes, and the beliefs it expresses concerning the transcendent, are effective because they are also making statements about (symbolize) and mirror society.

In practice most scholars identified as "symbolists" are interested in both the expressive and explanatory value of ritual. In Clifford Geertz's classic study of a Balinese cockfight, for example, the symbolic equivalence of the fighting cock with both the social and sexual status of its male owner is established ("cock" works in Balinese much as in English, with equivalent punning and *double entendre*). The cockfight is "about" social hierarchy, economic exchange, group solidarity, and rivalry. It is also, however, a means by which the Balinese male explains himself to himself. In Geertz's words, "In the cockfight, then, the Balinese forms and discovers his temperament and his society's temper at the same time. Or, more exactly, he forms and discovers a particular facet of them" (Geertz, 1993, p. 451).

Another so-called "symbolist," Maurice Bloch, looks at circumcision rituals in Madagascar (1986). Bloch traces the historical, social, and symbolic aspects of Merina ritual, but also its ability to address basic questions about what it means to be human. Because a ritual is not fully a statement and not fully an action (Bloch, 1986, p. 195), it allows its message to be simultan-eously communicated and disguised. As ritual action is not open to normal discursive processes of argumentation and contradiction it is able to convey a paradoxical message. For Bloch the key message (at least in initiatory rituals) is that death is better than life. Rituals attempt to overcome mortality by entering and absorbing or being absorbed by the transcendent.

> The reason the ritual does its ideological job is that it carries at its core a simple and general message, which can be recovered and used for almost any type of

domination. It is that this life is of little value, that it must be rejected, as far as is possible, and exchanged for the still transcendence where time has been vanquished by order and where therefore the relevance of birth, death and action has disappeared. It is only by this argument that power and violence can be made to appear necessary and desirable, and this applies to any power and violence that become indissolubly linked. (Bloch, 1986, p. 195)

Bloch bases his understanding of ritual on a universal biological process. Rituals play on the themes of vitality and mortality. They link time and transcendence. These processes are evident in rites of passage, which can be seen as the archetypal ritual process, encompassing in their simple threefold structure a pattern underlying all rituals. Bloch (like Durkheim) is therefore dealing with both local symbolic interpretations and fundamental explanatory facets of ritual.

Ritual as performance

We have noted that a ritual is in some sense a performance or cultural drama, but in what sense, and does this mean that it is in effect theater? One obvious difference between ritual and theater is that a ritual performance does not just repeat a received script, but is "a mode of action taken by real and familiar people to affect the lives of other real and familiar people. Participants in ritual may be 'acting,' but they are not necessarily 'just pretending.' They are 'enacting,' which contradicts neither the notion of belief nor the practice of theatrical acting" (Alexander, 1997, p. 154). Sir James Frazer and other nineteenth-century scholars of the "Cambridge School" believed that Greek tragedy (and the Western theater descended from it) had its origins in ritual. This view has been discredited by a total lack of empirical evidence, but this does not mean that ritual, theater, and other expressive genres, such as games, sport, dance, and music, do not have much in common. Performance theorist Richard Schechner (drawing heavily on the work of Victor Turner) has attempted to look at the links between these various types of performance, noting that play, games, sports, theater, and ritual all share several basic qualities. They involve a special ordering of time, a special, nonproductive value attached to objects, and often a special place set aside in which to perform (Schechner, 1994, pp. 6–16).

Whether a performance is to be classified as ritual or as theater depends (according to Schechner) on its context and function. At opposite ends of a continuum we have "efficacy" (the ability to effect transformations) and "entertainment." If the purpose of a performance is to be efficacious then the performance is a ritual. If its purpose is to entertain, then it is theater,

EFFICACY	⟵——⟶	ENTERTAINMENT
Ritual		Theater
results		fun
link to absent other		only for those here
symbolic time		emphasis now
performer possessed, in trance		performer knows what he or she is doing
audience participates		audience watches
audience believes		audience appreciates
criticism discouraged		criticism flourishes
collective creativity		individual creativity

Figure 6.1   Efficacy and entertainment as associated with other facets of performance.
Source: after Schechner (1994, p. 120).

although no performance is purely one or the other. Both efficacy and entertainment are associated with other facets of performance, which Schechner (1994, p. 120) sets out as in figure 6.1.

The boundaries between ritual and theater are not fixed and static. Schechner takes examples of ritual dances from Highland Papua New Guinea in order to trace the movement of performance along the continuum from efficacious ritual to theatrical entertainment. At Kurumugl in the Eastern Highlands this process can be seen in the ritual dancing, pig killing, and meat exchanges between villages. Formerly, the dancers were warriors who were transformed into allies by means of the performance. While the economic and social functions of the ritual have been preserved, the outlawing of intertribal warfare has moved the performance further toward the entertainment end of the spectrum. For the present, however, it remains efficacious in maintaining social relationships by alternating obligations between groups. The visiting dancers incur a debt of meat to the hosts that must be repaid at some future date when they have accumulated enough pigs to hold a dance in turn.

> As in all rites of passage something had happened during the performance. The performance both symbolized and actualized the change in status. The meeting at Kurumugl – killing pigs, dancing, giving–taking the meat – was the process of changing the valence of the relationship between hosts and invaders. This process was the only one other than war recognized by all the parties assembled at Kurumugl. Dancing and giving–taking the meat more than symbolized the changed relationship between hosts and invaders, it was the change itself. (Schechner, 1994, p. 118)

This type of ritual, which effects change and in which failure can have disastrous consequences (in this instance, warfare), is semantically heavily loaded – it really matters what happens, and whether the ritual "works." At the opposite extreme we may find rituals that appear to be devoid of meaning. Frits Staal (1989), for instance, has argued that Vedic rituals in India have retained their structure but lost their meaning. They have become action for its own sake, and as such more akin to play than efficacious action. Ritual performance may continue to function as a means of boundary maintenance between castes without the symbols themselves being resonant with deeper meanings for the actors.[5] Both extremes are represented in rites of passage. Celebrating a birthday, for instance, does not in and of itself make a person older. It merely acknowledges the fact and gives occasion for a party. A circumcision ritual or giving birth may, however, effect a change of status, turning a child into an adult. In both instances the body is accorded a symbolic significance, linking physical and social transformation with a particular event.

Rites of Passage

> **Rites of passage** (*rites de passage*) mark the transition from one stage of life, season, or event to another. Everyone participates in rites of passage, and all societies mark them in various ways.

The term "rite of passage" is often used to refer to "life cycle" or "life crisis" rituals, concerned with a change of status in the lives of individuals and groups. Rituals surrounding birth, initiation, marriage, and death would be typical examples of these life crisis rituals. Arnold van Gennep, however, thought of rites of passage in much broader terms, as a universal structuring device in human societies. He included seasonal festivals, territorial rituals, sacrifice, pilgrimage, and indeed any behavior, religious or secular, that displayed the same basic threefold pattern of separation, transition, and incorporation.

> **Arnold van Gennep** (1873–1957) has been described as "an outstanding scholar but unsuccessful academic" (Barfield, 1997, p. 221). He was born in Germany, and briefly held a chair in ethnography at Neuchâtel in Switzerland, but spent most of his life as an independent scholar in France, where he became known as the father of French folklore studies. As a prominent critic of Durkheim (particularly his focus on the social to the exclusion of the individual) it was impossible for van Gennep to aspire to an established academic post. Although van Gennep accepted

Durkheim's primary division of the sacred and the profane, he eschewed his distinction between magic and religion, regarding magic as the practical and religion as the theoretical aspect of a single magico-religious complex. His interests were broad, and his ideas often ahead of his time. Van Gennep's work on totemism and taboo, for instance, anticipated that of Lévi-Strauss, in viewing totemism as a means of classification rather than an early form of religion. He is best known in the English-speaking world for his 1909 study *The Rites of Passage* (first translated into English in 1960). Van Gennep looked at a wide range of customs not in order to amass data, but to see if he could discern their underlying structure. The basic threefold pattern of a rite of passage proposed by van Gennep (separation, transition, and incorporation) has been widely taken up and elaborated within many disciplines, including anthropology and religious studies.

The threefold structure of a rite of passage

Van Gennep noted that life does not proceed at a uniform rate, and that human experience is composed of stages and life crises, such as birth, puberty, marriage, childbirth, and death. There are periods when not much seems to happen, and other times when our lives seem to undergo a dramatic change, after which nothing is quite the same as before. The birth of a child or death of a parent, for instance, can bring about an irrevocable change in circumstances. Calendrical festivals mark seasonal changes, from the winter solstice and Christmas, through the spring equinox, Easter, midsummer, and so on. Agricultural cycles often form the basis of religious calendars and holidays (holy days), but the two do not necessarily coincide. Events such as journeys, or changes in status, are often marked by ritual, whether of national significance (like a royal coronation) or individual (like an eighteenth or twenty-first birthday party). As van Gennep noted:

> Transitions from group to group and from one social situation to the next are looked on as implicit in the very fact of existence, so that a man's life comes to be made up of a succession of stages with similar ends and beginnings: birth, social puberty, marriage, fatherhood, advancement to a higher class, occupational specialization, and death. For every one of these events there are ceremonies whose essential purpose is to enable the individual to pass from one defined position to another which is equally well defined. (van Gennep, 1960, p. 3)

The three stages of a rite of passage are given a variety of terms, all of which are intended to suggest the movement from one state to another. Van Gennep used two parallel sets of terms:

separation → transition → incorporation or reaggregation
preliminal → liminal → postliminal

Liminal: Latin *limen*, meaning "threshold."

Each stage has its own characteristic type of ritual. The first stage is concerned with separation from the previous state or situation and is marked by rituals that symbolize cutting or separating in some way. A novice monk or new recruit to the army, for instance, might have his hair cut short or his head shaved. A girl experiencing her first menses may be secluded in a special hut away from the rest of the community. A Muslim will ritually wash away all pollution, marking a break with ordinary space and time, before entering a mosque for communal prayer. The second stage is that of transition or marginality. The individual is neither one thing nor another, but "betwixt and between." Rituals characteristically mark this sense of ambiguity and confusion or disequilibrium. Normal rules of behavior may be suspended or exaggerated. Inmates or initiates may be required to wear a uniform, stripped of clothing, painted, or in some other way marked out as different, special. Certain rules on speech and movement may be imposed. Insignia or symbols are frequently used didactically to reinforce any verbal teachings. The third and final stage is that of incorporation or reaggregation, when the individual, in a life cycle ritual for instance, is reintegrated into society, but in a transformed state. Van Gennep also used the term "liminal" to highlight the performative, dynamic element of a rite of passage. The crossing of a threshold, real or symbolic, temporal or physical, is a key element in all rites of passage.

Not all three stages are equally well developed in every ceremonial pattern. The middle or liminal stage in particular can be elaborated or extended almost indefinitely. It is also possible to focus on the boundaries between stages and see the threefold pattern repeated at every stage. Van Gennep gives the example of betrothal, which forms a liminal period between adolescence and marriage. An act of betrothal will itself exhibit rites of separation, transition, and incorporation. In the West a couple may, for instance, begin the process of separating themselves from parental influences and hold a party for friends and family in which they are the hosts. Special clothes may be worn and gifts given to the couple. The woman may wear an engagement ring (a common symbol of being bound to someone). They are reincorporated into society with a new status – publicly recognized as an "engaged couple."

If one looks at marriage, these three stages are again visible. We could represent this diagrammatically as in figure 6.2. A "traditional" Western

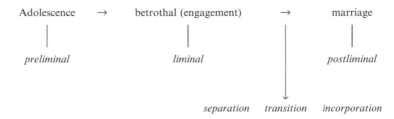

Figure 6.2 Elements of a traditional Western marriage.

marriage might include the elements shown in figure 6.3. The actual detail can and does vary enormously. What van Gennep sought to prove is that in whatever rite of passage one might wish to consider this same basic threefold structure is discernible.

Each rite of passage has its own specific aspects that are not centrally concerned with passage and transition. A marriage ceremony, for instance, takes fertility as its main theme. In a Western Christian wedding the words of the minister or priest usually allude to children as a prime reason for marriage.[6] The custom of throwing rice or rice paper over the bride and groom as they leave the church has its origins in fertility rituals. The wedding cake in white, representing the body of the bride in her matching white dress, is cut by the bride and groom as a symbolic slicing of her virginity, while the top tier of the cake may be kept for the christening of the as yet unborn child, symbolically present at the wedding feast.[7] At a funeral separation is symbolically marked and rituals are likely to be directed toward helping the deceased to make a safe and complete transition to the next world.[8] The

Figure 6.3 Elements of a traditional Western marriage.

focus may be on preventing the dead from haunting the living. Someone who has suffered a "bad death" (such as accident, suicide, or in childbirth) among the Bangwa of Southwest Cameroon will be buried on the far side of a stream or river to prevent his or her restless spirit from crossing back to the old compound in order to harm the living. Clothes or possessions may be burnt or discarded. Gypsies in Britain, for instance, will burn the trailer and possessions of someone who has died. Rites of passage surrounding childbirth are likely to contain rituals that stress protection. Special words and actions are performed to guard and strengthen the child. Gifts may be given to encourage it to stay and to make it welcome. The child may be given a protective amulet or cord. These specific aims will differ according to the purpose of the ritual and run alongside the threefold structure of a rite of passage.

In the second chapter of *The Rites of Passage* van Gennep pays particular attention to territorial passages and notes the importance of the threshold (*limen*) as the place which mediates between one physical space and another and between one social state and another. Whether it is carrying the bride across the threshold of the marital home, making the sign of the cross with water from the stoop at a church entrance, or removing one's shoes on entering a mosque, the crossing of the threshold is duly acknowledged. Van Gennep's interest in crossing from one stage or place to another can be seen in his description of the status of the stranger. Society is likened to a house divided into rooms and corridors. The inside constitutes, for its members, the realm of ordinary, everyday existence that is secular or profane. What lies outside is the realm of the unfamiliar and sacred. Strangers come from the outside, unknown (sacred), to the inside (profane) realm, and whether hostile or friendly they must be domesticated and contained. This is often achieved through offering hospitality, which in many societies is a highly formulized ritual act. The stranger is anomalous, neither insider nor outsider, and has the potential to bless or to threaten due to his or her ambiguous status.

Rites of incorporation or reaggregation in the third stage are often a mirror image of the first stage. Clothing removed during the initial rite of separation will be replaced, the believer who makes the sign of the cross with holy water on entering a church will do the same on leaving. The worshiper or initiate goes back into the world, but changed. One is not exactly the same as the person who embarked on the rite of passage. Rites of passage are processual dramas, not merely circular events. They mark the passing of time, as well as continuity with past traditions and generations.

Van Gennep formulates the general maxim that it is the first time that counts. Rites are more elaborated the first time a stranger enters a house or village. The birth of a first child (especially a son) is often marked by more elaborate rituals than the birth of subsequent children. A girl's first menses may be marked by ritual, and a first marriage tends to be a grander affair than subsequent weddings.

As a summary of his work on rites of passage van Gennep came to three general conclusions:

1 Beneath the multiplicity of forms a characteristic threefold pattern emerges. This recurs in all rites of passage and within different stages of a rite of passage.
2 The middle or transitional (liminal) stage can acquire a certain autonomy within a ceremonial whole.
3 The passage from one social position to another is identified with a territorial passage, such as the entrance to a village or house.

These points are summed up in the following statement:

For groups, as well as for individuals, life itself means to separate and to be reunited, to change form and condition, to die and be reborn. It is to act and to cease, to wait and to rest, and then to begin acting again, but in a different way. And there are always new thresholds to cross: the thresholds of summer and winter, of a season or a year, of a month or a night; the thresholds of birth, adolescence, maturity, and old age; the thresholds of death and that of the afterlife – for those who believe in it. . . . Our interest lies not in the particular rites but in their essential significance and their relative positions within ceremonial wholes – that is, their order. . . . The underlying arrangement is always the same. Beneath a multiplicity of forms, either consciously expressed or merely implied, a typical pattern always recurs: *the pattern of the rites of passage.* (van Gennep, 1977, pp. 189–91)

Victor Turner

Van Gennep had noted that the middle stage of a rite of passage could acquire a certain autonomy, an idea that proved especially fruitful in the work of Victor Turner.

Victor Turner (1920–83), Scottish born and English trained (under Max Gluckman in Manchester), spent most of his professional life teaching in the United States (at Cornell, Chicago, and Virginia). Victor Turner and his wife Edith carried out fieldwork among the *Ndembu* of Northern Rhodesia (Zambia) in the early 1950s, and in 1957 Victor Turner published his first major work on the Ndembu, *Schism and Continuity in an African Society.* Although trained in the

British structural-functionalist tradition, Turner's experience with the Ndembu led him to focus on religion, ritual, and symbols, key elements of social cohesion in an unstable society, fractured by matrilineal descent and virilocal residence (descent was traced through women and residence through men). The power struggles between various family and village heads led Turner to develop an emphasis on social drama rather than social institutions. This interest in performance and in performative aspects of ritual remained a feature of Turner's subsequent writings. Following their conversion to Roman Catholicism, Victor and Edith Turner researched and published an influential work on Christian pilgrimage, *Image and Pilgrimage in Christian Culture* (1978), that also used van Gennep's model of the rite of passage. Pilgrimage is described as "liminoid" or "quasiliminal," possessing parallels to the liminality of "tribal" rites of passage.

Turner developed his analysis of the middle stage of a rite of passage, most particularly in *The Ritual Process*, first published in 1969. Following her husband's death, Edith Turner (1921–) went back to Zambia and took part in a healing "tooth ritual," *Ihamba*, described in Victor Turner's *The Drums of Affliction* (1968). Her account of the *Ihamba*, described in *Experiencing Ritual* (1992), provides an interesting commentary on changing fashions in the anthropology of religion. The analysis pays much greater attention to insider (emic) accounts of the ritual, while Edith Turner herself is less concerned with maintaining a "scientific objectivity" than experiencing at first hand the spiritual healing power described by the Ndembu.

Victor Turner coined the term *communitas* (the Latin for "community") to describe the unstructured, egalitarian, human relatedness which he saw as typical of the middle, liminal, stage of a rite of passage. The use of the Latin term was intended to distinguish the ritual bonding of the rite of passage from the geographical, spatial connotations of a physical community. Rites of passage are seen as a movement from *structure* to *anti-structure* and back once more to structure. *Liminality* is anti-structural, "betwixt-and-between." This stage of a rite of passage may be fleeting or extended indefinitely, as in the case of pilgrims or religious communities who seek to live permanently outside the normal structures of society.

Key Turnerian terms

Liminality: the middle stage of a rite of passage; anti-structural, ambiguous, creative.

Communitas: spontaneous, immediate, and concrete relatedness typical of bonds formed between people in the middle, liminal stage of a rite of passage.

Normative communitas: the egalitarian model of relatedness typical of the liminal stage of a rite of passage, normally requiring time and a degree of institutional support to enable communitas to flourish, e.g. initiation rituals.

Spontaneous (or existential) communitas: a quality of relatedness that is most likely to arise in anti-structural situations, in the "interstices of the social structure." Unplanned and spontaneous, as might occur between strangers thrown together in a crisis or at an event that generates high emotions.

Ideological communitas: specifically formulated rules and regulations governing how people should live in harmony; developed in literate and complex societies. The outward form of the internal existential communitas, as in monastic communities.

Apocalyptic communitas: the apocalyptic mythology, theology, or ideology of "communitas-like" movements (anticipating future disaster or a catastrophic end to the world).

Liminoid/quasi-liminal: analogue of liminality characteristic of "post-industrial revolution" cultures (e.g. theater, ballet, film, music, art, poetry, and pilgrimage), which stand outside the mainstream and which possess transformative potential.

State: relatively fixed or stable condition, including legal status, profession, office, calling, rank, or degree.

Structure: systems of rank, office, organization, and hierarchy used to order society.

Anti-structure: egalitarian, unstructured, undifferentiated social relations.

Temenos: sacralized enclosure (often used for neophytes).

Sacra/sacerrima: the "most sacred things" usually exhibited in the most intense liminal moments of a rite of passage. They may be interpreted by cosmogonic myths.

Neophyte/initiand: person undergoing initiation. Compare *passenger* or *liminar* – the ritual subject.

Liminality

Turner's theoretical understanding is grounded in his knowledge of Ndembu ritual. From a description of the installation of a senior Ndembu chief, Kanongesha, for example, Turner (1991, pp. 102–6) draws out the following attributes that apply to liminality more generally. First of all, both the chief and his wife are dressed alike and referred to by the same term. Similar sexlessness and anonymity achieved by using the same clothing and terms for male and female initiands can also be seen in many Christian baptismal rites and in the Bwiti Cult of Gabon (Fernandez, 1982). The chief, like many other neophytes, is expected to remain silent and to adopt a servile posture, representing submission "to an authority that is nothing less than that of the total community." The community in turn "is the repository of the whole gamut of the culture's values, norms, attitudes, sentiments, and relationships" (Turner, 1991, p. 103). A third aspect of liminality is the use of ordeals and humiliations that "represent partly a destruction of the previous state and partly a tempering of their essence in order to prepare them to cope with their new responsibilities and restrain them in advance from abusing their new privileges" (Turner, 1991, p. 103). The neophyte is reshaped or molded physically and psychologically so that society's values can be inscribed on his or her body and mind. The Ndembu chief is expected to abstain from sexual relations during the rituals. In societies in which kinship is a major structuring factor, sexual relations symbolize ordered society, whereas the "undifferentiated character of liminality is reflected by the discontinuance of sexual relations and the absence of marked sexual polarity" (Turner, 1991, p. 104). Particularly in the case of installation to high office, but also in other situations, the initiand may be chastened and reminded of his or her worthlessness. The chief remains "one of the people" and must be instructed to serve rather than to pursue his own ends. The initiand is enjoined not to overstep his or her office, while values of human kindness are emphasized, often backed by divine sanctions. "The powers that shape the neophytes in liminality for the incumbency of new status are felt, in rites all over the world, to be more than human powers, though they are invoked and channeled by the representatives of the community" (Turner, 1991, p. 106).

The main characteristics of liminality and liminal *personae* are summed up by Turner in the following passage:

> Liminal entities are assigned and arrayed by law, custom, convention, and ceremonial. As such, their ambiguous and indeterminate attributes are expressed by a rich variety of symbols in the many societies that ritualize social and cultural transitions. Thus, liminality is frequently likened to death, to being in the womb, to invisibility, to darkness, to bisexuality, to the wilderness, and to an eclipse of the sun or moon. (Turner, 1991, p. 95)

Communitas and social structure

Turner developed the notion of a dialectic between communitas and structure. A rite of passage normally involves a movement from structure to anti-structure and back into structure. Communitas emerges "where structure is not," and is therefore commonly, but not exclusively, associated with the liminal stage of a rite of passage. Communitas does not refer to a territorially based community, but to unstructured and egalitarian bonds between people.

Communitas has an aspect of potentiality, generating symbols and metaphors. Its products are art and religion rather than legal and political structures.

> Communitas breaks through in the interstices of structure, in liminality; at the edge of structure, in inferiority. It is almost everywhere held to be sacred or "holy," possibly because it transgresses or dissolves the norms that govern structured and institutionalized relationships and is accompanied by experiences of unprecedented potency. . . . Liminality, marginality and structural inferiority are conditions in which are frequently generated myths, symbols, rituals, philosophical systems, and works of art. These cultural forms provide men with a set of templates or models which are, at one level, periodical reclassifications of reality and man's relationship to society, nature, and culture. But they are more than classifications, since they incite men to action as well as to thought. Each of these productions has a multivocal character, having many meanings, and each is capable of moving people at many psychobiological levels simultaneously. (Turner, 1991, pp. 128–9)

Neither structure nor anti-structure can exist in the absence of the other. Structure has a cognitive quality and consists of a set of classifications that provide a model for thinking about and living in a social and physical environment. Communitas, on the other hand, has an existential quality, involving the whole person in relation to other whole human beings.[9] If either structure or anti-structure is overemphasized there is likely to be a corresponding reaction and a move in the opposite direction. Such swings can be seen in many historical and contemporary movements. Turner cited the example of medieval Franciscans. Saint Francis (1182–1226) was radically anti-structural, rejecting wealth, status, and all the normal comforts of life. He sought to live in a small egalitarian community of like-minded men, dedicated to mendicancy and poverty. Within his lifetime, however, the swing toward structured hierarchy had already begun. The Franciscan Order that he had founded split, and the ownership of property and use of money, rejected by Francis, crept in.

Turner's understanding of structure and communitas bears the imprint both of the hippie movement ("flower power") and radical student protests of the late 1960s and early 1970s, with their demands for anarchic, global, non-hierarchical modes of relating, and of the academic Marxism that was influential in some social science faculties at this time. The Weberian understanding of the "routinization of charisma" is also apparent in the following statement:

> There is a dialectic here, for the immediacy of communitas gives way to the mediacy of structure, while, in *rites de passage*, men are released from structure

into communitas. What is certain is that no society can function adequately without this dialectic. Exaggeration of structure may well lead to pathological manifestations of communitas outside or against "the law." Exaggeration of communitas, in certain religious or political movements of the leveling type, may be speedily followed by despotism, overbureaucratization, or other modes of structural rigidification. (Turner, 1991, p. 129)

One of the most striking manifestations of communitas is that displayed by millenarian religious movements, whether of Christian origin or among the so-called "cargo cults" of Melanesia (in which people abandoned their homes and destroyed their crops and property in preparation for the arrival of European goods or "cargo").[10] In his influential study of medieval millennial thinking, Norman Cohn had referred to the people attracted to apocalyptic theologies, which emphasized the imminence of Christ's second coming, as the uprooted, poor, and desperate masses who had no place in mainstream society. They were the landless peasants and unemployed urbanites living on the margins of society.[11] Turner draws a series of parallels between the properties of liminality in the rituals of small-scale societies and these millenarian movements. Homogeneity, equality, and anonymity are emphasized, with an absence of property, or communal rather than individual ownership. Property rights stand for structural distinctions, and it is not uncommon for the followers of a millennial prophet to be instructed to destroy goods so as to get nearer to the required state of communion. (One could point to the early Christian community with their common property, waiting for the imminent destruction of the present order and the return of Jesus Christ to save the faithful.)

Members of millenarian movements are often reduced to the same status level – with the likely exception of their prophet or leader. They often wear the same unisex clothes and emphasize either sexual continence or sexual promiscuity, both of which have the effect of destroying ties of kinship (structure) by liquidating marriage and the family. There may be a disregard for personal appearance, accompanied by an ethic of unselfishness and total obedience to the leader and his or her sacred instruction. There is a maximization of religious, as opposed to secular, attitudes, with an emphasis on the transcendental nature of the community and its teaching. The sometimes violent or self-destructive logic of this form of extended communitas is developed by Maurice Bloch (discussed in the following section).

Women's initiation rituals

Bruce Lincoln regards van Gennep's and Turner's models of rites of passage as essentially masculine, with less salience for women, and therefore less universal than claimed. For Lincoln, ritual is "a coherent set of symbolic actions that has a real transformative effect on individuals and social groups" (Lincoln, 1991, p. 6). Most rites of passage, including male and female initiation rituals, "transform people, replacing old roles, statuses, and identities with new ones" (Lincoln, 1991, p. 6). According to Lincoln, however, women's initiation rituals do something more. As with other rites of renewal, they claim that "the cosmos itself is transformed along with the initiand" (Lincoln, 1991, p. 6).[12]

Five examples of women's initiation chosen by Lincoln in *Emerging from the Chrysalis* (1991) are arranged along a continuum displaying various degrees of coercion and control over women. When compared to male initiation, the emphasis on territorial passage is absent or much reduced. Women usually remain in or near their domestic dwelling throughout the period of the ritual. The women are usually initiated singly – so there is no opportunity for the bonding or communitas characteristic of the shared experience of male initiation. Whereas nudity is often a feature of male initiation – a leveling and humbling necessary before a new status can be achieved, women have no independent status to gain. The emphasis is more often on dressing and decoration than on stripping. There is usually little in the way of practical knowledge that initiands gain. What they learn is the attitude to adopt towards such tasks, rather than their actual content. Most girls have learnt from their mothers and other women how to procure and prepare food, look after children, and so on. As a married woman the initiand will continue to do these things, but must learn to do them willingly. Instead of separation, liminality, and incorporation, as the typical stages of a rite of passage for female initiands, Lincoln proposes an alternative structure:

enclosure → metamorphosis/magnification → emergence

In the original (1981) version of *Emerging from the Chrysalis*, Lincoln posed the question: who initiates women? If it is men, then initiation is something imposed on women from outside. He concludes, however, that it is society, or "the totality of the social order" (Lincoln, 1991, p. 93), that carries out the initiation, with men and women playing different roles.

> All the rites we have examined are open to men and women, and both sexes take active parts in all of them. It is society as a whole that acts, and thus the initiand experiences both the repressive force of men (who may cut her, rape her, or simply force her to run, work, or stay up all night) and the support of her fellow women (who may dress and adorn her, bring food to her, or keep vigil with her). (Lincoln, 1991, p. 93)

Among the Tukuna of the Northwest Amazon, for example, the men imper-
sonate demonic beings and seek to terrify and assault the initiand. The
women dress her and parade around her singing and tapping her with leaves.

> Later, most of the girl's hair is pulled out by a group of women seated around
> her, but the first and last locks are taken by her father's brother, who stands
> above her. The women are thus identified with the initiand: they sit as she sits,
> forming a group, and all of them have suffered what she now suffers. In contrast,
> the man is the instigator of the ordeal, and the only one who can put it to an
> end. He is set above the initiand, physically as well as hierarchically. What he
> does, he does as an individual rather than as part of a group, and never will he
> experience the pain he inflicts. (Lincoln, 1991, p. 93)

Lincoln describes the female initiand as the battleground on which antagonism between the sexes is enacted. Wider social tensions are, as Girard (see
below) suggests, focused on a scapegoat. In the case of conflicts regarding
female roles, the victim is the girl who is to be made into a woman. In his
original conclusion, however, Lincoln put a positive gloss on women's initiation rituals. Women learn how to accept socialized cultural roles, however
unfavorable for individuals they may be, and are better able to bear their lot
with good grace. The meaninglessness and numbing repetitiveness of so many
female tasks, which do after all engage with the continuation of life through
procreation and provisioning, are elevated to a cosmic plane.

> Such a sense of meaning is the greatest benefit that any ritual can bestow, and
> it is the ultimate function of all ritual to invest life with a deeper meaning than
> animal survival. A sense of meaning elevates life above boredom, mindlessness,
> and despair. It makes even the harshest existence worthwhile and bestows
> dignity on all of one's actions, however trivial they might otherwise seem.
> Whether the cosmos is renewed as a result, as is claimed within rites of women's
> initiation, is difficult for us to assess. But one can certainly say that a world in
> which individuals and societies find meaning in creative action is a very
> different world from one in which this has ceased to be the case. To this
> extent, rituals do live up to their claims, and the universe is made richer by
> their faithful performance. (Lincoln, 1991, p. 108)

In his afterword to the 1991 edition of *Emerging from the Chrysalis*, Lincoln
is more critical of the actual or implicit violence of women's initiation.
Feminist scholarship has highlighted the political dimensions of ritual, and
Lincoln describes his own thinking as having become more materialist and
less romantic. He is certainly more aware of the links between politics,
religion, and other aspects of social structure, stating that:

> I have come to view as immoral any discourse or practice that systematically operates to benefit the already privileged members of society at the expense of others, and I reserve the same judgement for any society that tolerates or encourages such discourses and practices. By these standards few, if any, rituals of women's initiation fare very well, and looking back, I fear that in some measure I was myself seduced by the elegant structures, well-wrought symbolism, and complex ideologies that are found within these rituals. (Lincoln, 1991, p. 112)

Women's initiation is about producing productive workers, docile faithful wives, nurturant mothers, and so on. Lincoln no longer regards society itself as a monolithic category, but as a series of competing interest groups. Critiquing his earlier conclusions, Lincoln concludes that:

> women's initiations, as practised by "society as a whole," have not always served women very well. More specifically, at those points where the collective interests of women *as women* diverge from those of "society as a whole," these rituals not only serve the latter interests, but make it very difficult for women to struggle against them. (Lincoln, 1991, p. 117)

If rituals are one way in which a society renews and reproduces itself, resisting and disrupting rituals can, suggests Lincoln, become a valid site of resistance. Alternatively, new rituals can be constructed that present an alternative pattern of gender relations. While these are projects with which Western gay, lesbian, and feminist interests engage, it should not be forgotten that for most women and disadvantaged groups opportunities for resistance may be limited and the costs high. Sudanese women, for example, often insist on their daughters' circumcision even when living in Western countries in which the practice is illegal. This may be a rational choice in view of the loss of status within the community from which an uncircumcised woman would suffer. Ellen Gruenbaum has noted that within the Sudan some women "have embraced systems of power based on social class privilege or on racial or ethnic discrimination, even though this requires accepting gender subordination" (Gruenbaum, 1998, p. 74), a subordination that may include severe "pharaonic" circumcision with all its attendant health problems. The alternative, forgoing male economic support or community membership, may be impossible for a woman if she is to survive.

Lincoln's conclusions (see below) are, however, pertinent, pointing as they do to the sociopolitical dimensions of ritual and the underlying violence rituals embody. This is not to say that his earlier responses are invalid – the production of meaning and endowment of the everyday with cosmic significance remains an important aspect of many people's experience.

I have tried to suggest three things. First, that rituals are involved not only in the construction of persons, but also in the construction of categories of persons, and in the construction of the hierarchic orders in which categories and persons alike are organized. Second, that such processes are not neutral, but have their victims, as well as their beneficiaries. And third, that those victims have means – creative and powerful – to react against the processes that victimise them. Among these are the disruption of existing rituals and the creation of novel rituals, to which one might add the critical study of ritual forms, with particular attention to their social contexts and consequences. (Lincoln, 1991, p. 119)

Ritual Violence

The linking of religion or ritual with violence may seem shocking to believers in a wholly loving and good God, in whose name the rituals are performed. For contemporary secularists, on the other hand, religious rituals are superstitions, and religions may be seen as responsible for most if not all the irrational, negative, and inhumane acts that people perpetrate on one another, on non-human creatures, and on the environment. Rather than adjudicate between these two extreme positions, this final section examines some of the evidence for the association of ritual with violence and the explanations for such a connection.

The Oedipal sacrifice

For Freud, religion is to society what neurosis is to the individual – an unresolved tension between the desire for pleasure and self-preservation on the one hand, and the demands of an ordered society on the other. It is this conflict, constantly re-enacted, that gives rise to civilization, although part of the tragedy of humanity is that civilization is based ultimately upon a delusion.

Sigmund Freud (1856–1939), the founder of psychoanalysis, qualified as a medical doctor in Vienna (Austria) in 1881. It was an interest in neurosis and its causes that led to Freud's exploration of the human mind, developing his key notions of the *unconscious* and *libido*. According to Freud, the motive force behind most of our actions lies not in conscious reasoning, but in the desires, fears, instinctual drives, and repressed, sublimated, or displaced thoughts and experiences that lie below the surface in the unconscious mind. One of the strongest of these drives is the libido, or psychosexual energy. The libido is an expression of an individual's life force and desire for pleasure and self-affirmation. Genital sexuality is one, powerful, form of this energy, but by no means its only expression.

Other key Freudian concepts include the following terms:

Id: the unconscious instincts driven by the "pleasure principle."

Ego: the conscious self that interacts with the external environment, representing the "reality principle."

Superego: an internal regulator or conscience – the internalization of parental values and expectations.

Fundamental to Freud's theories of human behavior and the origin of religion is his understanding of child sexuality and the *Oedipus complex*. In Greek myth Oedipus unwittingly fulfilled a prophecy that involved killing his father and marrying his mother, leading to the destruction of his native Thebes. Freud used this myth as a metaphor for a stage both in child development and in human social evolution. At about the age of four a boy becomes aware of his own sexuality. He perceives his father as a rival for his mother's love and wishes to kill him. He also fears castration by the father (thus becoming like the mother, who lacks a penis). The resolution of this conflict involves separation from the mother and identification with the father.

Influenced by Frazer (and Darwin), Freud believed that human society was originally patriarchal, with a powerful male jealously guarding his female(s) from other males. At a certain point the excluded younger males (brothers) joined together and killed their father so as to gain access to the women. The consequences of this action are worked out in a series of essays in his book *Totem and Taboo* (first published in 1913), in which Freud sees this original Oedipal action as the origin of the incest taboo (the men desired to have sex with their sisters and mothers but were prevented from doing so by guilt and fear of retribution from the murdered father), totemism (the father remained symbolically present in the clan totem animal or object), exogamy (because of the incest taboo totemic clans looked for women outside their own group), sacrifice (by means of which men sought to assuage their guilt for the original murder), religion (the totem/father is accorded sacred status, thus regaining his authority), and ultimately civilization itself (social life depends upon these self-imposed rules, elevated to the status of divine commands, if human beings are not to destroy one another).

Both religion and higher forms of culture (such as art) are therefore the result of displaced instinctual energies, which may find positive expression in the creative impulse, but which can also be restrictive and destructive. Although many Freudians have interpreted the notion of the primal Oedipal murder allegorically, Freud himself seems to have believed in an actual historical event. He sought to explain not just how individuals and societies think and act – the contours of the mind – but how and why they arrived at that point.

Freud's ideas have been extensively criticized. The emphasis on male sexuality, for instance, has been rejected or refashioned by feminist scholars. Anthropologists have pointed out that there is no evidence for the early forms of society imagined by Frazer and Freud (among others). Australian Aboriginal clans, with their totemic exogamous systems, were taken as exemplars of Freudian theory, but the case for the presupposed evolutionary sequences has never been demonstrated. Nevertheless, Freudian terminology has become part of the Western mental landscape, and whether or not anthropologists and others explicitly subscribe to Freud's ideas, their influence is ubiquitous, particularly where scholars are looking for universal explanations for human behavior or searching for the origin of religion and ritual.[13]

Violence and the sacred

One of the best known proponents of the view that violence is always implicit in and, indeed, lies at the heart of ritual is the French scholar René Girard, who puts forward an essentially functionalist, psychological argument. In his book *Violence and the Sacred* (1992), Girard argues that "In many rituals the sacrificial act assumes two opposing aspects, appearing at times as a sacred obligation to be neglected at grave peril, at other times as a sort of criminal activity entailing perils of equal gravity" (Girard, 1992, p. 1). Violence is universal, with easily recognizable physiological signs. When the object of violence is out of reach it is deflected onto a surrogate victim, something or someone closer to hand. Girard regards ritual sacrifice as "society seeking to deflect upon a relatively indifferent victim, a 'sacrifice-able' victim, the violence that would otherwise be vented on its own members, the people it most desires to protect" (Girard, 1992, p. 4). Sacrificial substitution entails a degree of obfuscation.

> Its vitality as an institution depends on its ability to conceal the displacement upon which the rite is based. It must never lose sight entirely, however, of the original object, or cease to be aware of the act of transference from that object to the surrogate victim; without that awareness no substitution can take place and the sacrifice loses all efficacy. (Girard, 1992, p. 5)

Sacrifice is therefore the community offering up a substitute for itself – protecting itself from its own violence. The purpose of the sacrifice is to restore harmony, and reinforce social bonds within the community. For Girard, this insight formed the basis of all cultural behavior.

> If once we take this fundamental approach to sacrifice, choosing the road that violence opens before us, we can see that there is no aspect of human existence foreign to the subject, not even material prosperity. When men no longer live in harmony with one another the sun still shines and the rain falls, to be sure, but the fields are less well tended, the harvests less abundant. (Girard, 1992, p. 8)

Following van Gennep, Girard sees religion – notions of deities, gods, or spirits – as the sacred, external to the mundanity of human society. Human violence is projected onto this sacred realm "out there," which can be neither fully unleashed nor ignored. To come too near the sacred (to the violence inherent in human society) is to risk getting burned. Too great a separation generates a backlash – the deflected violence demands acknowledgment and accommodation.

> The outcome of this relationship [with the sacred] is as follows: although men cannot live in the midst of violence, neither can they survive very long by ignoring its existence or by deluding themselves into the belief that violence, despite the ritual prohibitions attendant on it, can somehow be put to work as the mere tool or servant of mankind. The complex and delicate nature of the community's dealings with the sacred, the ceaseless effort to arrive at the ordered and uninterrupted accord essential to the well-being of the community, can only be expressed . . . in terms of optimum *distance*. If the community comes too near the sacred it risks being devoured by it; if, on the other hand, the community drifts too far away, out of the range of the sacred's therapeutic threats and warnings, the effects of its fecund presence are lost. (Girard, 1992, p. 268)

Girard is a literary scholar rather than an anthropologist. Although he draws widely on ethnographic, as well as classical, material to support his thesis, it would be fair to say that the examples are selected to illustrate the theory, rather than the theory arising from the ethnographic data. Anthropologists and other scholars looking at the links between sex and violence have also, however, noted the role of displacement. The perpetrator of violence is frustrated by his (or her) lack of ability to control others, particularly their sexual behavior, which jeopardizes a carefully constructed identity dependent on a self-image of power and authority. "Thus it is the perpetrator of violence who is threatened and experiences thwarting" (Moore, 1994, p. 153). If masculinity is predicated upon control and power, it is more vulnerable than femininity. In societies in which a dominant discourse of masculinity includes the superiority of men over women, children, and "nature" (as in most if not all human cultures), the reassertion of masculine values is achieved by the deflection of violence onto these weaker victims to hand.[14]

Rebounding violence

Maurice Bloch has also elaborated van Gennep's ideas on rites of passage. For Bloch a key feature of ritual is what he calls "*rebounding violence*" or "conquest." Bloch focuses on the notion of *vitality* and its transformation. In a rite of passage (indeed, in almost any ritual situation), the individual or group puts aside its ordinary vitality (energy, life force, power) in order to take on a superior, transcendental vitality – typically made available in the middle stage of a rite of passage. This is a "conquered vitality obtained from outside beings, usually animals, sometime plants, other peoples or women" (Bloch, 1992, p. 5). The final stage of a rite of passage involves a return to the mundane ("structure") but empowered by the divine. This return may lead to actual violence "because the recovered vitality is mastered by the transcendental" (Bloch, 1992, p. 5). Bloch (1986) gives examples of "rebounding violence" that occur in the circumcision rituals of the Merina of Madagascar, which can lead to the violent wounding of children, symbolic violence against women, and physical aggression directed toward those perceived as enemies. Like Lincoln, Bloch argues that rituals can serve to maintain the status hierarchies of a society, and, in line with Girard, proposes that human violence is displaced onto a transcendental power figure. A ritual will "feel right" because it reinforces a cultural message already familiar to participants, but also because it contains two key propositions: "(1) Creativity is not the product of human action but is due to a transcendental force that is mediated by authority, and (2) this fact legitimates, even demands, the violent conquest of inferiors by superiors who are closer to the transcendental ancestors" (Bloch, 1986, p. 189). If the elders, priests or power-holders in a society can identify themselves as key mediators of these transcendental forces they are able to justify their dominance.

For Bloch, the universal structure of a rite of passage is linked to the nature of human beings as biological and social animals. He argues that rituals involve a reversal of the normal processes of life, the progression from birth to maturation and eventually death. Rituals postulate the existence of a transcendental world or source of metaphysical power that lies beyond material existence and therefore negates death. Human beings can "borrow" or be conquered or consumed by some of this transcendental power via the ritual process, transforming themselves in the process.

> These irreducible structures of religious phenomena are ritual representations of the existence of human beings in time. In fact this ritual representation is simple transformation of the material processes of life in plants and animals as well as humans. The transformation takes place in an idiom which has two

distinguishing features: first, it is accomplished through a classic three-stage dialectical process, and secondly it involves a marked element of violence . . . or of conquest. (Bloch, 1992, p. 4)

Instead of human vitality being seen as the goal of life, ritual looks "beyond" or outside ordinary existence. Weakening and death lead to successful existence, as "by leaving this life, it is possible to see oneself and others as part of something permanent, therefore life-transcending" (Bloch, 1992, p. 4).

Bloch argues, interestingly, that in the case of millenarian movements the participants fail to enter the third stage of rite of passage, that of re-entering society imbued with the divine. Their rejection of the world is such that they undergo the classic rituals of separation from the world of structure, submitting themselves to the violence of that renunciation and submission to the divine. Having become "more like gods," there is, however, a refusal to take up their place in society once more, and such movements may become nihilistic and, as with the Heaven's Gate members, participants may eventually commit suicide in a definitive rejection of reproduction and ordinary vitality.

Arnold van Gennep and Victor Turner maintain a predominantly positive view of a rite of passage. For Turner especially, liminality and communitas convey the notion of potentiality, transformation, and solidarity. This is a rather different perspective from that of Maurice Bloch (perhaps a reflection of the differences between the optimistic counterculture of the 1960s and 1970s and a more cynical view of globalized violence of the 1980s and 1990s). Lincoln (1991) demonstrates this changing perspective in the different editions of *Emerging from the Chrysalis*. Turner and Bloch are interested in using history to help understand the mechanisms of symbolic structures, and are aware of the political implications of ritual. According to Bloch there are at least three "alternative avenues of legitimate practice" available through the symbolism of rebounding violence:

(1) the assertion of reproduction; (2) the legitimation of expansionism, which itself takes one of two forms: (a) it may be internally directed, in which case it legitimates social hierarchy or (b) it may be externally directed and become an encouragement to aggression against neighbours; (3) the abandonment of earthly existence. (Bloch, 1992, p. 98)

Bloch is interested in the continuity of rituals over time, and in the ways in which they incorporate and normalize violence, rather than the pedagogical dynamics of ritual. The mechanisms by which rites of passage, and in particular male initiation rituals, transform the initiands is a theme taken up by Harvey Whitehouse.[15]

Rites of terror

The violence of many male initiation rituals in Papua New Guinea has been well documented. The violence is not merely gratuitous, but can serve a psychological and social purpose. Harvey Whitehouse has utilized the concept of "flashbulb memories" to explain the way in which information can become imprinted on an individual's long-term memory if it was communicated while in a state of profound emotional shock, or accompanied by a peculiar emotional intensity. While fear may block access to certain parts of the brain (it is difficult to learn Latin verbs or mathematical equations while numbed with terror), where the information conveyed is of immediate interest and associated with intense relationships, the feelings, emotions, and content of the initiatory experience may be retained throughout life.

Whitehouse (1996) uses the example of Baktaman initiation in Papua New Guinea, in which everyday understandings are turned on their head. Baktaman men see themselves as involved in a continuous war with wild pigs, but in the initiatory rituals a wild pig mandible is placed among the *sacra* (the sacred objects) of the men's house.

> When a Baktaman novice first realizes that he is (in some sense) being made into a virile, aggressive pig – a warrior and a father – he is not only struck by the absurdity of his previous assumptions about pigs, but he associates this revelation with the terrifying and agonizing experience of being beaten with stones, whipped with nettles and dehydrated almost to the point of death. It is this combination of cognitive and emotional crises that produces the distinctive mnemonic effect. (Whitehouse, 1996, p. 710)

While this is hardly an emic explanation (Whitehouse is hypothesizing that the initiates are struck by the absurdity of their previous knowledge concerning wild pigs), it does go some way to accounting for the vividness of the initiatory experience, and the importance of ritually acquired embodied knowledge over simple verbal instruction. Human groups commonly devise violent rituals for their members as a means of cementing group loyalty, implanting esoteric knowledge, and initiating transformatory experiences. Whether we are talking about street gangs in Los Angeles, a Native American vision quest, a New Guinea initiation, or the fasting and asceticism associated with the Roman Catholic pilgrimage to Lough Derg in Ireland,[16] initiates will be familiar with the ordeals and emotional intensity involved in the rite of passage.

Conclusion

This chapter follows Arnold van Gennep in regarding the threefold structure of a rite of passage as a basic patterning of all ritual behavior. Rituals attempt to enact and deal with the most central and basic dilemmas of human existence – continuity and stability, growth and fertility, mortality and immortality or transcendence. It is the potential of rituals to transform people and situations that lends them their power. A ritual may create a docile wife or a fierce warrior, a loving servant or an imperious tyrant. The ambiguity of ritual symbols and the invocation of supernatural power magnifies and disguises human needs and emotions. Because rituals are performed, sometimes in terrifying circumstances, the messages they carry act at a psychobiological level that includes but exceeds the rational mind. Symbols and sacred objects are manipulated within ritual to enhance performance and to communicate ideological messages concerning the nature of the individual, society, and cosmos. Far from being an epiphenomenon of religious behavior, rituals are fundamental to human culture. They can be used to control, to subvert, to stabilize, to enhance, and to terrorize individuals and groups. The study of ritual can indeed provide a key to an understanding and interpretation of culture.

Notes

1   See Staal's (1989) discussion of Vedic rituals as empty of meaning (discussed at the end of this section).
2   For a discussion of ritual types and modes see Alexander (1997). Pascal Boyer (1994, chapter 7) outlines a cognitive approach to ritual, based on "ritualised religious episodes" that are central in transmitting and affirming religious beliefs.
3   Another way of approaching the history of ritual studies would be through the so-called "myth and ritual school." Some scholars have seen myth as prior to ritual, which is the acting out of the myth, while others claim that rituals create "reality" and are therefore concurrent with or antecedent to myth. For a discussion of the relationship between myth and ritual see Patton and Doniger (1996) and Segal (1998).
4   Eliade believed that "archaic" and contemporary simple societies share the same mental structures, and although he drew on anthropological material for his examples, these are as decontextualized as those in Frazer's *Golden Bough*.
5   Durkheim (1976, pp. 34–5) made a similar observation, noting that a rather mechanistic view of ritual was by no means confined to Vedic religion, and that it is not uncommon to find "practices which act by themselves, by a virtue which

is their own, without the intervention of any god between the individual who practices the rite and the end sought after."

6   In the Church of England liturgy for the "Solemnization of Matrimony," the minister gives as the first reason for marriage "the procreation of children, to be brought up in the fear and nurture of the Lord, and to the praise of his holy Name" (*The Book of Common Prayer*, p. 302).

7   See Charsley (1992).

8   *The Tibetan Book of the Dead*, a text instructing the soul of the deceased in their passage from one existence to the next, is one of the most developed examples of a transition liturgy.

9   Turner frequently refers to the Christian theologian Martin Buber (1958) and his description of an "I–Thou" relationship between the believer and God.

10   These "cargo cults" provide examples of syncretic millenarian thinking that combines Christian and traditional themes. See, for instance, Worsley (1970), Burridge (1971), Lawrence (1971), Wilson (1975), Trompf (1991), and Swain and Trompf (1995).

11   Cohn (1978). See also Cohn (1995). In *The Coming Deliverer: Millennial Themes in World Religions* (Bowie, 1997) I argue that millenarian thinking is actually part of orthodox teaching in all soteriological religions (which look for a coming savior). Whether this teaching is activated or not will depend largely on the degree of marginality experienced by particular groups, and the level of investment they have in mainstream society.

12   See Strathern and Stewart (1998, p. 249), who describe a correspondence between the body and cosmos in rituals from the Mount Hagen area of Papua New Guinea.

13   For an anthropological assessment of Freud's thesis see Fox (1967).

14   This argument is put forward and illustrated by most of the contributors to Harvey and Gow (1994).

15   For an excellent summary and critique of Bloch's description of the Orokaiva initiation ritual (described in chapter 2 of *Prey into Hunter*; Bloch, 1992), see Whitehouse (1996, pp. 704–8).

16   The pilgrimage, known as "St Patrick's Purgatory," involves both sleep deprivation and fasting.

References and Further Reading

Alexander, Bobby C. (1997) Ritual and current studies of ritual: overview. In Stephen D. Glazier (ed.), *Anthropology of Religion: a Handbook*. Westport, CT: Greenwood Press, pp. 139–60.

Asad, Talal (1993) *Genealogies of Religion: Discipline and Reasons of Power in Christianity and Islam*. Baltimore and London: Johns Hopkins University Press.

Barfield, Thomas (ed.) (1997) *The Dictionary of Anthropology*. Oxford and Malden, MA: Blackwell.

Beatie, John (1970) On understanding ritual. In B. R. Wilson (ed.), *Rationality*. Oxford: Basil Blackwell, pp. 240–69.

Beidelman, T. O. (1997) *The Cool Knife. Imagery of Gender, Sexuality, and Moral Education in Kaguru Initiation Ritual*. Washington, DC and London: The Smithsonian Institution Press.

Bell, Catherine (1992) *Ritual Theory, Ritual Practice*. Oxford and New York: Oxford University Press.

Bell, Catherine (1997) *Ritual Perspectives and Dimensions*. Oxford and New York: Oxford University Press.

Bloch, Maurice and Parry, Jonathan (eds) (1982) *Death and the Regeneration of Life*. Cambridge and New York: Cambridge University Press.

Bloch, Maurice (1986) *From Blessing to Violence. History and Ideology in the Circumcision Ritual of the Merina of Madagascar*. Cambridge and New York: Cambridge University Press.

Bloch, Maurice (1992) *Prey into Hunter. The Politics of Religious Experience*. Cambridge and New York: Cambridge University Press.

Book of Common Prayer (n.d.) Cambridge: Cambridge University Press.

Bowie, Fiona (1997) Equilibrium and the end of time: the roots of millenarianism. In Fiona Bowie (ed.), *The Coming Deliverer: Millennial Themes in World Religions*. Cardiff: University of Wales Press, pp. 1–26.

Boyer, Pascal (1994) *The Naturalness of Religious Ideas: a Cognitive Theory of Religion*. Berkeley: University of California Press.

Buber, Martin (1958) *I and Thou*, translated by R. G. Smith. Edinburgh: Clark.

Burridge, Kenelm (1971) *New Heaven, New Earth. A Study of Millenarian Activities*. Oxford: Basil Blackwell.

Charsley, Simon R. (1992) *Wedding Cakes and Cultural History*. London and New York: Routledge.

Cohn, Norman (1978) *The Pursuit of the Millennium*. St Albans: Paladin, Grenada Publishing (first published in 1957).

Cohn, Norman (1995) *Cosmos, Chaos and the World to Come. The Ancient Roots of Apocalyptic Faith*. New Haven, CT and London: Yale University Press.

Cox, James L. (ed.) (1998) *Rites of Passage in Contemporary Africa*. Cardiff: Cardiff Academic Press.

De Coppet, Daniel (ed.) (1992) *Understanding Rituals*. London: Routledge.

De Coppet, Daniel and Iteanu, André (eds) (1995) *Cosmos and Society in Oceania*. Oxford and Herndon, VA: Berg.

Durkheim, Émile (1976) *The Elementary Forms of the Religious Life*. London: George Allen & Unwin (first published in 1915).

Douglas, Mary (1973) *Natural Symbols*. Harmondsworth: Penguin.

Eliade, Mircea (1989) *The Myth of the Eternal Return: Cosmos and History*. London: Arkana, Penguin (first published in 1954).

Evans-Wentz, W. Y. (ed.) (1980) *The Tibetan Book of the Dead*. Oxford and New York: Oxford University Press.

Fernandez, James W. (1982) *Bwiti: an Ethnography of the Religious Imagination in Africa.* Princeton, NJ: Princeton University Press.

Fox, Robin (1967) *Totem and Taboo* Reconsidered. In Edmund Leach (ed.), *The Structural Study of Myth and Totemism.* ASA Monographs 5. London: Tavistock, pp. 161–78.

Freud, Sigmund (1985) Obsessive actions and religious practices. In Albert Dickinson (ed.), *The Origins of Religion.* The Pelican Freud Library, volume 13. Harmondsworth: Penguin, pp. 31–41 (first published in 1907).

Freud, Sigmund (1938) *Totem and Taboo: Resemblances between the Psychic Lives of Savages and Neurotics.* Harmondsworth: Penguin (first published in 1913).

Geertz, Clifford (1938) *The Interpretation of Cultures.* London: Fontana (first published in 1973).

Gell, Alfred (1975) *Metamorphosis of the Cassowaries: Umeda Society and Ritual.* London: Athlone.

Girard, René (1992) *Violence and the Sacred.* Translated by Patrick Gregory. Baltimore: Johns Hopkins University Press.

Glazier, Stephen D. (ed.) (1997) *The Anthropology of Religion: a Handbook. Part II, The Study of Ritual.* Westport, CT: Greenwood Press.

Grimes, Ronald L. (1982) *Beginnings in Ritual Studies.* Lanham, MD: University Press of America.

Gruenbaum, Ellen (1998) Resistance and embrace: Sudanese rural women and systems of power. In Margaret Lock and Patricia A. Kaufert (eds), *Pragmatic Women and Body Politics.* Cambridge and New York: Cambridge University Press, pp. 58–76.

Harvey, Penny and Gow, Peter (1994) *Sex and Violence: Issues in Representation and Experience.* London and New York: Routledge.

Horton, Robin (1979) Ritual man in Africa. In William A. Lessa and Evon Z. Vogt (eds), *Reader in Comparative Religion: an Anthropological Approach.* New York: HarperCollins, pp. 243–54.

Horton, Robin (1994) *Patterns of Thought in Africa and the West.* Cambridge: Cambridge University Press.

Jennings, Sue (1995) *Theater, Ritual and Transformation. The Senoi Temiars.* London and New York: Routledge.

Kaplan, Martha (1995) *Neither Cargo nor Cult: Ritual Politics and the Colonial Imagination in Fiji.* Durham, NC and London: Duke University Press.

Kratz, Corrine A. (1994) *Affecting Performance. Meaning, Movement, and Experience in Okiek Women's Initiation.* Washington, DC, and London: Smithsonian Institution Press.

La Fontaine, Jean S. (1985) *Initiation: Ritual Drama and Secret Knowledge across the World.* Harmondsworth: Penguin.

Lawrence, Peter (1971) *Road Belong Cargo. A Study of the Cargo Movement in the Southern Madang District New Guinea.* Manchester: Manchester University Press.

Lewis, Gilbert (1988) *Day of Shining Red: an Essay in Understanding Ritual.* Cambridge and New York: Cambridge University Press.

Lincoln, Bruce (1991) *Emerging from the Chrysalis: Rituals of Women's Initiation.* New York and Oxford: Oxford University Press.

Lincoln, Bruce (1989) *Discourse and the Construction of Society: Comparative Studies of Myth, Ritual, and Classification*. New York and Oxford: Oxford University Press.

Lutkehaus, Nancy C. and Roscoe, Paul B. (eds) (1995) *Gender Rituals: Female Initiation in Melanesia*. New York and London: Routledge.

Marvin, Carolyn and Ingle, David (1998) *Blood Sacrifice and the Nation: Totem Rituals and the American Flag*. Cambridge and New York: Cambridge University Press.

Moore, Henrietta (1994) The problem of explaining violence in the social sciences. In Penelope Harvey and Peter Gow (eds), *Sex and Violence: Issues in Representation and Experience*. London and New York: Routledge, pp. 138–55.

Morphy, Howard (1984) *Journey to the Crocodile's Nest: an Accompanying Monograph to the Film "Madarpa Funeral at Gurka'wuy"* (with an afterword by Ian Dunlop). Canberra: Australian Institute of Aboriginal Studies.

Morris, Brian (1987) *Anthropological Studies of Religion*. Cambridge and New York: Cambridge University Press.

Patton, Laurie L. and Doniger, Wendy (eds) (1996) *Myth and Method*. Charlottesville and London: University Press of Virginia.

Rappaport, Roy A. (1979) *Ecology, Meaning and Religion*. Berkeley, CA: North Atlantic Books.

Richards, Audrey (1982) *Chisungu. A Girl's Initiation Ceremony among the Bemba of Zambia*. Introduced by Jean La Fontaine. London and New York: Routledge (first published in 1956).

Rothenbuhler, Eric W. (1989) *Ritual Communication. From Everyday Conversation to Mediated Ceremony*. Thousand Oaks, CA and London: Sage.

Schechner, Richard (1994) *Performance Theory*. New York and London: Routledge.

Schechner, Richard and Appel, Willa (eds) (1990) *By Means of Performance. Intercultural Studies of Theater and Ritual*. Cambridge and New York: Cambridge University Press.

Segal, Robert, A. (ed.) (1998) *The Myth and Ritual Theory. An Anthology*. Malden, MA and Oxford: Blackwell.

Staal, Frits (1989) *Rules without Meaning: Ritual, Mantras and the Human Sciences*. Bern: Peter Lang.

Strathern, Andrew and Stewart, Pamela J. (1998) Embodiment and communication. Two frames for the analysis of ritual. *Social Anthropology*, 6(2), 237–51.

Swain, Tony and Trompf, Garry (1995) *The Religions of Oceania*. London and New York: Routledge.

Tambiah, S. J. (1979) *A Performative Approach to Ritual*. London: The British Academy and Oxford University Press.

Turner, Edith (1992) *Experiencing Ritual. A New Interpretation of African Healing*. With William Blodgett. Philadelphia: University of Pennsylvania Press.

Turner, Victor (1967) *The Forest of Symbols: Aspects of Ndembu Ritual*. New York: Cornell University Press.

Turner, Victor (1968) *The Drums of Affliction*. Oxford: Clarendon Press; London: The International African Institute.

Turner, Victor (1972) *Schism and Continuity in an African Society. A Study of Ndembu Village Life*. Manchester: University of Manchester Press (first published in 1957).

Turner, Victor (1974) *Dramas, Fields and Metaphors: Symbolic Action in Human Society*. Ithaca, NY and London: Cornell University Press.

Turner, Victor and Turner, Edith (1978) *Image and Pilgrimage in Christian Culture*. New York: Columbia University Press.

Turner, Victor (1979) Betwixt and between: the liminal period in *Rites de Passage*. In William A. Lessa and Evon Z. Vogt (eds), *Reader in Comparative Religion: an Anthropological Approach*. New York: HarperCollins, pp. 234–43.

Turner, Victor (1982) *From Ritual to Theater and Back: the Human Seriousness of Play*. New York: PAJ Publications.

Turner, Victor (1991) *The Ritual Process. Structure and Anti-structure*. Ithaca, NY: Cornell University Press.

Trompf, G. W. (1991) *Melanesian Religion*. Cambridge and New York: Cambridge University Press.

Tylor, Edward Burnett (1871) *Primitive Cultures* (2 volumes). London: Murray.

van Gennep, Arnold (1960) *The Rites of Passage*. London: Routledge and Kegan Paul (first published in 1909).

Werbner, Richard P. (1989) *Ritual Passage Sacred Journey: the Process and Organization of Religious Movement*. Washington, DC: Smithsonian Institution Press; Manchester: Manchester University Press.

Whitehouse, Harvey (1995) *Inside the Cult. Religious Innovation and Transmission in Papua New Guinea*. Oxford and New York: Oxford University Press.

Whitehouse, Harvey (1996) Rites of terror: emotion, metaphor and memory in Melanesian initiation cults. *Journal of the Royal Anthropological Institute*, 2(4), 703–15.

Wilson, Bryan (1975) *Magic and the Millennium*. St Albans: Paladin.

Worsley, Peter (1970) *The Trumpet Shall Sound. A Study of "Cargo" Cults in Melanesia*. London: Paladin.

Chapter 7

Shamanism

Introduction

The term "shaman" is frequently used nowadays in a variety of contexts. It is argued that "Jesus was a shaman," that "our ancestors practiced shamanic religions," that shamans can be found in Australia, Africa, and the industrialized world, as well as in the Arctic, Asia, and the Americas. This chapter seeks to deconstruct some of these very varied uses, looking at several *different approaches to the study of shamanism*, before going on to focus on *Arctic shamanism* as a key example of a shamanic complex. The final section takes a look at the popular rise of urban, core, or neo-shamanism – that is, at behavior described by practitioners or promoters as "shamanism" in the industrialized West.

What is shamanism?

> Shamanism . . . is not a religion. The spiritual experience usually becomes a religion after politics has entered into it. So the renewed interest in shamanism today can be viewed as democratization, returning to the original spiritual democracy of our ancestors in ancient tribal societies where almost everyone had some access to spiritual experience and direct revelation. We are now restoring ancient methods to get our own direct revelations, without the need of ecclesiastical hierarchies and politically influenced dogma. We can find things out for ourselves. (Harner, in Nicholson, 1987, pp. 15–16)

"Shamanism" is one of those terms (like "witchcraft" or "totemism") which is often used very broadly, referring to many different phenomena, some of which bear little relationship to one another or to any original derivation. Most writers are, however, agreed that shamanism is a technique rather than a religion, and that the shaman is a religious specialist existing within many different religious and cultural contexts. Shamanism may coexist with world religions, or be an important element within an animistic belief system. Shamanic experience is also being reclaimed by anthropologists such as Michael Harner (in the quotation above), and is finding a home in the United States, Canada, and Europe. The word *shaman* is thought to have originated with the Tungus (also known as the Evenk) of Eastern Siberia, where it refers to a religious specialist who has the ability to enter a trance state in order to communicate with and appease the "spirits" for the purposes of healing, fertility, protection, and aggression, and to act as a guide to the souls of the dead. Shamanism is sometimes regarded as an ancient, universal form of religious behavior, often coexisting with other formal religions (such as Buddhism in South East Asia). The popularity of Western shamanism, which draws largely on Native American traditions for inspiration, raises interesting questions as to the universality and comparability of shamanic phenomena. One might ask, for example, about the objective reality of the shamanic experience. Is it all in the mind, even if there are discernible physical effects? Are there really animal guardian spirits with which human beings can make contact? Is psychic healing a reality, and, if so, what is the relationship between the capacities of the human mind and external forces? This type of question is not easy to assess empirically, but the anthropologist can study what people say and think about their beliefs and practices, and the role that they play in structuring people's lives.

Different Approaches to the Study of Shamanism

We can identify four broad trends among writers on shamanism, although the categories are not discrete. Those who favor a loose definition, including contemporary Western shamanic practitioners and teachers, are likely to regard shamanism as both an ancient and a universal phenomenon. By way of contrast, there is a long tradition of scholarship that argues for a restricted use of the term, believing that to mean almost anything is ultimately to mean nothing. I have characterized these differing approaches as follows.

Shamanism: a widespread form of indigenous knowledge

For many writers, both popular and academic, "shamanism" refers to a wide range of religious specialists and various forms of ecstatic behavior wherever in the world they occur. This approach is particularly common in the English-speaking world. Ioan Lewis, for example, argues that witchcraft, spirit-possession, cannibalism, and shamanism are all closely related expressions of charismatic, mystical power. Fieldwork itself is described as "a form of shamanistic initiation" (Lewis, 1986, p. viii). A central definition of shamanism, for Lewis, is that it involves the domestication, rather than exorcism, of the spirits that possess the victim or initiate. The mastery of spirits, regarded by Lewis as a ubiquitous characteristic of shamanic initiation, is set alongside other spirit-possession cults which follow a similar "career structure" (Lewis, 1986, p. ix).[1]

Throughout his encyclopedic work, *Shamanism: Archaic Techniques of Ecstasy* (first published in 1964), Mircea Eliade treats shamanism as a distinct phenomenon with characteristics that are widely distributed throughout the ancient and contemporary world. Scriptural or world religions are regarded as having shamanic or closely parallel features. While acknowledging the central role of Arctic shamanism in any account of the phenomenon, Eliade sees shamanism more broadly as a "technique of ecstasy" (Eliade, 1988, pp. 4–5, 493). For Eliade (unlike Lewis),

> the specific element of shamanism is not the embodiment of "spirits" by the shaman, but the ecstasy induced by his ascent to the sky or descent to the underworld; incarnating spirits and being "possessed" by spirits are universally disseminated phenomena, but they do not necessarily belong to shamanism in the strict sense. (Eliade, 1988, pp. 499–500)

This leads Eliade to claim that Tungus shamanism "today" (i.e. in the 1930s, when Shirokogoroff produced his famous studies) "cannot be considered a 'classic' form of shamanism, precisely because of the predominant importance it accords to the incarnation of 'spirits' and the small role played by the ascent to the sky" (Eliade, 1988, p. 500). Eliade is led to postulate that there was an original "pure" shamanism in which ecstatic flight attempted to recover a primordial state before the "fall," normally accessible only through death. Most forms of shamanism actually recorded are thought to be "aberrant" or "degenerate," perhaps as a result of culture contact. Such claims are very difficult to verify, and owe more to nineteenth-century theoretical evolutionist debates than to contemporary anthropological discourse. Eliade's work has, however, been extraordinarily influential, and is widely quoted by writers on shamanism, most of whom accept his definitions and classification of shamanism without question.

Addressing a more popular audience, Joan Halifax describes shamanism as "an ecstatic complex of particular and fixed elements with a specific ideology that has persisted through millennia and is found in many different cultural settings" (Halifax, 1991, p. 3). Halifax identifies a number of defining features of shamanism, including: an initiatory crisis; a vision quest, ordeals, or experience of dismemberment and regeneration; the sacred tree or *axis mundi*; spirit flight, mastery of the lower, middle, and upper worlds and the ability to enter an ecstatic trance; a healer and intermediary between the community and non-ordinary reality (Halifax, 1991, chapter 1). The shamans whose stories are recorded by Halifax are drawn mainly from the Arctic and sub-Arctic regions, but include Australia, Africa, Borneo, and South and Meso-America. To give one final example of a broad definition of shamanism from the many possible, Piers Vitebsky, in his lavishly illustrated handbook *The Shaman: Voyages of the Soul, Trance, Ecstasy and Healing from Siberia to the Arctic*, claims that "shamanic motifs, themes and characters appear throughout human history, religion and psychology" (Vitebsky, 1995, p. 6). He goes on to state that "Shamanism is not a single, unified religion but a cross-cultural form of religious sensibility and practice. In all societies known to us today shamanic ideas generally form only one strand among the doctrines and authority structures of other religions, ideologies and practices" (Vitebsky, 1995, p. 11). While fully developed shamanic complexes are seen as being confined to the Arctic, Asia, and the Americas, Vitebsky discovers similar motifs and elements in Africa, New Guinea, and pre-Christian Europe (Vibetsky, 1995, pp. 50–1).

Shamanism: the oldest form of religion?

Writers who like to treat shamanism with a broad geographical brush usually trace the phenomenon back into humanity's prehistoric past, sometimes describing it as an *ur* religion or original, ancient form of human wisdom. Joan Halifax, for instance, sees continuity between religion as practiced by our Stone Age ancestors and contemporary shamanism:

> The shaman, a mystical, priestly, and political figure emerging during the Upper Palaeolithic period, and perhaps going back to Neanderthal times, can be described not only as a specialist in the human soul but also as a generalist whose sacred and social functions can cover an extraordinarily wide range of activities. (Halifax, 1991, p. 3)

In popular works of archaeology, in particular in descriptions of "the Celts," we frequently see shamanism appearing as a basic universal religious substrate, superseded by scripture-based world religions. Ancient carvings or rock paintings are labeled "shamanic," often with little attempt to define what is meant by the term.[2] Such are the difficulties surrounding any attempt to reconstruct the past, however, that scholars often turn to extant small-scale societies for clues concerning human social and spiritual evolution.

The Christian theologian Keith Ward, for example, utilizes examples of visionary intercessors from Australia, Africa, the Americas, and the Arctic to make the point that it is unlikely there was ever "one clear primeval revelation from an omnipotent creator" (Ward, 1994, p. 62). Ward is arguing a theological rather than a scientific point, but nevertheless concludes from observations of contemporary primal religions that "What is much more characteristic is a riotous plurality of presences – spirits, demons, and ancestors, of good and evil intent – whom the shamans or designated mediators can partly control or influence" (Ward, 1994, p. 62). Eliade, as already noted, adopts an evolutionary perspective, dominated by a Judeo-Christian monotheistic outlook. Unlike Ward, Eliade postulates that early human societies believed in the existence of a Supreme Being, with the ecstatic flight of the shaman (in its original "pure" form) an attempt to recapture the prelapsarian state (Eliade, 1988, pp. 504–7).

Shamanism as a northern–Arctic phenomenon

Russian and Scandinavian scholars, and others who have studied shamanism in northern societies, have largely eschewed a broad-based definition of shamanism in favor of a more restricted use, confining the term to the specific cultural features and world view characteristic of the Siberian–Arctic complex. A cultural continuum is acknowledged through the Americas and into South East Asia, although there are wide divergences between shamanic practices in the circumpolar region and in Korea or Brazil, for example. There is a long tradition of shamanic research in Russia, although with little reference to works in other languages. A. A. Popov, writing in 1932, for instance, cited some 650 papers on shamanism in his bibliography (Hultkrantz, 1993, p. 4).

Åke Hultkrantz insists, however, that shamanism should not be regarded as "a separate religion, the religion of Siberia," pointing out that "Siberian religions contain many elements which cannot be subsumed under the heading 'shamanism.' And there are many shamanisms in other areas showing a different constellation of traits, many of which do not occur in Siberian shamanism" (Hultkrantz, 1993, pp. 9–10). Shamanism with possession, for instance, is not common in Siberia, being more characteristic of Tibet and Central Asia. In these areas, however, the soul journey (Eliade's ecstatic flight, which for him is a central defining characteristic of shamanism) is little emphasized. There is not, according to Hultkrantz, any one "shamanism," but a constellation of characteristics that vary from one place to another (and over time). Hultkrantz distinguishes what he refers to as "general" or "simple" shamanism, which can be widely distributed, from the shamanism of the

Arctic, Siberia, and Mongolia. This minimum definition of simple shamanism consists of trance, direct contact with spiritual beings and guardian spirits, and mediation in a ritual setting (Hultkrantz, 1992, p. 10).

This goes little way to resolving the question as to how broadly the term "shamanism" can usefully be applied, and my own sympathies lie with those who would like to restrict the term to areas with a degree of cultural continuity. Parallels and contrasts between ritual specialists are more likely to be noted and described where an assumed affinity is not imposed by the use of a single term (the use of "witchcraft" to refer to phenomena in both Africa and Christian Europe leads to similar unwarranted assumptions of contiguity). Evans-Pritchard was clearly aware of the danger of the indiscriminate use of vernacular terms, noting that:

> One can standardize a word taken from a primitive vernacular, like *totem*, and use it to describe phenomena among other peoples which resemble what it refers to in its original home; but this can be the cause of great confusion, because the resemblances may be superficial, and the phenomena in question so diversified that the term loses all meaning. (Evans-Pritchard, 1972, p. 12)

The Russian Scholar S. M. Shirokogoroff, in his influential book *Psycho-mental Complex of the Tungus*, was equally conscious of the danger of applying the term "shamanism" to any ecstatic behavior, with a consequent loss of explanatory value, and argued strongly for restricted use of the term in its original context (1982, p. 271):

> I do not introduce a new term, because I hope that it will be possible to save the term "shaman" to be applied to the phenomenon here discussed. Without wearing out this term by the use in reference to very broad generalizations, and at the same time clearing it from various malignant tumours – theories which associated shamanism with sorcery, witchcraft, medicine-men, etc. – the term "shaman" shall still be preserved.

The desire to reserve the use of the term "shamanism" to the circumpolar regions, with the recognition of related complexes in Asia and the Americas, is, however, confined to scholars writing for the academic market. So handy a term, which can mean almost whatever you want it to mean, has achieved a broad currency in popular literature and in the popular imagination.

Can anyone be a shaman?

The past two or three decades have seen a considerable interest by industrialized Westerners in the "shamanic" practices of indigenous peoples, leading to a further broadening in the use of the term. The United States has led the way, with a focus on Native American traditions. Europeans draw both on Native American practices and on "Celtic" or other European pagan beliefs (as interpreted by a new body of practicing "shamanic" experts). The emphasis is less on the social role that the shaman plays in most small-scale societies, and more on the search for individual spiritual development and healing. Western shamanic teachers insist that anyone can become a shaman, or at least engage in shamanic practices. The techniques of soul journeying are available to all through shamanic workshops, or by means of a book and cassette of shamanic drumming. While many individuals who participate in shamanic workshops may adopt a world view that encompasses the existence of animal guides and soul journeying, even this is not necessary in order to experience the psychological effects of shamanism.[3] One of the best known proponents of Western or neo-shamanism (sometimes referred to as "core" shamanism) is Michael Harner, who wrote a bestselling "how to" manual, *The Way of the Shaman*, first published in 1980. Harner insists that a group or individual who seeks to enter a trance, to go on a soul journey, or to discover an animal spirit helper by means of a stereo cassette player, headphones, and drumming tape is not "playing Indian" but "going to the same revelatory spiritual sources that tribal shamans have traveled to from time immemorial" (Harner, 1990, p. xiv):

> They are not pretending to be shamans; if they get shamanic results for themselves and others in this work, they are indeed the real thing. Their experiences are genuine and, when described, are essentially interchangeable with the accounts of shamans from nonliterate tribal cultures. The shamanic work is the same, the human mind, heart, and body are the same; *only* the cultures are different. (Harner, 1990, p. xiv, *emphasis added*)

This approach, which is both individualistic and universalizing, with its minimization of cultural difference, is very much in tune with much of what is loosely described as New Age religion, with its eclecticism and its borrowings from psychoanalysis and psychotherapy. Neo-shamanism is in itself a fascinating object of study. It can throw new light on the powers of the human mind, while reminding us of the importance of the specific Western cultural and historical context that gives neo-shamanism its present form. Neo-shamanism also points to the ubiquity of certain religious themes, such as "soul" journeying and communication with the spirit world, in cultures that have quite disparate material cultures, lifestyles, social institutions, and languages.

Arctic Shamanism

The *locus classicus* of shamanism is the circumpolar region, although closely related beliefs and practices can be found throughout South East Asia (for instance, in Korea and China) and throughout the Americas. The derivation of the term "shaman" has been much debated. The word is probably Tungu-zian for a magician or conjurer (Hultkranz, 1993, p. 6), possibly deriving originally from Pali, Sanskrit, or Chinese, referring to one who is "excited," "moved," or "raised."[4] Shamanism is not a religion as such, but a cosmo-logical complex of beliefs, myths, rituals, practices, and paraphernalia cen-tered on the person of the shaman. This complex can continue to exist without the shaman (and indeed did so in much of the Soviet Union throughout the Stalinist period).[5]

Definitions

Tungus shamanism was described by Shirokogoroff in the following terms:

> In all Tungus languages this term refers to persons of both sexes who have mastered spirits, who at will can introduce these spirits into themselves and use their power over the spirits in their own interests, particularly helping other people, who suffer from the spirits; in such a capacity they may possess a complex of special methods for dealing with spirits. (Shirokogoroff, 1982, p. 269)

Paraphrasing Shirokogoroff (1982, p. 274), this leads us to the following five-point definition:

1 The shaman is a master (mistress) of spirits.
2 He or she has a group of spirits under his or her control.
3 There is a complex of methods and paraphernalia recognized and trans-mitted.
4 There is a theoretical justification of the practice.
5 The shamans assume a special social position.

Åke Hultkrantz has come up with a similar, comprehensive, list of features that typify Arctic shamanism:

> the shaman is "a social functionary who, with the help of guardian spirits, attains ecstasy in order to create a rapport with the supernatural world on behalf of his group members." . . . By "shaman" . . . I understand a person, male or female, who through his/her training or spiritual endowment is able to act as a mediator

between members of his/her social group (in some cases members of another social group) and the supernatural powers. The contact with the other world is realized through ecstasy or trance, two words for the same thing. The trance signals the entrance of the guardian spirits. In its full-blown forms, it may also mean the appearance of mighty spirits coming from distant places to give information and help. The flights of the shaman's own soul presuppose a deep, sometimes cataleptic trance. These flights could involve the retrieving of lost souls, the transporting of a dead person's soul to the land of the dead, a scouting expedition to places in this world or to the other world, or a visit to the high supernatural beings who control the fate and welfare of human beings. (Hultkrantz, 1993, p. 6)

The shaman functions as a healer and *psychopomp*, who guides the souls of the dead, but unlike other medical specialists the shamanic healer is invariably concerned with soul loss and recovery. Healing involves cooperation with guardian spirits, which are often in the form of animals. In northern societies, heavily dependent upon hunting for survival, the shaman must also seek the help of animal spirit guardians in order to persuade the game to surrender itself to the hunters. As an Inuit shaman reported to the Danish explorer and ethnographer Knud Rasmussen,

> The greatest peril in life lies in the fact that human food consists entirely of souls. All creatures we have to kill and eat, all those we have to strike down and destroy to make clothes for ourselves, have souls, souls that do not perish with the body and which must therefore be (pacified) lest they should revenge themselves on us for taking away their bodies. (Rasmussen, 1929, pp. 55–6)[6]

The skill of the hunter is to no avail if a bargain has not been struck with the animals' guardian spirits, allowing the souls of the animals killed to re-enter a new body, thereby guaranteeing the fertility of the species and a future supply of game.

Controlling the spirits

Central to any definition of shamanism is the ability to control the spirits which inhabit the seen and unseen worlds, and which affect the life, health, and fertility of the world. Healing cannot take place until the shaman has managed to domesticate a number of spirit helpers. Referring to Shirokogoroff, Ioan Lewis describes the central role of the shaman in Tungus society, and his or her relationship with the spirits:

> Tungus clans are small, scattered patrilineal units, rarely boasting more than a thousand members. As well as family and lineage heads, or elders, and

politically significant "big-men" who are primarily concerned with directing
the secular life of the group, each clan normally has at least one generally
recognised shaman. This "master of spirits" is essential to the well being of the
clan, for he [or she] controls the clan's own ancestral spirits and other foreign
spirits which have been adopted into the spirit hierarchy. In the free state,
these spirits are extremely dangerous . . . [to human beings]. Most are hostile and
pathogenic and are regarded as the sources of the many diseases which affect
the Tungus. (Lewis, 1989, p. 45)

The shaman's healing role is both preventative and curative, and depends on
a view of the world which holds that spirits are responsible for much of the
good and bad fortune which can befall individuals and society. Lewis continues his description of Tungus spirits by explaining that:

> Most diseases . . . are seen as having a mystical basis in the action of these
> noxious spirits. As long as the clan shaman is doing his [or her] job properly,
> however, in incarnating these spirits and thus controlling them by containing
> them, all is well. Indeed with the inducement of regular offerings, these tamed
> spirits are considered to protect the clan from attack by other alien spirits and
> also to ensure the fertility and prosperity of its members. These "mastered"
> spirits can thus be applied to fight off, or overcome, other hostile spirits
> which have not yet been rendered harmless by human incarnation. (Lewis,
> 1989, p. 45)

The tamed spirits become a kind of allied army which can be called upon by
the shaman to fight off or overcome other hostile spirits, not yet rendered
harmless by being "placed" in the body of a shaman. The tamed spirits also
aid the shaman in diagnosing and treating sickness, which is perceived in
terms of soul loss, with the shaman undertaking a perilous mystical flight to
recapture the patient's soul. The shaman is not, as in some contemporary
neo-shamanic groups, engaged in personal development. Shirokogoroff
stresses the dangerous and demanding character of the shaman's calling –
a vocation which may be resisted by the chosen individual, and which
involves considerable self-sacrifice and danger.

For the indigenous peoples of the Arctic and sub-Arctic region life was (and
is) harsh – a constant battle against the extremes of climate, latitude, and the
unpredictability of game. The physical and supernatural worlds are equally
capricious, and the spirits who determine the fate of human beings at best
neutral, but more often malevolent. An East Greenlandic man expressed this
sense of powerlessness in front of the forces of nature to Rasmussen in the
following terms:

I know nothing, but continuously life confronts me with forces that are stronger than me! As it is difficult to live we have the knowledge of our forefathers, and it is always the inexorable that becomes the fate of man and woman. Therefore we believe in evil. The good we do not have to consider as it is good in its own right and does not need to be worshipped. The evil on the other hand, which is lurking in the great darkness, threatening us through storm and bad weather and sneaking up on us in dank fog, has to be kept away from the path we walk. Human beings are capable of so little, and we do not even know whether what we believe is true. The only thing we do know for sure is that what has to happen will happen. (Rasmussen, 1921, p. 9)

The power of the shaman to combat evil spirits could be used to his or her advantage. While a necessary figure in Arctic societies, the shaman was also feared and sometimes a lonely, isolated figure. Rasmussen, in his book *Intellectual Culture of the Iglulik Eskimos*, recounts the measures taken by the Inuit to protect a child from the evil power of the shaman, and other malevolent acts and misfortunes:

> "If it is desired to render a boy invulnerable against animals and men, especially shamans and their attacks by means of witchcraft, if it is desired to prevent him from being bitten to death or otherwise killed by animals: walrus, bear, wolverine etc. and hinder shamans from causing him sickness of body by taking away his soul, then a shaman must be summoned as soon as the child is out of the womb." ... The shaman takes the soul out of the boy's body and lays it under his mother's lamp. The soul must then remain there as long as the boy lives. A ritual is performed in connection with the first seal: the flippers put in a grave "Then, when the young man later becomes a great hunter, and some shaman or other grows envious, and endeavours to take away his catch by magic, i.e. steal the souls of the animals he gets, the attempt will prove fruitless. The shaman's helping spirits will be afraid of the outer part of the flippers placed in the grave, and will then protect the boy's catch against all evil." (Rasmussen, 1929, pp. 172, 178)[7]

Greenland shamans were often implicated in murders, and could become victims themselves. Release from the power of the shamans was, in fact, cited as a motive for conversion to Christianity, and eighteenth- and nineteenth-century missionaries often regarded undermining the authority of shamans as a key element in their success.[8]

The trance séance

The main focus of shamanic activity is the trance séance, in which the shaman makes contact with the spirits, sending out his or her soul to heal, exorcise, mediate, divine, or perform acts of vengeance. The séance could be

a low-key affair consisting of a consultation between a shaman and peti-
tioner, or a major public ceremony in which theatrical rituals and the
performance of various "tricks" of perception on the audience all aid the
dramatic effect and help to bring about the desired result.

Lewis, referring to the Tungus, writes:

> Séances may be held to make contact with the spirits of the upper or lower worlds.
> For instance, the shaman may be consulted by his [or her] clansmen [or women] to
> reveal the causes of an outbreak of disease, or to discover the reason for a run of bad
> luck in hunting. This requires him [or her] to call up the spirits into himself [or
> herself] and, having established the cause of the misfortune, to take appropriate
> action. He [or she] may, for example, consider it necessary to take a sacrificial
> reindeer to the spirits of the lower world and seek to persuade them to remove the
> difficulties his [or her] kin are experiencing. (Lewis, 1989, p. 46)

The atmosphere may be highly charged, with drumming, singing, dancing,
and the wearing of an elaborate costume all adding to the dramatic effect.
The theatrical quality of the séance comes through in the following description given by Shirokogoroff:

> The rhythmic music and singing, and later the dancing of the shaman, gradually
> involve every participant more and more in a collective action. When the
> audience begins to repeat the refrains together with the assistants, only those
> who are defective fail to join the chorus. The tempo of the action increases, the
> shaman with a spirit is no more an ordinary man or relative, but is a "placing"
> (i.e. incarnation) of the spirit; the spirit acts together with the audience, and this
> is felt by everyone. The state of many participants is now near to that of the
> shaman himself, and only a strong belief that when the shaman is there the spirit
> may only enter him, restrains the participants from being possessed in mass by
> the spirit. This is a very important condition of shamanizing which does not
> however reduce mass susceptibility to the suggestion, hallucinations, and un-
> conscious acts produced in a state of mass ecstasy. When the shaman feels that
> the audience is with him and follows him he becomes still more active and this
> effect is transmitted to his audience. After shamanizing, the audience recollects
> various moments of the performance, their great psychophysiological emotion
> and the hallucinations of sight and hearing which they have experienced. They
> then have a deep satisfaction – much greater than that from emotions produced
> by theatrical and musical performances, literature and general artistic phenom-
> ena of the European complex, because in shamanizing the audience at the same
> time acts and participates. (Cited in Lewis, 1989, pp. 46–7)

Numerous skeptical missionaries and travelers have sought to expose the
shaman-magician's skill, often with some success. On occasion, however,

the ability of shamans to alter the physical world around them, or the audience's perception of it, defies easy explanation. Waldemar Bogoras, a traveler in Siberia at the beginning of the twentieth century, is typical of those who, while skeptical of the claims made by shamans and not sharing their world view, cannot help but admire the magician's skill. In 1901, Bogoras visited the village of Chibukak on St Lawrence Island, where he was introduced to an old man of shamanic stock called Abra. When Bogoras asked Abra to demonstrate his shamanic skills he first refused for fear of the American Baptist preacher, the only official in the community and its physician and school teacher. Bogoras eventually managed to obtain the preacher's permission on the grounds that both he and Abra were beyond the saving grace of God, so no more harm could come to their reprobate souls.

> So we two were left, the shaman and I, in the sleeping-room of his underground house. Abra had removed nearly all of his clothing. He took my best American double blanket and placed two corners of it on his own naked shoulders. The other corners he gave me to hold. "Do not let them go!" he warned as he began to crawl out of the sleeping-room, which was some ten feet wide. The blanket seemed by some strange power to stick fast to his shoulders. It tightened and I felt the corners that I held on the point of escaping from my hands. I set my feet against a kind of cross-beam that ran along the flooring, but the tension of the blanket almost raised me to my feet, entirely against my will. Then all at once I made a sudden movement and dug both my arms, blanket and all, deep behind the wooden frame that supported the skin cover of the sleeping-room; I and the sleeping-room were practically one. "Now we shall see," said I to myself.
>   The tension continued to increase, and lo, the framed wall rose on both sides of me, right and left. The rays of moonshine entered the room and cut athwart the darkness. A flat tank to the right of me, full of water and half dissolved snow, was overturning and the ice-cold water was spilling on my knees. A heap of iron pans and dishes and ladles and spoons, on my right, was breaking down with much noise and clangor. I had a feeling that in a moment the whole house would tumble in about my ears, and from a sheer instinct of self-preservation I let go of the blanket. It skipped across the space just like a piece of rubber. Then, all at once, I came to myself and looked round. The water-tank was in its proper place. Likewise pans and dishes. Everything was just as it should be. The awful old shaman had worked on me by will power and made things look queer. (Cited in Halifax, 1990, pp. 15–16)[9]

Bogoras records his admiration for the shaman's skill, even if he remains convinced that the séance involved sleight of hand rather than mystical powers:

This neat piece of work was the more remarkable in that it was practiced on a skeptic like myself who was, so to speak, filled with a spirit of personal resistance against the trickery, and in the absence of the usual crowd of believers, which gives the shaman a terrible tenfold impetus. Abra had been able to curb my will and intelligence altogether single-handed. And now he was calling from the outer room with a note of exaltation. "But the blanket is for me!" For the objects handled by the spirits become wholly unfit and even dangerous for the use of average human beings, and must be given over to the shaman. (Cited in Halifax, 1990, p. 16)

Whatever sleight of hand or other means used by the shaman to achieve dramatic effects, many observers, like Shirokogoroff, were convinced of a séance's therapeutic effects. Sick individuals become, for a while, the focus of attention and their will to live is strengthened. Community tensions can be brought into the open and resolved, and the séance itself acts as a cathartic event.

The shamanic calling

When a Westerner joins a shamanic drumming group or takes part in a shamanic workshop, he or she may do so out of curiosity, or be driven by some deeper sense of purpose. The Westerner is, however, drawn to shamanism in a society in which the shaman's role is hardly recognized. There will probably be an expectation that all those present can learn to "be" shamans and to have shamanic experiences. In cultures in which shamanism is (or was) a central expression of religious behavior, the shamanic vocation has a different meaning. Most members of the society are not and do not want to be shamans. Those who take on this role may conform to the image of the "wounded healers," those individuals whose sickness, psychosis, or possession drove them to seek healing. They must learn to tame the spirits that are troubling them and in turn learn to heal others. In some instances a lonely person, or one who seeks power over others, may set out to confront the spirits in the search for shamanic power. In other instances family or community members may apprentice a child or young person to an established shaman. A community without a shaman may interpret signs of a shamanic vocation in one of its members and seek to persuade him or her to undergo initiation. Although an apprenticeship with an older shaman is common in Arctic societies, the spirits may call someone who has no access to a mentor. Rasmussen records the experience of an Inuit shaman who had tried in vain to apprentice himself to an older shaman and who, finally, had sought initiation alone, through solitude in the wilderness:

I soon became melancholy. I would sometimes fall to weeping and feel unhappy without knowing why. Then for no reason all would suddenly be changed, and I felt a great, inexplicable joy, a joy so powerful that I could not restrain it, but had to break into song, a mighty song, with room for only one word: joy, joy! And I had to use the full strength of my voice. And then in the midst of such a fit of mysterious and overwhelming delight I became a shaman, not knowing myself how it came about. But I was a shaman. I could see and hear in a totally different way. I had gained enlightenment, the shaman's light of brain and body, and this in such a manner that it was not only I who could see through the darkness of life, but the same bright light also shone out from me, imperceptible to human beings but visible to the spirits of earth and sky and sea, and these now came to me to become my helping spirits. (Rasmussen, 1929, p. 119)[10]

Shamanic initiation is a dangerous event in which the spirits test the strength of the *neophyte*. The motif of death and dismemberment is common, and is often reflected in the skeletal images on a shaman's costume. Among Greenlanders shamanic initiation could be a long drawn-out process, which the neophyte had to keep secret from the rest of society. For a woman childbearing could put an end to her shamanizing, and the spirits might suggest ways in which she could dispose of her husband! The would-be shaman had to summon the help of spirits sufficiently powerful to help him or her, but their strength was also a threat to the initiate. Not all those seeking spirit helpers would finally succeed in becoming fully fledged shamans. Being discovered in the quest could, for instance, put an end to the quest for shamanic power, as could breaking one of the many food or other taboos imposed on the neophyte. For some shamans, their calling takes place even before birth in a premonition to their mother. Vitebsky recounts the story of Dyukhade, from the Nganasan people of Northwest Siberia, who was renowned as a great shaman in the 1930s:

I became a shaman even before I saw the light of day. Before she became pregnant, my mother had a dream in which she became the wife of the Smallpox Spirit. She woke and told her family that her future child was to become a shaman through this spirit. When I grew up a little I fell ill for three years. During this illness I was escorted through various dark places where I was thrown now into water, now into fire. At the end of the third year I was dead to the world and lay motionless for three days. It was only on the third day that I woke up again, when they were getting ready to bury me. During those three days, while the people around thought I was dead, I went through my initiation. I reached the middle of the sea and heard a voice saying, "You will receive your gift from the Master of the Water. Your shamanic name will be Loon [a diving bird]." I came out of the water and went along the shore. I saw a naked woman lying on her side. This was the Mistress of the Water. I began to suck her breast. She said, "So my child has appeared. I'll let him drink his fill, my child has surely come out of great need and exhaustion." (Vitebsky, 1995, p. 58)

While no two accounts of shamanic initiation are the same, several themes are common. The initiate must contact spirits who will become helpers. These will usually eat, dismember, or kill the initiate, before he or she is reconstituted as a shaman. The initiate is often ill or possessed prior to initiation, and may lose consciousness or appear dead to others. The quest for shamanic power may take many years, or be an almost instantaneous event. However long the process takes, the fully fledged shaman acquires the power to see and travel in the spirit world and to summon the aid of the animal (or other) spirit guides. Being able to see the spirits means that the shaman can also be seen. He or she must continue to exercise and build up power so as not to be overcome by the spirits that have been invoked.

The shamanic career

It can take an initiate more than a decade to become a shaman, or the mastery of spirits and knowledge of the upper and lower worlds may occur in an instant. In many cases, however, initiates pass through a similar sequence of stages on the way to becoming shamans.[11] The first phase or stage is that of involuntary, uncontrolled, or unsolicited possession, or some life crisis such as an illness, which is interpreted as the action of malevolent spirits. In some cases there may be a childhood trauma, such as a beating, which impels the individual toward a shamanic career.

In the first stage of possession or illness the neophyte is merely a patient. It is possible that a cure will be sought, or that the spirits troubling the person will be exorcised. If the cure or exorcism is successful this is likely to be the end of the matter, and the individual returns to normal life. On occasion, however, all cures may fail, or the type of illness or possession suggests to the patient and to those around that he or she may have a shamanic vocation. As the spirits are tamed or domesticated, or the illness is overcome, the patient moves onto the second stage. Having been through a powerful transformative experience, the wounded healer begins to acquire shamanic powers. As the ability to control the spirits – to summon them at will and to use them as guides – increases, so the shamanic vocation becomes more stable and formalized. In the third and final stage the individual is able to use his or her powers to heal or to harm others. Once recognized as a fully fledged shaman, the person is marked for life. It is not possible to change one's mind or to retire. The shaman can see and be seen by spirits in the upper and lower worlds, and must live hereafter in a world of potentially hostile and dangerous forces. Whether loved or feared by the community, the shaman remains at its service, an essential if ambivalent character existing on the edge of society.[12]

Shamanic regalia

In Arctic shamanism certain items of shamanic equipment are ubiquitous (although not confined to this region). A recurrent feature of the trance-séance, for instance, is an *axis mundi*, a ladder, pole, or tree used to represent the center of the world.[13] In his or her ecstatic journey to the upper and lower worlds the shaman may climb this symbolic tree which unites the world of human beings and non-human forces. The most important single piece of equipment in many Arctic societies is the shaman's drum, sometimes referred to as a mount (or horse). The rhythm of the drum, perhaps accompanied by the singing of the shaman and audience, enables the shaman to enter the trance-state. A shaman's drum is a powerful and respected item of equipment, often passed down through many generations. Costume is also important. Although some shamans may work naked or nearly naked, others have elaborate cloaks or tunics, often depicting a skeleton, representing the dismemberment and regeneration the initiate suffered at the hands of the spirits. The costume will probably be made from animal skins, decorated with items of particular significance to the shaman. Bones, feathers, and pelts of animals from the same species as the shaman's spirit helpers may hang from the costume. An animal headdress can add to the awe-inspiring sight of the dancing, whirling, trancing shaman. In some areas psychotropic substances are ingested or inhaled to help the shaman enter the spirit world. Finno-Ugrian shamans, for instance, used the mushroom *Amanita muscaria* (although alcohol may now serve instead).

The songs or chants of the shaman can indicate the purpose of the soul-journey, perhaps indicating the power of the possessing spirits and reminding onlookers that the shaman is now a vehicle for their action, and no longer an ordinary human being. Joan Halifax records the healing song of a Yukaghir shaman from Siberia:[14]

> listen
> I'm a shaman
> spirits rise for me
> draw near me now
> help me

listen you
invisible one
my scream's a storm
covering this world
leave this man
this sick one here
leave this man
alone

Shamanism in the Industrialized West

Recent years have witnessed a rapid growth of interest in "shamanism" and shamanic practices, most notably in the United States, but also throughout Europe. There are now a number of popular glossy magazines dedicated to shamanism, or which regularly include items on shamanism, and each year sees the publication of new books, from the academic monograph to the more popular coffee-table variety. One can buy shamanic drums and other associated paraphernalia in specialist shops, by mail order, or via the Internet, and an increasing number of organizations and individuals advertise shamanic workshops – all of which attest to the current marketability of shamanism.[15]

Piers Vitebsky succinctly contextualizes contemporary interest in shamanism in the following passage:

> From the 1970s, new shamanic movements have sprung up in the USA and Europe. These combine the legacy of the drug culture of the 1960s with a long-standing interest in non-Western religions, current environmentalist movements, strands of the New Age movement and all the various forms of self-help and self-realization. Popular anthropology has also contributed, especially via the work of Castaneda. These movements take the strongest form of the view that shamanism is opposed to institutionalized religion and political systems and speak of a democratization of shamanism in which every person can be empowered to become their own shaman. They think of shamanism not so much as a religion but as a view of reality and an effective technique. (Vitebsky, 1995, pp. 150–1)

Western shamanism does not always sit easily with the indigenous models to which it looks for inspiration and guidance. Vitebsky goes on to warn that:

> Traditional cultures form almost the entire history of shamanism and provide the basis for our knowledge about it, yet they contain integral elements which are incompatible with other New Age values such as vegetarianism, feminism

or a desire to separate healing completely from sorcery. There is a risk that the new shamanists may create their own ideal image of shamanism and then judge traditional societies as failing to live up to this image. (Vitebsky, 1995, p. 151)

This is what has happened in Eliade's work, with its evolutionary stages of "authentic shamanism," in which celestial ascent was foregrounded, succeeded by a "diluted" or "subsidiary" shamanism in which spirit possession is more common – virtually all documented cases falling into the latter category. Another possible risk is that indigenous peoples feel that their knowledge has been "stolen" or hijacked by Westerners for their own purposes. Tensions have arisen in particular in the relationships between some white and Native Americans, with the former accused of neo-imperialism in respect of Native American knowledge. Skills and formulae that are traditionally restricted to initiates are disseminated, and often commercialized, leaving indigenous peoples feeling belittled and betrayed. In response, urban practitioners sometimes argue that shamanic techniques are not the property of one particular people, but of humanity as a whole; others emphasize their pedigree as an indigene, either via an apprenticeship, by adoption, or through genetic inheritance, giving them a claim to authenticity and the right to teach others their techniques.

Carlos Castaneda and Don Juan

The first introduction to shamanism for many Westerners is via the printed word. One of the most influential sources remains the work of Carlos Castaneda, author of a series of highly successful books featuring a Yaqui Indian, Don Juan Matus. Castaneda claimed that while carrying out research in Arizona on the use of medicinal plants he was introduced to the white-haired old Indian sorcerer, "Don Juan," and became his apprentice. The first book, *The Teachings of Don Juan: a Yaqui Way of Knowledge*, published by the University of California Press in 1968, became an immediate bestseller. The "autobiographical" account of Castaneda's adventures in the first part of the book are followed by a shorter section entitled "A Structural Analysis," which is presumably intended to signal the academic credentials of the work. Castaneda's Ph.D. thesis in anthropology (1973) from the University of California, Los Angeles, consists largely of the text of this previously published work. *The Teachings of Don Juan* became the first of a series of ten books in which the narrative element remained uppermost. Some academics, among others, have subsequently expended considerable time and energy "exposing" Castaneda as a fraud – or at least demonstrating that whatever else his writings are, they cannot be considered as serious ethnography.[16] There are other scholars, however, who are happy to extend the term "ethnography" to include imaginative and fictive genres, including the adventures of the young Carlos and his mentor Don Juan. Castaneda was not the first writer to use mind-altering drugs, which feature prominently in Don Juan's teachings, to experience non-ordinary reality, and to seek to describe those experiences to others. Where Castaneda scored over other authors was in the added element of romantic exoticism, derived from situating his experiences within the cosmological framework of an indigenous small-scale society.[17]

Castaneda himself remained an enigmatic figure to the end. He was rarely photographed, tape-recorded, or interviewed, and was evasive about his personal life.[18] His former wife, Margaret Runyan Castaneda, seems to indicate in her autobiographical account *A Magical Journey with Carlos Castaneda* (1996) that fact and fiction were interwoven in Castaneda's accounts of his apprenticeship with Don Juan. Castaneda himself, however, maintained that the accounts were true – and that it was the very otherness of the world view described that challenged the reader's sense of the real. The knowledge Castaneda claimed to have gained through his training as a *nagual* (sorcerer) is synthesized in a new martial arts technique, *Tensegrity*, aimed at increasing awareness of the energy fields of which human beings are comprised. Through his books and Tensegrity workshops Castaneda is regarded by many Americans as the father of neo-shamanism. A quick browse of the Internet will reveal dozens of organizations, books, periodicals, and workshops claiming to link secularized, urbanized men and women to the wisdom of their prehistoric ancestors, a wisdom thought to be perilously preserved in a few remaining traditional shamans in indigenous small-scale societies.

Michael Harner and the Foundation for Shamanic Studies

Arguably the best known and most influential of Castaneda's successors is Michael Harner, an academic anthropologist who has spent many years researching shamanic techniques in the Americas and in northern Europe (Saamiland). Harner received training in shamanic techniques from the Jivaro in the Upper Amazon during his fieldwork in the early 1960s, and became convinced that the insights he gained were applicable to all people, and that the forebears of white Americans and Europeans had once had similar abilities. In 1980 Harner published his self-help manual for would-be Western shamans, *The Way of the Shaman*, which became an immediate best seller. The book was based on the experience gained from nearly a decade of leading workshops on what Harner terms "core" shamanism. In 1987, two organizations founded by Harner for the preservation and dissemination of shamanic knowledge were amalgamated into the non-profit-making *Foundation for Shamanic Studies*. Although the use of drugs was central to Harner's own early experiments in shamanism, this is not publicly acceptable in contemporary America or Europe, and Harner encourages instead the use of drumming to reach an altered state of consciousness (ASC) in which it is possible to experience non-ordinary reality. In his introductory text, *The Elements of Shamanism*, Neville Drury claims that he was attracted to Harner's shamanism by its simplicity and democracy. From his own experience of running workshops, Drury states that:

> However, one thing never ceases to amaze me – that within an hour or so of drumming, ordinary city folk are able to tap extraordinary mythic realities that they have never dreamed of. It is as if they are discovering a lost fairyland of cosmic imagery from within the depths of the psyche. During the "sharings" which are a part of the workshops, all these marvellous revelations pour forth. (Drury, 1992, pp. ix–x)

Shamanic counseling

As in traditional small-scale societies, Western shamans often use their skills to heal others. Many of those who participate in shamanic workshops or who otherwise seek to acquire shamanic powers work in the caring professions, and want to enhance the service they can offer to clients (see Jakobsen, 1999). It is not uncommon for individual Westerners to set themselves up as shamanic healers, perhaps after serving an apprenticeship with or observing indigenous shamans at work. One of the key differences between Western and traditional shamanic counseling or healing, however, is the nature of the shamanic vocation. In most "traditional" societies shamanic powers are restricted to a few individuals, and may be regarded as a menace as much as a blessing. According to neo-shamanic teachings, however, we are all encouraged to access a "shamanic state of consciousness" (SSC). Shamanism becomes a means of making sense of and gaining control over one's life, of expanding one's view of reality, and of getting in touch with aspects of an inner mental world. Almost anyone, using the right techniques, can find his or her own power animals and places and use them for self-healing. The shamanic counselor may go on a soul journey on behalf of the client (patient), or may act rather as a midwife or facilitator, encouraging the client to find and deal with the cause of the malaise himself or herself. Clients can achieve an altered state of consciousness so as to journey to the upper and lower worlds and meet their spirit animals in the comfort of their own homes, and then recount their experiences to the shamanic counselor in a formal therapy session.[19] The publicity surrounding "shamanic" healing in the Philippines, in which the healer removes objects from the patient's body without actually using surgical techniques, has also attracted followers in theWest, and forms part of the repertoire of some independent shamanic healers.[20]

Conclusion

In this chapter I have focused on two main aspects of shamanism. After alerting the reader to very different uses of the term shamanism, I looked at its "traditional" northern form as found among the natives of Siberia, Green-land, northern Scandinavia and the Inuit of Canada and Alaska. In the second part of the chapter I explored some aspects of the recent rise of New Age, urban or core shamanism. Whether one wishes to apply the same term to both these phenomena is a matter of personal judgment – they are certainly very different, although neo-shamanism is heavily dependent on the real or imagined sha-manic practices of indigenous peoples. In her book *Shamanism: Traditional and Contemporary Approaches to the Mastery of Spirits and Healing*, Merete Demant Jakobsen makes some interesting comparisons between the shamanism of eighteenth- and nineteenth-century Greenland, and that encountered in workshops led by a former colleague of Harner. The democratic element of self-improvement characteristic of urban shamanism has already been noted. Another difference between core shamanism and that of the Greenlanders is in their fundamentally differing world views.

> It is crucial to understand the difference between the concept of spirits among the Greenlanders, where they are seen at best as neutral, at worst as malevo-lent, and where they have to be controlled in order to be helping spirits, and core-shamanism where the spirits are mostly benevolent and are easily attracted to the assistance of the questing course participant. The relationship between fear and accumulation of spirits is played down in the courses and although the participants are aware of their own fears, the experience of the journey mostly confirms the harmonious relationship that the courses aim to establish with non-ordinary reality. (Jakobsen, 1999, p. 218)

For these Western shamans the spirits are allies, and gently guide the participant. They are not dangerous forces that have to be mastered and controlled. Jakobsen consequently advocates making a clear distinction between shamanism as found in Greenland and other circumpolar societies and the shamanic behavior of urban shamans.

What such comparisons do teach us is that religious behavior may have universal elements, but that it is also highly dependent upon its social and physical environment. Carlos Castaneda's descriptions of altered reality and Michael Harner's drumming groups appeal to urbanized Westerners because they draw on motifs familiar in Western cultures. They successfully integrate elements of New Age thinking, psychoanalytic practice, and popular culture with the exoticism of the prehistoric and indigenous "other" – with the search for roots and for ancient wisdom. And, for many people, it works. Shamanism in China, Greenland, or among the Tungus is also dependent on its cultural context for meaning. In a cold, barren, and inhospitable environment the spirits are hostile, not allies of an ecologically friendly earth mother. Beliefs and practices do not exist in an abstract world apart from the people who embody them, and act them out in rituals and in the minutiae of their daily lives. The study of shamanism in different societies, including the West, requires the scholar of religion to pay due attention to the social and cultural worlds that sustain the shaman.

Notes

1   Jakobsen (1999) makes the distinction between being possessed and possessing central to a definition of the shaman's role. Lewis employs the idiom of domestication to distinguish between passive and active spirit possession.

2   See, for example, Ellis Davidson (1988, pp. 96, 161), Low (1996, p. 110), and, at a more popular level, Drury (1992, pp. 2–3). The neolithic pastoralist who perished while crossing the Alps was initially claimed to be a shaman, following the widespread tendency among archaeologists to assign a religious significance to an individual, artifact, or site when no more obvious utilitarian use is apparent, or which is poorly understood.

3   For an informative and scholarly account of contemporary shamanic workshops, see Jakobsen (1999).

4   See Eliade (1988, pp. 4, 495–6).

5   It could be argued, alternatively, that neo-shamanism focuses on the shamanic practitioner, with little reference to the cosmological belief system which traditionally supports it, despite the popularity of ritual paraphernalia, such as drums, costumes, and incense. Psychotropic drugs, which figured prominently in the shamanic experiences of Castaneda and Harner, are not normally advocated in neo-shamanic workshops.

6   Cited in Halifax (1990, p. 6).

7   Jakobsen (1999, p. 133, n.9). The quotations are from pages 172 and 178 of Rasmussen's text. The comments between the quotations from Rasmussen are Jakobsen's gloss on the text.

8   See Jakobsen (1999) and Mousalimas (1995).

9   Originally published in *Asia*, 24(4), 1929, pp. 335–6.
10 Quoted in Lewis (1989, p. 32).
11 I am following Lewis (1986, chapter 5, "The Shaman's Career"). Lewis links
    these stages to possession cults more generally.
12 In South America shamanic and political power are more likely to coexist in the
    same individual, such as a village headman (see Chagnon, 1968).
13 In Greenland, where there are no trees, an *axis mundi* is not a feature of the
    trance séance (Merete Demant Jakobsen, personal communication). In other
    parts of the Arctic, however, a ladder or pole may substitute for a tree.
14 Halifax (1990, p. 57). Taken from Cloutier (1973, p. 11).
15 Examples of shamanic or other relevant journals include *Shaman's Drum:
    a Journal of Experiential Shamanism*, published by the Cross Cultural Shamanism
    Network, Oregon (USA), *Sacred Hoop*, published in Evesham (England), and
    Kindred Spirit, published in Totnes (England).
16 One of Castaneda's most persistent critics, Richard de Mille (1976, 1980), decon-
    structed Castaneda's sources to the extent that it would be very difficult to
    maintain that they were based on ethnography rather than fiction. Daniel Noel
    (1998, pp. 83ff) is wrong, however, in imagining that anthropology's literary turn
    or its various novelistic experiments are analogous to Castaneda's fiction. In the
    latter case the fiction was masquerading as fact. Most mainstream anthropology
    distinguishes clearly between ethnography and fiction, or where the two are
    intentionally interwoven, is up-front about this. Experimentation with different
    genres may give access to a more rounded picture of a society, and it is recognized
    that the most accurate descriptions possible are still literary constructs. This is very
    different, however, from an intention to deceive the reader.
17 Writers such Aldous Huxley, Timothy Leary, and Gordon Wasson also wrote
    about their experiments with hallucinogenic drugs in the 1950s and 1960s, and
    became cult figures in the student movements of the 1960s and 1970s.
18 Castaneda died of liver cancer on April 27, 1998, according to his executor
    Deborah Drooz, and was cremated, with his ashes being taken to Mexico. Little is
    known of his origins, although immigration records indicated that he was born
    on December 25, 1925, in Cajamarca, Peru. A volume of *Contemporary Authors*,
    on the other hand, records his birth as December 25, 1931, in São Paulo, Brazil
    (www.dailynews.com/sections/us/DailyNews/castaneda).
19 We can see a parallel here with the relationship between psychoanalyst and
    analysand.
20 Similar techniques are used by Native Americans in the United States and
    elsewhere.

References and Further Reading

Ahlbäck, Tore (ed.) (1987) *Saami Religion*. Based on papers read at the Symposium on
    Saami Religion, Åbo, Finland. Åbo: The Donner Institute for Research in Religious

and Cultural History. Distributed by Almqvist and Wiksell International, Stockholm.

Balzer, Marjorie Mandelstam (ed.) (1997) *Shamanic Worlds: Rituals and Lore of Siberia and Central Asia*. New York and London: North Castle Books.

Castaneda, Carlos (1976) *The Teachings of Don Juan: a Yaqui Way of Knowledge*. Harmondsworth: Penguin (first published in 1968).

Castaneda, Margaret Runyan (1996) *A Magical Journey with Carlos Castaneda*. New York: Book World Press.

Chagnon, Napoleon (1968) *Yanomamo: the Fierce People*. New York: Holt, Rinehart and Winston.

Cloutier, D. (1973) *Spirit, Spirit*. Providence, RI: Berg.

De Mille, Richard (1976) *Castaneda's Journey: the Power and the Allegory*. Santa Barbara, CA: Capra.

De Mille, Richard (ed.) (1980) *The Don Juan Papers: Further Castaneda Controversies*. Santa Barbara, CA: Ross-Erickson.

Drury, Nevill (1992) *The Elements of Shamanism*. Shaftesbury: Element Books.

Eliade, Mircea (1988) *Shamanism: Archaic Techniques of Ecstasy*. London: Arkana, Penguin (first published in 1964).

Ellis Davidson, H. R. (1988) *Myths and Symbols in Pagan Europe: Early Scandinavian and Celtic Religions*. Manchester: Manchester University Press.

Evans-Pritchard, E. E. (1972) *Theories of Primitive Religion*. Oxford: Oxford University Press (first published in 1965).

Glazier, Stephen D. (ed.) (1997) *Anthropology of Religion: a Handbook. Part IV: Shamanism and Religious Consciousness*. Westport, CT and London: Greenwood Press.

Grim, John A. (1987) *The Shaman: Patterns of Religious Healing Among the Ojibway Indians*. Norman and London: University of Oklahoma Press.

Halifax, Joan (1990) *Shaman: the Wounded Healer*. London: Thames & Hudson.

Halifax, Joan (1991) *Shamanic Voices: a Survey of Visionary Narratives*. New York: Arkana, Penguin.

Harner, Michael (1990) *The Way of the Shaman*. New York: HarperCollins (first published in 1980).

Holm, Gustav (1914) *Legends and Tales from Angmagsalik*. Collected by G. Holm. *Meddeleelser om Grønland*, Bd. 39.

Hultkrantz, Åke (1992) *Shamanic Healing and Ritual Drama: Health and Medicine in Native North American Religious Traditions*. New York: Crossroad.

Hultkrantz, Åke (1993) Introductory remarks on the study of shamanism. *Shaman: an International Journal for Shamanistic Research*, 1(1), 3–14.

Humphrey, Caroline, with Urgunge Onon (1996) *Shamans and Elders: Experience, Knowledge and Power among the Daur Mongols*. Oxford: Clarendon Press.

Goodman, Felicitas D. (1990) *Where Spirits Ride the Wind: Trance Journeys and Other Ecstatic Experiences*. Bloomington and Indianapolis: Indiana University Press.

Jakobsen, Merete Demant (1999) *Shamanism: Traditional and Contemporary Approaches to the Mastery of Spirits and Healing*. Oxford: Berghahn.

Kalweit, Holger (1992) *Shamans, Healers, and Medicine Men*. Boston and London: Shambhala.

Kressing, Frank (1997) Candidates for a theory of shamanism. A systematic survey of recent research results from Eurasia and Native America. *Shaman*, 5(2), 115–41.

Lewis, I. M. (1986) *Religion in Context: Cults and Charisma*. Cambridge: Cambridge University Press.

Lewis, I. M. (1989) *Ecstatic Religion: a Study of Shamanism and Spirit Possession*, 2nd edn. London and New York: Routledge (first published in 1971).

Low, Mary (1996) *Celtic Christianity and Nature: Early Irish and Hebridean Traditions*. Edinburgh: Edinburgh University Press.

Merkur, Daniel (1985) *Becoming Half Hidden: Shamanism and Initiation among the Inuit*. Stockholm Studies in Comparative Religion 24. Stockholm: Almqvist and Wiksell International.

Mousalimas, S. A. (1995) *The Transition from Shamanism to Russian Orthodoxy in Alaska*. Providence, RI and Oxford: Berghahn.

Nicholson, Shirley (compiler) (1987) *Shamanism: an Expanded View of Reality*. Wheaton, IL: Quest Books.

Noel, Daniel C. (1998) *The Soul of Shamanism: Western Fantasies, Imaginal Realities*. New York: Continuum.

Rasmussen, Knud (1921) *Myter og Sagn fra Grønland I*. Copenhagen: Gyldendalske Boghandel.

Rasmussen, Knud (1929) *Intellectual Culture of the Iglulik Eskimos*. Report of the Fifth Thule Expedition. Copenhagen: Gyldendalske Boghandel, Nordisk Forlag.

Reichel-Dolmatoff, Gerardo (1997) *Rainforest Shamans: Essays on the Tukano Indians of the Northwest Amazon*. Dartington: Themis Books.

Riches, David (1994) Shamanism: the key to religion. *Man* (new series), 29(2), pp. 381–405.

Rutherford, Ward (1986) *Shamanism: the Foundations of Magic. A History of the Shamanic Tradition from Its Origins to the Present Day*. Wellingborough: The Aquarian Press.

Rydving, Håkan (1993) The end of drum-time: religious change among the Lule Saami, 1670s–1740s. Doctoral dissertation, Uppsala. Distributed by Almqvist and Wiksell International, Stockholm.

Shirokogoroff, S. M. (1982) *Psychomental Complex of the Tungus*. London: Kegan Paul, Trench, Trubner & Co. Ltd (first published in 1935).

Siikala, A. L. (1978) *The Rite Technique of the Siberian Shaman*. Helsinki: FF Communications.

Vitebsky, Piers (1995) *The Shaman: Voyages of the Soul, Trance, Ecstasy and Healing from Siberia to the Amazon*. London and Basingstoke: Macmillan in association with Duncan Baird Publishers.

Ward, Keith (1994) *Religion and Revelation: a Theology of Revelation in the World's Religions*. Oxford: Clarendon Press.

Chapter 8

Witchcraft and the Evil Eye

Introduction

Studies of witchcraft and the evil eye may seem to represent the "exotic" end of anthropological studies of religion, where people are least like "us" (the Western, rational, post-Enlightenment individual) and at their most illogical, romantic, or mysterious. In fact, beliefs and practices concerning witchcraft and the evil eye reveal an attitude to the natural world and to moral relationships within it that is both pervasive and enduring. In the West this way of thinking is mainly associated with peasant cultures, but it can also be found to some extent within the revival of contemporary Paganism, which draws largely on an educated, urban clientele. So what does this cosmology consist of? One of its most fundamental ideas is that of a life force, essence or energy within people. This is commonly extended to non-human animals, other living creatures, and even inanimate and invisible, or seldom visible, objects, such as rocks, rivers, and spirits of various kinds. This life force can be captured or harmed by others whose own life force is more powerful, malevolent, or in some way out of control. The metaphor is often one of cannibalistic consumption or draining of the victim's life. This harm is effected at the psychic level, but will be reflected in the biological and material state of the victim. The aggressor may use instruments, such as incantations, spells, ritual objects, and actions in order to steal or harm the life force of victims, or may injure them unwittingly. It is prudent to protect oneself from psychic attack, but if overcome a specialist is usually called upon to counteract the effects of psychic aggression. The specialist may seek to deflect the attack away from the victim, possibly back onto the aggressor, or to identify the aggressor and force him or her to take counter actions to remove the harm done.

Another fundamental notion is that of limited good. There is only a certain finite amount of health, wealth, and happiness to go around. If someone is particularly successful, fertile, and fortunate in life there is an assumption that they have profited at someone else's expense. The prosperous may fear those who are less well-off, because of the power of their jealousy, and perhaps from a sense of guilt and arising from the shared assumption that in a zero-sum game the only "fair" system is one in which good fortune is distributed as evenly as possible.

Different parts of the world have their own cultural elaborations of this form of thinking. In much of sub-Saharan Africa the idiom is one of witchcraft or sorcery. The witch seeks to "eat" the flesh of the victim, causing him or her to sicken. Witchcraft is "hot" and needs to be "cooled." In India, Europe, and Semitic countries (the Arab and Jewish worlds and diaspora), the dominant idiom is one of wet and dry rather than hot and cold.[1] The vital essence is conceived as liquid and the victim is drained. Recovering moisture is a vital part of recovering one's life force. These ideas are commonly expressed through belief in the "evil eye," although this may coexist with belief in the actions of witches and sorcerers.

All that we have said in previous chapters concerning the problems of translation also applies in this case. Using terms like "witchcraft" or "sorcery" implies similarity where it may not exist. There is always a tension in anthropology between the desire to understand cultural phenomena in context, favoring the use of the vernacular, and the comparative project, which attempts to make broader theoretical statements.[2] The term "witchcraft" and designation "witch" are used, for instance, in at least four very distinct ways. Although there are common threads it is important to distinguish between them.

1 In medieval and early modern Europe the older village practices of cursing and blessing, healing and manipulating people and objects, sometimes referred to as *malefice*, became inextricably linked with Christian theology.[3]

2 Church reformers identified witches or sorcerers as adversaries of Christianity and agents of Satan, projecting onto those identified an inversion of all that was considered holy and civilized.

3 African witchcraft and sorcery is closer to older European notions of *malefice* and the evil eye than it is to this Christianized "shadow" version of its own image (that continues to haunt the popular European imagination and to manifest itself in anti-witchcraft scares). In Africa too, European missionaries tried to fit the African world view, which in many instances included belief in the power of witches, into a Christian (or anti-Christian) framework.

4 In recent years we have seen the growth of Western "Pagan" forms of witchcraft. These may be consciously experimental, drawing eclectically

on many traditions and creating new ones, as with Wicca and some other forms of the Craft, or they may claim continuity with a hidden tradition that is said to have survived years of persecution through secrecy and oral transmission, primarily within families.

To describe village *malefice*, the witches of the church inquisitors, contemporary African witchcraft, and Wicca with a single term is evidently a risky business. Each reader will have in his or her mind a particular image of a witch, based upon previous reading and experience, and this can color and distort the phenomena described. In this chapter I therefore attempt to make clear what I am referring to when using such common but misleading terms as witchcraft or sorcery. The argument for retaining their use is to point to similarities that do exist, as well as to fall in with conventional usage. Despite the drawbacks inherent in retaining witchcraft as a descriptive and analytical category, it continues to serve as a useful shorthand.

The main focus of this chapter is *African witchcraft*, looking at Evans-Pritchard's famous work *Witchcraft, Oracles and Magic among the Azande*. Zande notions of witchcraft are compared to those from elsewhere in sub-Saharan Africa, particularly Cameroon. Moving to Europe, Jeanne Favret-Saada's work on *witchcraft in rural France* provides a link between both contemporary Africa and older village *malefice* as understood in Western societies. There are also parallels between the notion of the *evil eye* and witchcraft as experienced and described by Favret-Saada. The third section of the chapter focuses on the evil eye, including Alan Dundes's attempt to synthesize various explanations into a framework of "wet" and "dry." The final section addresses the *debate on mentalities*, already touched upon in earlier discussions of Evans-Pritchard's work on the Azande. Lucien Lévy-Bruhl suggested that there were two ways of thinking, one rational in developed societies, and the other prelogical and mystical in primitive societies. Although he later modified his views, the debate Lévy-Bruhl initiated on comparative cognition continues, with rationality still a hotly debated issue within anthropology.

Witchcraft in Africa

Nigerian writer E. B. Idowu gives a succinct definition of African witchcraft, although it is not true to suggest, as Idowu implies, that his description applies to the whole continent. The following account fits Bantu and West African peoples best, although there are similar beliefs elsewhere in the continent.

The observer from elsewhere outside African culture may hold whatever theory appeals to him most on the subject. To Africans of every category, witchcraft is an urgent reality. There are African investigators who have come to the realisation that in speaking or writing about witchcraft, the *actual* belief of Africans must come first. African concepts about witchcraft consist in the belief that the spirits of living human beings can be sent out of the body, mind or estate; that witches have guilds or operate singly, and that the spirits sent out of the human body can act either visibly or through a lower creature – an animal or bird. . . . It is generally believed that the guild of witches have their regular meetings and ceremonies in forests or in open places in the middle of the night. The meeting is the meeting of "souls," "spirits," of the witches. In several places in Africa, it is believed that the spirits leave the bodies of witches in the form of a particular kind of bird. Their main purpose is to wreak havoc on other human beings; and the operation is the operation of spirits upon spirits, that is, it is the ethereal bodies of the victims that are attacked, extracted, and devoured; and this is what is meant when it is said that witches have sucked the entire blood of the victim. Thus, in the case of witches or their victims, spirits meet spirits, spirits operate upon spirits, while the actual human bodies lie "asleep" in their homes. (Idowu, 1978, pp. 175–6)

Evans-Pritchard and the Azande

The most influential work on African witchcraft remains Edward Evans-Pritchard's 1937 classic *Witchcraft, Oracles, and Magic among the Azande*. Although it was only one of several books that Evans-Pritchard wrote about the Azande, it is undoubtedly the most widely read. Oxford University Press produced an abridged paperback version in 1976, and extracts from the book have been widely anthologized. The Azande, when Evans-Pritchard studied them in the 1920s and 1930s, numbered about half a million. They are still mainly agriculturists, living in the southern Sudan and eastern Congo. In some societies witchcraft is hidden or denied, but not among the Azande. As Evans-Pritchard records:

I had no difficulty in discovering what Azande think about witchcraft, nor in observing what they do to combat it. These ideas and actions are on the surface of their life and are accessible to anyone who lives for a few weeks in their homesteads. Every Zande is an authority on witchcraft. There is no need to consult specialists. There is not even need to question Azande about it, for information flows freely from recurrent situations in their social life, and one has only to watch and listen. *Mangu*, witchcraft, was one of the first words I heard in Zandeland, and I heard it uttered day by day throughout the months. (Evans-Pritchard, 1976, p. 1)

The Azande distinguish between witches and sorcerers, although this is by no means the case everywhere in Africa.[4]

Witchcraft: for the Azande, a psychic power inherited from a parent of the same sex. Witchcraft substance can be detected in the body by autopsy after a person has died. Witchcraft may be used to harm others either consciously or unconsciously by sending out or activating witchcraft substance. The Azande refer to witchcraft as *mangu* and a witch as *boro (ira) mangu*.

Sorcery: bad or illicit magic involving the conscious use of medicines in order to harm others. Sorcery is a skill that can be learnt, rather than a disposition that is inherited. The Azande terms used to describe sorcery are *gbegbere (gbigbita) ngua* or *kitikiti ngua*. A sorcerer is *ira gbegbere (kitikiti) ngua* (Evans-Pritchard, 1976, pp. 227–8).

The word *ngua* is used for magic more generally, with the Azande distinguishing between good and bad magic. It is, however, witchcraft that most concerns the Azande. It is not an infrequent and frightening event, but part of everyday life. Hunting, fishing, agriculture, the domestic life of the homestead, and the communal life of the village and court are all arenas for the activity of witches. Almost anything that happens may be referred to in terms of witchcraft.

> If blight seizes the ground-nut crop it is witchcraft; if the bush is vainly scoured for game it is witchcraft; if women laboriously bale water out of a pool and are rewarded by but a few small fish it is witchcraft; if termites do not rise when their swarming is due and a cold useless night is spent in waiting for their flight it is witchcraft; if a wife is sulky and unresponsive to her husband it is witchcraft; if a prince is cold and distant with his subject it is witchcraft; if a magical rite fails to achieve its purpose it is witchcraft; if, in fact, any failure or misfortune falls upon anyone at any time and in relation to any of the manifold activities of his life it may be due to witchcraft unless there is strong evidence, and subsequent oracular confirmation, that sorcery or some other evil agent has been at work, or unless they are clearly to be attributed to incompetence, breach of a taboo, or failure to observe a moral rule. (Evans-Pritchard, 1976, p. 18)

The reaction is one of annoyance rather than terror, and the Zande man has means at his disposal to deal with the attack (a woman must ask her husband or a kinsman to act on her behalf). When witchcraft is suspected a man will consult an oracle in order to confirm that witchcraft is the cause of the misfortune and to identify the witch or witches. Once the witch is known, preventative action can be taken, forcing the witch to withdraw the attack by cooling his or her witchcraft substance. The oracles vary, starting with the poor man's termite oracle, in which two sticks are inserted into a termite mound while the man asks specific questions such as "If X is a witch then eat the stick." The rubbing board oracle involves a specialist operator who slides one piece of wood over another as similar yes/no questions are posed, the friction of the wood giving the answers. The most prestigious oracle is the poison oracle *benge*, which can be used only with the authority of the chief. The poison, with a strychnine base, is found in a wild forest creeper and is administered to chicks as the operator puts the questions to the oracle. There is a double check on the procedure. If the question was initially phrased, "If Y is a witch, then let the fowl die," and the chick were to die, then the same question would be repeated a second time, but with the injunction to let the chick live. If witchcraft is confirmed, the accused is presented with the bird's wing as a sign of his or her guilt, and may be summoned to the chief's court to answer the charges.

One reason why witchcraft beliefs have continued to thrive in much of sub-Saharan Africa among Christianized populations is that Christianity sometimes offers little in the way of explanation for life's exigencies.[5] In the West and in Islamic countries people may speak of good or bad luck, fate or the will of God, or perhaps regard misfortune as punishment, or as meaningless chance. The Azande and many other African peoples, however, can draw on a much more comprehensive hermeneutical system that also gives people the possibility of doing something about it. As Evans-Pritchard put it, witchcraft explains unfortunate events. Control is re-established in an otherwise uncertain world. Evans-Pritchard is at pains to point out that the Azande are not ignorant of cause and effect. They are simply "foreshortening the chain of events and in a particular social situation are selecting the cause that is socially relevant and neglecting the rest" (Evans-Pritchard, 1976, p. 25). Thus, if a man is killed by a spear in a skirmish with enemies the physiological cause of death is not socially relevant, as there is nothing that can be done to bring the man back to life. What can be done is to identify the witch who guided that particular spear to that particular man and to punish him (or her). "Hence if a man is killed by an elephant Azande say that the elephant is the first spear and that witchcraft is the second spear and that together they killed the man" (Evans-Pritchard, 1976, p. 26). Some of Evans-Pritchard's vivid examples serve to give a flavor of the way in which the Azande reason concerning witchcraft, an idiom that Evans-Pritchard found he soon adopted himself:

A boy knocked his foot against a small stump of wood in the centre of a bush path, a frequent happening in Africa, and suffered pain and inconvenience in consequence. Owing to its position on his toe it was impossible to keep the cut free from dirt and it began to fester. He declared that witchcraft had made him knock his foot against the stump. I always argued with Azande and criticized their statements, and I did so on this occasion. I told the boy that he had knocked his foot against the stump of wood because he had been careless, and that witchcraft had not placed it in his path, for it had grown there naturally. He agreed that witchcraft had nothing to do with the stump of wood being in his path but added that he had kept his eyes open for stumps, as indeed every Zande does most carefully, and that if he had not been bewitched he would have seen the stump. As a conclusive argument for his view he remarked that all cuts do not take days to heal but, on the contrary, close quickly, for that is the nature of cuts. Why, then, had his sore festered and remained open if there were no witchcraft behind it? This, as I discovered before long, was to be regarded as the Zande explanation of sickness. (Evans-Pritchard, 1976, pp. 19–20)

Evans-Pritchard shows how explanations of witchcraft provide the "missing link" in a chain of causation. There may be straightforward "natural" explanations for events, but these do not account for the element of synchronicity or chance that leads natural events and people to collide in time and space. Azande thought is presented as logical and rational (if mistaken according to Western scientific precepts). It is not that the Azande have no knowledge of natural causation and live in a mystical world, but that their philosophy fills the gaps in such a theory, so that the whole of life, and death, is imbued with meaning.

Evans-Pritchard managed to enter into Zande thinking, adopting the use of oracles in order to arrange his daily life (essential if he was to be effective in carrying out his fieldwork), while always seeking to relate Zande notions to his own. His style has sometimes been read as patronizing – he describes his arguments with the Azande over questions of logic, and is not prepared simply to accept and record their beliefs (as a proponent of the phenomenological method of the study of religion might try to do). Evans-Pritchard is fully engaged in his fieldwork experience and manages to present Zande ideas in a way that shows why they make perfect sense to those raised within that culture. Indeed, his arguments with the Azande can be seen as a sign of respect. He treated them as rational human beings who were perfectly capable of coming up with convincing explanations for their beliefs and actions, and he was interested to discover what these might be.

One example of Evans-Pritchard's attempts to make sense of his experience both in terms of Zande logic and in relation to his own background and epistemology concerns his sole physical encounter with witchcraft. Moving lights are said to emanate from the body of the sleeping witch as his or her activated witchcraft substance stalks its prey.

I have only once seen witchcraft on its path. I had been sitting late in my hut writing notes. About midnight, before retiring, I took a spear and went for my usual nocturnal stroll. I was walking in the garden at the back of my hut, amongst banana trees, when I noticed a bright light passing at the back of my servants' huts towards the homestead of a man called Tupoi. As this seemed worth investigation I followed its passage until a grass screen obscured the view. I ran quickly through my hut to the other side in order to see where the light was going to but did not regain sight of it. I know that only one man, a member of my household, had a lamp that might have given off so bright a light, but next morning he told me that what I had seen was witchcraft. Shortly after-wards, on the same morning, an old relative of Tupoi and an inmate of his homestead died. This event fully explained the light I had seen. I never discovered its real origin, which was possibly a handful of grass lit by someone on his way to defecate, but the coincidence of the direction along which the light moved and the subsequent death accorded well with Zande ideas. (Evans-Pritchard, 1976, p. 11)

Evans-Pritchard's account of Zande witchcraft is framed in terms of *structural-functional* explanations. He shows how accusations follow lines of tension, which in turn relate to Azande social institutions. Thus, although a prince may be suspected of witchcraft, he will never actually be accused by a commoner. A woman must ask her husband, or more occasionally a male relative, to consult oracles on her behalf. Not surprisingly, therefore, Evans-Pritchard never came across a case in which a woman accused her husband of witchcraft. Men, on the other hand, frequently put the names of their wives before the oracles as suspected witches. Evans-Pritchard saw witchcraft, in bringing tensions into the open and dealing with them publicly, as an institution that was a kind of safety valve, facilitating the smooth functioning of society and supporting the status quo.[6]

Child witches among the Bangwa

Another interesting functional account of witchcraft is Robert Brain's (1970) account of child witches among the Bangwa of South West Province in Anglophone Cameroon. The Bangwa make no distinction between sorcerers and witches, the term *lekang* (plural *begang*) being used to translate the English terms "witch," "sorcerer," and "spirit." Witchcraft accusations clearly follow lines of social tension, as among the Azande. The Bangwa are patrilineal, but do not practice primogeniture. Sons do not know which of their number will inherit their father's titles, widows, and various rights and powers until after his death. As a man does not trust his sons, the name of his successor is given to retainers (formerly captured slaves who did not have

kinship links in the area). Due to fear of witchcraft, Bangwa compounds are
built as far apart as is compatible with inheriting the right to farm in
a common territory, and half-brothers (children of the same father but
different mothers) are among those most feared as witches. Children of the
same mother, on the other hand, and kin related through the mother, form
a solidarity group (the *atsen'ndia*, literally the "buttocks" or "loins" of the
house) and rarely if ever accuse one another of witchcraft. Co-wives, who are
in constant competition for their husband's attention and the allocation of
resources – access to farm land, school fees, clothes, salt, and oil, for instance
– are always potential rivals and therefore potential witches.[7]

The presence of child witches cannot, however, be explained simply by
looking at social tensions, although accusations also followed structural
patterns, with half-siblings accusing one another of witchcraft.[8] Brain
comes up with an alternative theory, based on access to food resources.
When Robert Brain carried out his fieldwork among the Bangwa in the
1960s most meat and other high sources of protein such as eggs were, due
to a series of food taboos, reserved almost entirely for men. Witches, however, would be given meat in order to persuade them not to eat their victims
in the witchcraft realm.[9] Child sickness, very common in this area,[10] might
be attributed to the action of witches, but just as often it was assumed that
the child himself or herself was a witch, suffering for his or her actions.
According to the Bangwa a witch would transform into a "were animal," and
if this witch self was injured or encountered anti-witchcraft medicines, the
witch would suffer an appropriate reaction. Confession could lead to an
amelioration of the condition and, provided the actions the child confessed
to were not too serious, did not carry a heavy penalty. Children sometimes
confessed to being witches spontaneously (even if not sick), but others were
encouraged to do so, and when ill would be in a suggestible condition. Brain
paints a vivid picture of the conditions that might lead a child to admit to
being a witch:

> The atmosphere of the sick-room is conducive to confession. Disturbed by pain,
> delirious with fever, a child stops distinguishing between reality and hallucin-
> ation. A sick person is never left alone: crowds of kin and sympathizers pester
> him with well-meaning inquiries; he repeats his symptoms over and over again.
> What the visitors want to know, of course, are the real, the supernatural, causes
> of the illness. Veiled and not so veiled questions are put to the child: Where did
> you go? Did you change into a were-animal: Confess! Confess! In such an
> atmosphere confession may bring peace, and relief to a disordered mind.
> Throughout the illness the normal domestic activities of the one-roomed
> Bangwa hut continue for fifteen to twenty hours a day: small children crawl
> around the floor, visitors are fed, chickens fly over the raised threshold.

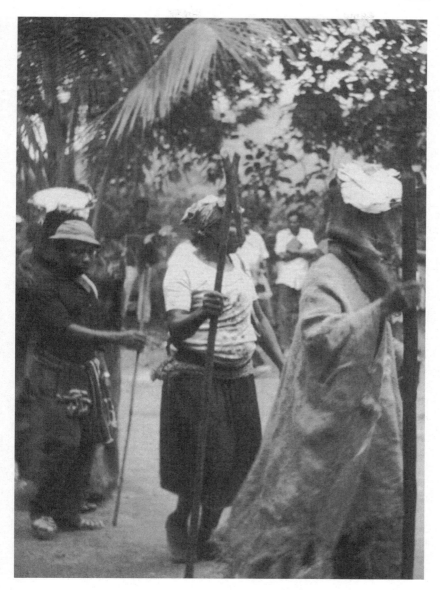

Figure 8.1 Masked members of a dead chief's Night Society at a "cry die" (funeral) in Fontem, Cameroon. The feared Bangwa Night Society (*tro*) are said to accompany a chief on his nightly witchcraft exploits.
© Fiona Bowie.

The mother prepares food, or goods to sell in the market. The sick child shares a bed with his brothers or sisters, or, if he is the last-born, with his mother; she copulates with her husband in the same bed. It is not only the European who finds the crowded, disturbed room oppressive during illness. (Brain, 1970, p. 170)

A confession of witchcraft normally meant a good meal. Relatives would bring chickens for the child to "bring him, or her, back out of the sky," the sky being the abode of witches. Robert Brain gives an example of the significance of protein for child witches. A boy of about fourteen confessed to his father that he and his witch companions – identified as other children and adults of the same neighborhood – had been to the sky, where they were eating his small sister, a girl who was at the time very ill. The Fon of Fontem (the paramount chief) was told, and at the next market day the Fon's retainers summoned the boy and his accomplices to attend the palace.[11] A goat was butchered and the boy demonstrated precisely how his sister had been eaten and the pieces divided among them in the witch-bush. Brain concludes the tale by relating that "The goat was divided accordingly, and to the accompaniment of hoots from the spectators the witches were told to go home and eat their meat, and leave the child alone. Not one of the group protested, but took his share and quietly went away. The girl, of course, recovered" (Brain, 1970, p. 174).

Some children learned to "play the system" and would give lurid accounts of their witchcraft activities, always stopping short of admitting to anything too serious. On other occasions, however, the results were more tragic. In one incident in which Robert Brain was himself involved, for instance, a child with tetanus was left untreated until it was too late as he confessed to having "eaten" a half-sibling, the child of a co-wife with whom his mother was having a dispute. When he died visitors congratulated the parents on losing a "child of the sky." Brain speculates that this could ease the pain for the mother, if she thought of her dead child as a witch (although as all Bangwa are thought to inherit their witchcraft substance from their mother, and only a successor his father's witchcraft in addition to that of his mother, this would be an ambivalent form of comfort, if, indeed, comfort at all).

Witchcraft as a social threat

While there is undoubtedly some merit in structural-functional accounts of witchcraft confessions and accusations, they can underplay the disruptive and often tragic nature of witchcraft in Africa. Uncertainty and rapid change have led to an increase in witchcraft accusations in many areas, and suspected witches may be attacked and killed. The local forces of law and order are often at a loss as to how to react, in some cases upholding accusations, treating the alleged witches as criminals, and in other cases dismissing accusations, regarding the accused as the victim. In Cameroon, fear of witchcraft generates numerous witch-curing societies that cross linguistic and ethnic lines. In one incident in Manyu Division (South West Province), described in the anglophone Cameroonian newspaper *The Herald* (June 5, 1995, p. 3), soldiers arrested the entire population of the village of Kesham and detained them at the divisional capital, Mamfe. The villagers were suspected of having buried alive a woman and her lover who were believed to be "responsible for the surprise death of 22 people within two weeks in the village." The couple had been identified by the village *obasinjom*, a secret witch-curing society, and given a beating. When the deaths continued, the villagers "decided to have both Anthony and Mary tried by the traditional council and reportedly taken to 'Ekpe Bust,' a dense forest where there were speculations that the lovers were either buried alive or tied to large stones and dumped into a river called Mah." The mother of the murdered woman was forced to leave the area for her own safety.[12] The newspaper reporting the incident sided with the villagers rather than the murdered couple, suggesting that the human rights of the arrested villagers had been violated, although they had subsequently been released for lack of evidence.

This not uncommon example indicates the dilemma faced by the authorities, torn between upholding a law based on individual rights and popular notions of justice that require witches to be punished.[13] In some areas state courts (as opposed to the less powerful "traditional" courts of local chiefs) have started to convict those accused of witchcraft, accepting the accusers' descriptions of how witches devoured the soul of their victims. Those who set themselves up as witch finders (in Cameroon often referred to by the widespread Bantu term *nganga*) acquire considerable power in such an environment.

Several writers have referred to the links between witchcraft and modernization.[14] In southern and western Cameroon, for instance, a new type of witchcraft, known as *ekong, kupe* (after Mount Kupe, where it is sometimes located), or *famla*, involves turning people into zombies and using them as slave labor. In return for wealth and success the witches must provide a victim from among their own family. The most numerous and economically (but not politically) powerful ethnic group in Cameroon are the Bamileke, and *famla* is sometimes put forward as an explanation for Bamileke success as traders, both expressing and fueling inter-ethnic tensions. In some areas physical locations are identified as witch markets – places where witches can go and exchange the flesh of their victims. Witches may also go to such places to take a kind of lucky dip package – it may contain riches and success or sickness and misfortune (see Pool, 1994, pp. 159–64). The notion of limited good and the leveling mechanisms often associated with witchcraft are combined with experience of and the fears associated with the growth of a capitalist economy.

It is not the case that all sub-Saharan peoples live in fear of witchcraft or blame it for their misfortunes. Colin Turnbull lived among the Mbuti pygmies of the Ituri forest (when it was part of the Belgian Congo), and contrasted the Mbuti lack of interest in witchcraft with its prominent role in the lives of their Bantu neighbors. The Mbuti, who are primarily forest hunter-gatherers, believe in malevolent supernatural powers, but not in inherited witchcraft substance. Both are seen as belonging to the world of the village, and they have no need of such concepts in the forest. The Mbuti's Bantu neighbors, who are farmers, use witchcraft as a mechanism for social control. The villagers believe that their superior understanding of witchcraft places the Mbuti in a position of dependence, as when a death occurs among the Mbuti the pygmies are ignorant of the appropriate mechanisms for divining who is responsible. Turnbull, however, argues that, far from increasing Mbuti dependence, witchcraft illustrates the pygmies' distance from the world of the village. The Mbuti have no need of witchcraft as an explanation for death. They have other mechanisms of social control and look for natural rather than supernatural causes to explain misfortune (Turnbull, 1976, pp. 59–60). These interesting contrasts point to the interrelationship of environment and social structure (see chapter 5) and their role in the formation of cosmological systems. Witchcraft in Europe has similarly been associated with an agricultural, peasant, subsistence economy and world view, and it is these links that we will explore next.

Witchcraft in Rural France

Jeanne Favret-Saada is a Parisian anthropologist who spent two and a half years studying witchcraft in north-western France, in what she termed the *bocage* or "hedge country," in the late 1970s. Favret-Saada faced a very different challenge from Evans-Pritchard or other anthropologists studying witchcraft in Africa, where most people never question its existence and talk about it constantly. She noted that most French work on witchcraft has been undertaken by folklorists. They have amassed data on witchcraft and unwitching rituals, but these tend to be abstracted from any social context. The person performing the ritual is seen as the least important factor, and his or her social relationships are ignored. Witchcraft was something that credulous peasants "believed in," which, by definition, could not be true. It was also the case that peasants in north-west France, like their Parisian neighbors, were educated in the dominant positivistic, scientific discourse of post-Enlightenment Europe. Favret-Saada's informants were well aware that to discuss witchcraft invited disbelief and invoked notions of backwardness.

> **Ensorceller,** "to bewitch." The term does not distinguish between witchcraft and sorcery. The witch, who is always identified as the male head of a family, is thought to use spells and ritual to achieve his ends.
> **Désorcelleur,** "unwitcher" – the person, male or female, who counters the power of the witch with his or her own power or "force."

The problem for Favret-Saada was where to start, as direct questions concerning witchcraft were met with denial and protestations of ignorance. She began by observing the words people used to express biological misfortune, such as death, sterility, and illness in animals and humans, in everyday conversations. The first thing she noticed was that people distinguished between ordinary misfortunes, which were accepted as a "one-off" and natural, and a series of misfortunes, which implied something more sinister. When several unfortunate events follow one another – a cow dies, a wife has a miscarriage, a child develops spots, the car runs into a ditch, the butter won't churn, the bread won't rise, and so on – then a couple will begin to ask themselves: what will happen next? Like everyone else they first consult the doctor, the vet, or the mechanic, looking for an explanation and a cure, but the professionals treat the incidents as separate events and fail to address the anxiety provoked by the series. The couple are left with the feeling that the symptoms may have been dealt with but that the cause of their misfortune has not been addressed.

If the couple approach a priest, perhaps fearing that they are going mad, they can meet with a range of possible responses. (1) The priest (like the doctor or the vet) may dismiss the misfortunes as part of the natural order and deny them any religious significance. In effect he is dismissing the couple's anxiety as superstition. (2) He can admit that there might be a supernatural explanation for their misfortunes, but view them as trials from God, rather than as the curse of a neighbor. (3) The priest may accept that there is evil intent and interpret the misfortunes as the work of the devil. He can then perform an exorcism, or call in the diocesan exorcist to perform one. In this way he is seen by the people as a small-scale unwitcher. He can protect people from evil spells but without sending them back on the witch. This might work if the spell is a small one, but if unsuccessful a more powerful unwitcher must be found.

The task of the unwitcher is to put him or herself between the witch and the victim, with the intention of deflecting the spell so that it rebounds on the witch. If the witch is more powerful than the unwitcher, the unwitcher may also be hurt by the spell. Favret-Saada was living with a family who believed themselves bewitched. When she suffered an accident she was seen as an unwitcher – but one whose lack of power meant that she herself had been harmed by the force that she had tried to block. Having been physically drawn into the witchcraft discourse, Favret-Saada was able to learn more about it and became apprenticed to a woman recognized as a more powerful unwitcher. She became her own informant, and observed the ways in which she was positioned by others. If witches did not exist, the discourse on witchcraft certainly did, and to that extent it was a reality in people's lives.

Favret-Saada found that the logic of witchcraft had to be sought in the economic and social relations of her informants. It was a peasant economy based on family-run farms. A man, his wife, children, livestock, and goods were considered as a single unit. As only one son, or sometimes a son-in-law, could inherit the family farm, there was inevitably tension within families concerning succession. Considerable personal skills and a rather thick skin were required by the one who inherited the farm to see off competing claims to the property, and to make a success of it. The rationale of witchcraft is dependent on a view of limited good and of a life force that can be attacked by others.

> It is presumed that a witch is "draining the force" from a farmer whose farm is affected by repeated misfortunes. (It is very likely that no one in the Bocage throws spells, which does not prevent people from being hit by them.) The witch is also head of a farm and family. Close, but not related to the bewitched, he is supposed to want to drain the normal or vital "force" of the bewitched, that is to say, the latter's capacity to produce, reproduce and survive. The witch is attributed an "abnormal force," always evil, which he is supposed to use by practising precise rituals, or through the ordinary means of communication – looking, speaking, and touching. . . . The "abnormal force" of the witch, draining the normal "force" of his victim makes the farms function like two communicating vessels: as one fills up with riches, health and life, the other empties out to the point of ruin or death. (Favret-Saada, 1989, p. 43)

Favret-Saada suggests that witchcraft therapies should be seen within a broader category of "remedial institutions." In the *bocage* the male head of the farm is always the primary target of an attack, but the wife is invariably the one who seeks a cure. She attempts to take back control of the situation by seeking out and then following the prescriptions of the unwitcher. This has a beneficial effect, first on the woman, and then on her husband as well. Although the witch is always identified as a neighbor (just far enough away to prevent the breakdown of reciprocal labor obligations from damaging the farm), Favret-Saada argues that the lines of tension exposed are not between neighbors but within families, particularly when succession is at stake. The misfortunes suffered may be the result of difficulties the heads of farms and families can have in establishing their claims to their house and land, and the discourse of witchcraft and the outside help it offers may enable them to take the necessary steps. Favret-Saada even suggests that those who seek the help of an unwitcher have usually been accused of being witches themselves. Becoming a victim and seeking curative action may therefore be another way of dealing with the practical and psychological pressures inherent in the economic life of the *bocage*.[15]

The Evil Eye

The evil eye is a widespread, but not universal, belief, confined mainly to India, the Middle East (including North Africa), Europe, and areas settled by people from these parts of the world. It is also far from dead. Students from the Channel Islands (which lie between the South of England and France) assure me that the evil eye is alive and well there, and even sophisticated Europeans or Americans who regard the evil eye as a quaint superstition often use phrases and perform actions, such as toasting someone's health, indicative of residual cultural belief in the evil eye.[16]

Alan Dundes gives a comprehensive general description of the evil eye in his article "Wet and Dry, the Evil Eye":

> The evil eye is a fairly consistent and uniform folk belief complex based upon the idea that an individual, male or female, has the power, voluntarily or involuntarily, to cause harm to another individual or his property merely by looking at or praising that person or property. The harm may consist of illness, or even death or destruction. Typically, the victim's good fortune, good health, or good looks – or unguarded comments about them – invite or provoke an attack by someone with the evil eye. If the object attacked is animate, it may fall ill. Inanimate objects such as buildings or rocks may crack or burst. Symptoms of illness caused by the evil eye include loss of appetite, excessive yawning, hiccoughs, vomiting, and fever. If the object attacked is a cow, its

milk may dry up; if a plant or a fruit tree, it may suddenly wither and die. Preventative measures include wearing apotropaic amulets, making specific hand gestures or spitting, and uttering protective verbal formulas before or after praising or complimenting a person, especially an infant. Another technique is concealing, disguising, or even denying good fortune. (Dundes, 1981, p. 258)

Apotropaic: turning away, or intending to deflect, evil. From the Greek *apo*, "from," plus *trope*, "turning."

Anthropological interest in the evil eye goes back to Edward Tylor (1890), and it is still the subject of debate between anthropologists.[17] Most documented instances of the evil eye, however, have been the work of folklorists. In the nineteenth century, Alexander Carmichael, a Scottish tax collector with a passion for oral literature, toured the Highlands and Islands of Scotland recording the Gaelic songs, incantations, prayers, and stories of the people. The results of his labors were eventually published under the title *Carmina Gadelica* ("Gaelic Songs"). Among Carmichael's blessings and curses are several on the evil eye, many interwoven with Christian elements. In the following example a verse to counter the effects of the evil eye ends with the words:

> If it be a man that has done thee
> harm,
> With evil eye,
> With evil wish,
> With evil passion,
>
> Mayest thou cast off each ill,
> Every malignity,
> Every malice,
> Every harassment,
> And mayest thou be well for ever,
> While this thread
> Goes round thee,
> In honour of God and Jesus,
> And of the Spirit of balm
> everlasting.[18]

Arnold van Gennep parodied the scholar who spent his entire life amassing material on the evil eye, which by the age of 54 had involved his mastering 843 languages and dialects, and who died at his library seat leaving eighteen million notes of no use to anyone.[19] More recently, however, different disciplinary perspectives have been applied to the phenomenon in an attempt to provide some type of explanation. Richard Coss (1981), for example, looked at psychological studies of eye contact and aversion in the search for a universal basis for beliefs concerning the evil eye. Coss notes that mammals, including humans, regard staring eyes as aggressive. The large, staring, less focused gaze of a baby, on the other hand, is regarded as appealing and as an invitation to bonding. In one experiment cited by Coss, large transparent panels displaying a single column of abstract, frowning eyes were hung in several shop entrances in an effort to reduce shoplifting. Apparently, potential shoppers walked briskly into the shop without looking at the goods near the panels. Shoplifting dropped dramatically during the test period, while total sales remained the same. Rupert Sheldrake (1994) has attempted to go one step further and find out whether people can sense they are being looked at, even via hidden security cameras. The results seem to indicate that a significant number of us are aware of the gaze of others, whether or not the observer is physically present.

Howard Stein, in his article on Slovak-Americans, focuses on another very frequently cited component of the evil eye – jealousy. His study looks at the way in which a discourse of jealousy and the evil eye manifests in childrearing practices, particularly weaning.

> In the folk idiom, "jealousy" is an act of will, secretly wanting what is not yours, wanting something you cannot have. One covetously desires to possess what one should not even want; one ambivalently remembers that distant "object" once tenuously "possessed," which in turn generates a boundless rage against the ambivalent object. Thus the very act of admiration can destroy the object of admiration. The only way to neutralize the effect of "jealousy" is to spit before uttering admiration; or if you suspect someone has put the Evil Eye on you, to perform the flotation experiments [which involve dropping hot coals or burning matches into water and seeing if they sink or float]. The Slovak explanation holds that the first "jealousy" is wanting the mother's breast when she does not wish to give it – when it has been withdrawn. One wishes to take when one is no longer given. But one must absolutely not give in to another's will. One remains steadfast, resolute, strong. The mother's will prevails over the child's wish and pleading. The rationale: if you get what you want (even) once, you will think you can have what you want every time you want something. The child, as the mother, learns to be alternately *will-less* and *wilful*. (Stein, 1981, pp. 244–5)

David Pocock (1981), an anthropologist, looked at the evil eye or *najar* among the Patidar caste in Gujarat, India. Pocock linked fear of the evil eye to tensions within the caste, particularly concerning differences of wealth and status. The evil eye is depicted as operating much like witchcraft in Africa or in north-west France. Ideally members of a single caste should enjoy a similar level of wealth, but in practice considerable differences exist. Fear of the envy of a poorer kinsman helps to ensure that wealth is enjoyed modestly rather than ostentatiously, and places the wealthy under an obligation to help caste members who are less well off.

Rather than looking at specific case studies, Alan Dundes attempts to synthesize data on the evil eye and to suggest some underlying principles. Etymologically there is a connection between the evil eye and jealousy. The English word "envy" is derived from the Latin *invidia*, which in turn derives from *in videre*, "to see." There is an assumption that to see something is to want it. A common reaction to seeing a desirable object is to praise it, and praise may well be tinted with envy. The existence of envy is, however, universal, whereas the evil eye is not. Dundes comes up with four interrelated folk ideas common to Indo-European and Semitic cultures. They may not be consciously articulated, but Dundes claims that they operate as underlying structural principles of thought, and help to make sense of an otherwise disparate range of phenomena. These four principles can be summarized as follows:

1   Life depends upon liquid. From the concept of "the water of life" to semen, milk, blood, bile, saliva, and the like, the consistent principle is that liquid means life while loss of liquid means death. Liquids are living; drying is dying!
2   There is a finite, limited amount of good – health, wealth, etc. – and because that is so, any gain by one individual can only come at the expense of another. If one individual possesses a precious body of fluid, semen, for instance, this automatically means that some other individual lacks that same fluid.
3   Life entails an equilibrium model. If one has too little wealth or health, one is poor or ill. Such individuals constitute threats to persons with sufficient and abundant wealth and health. This notion may be in part a projection on the part of well-to-do individuals. They think they should be envied and so they project such wishes to the have-nots. On the other hand, the have-nots are often envious for perfectly good reasons of their own.
4   In symbolic terms, a pair of eyes may be equivalent to breasts or testicles. A single eye may be the phallus (especially the glans), the vulva, or occasionally the anus. The fullness of life as exemplified by such fluids as mother's milk or semen can thus be symbolized by an eye, and accordingly

threats to one's supply of such precious fluids can appropriately be manifested by the eye or eyes of others (Dundes, 1981, pp. 266–7).

Dundes turns to Richard Broxton Onions (1951) for elaboration of the notion that liquid is life. Part of the rationale behind cremation, for instance, is said to be that burning speeds up the drying process – the final removal of the liquid of life. Onions noted that for the Greeks aging is seen as the gradual removal of liquid, and Dundes suggests that the observation of grapes drying into raisins and plums into prunes can be seen as analogous to the wrinkling of the human face with age. In support of this theory, Dundes points out that the drinking of a toast (the taking in of vital liquids) is accompanied by verbal formulae such as "here's to your health" or "long life to you." In terms of a notion of limited good, such phrases can be interpreted as reassuring the assembled company that the drinker does not wish to replenish his or her own liquid (life force) at the expense of others. Without such a rationale there is no compelling reason to associate drinking with the need to affirm the *good health* of others. A further example cited by Dundes comes from a piece of fieldwork carried out by Claude Lévi-Strauss in the south of France (1969). In cheaper restaurants each table setting includes a small bottle of wine, which is poured not into one's own glass, but into that of someone at a neighboring table. This practice could similarly be interpreted as a response to a notion of limited good. "If one drinks without regard to one's neighbors, one risks being envied and becoming the object or victim of the evil eye" (Dundes, 1981, p. 268). Even tipping a waiter can be seen as buying off possible envy (see Foster, 1972), and in Scotland it used to be said that offering a stranger at an inn a little milk would counteract any possible effects of the evil eye, an effect enhanced if one first took a little oneself (Maclagan, 1902). This leads Dundes to speculate on the links between breastfeeding and the common belief that a greedy child will grow up to have the evil eye. If weaning takes place, as was more commonly the case in the past (before contraception limited family size), because a new baby requires the milk, we can clearly see the roots of sibling rivalry and competition over the scarce resource of the mother's milk. For an older sibling to deprive a baby of the milk it needs could literally mean that its essential liquids and therefore life are being denied.[20] Dundes goes further to suggest a connection between the words "tip," "tipple" (drink) and "nipple" (mother's milk), and notes that yawning, frequently taken as a means of diagnosing someone with the evil eye, might be reminiscent of the infant's open mouth, wanting its mother's breast.

While Dundes's attempts to look for an underlying rationale to the wide range of phenomena concerning the evil eye is fascinating, and sometimes convincing, it is important to remember that customs don't exist in the abstract.[21] Such etic (outsider) or abstract explanations need to be balanced by emic (insider), experience-near observations. Jeanne Favret-Saada's work reminds us that knowledge of the individuals involved in the witchcraft discourse, and their relationships with one another, is essential if one is to make sense of people's beliefs and actions. Dundes seeks to do for the evil eye what Evans-Pritchard did for witchcraft – to point to its underlying rationale and logic. The final section of this chapter returns to discussions concerning the rationality of seemingly illogical beliefs.

The Mentalities Debate

Evans-Pritchard described participant observation as both entering into and withdrawing from another culture. The anthropologist "lives in two different worlds of thought at the same time, in categories and concepts and values which often cannot easily be reconciled" (Evans-Pritchard, 1976, p. 243). When asked whether he accepted Azande ideas of witchcraft, Evans-Pritchard gave the "yes and no" type of answer that must be familiar to many field anthropologists:

> In my own culture, in the climate of thought I was born into and brought up in and have been conditioned by, I rejected, and reject, Zande notions of witchcraft. In their culture, in the set of ideas I then lived in, I accepted them; in a kind of way I believed them. . . . If one must act as though one believed, one ends in believing, or half-believing as one acts. (Evans-Pritchard, 1976, p. 244)

The type of society in which one is raised self-evidently affects the way one views the world. Are there, therefore, fundamentally different ways of thinking in different societies?

Lucien Lévy-Bruhl

Debates surrounding the way people think and the relationship between mental processes and social conditioning have occupied anthropologists for much of the twentieth century. The questions raised often focus on the issue of rationality. Do only the inheritors of a Western scientific tradition think rationally, or is rational thought universal? Another way of looking at the debate is to question whether Western thought is as logical, analytical, and rational as some positivist scholars like to think. One man who spent his life pondering the question of mentalities was Lucien Lévy-Bruhl.

Lucien Lévy-Bruhl (1857–1939) was born into a middle-class Parisian Jewish family. In 1896 he was appointed Professor of Modern Philosophy at one of France's premier academic institutions, the Sorbonne. Like his contemporary, Durkheim, Lévy-Bruhl thought that religion was socially based, but he increasingly distanced himself from the Durkheimian school, the *Année Sociologique*. Lévy-Bruhl wanted to establish a "science of morals" by comparing ethical codes in different societies. He is considered one of the founders of *cultural relativity*, the need to view each culture as a whole, on its own terms, in order to uncover the relationships and assumptions that govern it, an approach developed in the United States by Franz Boas. It was his 1910 work *Les Fonctiones mentales dans les sociétés inférieures* (translated into English in 1926 as *How Natives Think*) and his 1926 *Mentalité primitive* (translated in 1923 as *Primitive Mentality*) that both made and to some extent destroyed Lévy-Bruhl's reputation. He later modified the notion put forward in these works that there are two different types of "mentality," one primitive and the other modern, but it is with his initial proposal that Lévy-Bruhl remains most closely associated.

Nineteenth-century evolutionary theorists such as Herbert Spencer, Edward Tylor, and Sir James Frazer shared three common assumptions: (a) the idea of progress; (b) an unquestioned faith in the efficacy of the comparative method; and (c) the notion of a psychic unity among all peoples. If left alone, all human communities would pass through the same stages of social evolution. The supposition was that eventually all societies would reach the same peak of rational, civilized thought and behavior that characterized Victorian Britain. Lévy-Bruhl was particularly concerned with this third proposition, the psychic unity of different peoples. From his studies Lévy-Bruhl concluded that the formal rules of logic that governed rational thought did not actually apply in many simpler societies.

Aristotelian logic (deriving from the classical Greek philosopher Aristotle, 384–322 BCE) is based on two rules of rational thought: (a) the law of non-contradiction (something cannot be both x and not-x at the same time and in the same sense); and (b) the law of the excluded middle (two objects cannot occupy the same space at the same time).[22]

According to Lévy-Bruhl, the West has an intellectual tradition based on the rigorous testing and analysis of hypotheses going back centuries, so that Europeans are logically oriented and tend to look for natural explanations to events. The "collective representations" of "primitive" peoples, on the other hand, tend to be "prelogical" or "mystical." In *How Natives Think*, Lévy-Bruhl stated that "the reality surrounding the primitives is itself mystical. Not a single being or object or natural phenomenon in their collective representations is what it appears to be to our minds" (Lévy-Bruhl, 1985, p. 38). He concluded that differences in ways of thought violate the notion of a psychic unity of human beings, and that in simple societies Aristotelian logic simply does not apply.

Collective representations: a way of looking at the world that is common to members of a social group. Representations are transmitted from one generation to another rather than invented anew by individuals, who are born into them. Although they only exist in and through individuals, collective representations imply a unity beyond the distinct individuals who compose a group (see Lévy-Bruhl, 1985, p. 13).

Lévy-Bruhl's ideas were subjected to a storm of criticism. He was a philosopher with a background in psychology rather than a fieldwork anthropologist, and many of his data were shown to be inadequate. He was also understood to have said that "primitive" peoples are not able to make objective causal connections between events. The line drawn between "primitives" and "us" was criticized as vague and indefensible. In fact Lévy-Bruhl never denied that all people everywhere use logical thought in relation to practical and technical matters, but claimed that the mystical interpretation of an event will always predominate in a "primitive mentality." Lévy-Bruhl used the example of Australian Aboriginals. They may be aware that the birth of a child results from the coupling of a man and a woman, but they will also view the baby as a reincarnation of one or more totemic spirits. It could be argued that this is no different from the ancient Greek (and contemporary Christian, Jewish, and Islamic) belief that while conception takes place through the union of the sexes, a preexistent soul is transported into the fetus. Lévy-Bruhl claimed that Westerners differ from people in simple societies in that the former are aware of the contradiction, whereas the latter are not. The notion of faith depends upon believing something that cannot be proved, and invokes the language of paradox and mystery as a way of dealing with contradictions.[23]

In his search for a comparative understanding of "mentalities," Lévy-Bruhl succeeded in annoying the intellectualist school of Tylor and Frazer, by stating that mental processes are not everywhere the same, and the cultural relativists like Boas, who rejected any attempt to make generalizing statements about peoples. Malinowski had claimed that the apparently ir-rational behavior of primitives is due to a faulty logic, a misapplication of the rules of reason, not wholly different assumptions concerning the way the world works. Lévy-Bruhl rejected Malinowski's search for individual, psycho-logical explanations of human behavior, preferring the collectivist approach of Durkheim.

Lévy-Bruhl accepted that the division he had sought to make between different types of thought in different types of society was too rigid, and by the 1930s no longer sought to defend this position. In his *Carnets* or *Note-books* in an entry dated August 29, 1938, he proposed:

> let us entirely give up explaining participation by something peculiar to the human mind, either constitutional (in its structure and function) or acquired (mental customs). In other words, let us expressly rectify what I believed correct in 1910: there is not a primitive mentality distinguishable from the other by *two* characteristics which are peculiar to it (mystical and prelogical). There is a mystical mentality which is more marked and more easily observable among "primitive peoples" than in our own societies, but it is present in every human mind. (Lévy-Bruhl, 1975, pp. 100–1)

Lévy-Bruhl's conclusion, that there are different types of thinking ("lo-gical" and "mystical") coexisting in all societies, although to different de-grees, has continued to excite interest from anthropologists interested in cognition. Two major scholars invited to give the Morgan Lectures in the United States recently returned to the "mentalities debate." Stanley Jeyaraja Tambiah's lectures were published in 1993 under the title *Magic, Science, Religion and the Scope of Rationality*. Byron J. Good published his lectures the following year as *Medicine, Rationality and Experience*. In order to illustrate some of the directions this debate has taken, we will now look at some of Good's arguments concerning rationality and medical science, as the latter is often thought to typify notions of objectivity, progress, pure knowledge, and value-free judgments.

Rationality and Western science

For Lévy-Bruhl, logical, rational, scientific thought was opposed to "prelogi-cal" thought based on "mystical participation." Religion belonged to pre-logical thought, whereas medicine would be classified as logical. Byron Good (1994), on the other hand, claims that there is a close relationship between science, including medicine, and religious fundamentalism. The relationship turns in part on our concept of "belief."

For fundamentalist Christians, salvation is often seen to follow from belief, and mission work is conceived as an effort to convince the natives to give up false beliefs and take on a set of beliefs that will produce a new life and ultimate salvation. Ironically, quite a-religious scientists and policy makers see a similar benefit from correct belief. Educate the public about the hazards of drug use, our current Enlightenment theory goes . . . get them to believe in the right thing and the problem will be licked. Educate the patient, medical journals advise clinicians, and solve the problems of noncompliance that plague the treatment of chronic disease. . . . get people to believe the right thing and our public health problems will be solved. Salvation from drugs and from preventable illness will follow from correct belief. (Good, 1994, p. 7)

Evans-Pritchard distinguished between what Azande "believe," as in "Azande believe that some people are witches," and what they "know," the verb used to describe Azande leechcraft – their medical knowledge of diseases and healing. Thus Evans-Pritchard organized his monograph on Zande witchcraft "around a distinction between those ideas that accord with objective reality . . . and those that do not; the language of knowledge is used to describe the former, the language of belief the latter" (Good, 1994, p. 13). Good turns to Wilfred Cantwell Smith (1977, 1979) in order to explore further the etymology of the term "belief," concluding that our understanding of the term is relatively recent. In Old English "to believe" meant to "hold dear," and for Chaucer it was "to pledge loyalty." Belief in God was not therefore a claim to hold to something that could not be proved, but a promise to live one's life in the service of God, like a bondsman to his lord. Only by the end of the seventeenth century did "belief" indicate a choice between two possible explanations or propositions, so that "I believe in God" implied a choice between believing that God existed and claiming that God was a human creation, a fantasy. As Evans-Pritchard indicated, for the Azande to "believe" in witchcraft was a very different proposition than it was for him. As in pre-Enlightenment Europe, there was a single hegemonic world view. The possibility that witches might not exist was not part of Zande "collective representations" (to use Lévy-Bruhl's phrase). Both medical scientists and fundamentalist Christians, according to Good, use "belief" in this contemporary sense of choosing between two options, one true and one false. The matter of "correct belief" is of vital importance, implying the choice between a right and a wrong way of seeing the world.

The concept of belief as currently understood and used in English may be difficult or impossible to translate into other languages. Mary Steedly (1993) worked among the Karobatak in Sumatra. They kept asking her a question that she interpreted as "do you believe in spirits?" Steedly did not want to say "no" in case this damaged her relation with the people, but felt unable to answer "yes" as this would constitute a lie. It was only after some months that she realized the Karobatak were not asking her "do you believe spirits exist?" but "do you trust the spirits?" They wanted to know whether she maintained a relationship with them (in the way that Evans-Pritchard and Paul Stoller used oracles to determine everyday life in Africa). Medieval Christians who asserted belief in God did not proclaim God's existence, but their loyalty to God's service. The key difference between Evans-Pritchard and Mary Steedly on the one hand, and the Azande, Karobatak, and medieval European Christians on the other, is the presence or absence of alternative views of the world. Good refers to Jeanne Favret-Saada's *Deadly Words* as the first truly postmodern ethnography on witchcraft. Favret-Saada was not able to stand aside and distinguish mystical belief from "real" knowledge. As Good comments, "for those attacked by a sorcerer, for those peasants – and Favret-Saada herself – whose very lives were at stake, *belief* in witchcraft is not the question. How to protect oneself, how to ward off the evil attacks producing illness and misfortune, is the only significant issue to be addressed" (Good, 1994, p. 14).

As a medical anthropologist, familiar with both clinical medicine and notions of health and disease in a cross-cultural context, Good is extremely critical of the claims of the Western biomedical world view.

> Clinical medicine all too often instantiates a narrowly conceived instrumental reality. It does so quite subtly . . . through the force of everyday practices – like writing in charts – through which the objects of medicine are constituted. It does so also by narrowing the scope of the clinical gaze to such an extent that many of the most crucial aspects of medical care – addressing social and economic conditions that produce a patient's disease and trigger costly interventions, placing priority on helping patients achieve a good death – are simply ignored as irrelevant to the domain of clinical practice. (Good, 1994, p. 180)

Good contrasts the biomedical world view, limited but self-confident, with the much more tentative and questioning approach of anthropology, referring to Clifford Geertz's (1988, p. 146) description of Western society's "salvational belief in the powers of science." However untried, untested or illogical a medical procedure or scientific hypothesis might be, there is considerable investment in *believing* that it is rational and wholly different from the claims of religion and thought worlds of "primitive" peoples. Most anthropologists would agree with Lévy-Bruhl's later conclusions that there are different ways of thinking common to all peoples. There is a scientific way of thinking that tests hypotheses against everyday reality and experience, essential to technical advances, and a more "mystical" or non-logical mode of thought that works

via metaphor and analogy to make sense of the complexity of human existence. In practice these may not be distinguishable from one another, or may
both come into play in the same situation. Philosophers and theologians, for
instance, have argued for the rationality of believing in God, and supposedly
irrational beliefs, such as witchcraft, may appear to be supported by empirical
evidence. Radcliffe-Brown (1952) also saw the same processes at work in
"primitive" and Western societies. All religions, according to Radcliffe-
Brown, tend to incorporate natural phenomena and human activities into
a single cosmological schema. Objects and events acquire *ritual value* (i.e. they
are seen as sacred) if they impinge upon or come to symbolize some aspect of
human experience. There may be a difference of degree between peoples
regarding the extent to which this principle operates, but not in kind.

Mary Douglas is a strong advocate of the view that there is indeed
a psychic unity to human beings. Both "primitive ritual" and "secular
rites," for instance, serve as focusing mechanisms or mnemonics and
a control for experience. Obsessively packing and repacking a suitcase before
a holiday will not make the weekend come any sooner, but can help the
traveler exclude all that is not necessary for the enjoyment of the holiday,
both physically and mentally. In the same way, a Dinka herdsman who knots
a bundle of grass at the wayside as he hurries home to supper does not expect
the action alone to mean that he is in time for supper. The knotted grass
helps to focus his mind and he redoubles his efforts to be home on time
(Douglas, 1966, pp. 63–4). In both these examples what might be termed
illogical (ritual, mystical) actions have a practical, rational effect. To draw
too tight a distinction between modes of thought is to misunderstand human
psychology and therefore rationality. For Douglas, as for Good, "The right
basis for comparison is to insist on the unity of human experience and at the
same time to insist on its variety, on the differences which make comparison
worth while" (Douglas, 1966, p. 77). It is the greater differentiation,
the choices available to us, that really distinguish modern from simpler
societies.

Mary Douglas characterized one of the principal differences in modes of
thought as personalized versus impersonal. Some cosmologies (she includes
China as well as sub-Saharan Africa) relate the universe very directly to
human behavior. Geomancy and *feng shui*, for instance, work on the assumption that the earth and its energies and human fortune are intimately related
to one another. Robert Pool (1994), in his study of witchcraft in the
Cameroon grassfields, concludes that notions of witchcraft come back to
issues of personal responsibility. It reflects a personalized world in which
the actions and even thoughts of individuals have repercussions in both
social and "supernatural" spheres.

Pierre Bourdieu (1977, pp. 110–12) points out that the "fictitious" rationality of academic scholarship (and the Western philosophical tradition as a whole), with its desire to order relations in the abstract, is very different from the "fuzzy" logic of everyday life, in which apparently contradictory systems may never actually come into view at the same time. Bourdieu therefore contrasts the "universe of practice" with the "universe of academic discourse." Once more, we are not dealing with "primitive" versus "civilized" societies. Outside the world of academia we all function successfully with notions that make sense within their own realm. To give one often cited example, a Christian might have no problems "believing in" the account of creation in the Book of Genesis and in scientific explanations in terms of the "big bang." If the contradiction is pointed out, the individual will probably respond that each belongs to a different discourse. The biblical account speaks in the language of poetry and myth, and addresses questions of meaning and human responsibility, whereas the scientific version of creation is concerned with mechanisms and physical laws.[24] This is similar to the Zande who holds both that witchcraft caused a stilted granary to collapse and injure someone sitting in its shade (the meaning of the event) and that the support gave way because it had been eaten by termites (the mechanism which caused it).

We should not forget, however, the impact of the Enlightenment on Western thought, including European Christianity. As Paul Gifford states,

> The supernaturalistic has largely disappeared (we will use this term to distinguish between the realm of demons, spirits, witches and so on from the supernatural – God, heaven, prayer, the resurrection of Christ, sacraments – which has largely persisted in the Western churches)....Reality is generally not experienced in terms of witches, demons and personalised spiritual powers, and Christianity has changed to take account of this....In Africa most Christians operate from a background little affected by the European Enlightenment; for most Africans, witchcraft, spirits and ancestors, spells and charms are primary and immediate and natural categories of interpretation....Most Africans have an "enchanted" worldview. (Gifford, 1998, pp. 327–8)

This leads to a situation in the mainline Christian churches in Africa in which its leaders publicly espouse Enlightenment thinking, while most ordinary Christians hold a much more "traditional" supernaturalistic view of the world, as was common in Europe prior to the Enlightenment (see Thomas, 1971). The fastest growing churches in Africa, as in Latin America, are those that preach a prosperity and deliverance Gospel – if you believe (and give or "seed" money) you will be blessed with health and wealth. Failure to achieve your goals is blamed on spirits, witchcraft, curses, involvement with traditional healers ("fetish priests"), and so on. These newer

Pentecostal churches reject traditional culture, but also have a supernaturalistic vision of reality, with a discourse of God and the Devil, miraculous
interventions, and an instrumental understanding of religion, all of
which accord with aspects of traditional thinking, including the dynamics
of witchcraft.[25]

Robin Horton (1994) picks up the theme of rationality and choice
ushered in by the Enlightenment, contrasting the "closed" nature of African
traditional thought with the "open" world view of modern Europe and
America. We have already seen that Tylor, Malinowski, and others were
wrong when they believed that science would eventually put paid to both
magic and religion. Science merely provided one more element, albeit an
immensely powerful and significant one, in the cosmological choices available.[26] It is clear that not everyone can cope with the developing awareness
of alternatives, which erode certainties and absolute values.

> These people still retain the old sense of the absolute validity of their belief-
> systems, with all the attendant anxieties about threats to them. For these
> people, the confrontation is still a threat of chaos of the most horrific kind –
> a threat which demands the most dramatic measures. They respond in one of
> two ways: either by trying to blot out those responsible for the confrontation,
> often down to the last unborn child; or by trying to convert them to their own
> beliefs through fanatical missionary activity.... Some adjust their fears by
> developing an inordinate faith in progress towards a future in which "the
> Truth" will be finally known. But others long nostalgically for the fixed,
> unquestionable beliefs of the "closed" culture. They call for authoritarian
> establishment and control of dogma, and for the persecution of those who
> have managed to be at ease in a world of ever-shifting ideas. Clearly, the
> "open" predicament is a precarious, fragile thing. (Horton, 1994, pp. 256–7)

We can probably all think of examples of both types of reaction, from blind
faith in science and progress to the restrictive Islam of Afganistan's Taliban
and Christian fundamentalists who believe that they alone are "saved." The
competing marketplace of ideas that constitutes modernity is not the home of
rational scientific thought, so much as a jumble of assorted ideas, some
compatible, others contradictory. Where the developed world differs from
that of indigenous peoples is in its proselytization. Traditional peoples rarely
try to convince others of the rightness of their world view, as it is self-
evident.[27] Once choice is introduced so is uncertainty. Being social animals,
we react to doubt by attempting to recruit others to our side, finding security
in numbers, or, failing that, in ever tighter boundaries that exclude the
outside world with its "wrong" way of seeing. It is also possible, however,

for quite different world views to coexist. One can be a religious believer and a scientist, or a modern post-Enlightenment Frenchman who believes himself bewitched. We may not be consciously aware of the processes involved, but we are all familiar with syncretic religious ideas and practices. Whether chance is sought or resisted, religions continue to interact and develop and contest their ground whenever and wherever human beings and cultures meet together.

Notes

1 I would like to thank an anonymous publisher's reader for pointing out that the witchcraft/evil eye idiom of "wet" and "dry" in India is not to be confused with the *ayurvedic* system of medicine, which classifies the effect of substances on the body and spirit with "hot" and "cold" terminology.

2 This conundrum is expressed by Bruce Kapferer in his book on Sinhalese Buddhists in Sri Lanka, *The Feast of the Sorcerer*. Kapferer states that "I should make it clear from the start that although I begin with the general category of sorcery, my objective is effectively to demolish the value of the descriptive and phenomenal category of sorcery as a thing in itself. In other words, I address a kind of human practice which anthropologists and other scholars can recognize and delineate as being of a distinct order but which in the final analysis refuses the final categorical or phenomenal confinement that is imposed on it" (Kapferer, 1997, p. 8). If the anthropologist insists on cultural specificity, using only vernacular terms, it is very difficult to draw wider theoretical conclusions concerning human cultures and institutions. For this reason, despite the dangers of misrepresentation, most ethnographers try to combine vernacular explanations with the use of shorthand terms that have a wider currency. For Kapferer, for instance, the word "sorcery" is used "very broadly to cover those practices, often described as magical, that are concerned to harness and manipulate those energies and forces which are centred in human beings and which extend from them to intervene – heal, harm, or protect – in the action and circumstance of other human beings" (ibid.).

3 The linking of *malefice* with village life reflects tensions within a face-to-face or small-scale society that can result in accusations of witchcraft (see Macfarlane, 1970a; Favret-Saada, 1980). Where people are able to move away from sources of conflict and find employment or security elsewhere, accusations of witchcraft are unlikely. Turnbull (1976) argued that the mobility and relative independence of pygmy bands in the forests of Central Africa was one reason why they did not "need" witchcraft as an outlet for social tensions. They had alternative means (e.g. ostracism) of dealing with people who offended against cultural mores.

4 Due to the influence of Evans-Pritchard's work these categories are sometimes treated as normative (at least in Africa).

5 Paul Gifford (1998, pp. 97–109) gives a fascinating description of Pentecostal Christian "deliverance ministries" in Ghana, which draw on traditional idioms of witchcraft and spirit possession in order to account for bad health or misfortune. This is an example of the transformation of certain types of American evangelical Christianity that changes its emphasis and resonances on African soil.

6 Clyde Kluckhohn (1944) studied Navaho witchcraft in the United States in terms of the anxieties and tensions generated within small-scale communities. Destructive impulses are projected outward onto others, who are then accused of being witches and stigmatized (see Girard, 1992, discussed in chapter 6). The relationship between the insecurity and aggression of the "victim" and the likelihood that he or she will accuse others of witchcraft has been widely recognized in both emic (insider explanations) and etic ethnographic accounts.

7 See Brain (1972) and Bowie (1985) for general information on the Bangwa. For more details on Bangwa witchcraft see Bowie (1999).

8 Robert Brain describes a poignant response from a Bangwa child to his assertion that he did not believe in witchcraft: "Europeans do not know jealousy; they don't hate their brothers so they do not need witchcraft to harm them" (Brain, 1970, p. 167).

9 Monica Wilson (1951, p. 308), referring to the Nyakusa in East Africa, also records giving meat to witches as a countermeasure to "cool" their witchcraft.

10 When the Focolare mission arrived in Fontem in 1966 the infant mortality rate in some areas was said to have reached 80 percent. The first Focolarini to work in the area were medical personnel and they immediately opened a dispensary in a disused compound, before raising funds to build the hospital (see Bowie, 1985).

11 The current Fon of Fontem still sees hearing witchcraft trials as one of his main functions, and his new office block has a court room specifically for that purpose.

12 She had reported the matter to the administration, but as witchcraft is commonly said to pass from mother to daughter and father to son, a woman identified as the mother of a witch is also vulnerable to accusations of witchcraft if she remains in her home community.

13 Similar choices had to be made in Europe in the late medieval and early modern period. In the early Middle Ages judges and churchmen assumed that witches did not exist, or at least did not do what they were accused of. Cases were therefore normally dismissed. By the early modern period, however, the assumption was that witches did exist and that they could perform anti-social acts. Those accused were far more likely to be tried and executed for their alleged crimes.

14 See, for instance, Ardener (1970), Rowlands and Warnier (1988), Geschiere and Fisiy (1994), and Geschiere (1997), all of whom refer to fieldwork examples in Cameroon. For examples from East Africa, see Brain (1983).

15 Alan Macfarlane (1970a, b) reaches similar conclusions in his historical study of witchcraft in Tudor and Stuart Essex in England. Witchcraft accusations were primarily between people who were expected by obligations of neighborliness to show concern for one another, but whose family and economic situation promoted competition. Disproportionately poorer, but not destitute, older women,

who in earlier times might have expected the community to support them, were identified as witches. The Church and civil authorities encouraged the transition to a more individualistic ethic. "Once workhouses had been established, when it had become a Christian's duty to abstain from indiscriminate charity, as soon as there had been a change from the informal, day-to-day, treatment of the poor and old to a more conscious and formal situation, the anxieties may have lessened" (Macfarlane, 1970a, p. 206). In the *bocage* there is a similar tension between the obligations to one's kin and the logic of the inheritance system, but with accusations of witchcraft displaced onto a neighbor. The affective and moral ties to one's family are therefore preserved, while allowing those suffering misfortune to assert control over their situation.

16 There are some recorded influences of the evil eye in sub-Saharan Africa. Middleton and Winter (1963, p. 194), for instance, record that the Gisu believe that someone with the evil eye can harm others by showing excessive admiration or by staring. This is very similar to recorded examples from Europe and the Middle East.

17 See, for instance, Herzfeld (1981, 1984) and Galt (1982, 1985).

18 Carmichael (1928). See also Davies and Bowie (1995).

19 It is suggested that van Gennep had in mind Jules Tuchmann, who did indeed spend his life compiling material on the evil eye. Van Gennep's article, with an introductory commentary, is reprinted in Dundes (1981). Evans-Pritchard (1976, p. 243) was also at pains to stress that the amassing of data devoid of theoretical content is a waste of effort.

20 See Pat Caplan's description of childrearing on Mafia Island, Tanzania, in chapter 4.

21 Dundes continues by seeking to make an analogy between the evil eye and genitalia, perhaps the least convincing element of his argument, although he does find some interesting and at times explicit connections.

22 See Schrempp (1989) for a discussion of Aristotelian logic and its relevance for social anthropology.

23 See the discussion on virgin birth between Edmund Leach (1966, 1968) and David Schneider (1968).

24 Of course, many biblically based Christians and Muslims would come to different conclusions concerning the coherence of scriptural and scientific ideas, and might well find that the latter do clash with the former.

25 Gifford (1998) provides an excellent analysis of the role of Pentecostal churches in Africa, including the transformations that take place when a basically American Gospel is transplanted into African soil. See also David Martin (1990) for a description of the rise of Pentecostalism in South America.

26 Macfarlane (1970a, pp. 200–6), in his study of witchcraft in sixteenth- and seventeenth-century Essex (England), also regarded scientific knowledge, or the lack of it, as less significant as an explanation for witchcraft beliefs than personalized relationships. When people stopped caring, or being forced to care by the face-to-face nature of their interactions and mutual dependence, what neighbors

thought of them, witchcraft accusations started to decline. Similarly, religious beliefs alone could not account for the presence or absence of witchcraft as an explanation for misfortune. Macfarlane (1970a, p. 188) states that "People did not accuse their neighbours of witchcraft out of religious fervour." It was because they had slighted them, or had obligations toward them that they had difficulty fulfilling, that they accused neighbors of bewitching them.

27 What terms are we to use? "The West," "the industrial world," "post-Enlightenment societies," as opposed to "traditional," "indigenous," or "less-developed" societies? The absence of a satisfactory terminology points to the fluid nature of any categorical distinctions.

References and Further Reading

Ankarloo, Bengt and Henningsen, Gustav (eds) (1993) *Early Modern European Witchcraft: Centres and Peripheries*. Oxford: Oxford University Press.

Ardener, Edwin (1970) Witchcraft, economics and continuity of belief. In Mary Douglas (ed.), *Witchcraft Confessions and Accusations*. London: Tavistock, pp. 141–60.

Badone, E. (1990) *Religious Orthodoxy and Popular Faith in European Society*. Princeton, NJ: Princeton University Press.

Bayart, J. F. (1993) *The State in Africa: The Politics of the Belly*, translated by M. Harper, C. and E. Harrison. London: Longman.

Bloch, Maurice E. F. (1998) *How We Think They Think: Anthropological Approaches to Cognition, Memory and Literacy*. Boulder, CO and Oxford: Westview Press.

Bocock, R. and Thompson, K. (eds) (1985) *Religion and Ideology*. Manchester: Manchester University Press

Bourdieu, Pierre (1977) *Outline of a Theory of Practice*, translated by R. Nice. Cambridge: Cambridge University Press.

Bowie, Fiona (1985) A social and historical study of Christian missions among the Bangwa of South West Cameroon. D.Phil. thesis, Oxford.

Bowie, Fiona (1999) Witchcraft and healing among the Bangwa of Cameroon. In Graham Harvey (ed.), *Indigenous Religions: a Companion*. London: Cassell.

Brain, James Lewton (1983) Witchcraft and development. *African Affairs*, 82, 371–84.

Brain, Robert (1970) Child witches. In Mary Douglas (ed.), *Witchcraft Confessions and Accusations*. London: Tavistock, pp. 161–79.

Brain, Robert (1972) *Bangwa Kinship and Marriage*. London: Cambridge University Press.

Carmichael, Alexander (1928) *The Carmina Gadelica*. Edinburgh: Scottish Academic Press.

Cohn, Norman (1970) The myth of Satan and his human servants. In Mary Douglas (ed.), *Witchcraft Confessions and Accusations*. London: Tavistock, pp. 3–16.

Coss, Richard G. (1981) Reflections on the evil eye. In Alan Dundes (ed.), *The Evil Eye: a Casebook*. New York and London: Garland, pp. 181–91.

Crick, Malcolm (1982) Recasting witchcraft. In Max Marwick (ed.), *Witchcraft and Sorcery: Selected Readings*. Harmondsworth: Penguin, pp. 343–64.

Davies, Oliver and Bowie, Fiona (eds) (1995) *Celtic Christian Spirituality*. London: SPCK; New York: Crossroad.

Douglas, Mary (1966) *Purity and Danger: an Analysis of Concepts of Pollution and Taboo*. London: Routledge and Kegan Paul.

Douglas, Mary (ed.) (1970) *Witchcraft Confessions and Accusations*. ASA Monographs 9. London: Tavistock.

Dundes, Alan (1981) Wet and dry, the evil eye. In Alan Dundes (ed.), *The Evil Eye: a Casebook*. New York and London: Garland, pp. 257–312.

Evans-Pritchard, E. E. (1934) Lévy-Bruhl's theory of primitive mentality. *Bulletin of the Faculty of Arts* (Egyptian University, Cairo), 2.

Evans-Pritchard, E. E. et al. (eds) (1954) *The Institutions of Primitive Society*. Oxford: Basil Blackwell.

Evans-Pritchard, E. E. (1976) *Witchcraft, Oracles and Magic among the Azande*. Abridged with an introduction by Eva Gillies. Oxford: Clarendon Press (first published in 1937).

Evans-Pritchard, E. E. (1981) *A History of Anthropological Thought*. London and Boston: Faber and Faber.

Favret-Saada, Jeanne (1980) *Deadly Words: Witchcraft in the Bocage*. Cambridge: Cambridge University Press.

Favret-Saada, Jeanne (1989) Unwitching as therapy. *American Ethnologist*, 16 (1), 40–56.

Foucault, Michel (1973) *The Birth of the Clinic: an Archaeology of Medical Perception*. New York: Random House.

Foster, George M. (1965) Peasant society and the image of limited good. *American Anthropologist*, 67, 293–315.

Foster, George M. (1972) The anatomy of envy: a study in symbolic behavior. *Current Anthropology*, 13, 165–202.

Galt, Anthony H. (1982) The evil eye as synthetic image and its meanings on the Island of Pantelleria, Italy. *American Ethnologist*, 9, 664–81.

Galt, Anthony H. (1985) Does the Mediterraneanist dilemma have straw horns? *American Ethnologist*, 12(2), 369–71.

Geertz, Clifford (1988) *Works and Lives: the Anthropologist as Author*. Stanford, CA: Stanford University Press.

Geschiere, Peter (1988) Sorcery and the state. Popular modes of action among the Maka of Southeast Cameroon. *Critique of Anthropology*, 8(1), 35–63.

Geschiere, Peter and Fisiy, Cyprian (1994) Domesticating personal violence: witchcraft, courts and confessions in Cameroon. *Africa*, 64(3), 323–41.

Geschiere, Peter (1997) *The Modernity of Witchcraft: Politics and the Occult in Postcolonial Africa*. Charlottesville and London: University of Virginia Press.

Gifford, Paul (1998) *African Christianity: Its Public Role*. London: Hurst & Co.

Ginzburg, Carlo (1992) *The Night Battles: Witchcraft and Agrarian Cults in the Sixteenth and Seventeenth Centuries*. Baltimore: Johns Hopkins University Press.

Girard, René (1992) *Violence and the Sacred*. Translated by Patrick Gregory. Baltimore: Johns Hopkins University Press.

Good, Byron J. (1994) *Medicine, Rationality and Experience: an Anthropological Perspective*. Cambridge: Cambridge University Press.

Herzfeld, Michael (1981) Meaning and morality: a semiotic approach to evil eye accusations in a Greek village. *American Ethnologist*, 8, 560–73.

Herzfeld, Michael (1984) The horns of the Mediterraneanist dilemma. *American Ethnologist*, 11, 439–54.

Horton, Robin (1975) On the rationality of conversion. *Africa*, 45, 3–4.

Horton, Robin (1994) *Patterns of Thought in Africa and the West*. Cambridge: Cambridge University Press.

Horton, Robin and Finnigan, Ruth (eds) (1973) *Modes of Thought*. London: Faber and Faber.

Idowu, E. Bolaju (1978) *African Traditional Religion*. London: SCM.

Kapferer, Bruce (1997) *The Feast of the Sorcerer: Practices of Consciousness and Power*. Chicago and London: University of Chicago Press.

Kluckhohn, Clyde (1944) *Navaho Witchcraft*. Peabody Museum Papers, Harvard University, 22(2).

Leach, Edmund R. (1966) Virgin birth. *Proceedings of the Royal Anthropological Institute*, 39–49.

Leach, Edmund R. (1968) Correspondence. *Man*, 3(1), 129.

Lett, James (1998) *Science, Reason and Anthropology: the Principles of Rational Inquiry*. Lanham, MD: Rowman and Littlefield.

Lévi-Strauss, Claude (1969) *The Elementary Structures of Kinship*. London: Eyre and Spottiswoode.

Lévy-Bruhl, Lucien (1975) *The Notebooks on Primitive Mentality*. Translated by Peter Rivière. Oxford: Blackwell (first published in 1949).

Lévy-Bruhl, Lucien (1985) *How Natives Think*. Translated by Lillian A. Clare, with a new introduction by C. Scott Littleton. Princeton, NJ: Princeton University Press (first published in 1910).

Lloyd, G. E. R. (1993) *Demystifying Mentalities*. Cambridge: Cambridge University Press.

Luhrmann, Tanya (1989) *Persuasions of the Witch's Craft*. Oxford: Basil Blackwell.

Macfarlane, Alan (1970a) *Witchcraft in Tudor and Stuart England: a Regional and Comparative Study*. London: Routledge and Kegan Paul.

Macfarlane, Alan (1970b) Witchcraft in Tudor and Stuart Essex. In Mary Douglas (ed.), *Witchcraft Confessions and Accusations*. London: Tavistock, pp. 81–99.

Maclagan, R. C. (1902) *Evil Eye in the Western Highlands*. London: David Nutt.

Martin, David (1990) *Tongues of Fire: the Explosion of Protestantism on Latin America*. Oxford: Blackwell.

Marwick, Max (ed.) (1982) *Witchcraft and Sorcery*. Harmondsworth: Penguin.

Mbembe, Achille (2001) *On the Postcolony*. Berkeley and London: University of California Press.

Meyer, Birgit (1992) "If you are a devil, you are a witch, and if you are a witch, you are a devil." The integration of "pagan" ideas into the conceptual universe of the Ewe in Southeastern Ghana. *Journal of Religion in Africa*, 22, 98–132.

Middleton, J. and Winter, E. H. (eds) (1963) *Witchcraft and Sorcery in East Africa*. London: Routledge and Kegan Paul.

Needham, J. (ed.) (1928) *Science, Religion and Reality*. London: Sheldon Press.

Needham, Rodney (1972) *Belief, Language and Experience*. Chicago: University of Chicago Press.

Onions, Richard Broxton (1951) *The Origins of European Thought about the Body, the Mind, the Soul, the World, Time and Fate*. Cambridge: Cambridge University Press.

Overing, Joanna (ed.) (1985) *Reason and Morality*. London: Tavistock.

Pocock, David F. (1981) The evil eye – envy and greed among the Patidar of Central Gujerat. In Alan Dundes (ed.), *The Evil Eye: a Casebook*. New York and London: Garland, pp. 201–10.

Pool, Robert (1994) *Dialogue and the Interpretation of Illness: Conversations in a Cameroon Village*. Oxford and Providence, RI: Berg.

Popper, Karl (1972) *Objective Knowledge: an Evolutionary Approach*. Oxford: Clarendon Press.

Radcliffe-Brown, Alfred Reginald (1952) *Structure and Function in Primitive Society*. London: Cohen and West.

Rowlands, Michael and Warnier, Jean-Pierre (1988) Sorcery, power and the modern state in Cameroon. *Man*, 23, 118–32.

Sahlins, Marshall (1976a) *Culture and Practical Reason*. Chicago: University of Chicago Press.

Sahlins, Marshall (1976b) *The Use and Abuse of Biology: an Anthropological Critique of Sociobiology*. Ann Arbor: University of Michigan Press.

Schneider, David M. (1968) Virgin birth. Correspondence *Man*, 3(1), 126–9.

Schoeck, Helmut (1997) The evil eye: forms and dynamics of a universal superstition. In Arthur C. Lehmann and James E. Myers (eds), *Magic, Witchcraft and Religion: an Anthropological Study of the Supernatural*, 4th edn. Mountain View, CA: Mayfield Publishing Co., pp. 227–30.

Schrempp, Gregory (1998) Aristotle's other self: on the boundless subject of anthropological discourse. In George W. Stocking Jr (ed.), *Romantic Motives: Essays on Anthropological Sensibility*. History of Anthropology, Volume 6. Madison: University of Wisconsin Press, pp. 10–43.

Shaw, Rosalind (1997) The production of witchcraft/witchcraft as production: memory, modernity, and the slave trade in Sierra Leone. *American Ethnologist* 24(4), 856–76.

Shaw, Rosalind (2002) *Memories of the Slave Trade: Ritual and the Historical Imagination in Sierra Leone*. Chicago and London: University of Chicago Press.

Sheldrake, Rupert (1994) *Seven Experiments that Could Change the World: a Do-it-yourself Guide to Revolutionary Science*. London: Fourth Estate.

Skorupski, J. (1973) Science and traditional religious thought. *Philosophy of the Social Sciences*, 3.

Smith, Wilfred Cantwell (1977) *Belief and History*. Charlottesville: University of Virginia Press.

Smith, Wilfred Cantwell (1979) *Faith and Belief*. Charlottesville: University of Virginia Press.

Sperber, Dan (1985) *On Anthropological Knowledge*. Cambridge: Cambridge University Press.

Spooner, Brian (1970) The evil eye in the Middle East. In Mary Douglas (ed.), *Witchcraft Confessions and Accusations*. London: Tavistock, pp. 311–19.

Steedly, Mary Margaret (1993) *Hanging without a Rope: Narrative Experience in Colonial and Neocolonial Karoland*. Princeton, NJ: Princeton University Press.

Stein, Howard, F. (1974) Envy and the evil eye among Slovak-Americans: an essay in the psychological ontogeny of belief and ritual. *Ethnos*, 2(1), 15–46. Reprinted in Alan Dundes (ed.), *The Evil Eye: a Casebook*. New York and London: Garland, pp. 223–56.

Stewart, Charles and Shaw, Rosalind (eds) (1994) *Syncretism/Anti-Syncretism: the Politics of Religious Synthesis*. London: Routledge.

Tambiah, Stanley Jeyaraja (1991) *Magic, Science, Religion and the Scope of Rationality*. Cambridge: Cambridge University Press.

Thomas, Keith (1971) *Religion and the Decline of Magic*. London: Weidenfeld & Nicolson.

Turnbull, Colin (1976) *Wayward Servants: the Two Worlds of the African Pygmies*. Westport, CT: Greenwood Press.

Tylor, Edward Burnett (1890) Notes on the survival of ancient amulets against the evil eye. *Journal of the Royal Anthropological Institute*, 19, 54–6.

van Gennep, Arnold (1981) The research topic: or, folklore without end. In Alan Dundes (ed.), *The Evil Eye: a Casebook*. New York and London: Garland, pp. 3–8.

Wilson, Brian (ed.) (1970) *Rationality*. Oxford: Basil Blackwell.

Wilson, Monica (1951) Witch beliefs and social structure. *American Journal of Sociology*, 56(4), 307–13.

Winch, Peter (1958) *The Idea of a Social Science, and Its Relation to Philosophy*. London: Routledge & Kegan Paul.

Chapter 9

Pilgrimage

Introduction

Pilgrimage is not a classical anthropological topic like witchcraft or shaman-ism, and until the 1970s received relatively little attention. Many ethno-graphic accounts center on a particular shrine and its devotees, which provide a geographical focus akin to the small community of traditional anthropology. More recent studies have looked at the personal experiences of pilgrims on the road (Frey, 1998) or at the role of a shrine in maintaining a national diasporic identity (Tweed, 1997). Gananath Obeyesekere (1984) adopted a less conventional approach in his psychological case studies of female ascetics at the shrine of Kataragama in Sri Lanka. Obeyesekere's main interest was not the actual pilgrimage as an event, but the symbolic role of the women's matted hair, and the way this related to their life stories (see chapter 2).[1] Anthropology has few tools for dealing with personal experi-ence, and pilgrimage, with its enactment of a physical, spiritual, and emotional journey, and a search for transformation, healing, or sociality, presents a particular challenge. There is a danger that anthropologists either ignore the transitory process of the actual pilgrimage, or map only its social and cultural dimensions. The study of pilgrimage therefore calls for a combination of approaches, ideally drawing on a variety of disciplinary perspectives. We need to take into account the history of a particular shrine; the psychological and spiritual experience of the individual; political, economic, and cultural factors; the interactions between home, journey, and shrine; the theological rationale of a particular site and the religious and cultural meanings it holds for its devotees; and the wider economic and social effects that pilgrimage has on sending and receiving communities, and those on pilgrimage routes.

We will begin by examining existing approaches to the study of pilgrimage and some of the typologies devised to classify them. We will then look at pilgrimages as an arena of competing discourses, a domain in which different views and expectations coexist, using the example of the Roman Catholic shrine of Our Lady of Lourdes in France. We will also apply the study of pilgrimage to the notion of religious synthesis or syncretism. All religions and cultures reflect contact with others, and even the most conservative regimes change over time. Some, however, openly embrace change and are happy to incorporate new elements, while others see this as polluting or dangerous and resist what they regard as foreign influences. It is quite possible for a tradition to be extremely welcoming to new ideas while maintaining a discourse of tradition and stability. The opposite is also true. A religion or culture may see itself as pluralistic whilst in fact remaining relatively static. The fact of synthesis is not an issue, but how it is dealt with and the politics of syncretism are of considerable interest to anthropologists. The theme of syncretism is illustrated by pilgrimage in the Andes in South America, where indigenous Indian and Hispanic Roman Catholic elements are constantly reworked, depending on the political, religious, and social needs at any one moment. Although the examples chosen are primarily within a Christian context, pilgrimage is a major theme in most religious traditions, and has parallels in virtually all religions.

Approaches to the Study of Pilgrimage

Pilgrimage is not an epiphenomenon of modern life. It has the power to move vast numbers of people across the world, to transform the economies of countries and regions, and to disseminate political as well as religious messages. The Islamic pilgrimage to Mecca in Saudi Arabia, known as the *Hajj*, one of the best known and highest profile pilgrimages in the world, attracts around two million visitors each year. Rome, the center of the Roman Catholic world, attracted several million visitors for the millennium, and lodgings in and around the city were booked up years in advance. Pope John Paul II could pull crowds of young people numbering in millions for international youth days held in various parts of the world, as well as for his funeral mass at the Vatican City in Rome. In 1958, the centenary year of the apparitions of the Virgin Mary to Bernadette Soubirous, over five million pilgrims visited Lourdes, and in 1987 the number was over four and a half million.[2] India, however, can boast the most popular pilgrimage sites. Every 12 years the pilgrimage of Kumbha Mela, held at the sacred river confluence at Allahabad, draws over 10 million pilgrims.[3]

Discomfort and danger, far from discouraging pilgrims, can add to a site's reputation and increase the merit attached to visiting a shrine. James Preston

(1992, p. 35) records that the Shaivite shrine of Amarnath in Kashmir, situated at 12,725 feet above sea level, continues to attract pilgrims despite the dangers of the journey. In 1928 over five hundred people died negotiating the final precipitous 30-mile trek, and in 1970 18 people died in a blizzard. The *Hajj* has seen its share of disasters from a variety of causes: fire, civil unrest, and suffocation caused by panic in massive crowds. Even in Ireland pilgrimage has its challenges. The Stations of the Cross on the ancient monastic island of Skellig Michael are now out of bounds to the public as they are considered too precipitous, but pilgrims on the mainland continue to ascend the 2,510-foot mountain known as Croagh Patrick every year. In 1106 the Bishop of Ardpatrick was killed, and in 1972, when 40,000 pilgrims ascended the mountain, 15 had to be stretchered down. Lightning has also been responsible for the deaths of pilgrims praying on the exposed summit (Turner and Turner, 1978, p. 208; Preston, 1992, p. 36). Many of the world's most popular shrines record their share of tragedies, and as the number of pilgrims continues to increase, so does the potential for disaster.

Early anthropological studies of pilgrimage are few and far between. The Semitic scholar William Robertson Smith dealt briefly with the topic in his 1907 work, *The Religion of the Semites*, and Robert Hertz published one of the first sociological studies of a pilgrimage shrine in 1913 when he wrote a brief work on the Alpine shrine of St Besse. Eric Wolf's short piece on the Virgin of Guadalupe in Mexico (1958) was among the first anthropological studies based on a New World shrine. Émile Durkheim's classic study *The Elementary Forms of the Religious Life* ([1915] 1976), although not dealing specifically with pilgrimage, has proved extremely influential. Durkheim regarded religious festivals as occasions for social regeneration and moral unity, and many studies have followed Durkheim in emphasizing the ways in which pilgrimages weld together diverse communities and various social strata into more collective entities. To some extent this is evidently the case. The Muslim *Hajj*, one of the Five Pillars of Islam, can be seen as one example in which individual partici-pants from all over the Islamic world and of all social classes are removed from their locality and become conscious of a wider and more inclusive identity.[4] The American Black Muslim leader Malcolm X, for instance, preached anti-white Islam until he experienced the universal, leveling effect of the pilgrim-age to Mecca, and became convinced that there could be no such thing as an exclusive black Islam.[5] Marxist approaches to pilgrimage have been equally functionalist, except that in place of social integration, religious cults are implicated in the generation and maintenance of ideologies that legitimize domination and oppression. In the case of the *Hajj*, for instance, it could be argued that by presenting the myth of social equality for the duration of the pilgrimage real inequalities are preserved and legitimated.

Victor Turner, in his book *Dramas, Fields and Metaphors* (1974),[6] also developed a functionalist approach, dealing with pilgrimage as a social process. Turner linked pilgrimage to the middle, liminal, anti-structural stage of a rite of passage (see chapter 6).[7] In the liminal stage of a rite of passage the bonds of communitas or egalitarianism are uppermost. According to Turner, pilgrimage takes people out of normal society and throws individuals together, united by a common purpose. It is at odds with the normal social hierarchies and institutional norms and ideas. It is anti-structural, creative, and transformative. Pilgrimage supports social structures inasmuch as anti-structure is needed as a corrective to overweening structure, but is not to be identified with structured society. There are obviously occasions when Turner's analysis holds good. A well-paid New York journalist who felt the urge to leave his job, sell his apartment, and rethink his life and priorities described to a radio audience recently how he ended up as a pilgrim on the road to the shrine of Saint James of Compostela (Santiago de Compostela) in Spain. He described the companionship of fellow pilgrims along the way, and the lack of interest in what people did or how much they earned in their "other" life. For the duration of the journey, all pilgrims were equal and shared a common goal (cf. Frey, 1998).

The problem with all three of these functionalist approaches, which focus on the role of pilgrimage in relation to the structure of society, is that while pilgrimages *may* act as a force of moral regeneration (Durkheim), *may* make people content with their lot in their everyday life so that they no longer struggle to improve their condition (Marx), and *may* cement bonds of communitas (Turner), equally they may not. As universal paradigms functionalist approaches are wanting, telling only part of the story. If we take the *Hajj* as an example, the pilgrimage is as likely to highlight ethnic and religious tensions as it is to create feelings of commonality. Existing differences can be thrown into the spotlight and old enmities may come to a head during a pilgrimage. The Church of the Holy Sepulchre, the reputed site of Jesus's death and burial in Jerusalem, has become the arena of fierce competition between various factions, each with its own interests to protect. The Marian shrine of Walsingham in Norfolk (England) has parallel Roman Catholic and Anglican pilgrimage sites and facilities, and few people who visit the small village on church-organized trips are fully aware of the holy places of the "other side," despite the fact that they form part of a single shrine complex.[8] The more recent site of Marian apparitions and popular pilgrimage destination of Medjugorje in Bosnia-Herzegovina cannot be fully understood outside the context of tensions between Christians and Muslims and between Serbian-Orthodox and Croat-Roman Catholic Christians.[9]

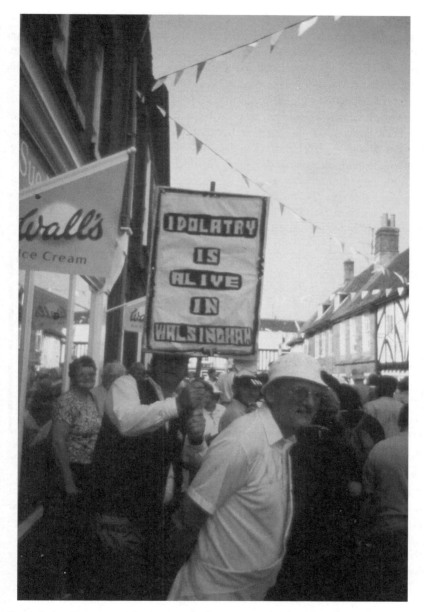

Figure 9.1 Competing discourses of pilgrimage in Walsingham, Norfolk.
© Simon Coleman

In an effort to overcome the limitations of functionalist approaches, some anthropologists have attempted to look at the very different conceptions of pilgrims and other people connected with a particular pilgrimage locale. John Eade, Michael Sallnow, and other contributors to *Contesting the Sacred* (1991) use the term "competing discourses" to describe the various agendas and world-views that operate at a pilgrimage site. From this perspective Victor Turner's view of pilgrimage as communitas can be seen as representing one particular discourse concerning pilgrimage rather than an empirical description of it (cf. Eade and Sallnow, 1991, p. 5). The discourse of communitas might well coexist or compete with alternative discourses. With the *Hajj*, for instance, a discourse of universal brotherhood and sisterhood coexists with a discourse of intra-Muslim divisions. The Shiite–Sunni split, which always has the potential to erupt into violence and which requires a massive military presence, can hardly be accommodated within a Turnerian model of communitas.

---

discourse – speech or language, and by extension the worldview associated with a language. In anthropology, and literary and cultural studies more generally, the term discourse has been greatly extended in its referents.
discourse theory – Mikhail Bakhtin (see chapter 3) viewed all "texts," which can include social situations as well as written or oral texts, as plural or **dialogic**. The voice of the author or anthropologist is just one among many. Michel Foucault (see chapter 2) pointed not just to the plurality of voices in any situation but also to the power differentials between various parties. Looking at **competing discourses** therefore involves sensitivity to power relations as well as recognition of different perspectives.

In shifting the focus to the multiplicity of meanings and motivations associated with any pilgrimage site, Eade and Sallnow have opened up a fruitful line of study. It should be noted that the term "competing" does not necessarily imply conscious or antagonistic contests between various interest groups, although these may occur. It is the plurality of views and the importance of interpreting social fields as textured or multi-faceted rather than homogenous that comes to the fore. As Eade and Sallnow write in their Introduction to *Contesting the Sacred*:

> What, then, is the new agenda for pilgrimage studies that emerges from these chapters? Put briefly, it amounts to a recognition that pilgrimage is above all an arena for competing religious and secular discourses, for both the official co-option and the non-official recovery of religious meanings, for conflict between orthodoxies, sects, and confessional groups, for drives towards consensus and communitas, *and* for counter-movements towards separateness and

division. The essential heterogeneity of the pilgrimage process, which was marginalized or suppressed in the earlier, deterministic models of the correspondence theorists [following a Durkheimian reading] and those who adopted a Turnerian paradigm, is here pushed centre-stage, rendered problematic. As a direct consequence, the theoretical discourse *about* pilgrimage becomes more diversified and discrepant, being less concerned to match empirical instances with a preconceived ideal – whether analytically or theologically inspired – than to deconstruct the very category of "pilgrimage" into historically and culturally specific behaviours and meanings. For, if one can no longer take for granted the meaning of a pilgrimage for its participants, one can no longer take for granted a uniform definition of the phenomenon of "pilgrimage" either. (Eade and Sallnow, 1991, pp. 2–3)

We also find approaches to the study of pilgrimage vary according to an author's interests. Some writers focus on the experience of pilgrims (as in Geoffrey Chaucer's *Canterbury Tales* or Nancy Frey's *Pilgrim Stories*), or a cult, with all its historical and sociological dimensions (as in Robert Hertz's study of St Besse), or the shrine or pilgrimage locale itself. Mircea Eliade (1959, 1963) has developed the notion of a sacred center with an intrinsic pulling power. It is true that sacred sites often remain remarkably constant while the uses to which they are put changes. Christian churches and shrines in Europe and elsewhere are frequently built over or incorporate earlier pre-Christian sites. Some writers have sought to explain the attraction of certain places in terms of the earth's magnetism or other topographical features.[10] Most anthropologists have, however, been rather skeptical of explanations of a site's popularity based on some intrinsic qualities, especially if they fail to take account of more human factors, and on the whole dislike anything that could smack of essentialism or reductionism. Rather confusingly, James Preston (1992) has adopted the term "spiritual magnetism" to describe the accumulative sanctity of many shrines. Alan Morinis seeks to clarify this expression by relating it to a whole host of factors, thereby avoiding an oversimplified or materialist (Eliadian) interpretation of the shrine's power:

It is because pilgrimage centres are repositories for a culture's ideals that they have been so commonly and extensively supported. Political patronage has been common . . . Celebrated pilgrimage places often enshrine relics of the most revered saints or most authenticated apparitions of the divine. These centres have been glorified with the highest expressions of religious art and architecture that cultures have evolved. The result is that the shrine incarnates the ideal it embodies. The message that this place is the holy of holies is strongly reinforced for the pilgrim in the art, architecture, music, drama, and so on that embellish the centre. In fact, once the "spiritual magnetism" of the place develops . . . , it can become so powerful that it overwhelms group or cultural boundaries and so draws pilgrims of many affiliations, who come because of the reputation for power the place projects and manifests through material representations. (Morinis, 1992a, p. 5)

This view could be regarded as similar to Durkheim's notion of the shrine as the embodiment of a society's highest goals and ideals. Morinis would, however, wish to argue that it is less deterministic. It does not assume that the god that is worshiped is society's representation of itself, nor that religion is necessarily the only or even the most important factor in enhancing the reputation of a shrine. Neither does Morinis wish to prejudge the motivations of those who are drawn to such a site. Some may wish to conform to a society's ideals as manifested by a shrine, others may come out of curiosity, compulsion, or habit, or in the hope of extracting some of its putative power for their own ends.

Typologies

We have not as yet attempted to define pilgrimage, or to look at various ways in which pilgrimages or pilgrims can be classified. As the title of his edited book *Sacred Journeys* suggests, Alan Morinis uses the term "wherever journeying and some embodiment of an ideal intersect" (1992a, p. 3). This would include Australian Aboriginals visiting sacred places associated with the Dreamtime (see chapter 5), or Zuni in the southwestern United States visiting shrines on their sacred Corn Mountain. The Incas, as we will see below, had well-established pilgrimage trails linking all parts of their former Andean empire. The connection between pilgrimage and tourism often arises as an issue (cf. Cohen, 1992) and it would be fair to say that we are talking about a continuum rather than an absolute difference between the two. Visitors to Rome may describe themselves as "spiritual tourists," popping into the odd church and admiring the frescos as part of a cultural tour. Whether or not they regard themselves as pilgrims may depend upon where they are at any one moment and their attitude towards a site. Someone who goes regularly to the Vatican for Mass is unlikely to describe him or herself as pilgrim (other than in the sense of being on the pilgrimage of life). For others, being in the holy city and visiting its religious sites will be their specific aim, possibly with the intention of earning the indulgences dispensed via the Roman Catholic Church.[11] Morinis points out that distinguishing pilgrims from travelers or tourists is made easier by the fact that in most cultures pilgrims tend to be "self-labeling." At times company and destination may be less important than a person's inner disposition, although in other instances the formal designation of an event as a pilgrimage is what makes it one for its participants.

We tend to think of pilgrimage in terms of physical journeys to geograph-
ically located places, but the term is used in the vernacular of many languages
and cultures much more widely. The journey may be metaphorical, internal,
and spiritual with no physical movement. The goal may be mapped out, or
pilgrims may set off on their journey as wanderers with no fixed destination,
led only by chance or the hand of God. In the early medieval Irish, Scottish,
and Welsh tradition the ideal of the "desert" was taken over from the ascetic
hermits of the early Christian centuries, who were known as the Desert
Fathers. The lives of the saints often recount how the holy men and
women would leave home and family as an act of penitence or asceticism.
They might become missionaries in foreign lands, forever exiled from kin and
country, or live in a remote and desolate place, cut off from all creature
comforts. Morinis emphasizes the importance of ideology in defining
a pilgrimage. The goal should embody valued ideals. This would not limit
the use of the term to religious gatherings. For a football fan a visit to the
home of their club side may be regarded as a pilgrimage. Grace Davie (1993)
describes how in the case of Anfield, the ground of Liverpool football club in
England, the secular and religious have become entwined. Following the
tragedy at Hillsborough stadium in Sheffield in 1989, in which 94 Liverpool
supporters watching an away game were crushed to death in the crowd, the
home ground at Anfield became a center of pilgrimage, with religious leaders
taking a prominent role in expressing and channeling people's grief. With the
death of Diana, Princess of Wales, a similar conflation of the sacred and
secular was evident (illustrating the difficulties with Durkheim's rather rigid
dichotomy between the sacred and profane). Diana has been accorded semi-
divine status by both the popular press and many people in Britain,
and anticipating the disruption her cult status could cause to local people,
she was buried on an island, formerly a pets' cemetery, on her brother's
family estate. Here access to her grave can be controlled in a way that
would not be possible in the family crypt in the local church. The United
States has long been familiar with this celebrity phenomenon in the shape
of the cult of Elvis Presley and Graceland, his former home at Memphis
in Tennessee (cf. King, 1993; Clift and Clift, 1996). Bearing in mind this
wide variation and broad usage of the term, Morinis tenders the following
definition:

> [T]he pilgrimage is a journey undertaken by a person in quest of a state that he or
> she believes to embody a valued ideal. At its most conventional, the end of
> the pilgrimage is an actual shrine located at some fixed geographical point.
> The place has acquired a reputation that draws pilgrims...One who journeys
> to a place of importance to him or herself alone may also be a pilgrim.

> The allegorical pilgrimage seeks out a place not located in the geographical
> sphere. Some sacred journeys are wanderings that have no fixed goal; the
> pilgrimage here is the search for an unknown or hidden goal. (Morinis 1992a:
> 4, emphasis added)

The typologies of pilgrimage that have evolved are dependent upon the
background and intentions of the writer. A Christian theologian, J. G. Davies
(1988, p. vi), focusing on pilgrimage as a spiritual phenomenon, identifies
four themes in contemporary pilgrimages, with chapters entitled "Pilgrimage
as a Spiritual Exercise," "Pilgrimage as an Imitation of Christ and His Saints,"
"Pilgrimage, Identity and Unity," and "Pilgrimage and the Bible." Simon
Coleman and John Elsner, in *Pilgrimage Past and Present* (1995) adopt an
approach consistent with a comparative religious studies perspective, with
chapters on the classical world, Jewish, Muslim, Christian, Indian, and
Buddhist pilgrimage. We can also usefully produce a typology of pilgrimage
based on destination, which serves to remind us that the "sacred place" is
only one possible goal, and that sacred places themselves can be extraordinarily varied. I would identify at least five foci – although in themselves these
tell us nothing of the motivation or experience of the pilgrim or the process
of pilgrimage (cf. Nolan and Nolan, 1989):

1   Pilgrimage to a sacred place.
2   Pilgrimage to a sacred person.
3   Pilgrimage related to a sacred object.
4   Pilgrimage as a sacred text.
5   Pilgrimage as an allegorical journey.

In order to explore further the nature of pilgrimage we can consider each
category in turn.

1   *Pilgrimage to a sacred place.* The pilgrimage locale may be a physical
    structure such as a building or some other construction, for example,
    the Holy Sepulchre in Jerusalem, Graceland in Tennessee, or Anfield
    football ground in Liverpool. It could be a feature of the landscape, like
    Ayres Rock (Uluru) in central Australia or the River Ganges in India, or
    a place in which natural features have been enhanced by human efforts,
    such as holy wells with steps and canopies. These constructions may be
    quite elaborate, like the Roman baths at the shrine of Sulis Minerva in
    Bath, England. With the resurgence of Paganism in the West, attention is
    increasingly paid to sites thought to focus natural energies, such as stone
    circles or standing stones, or to natural features such as trees.[12] Many of

the most popular contemporary Roman Catholic shrines are associated with a theophany, the manifestation of a deity or some aspect of the divine to human beings. Lourdes in France, Fatima in Portugal, Knock in Ireland, Medjugorie in Bosnia-Herzogovina, and Guadalupe in Mexico are among many sites associated with the appearance of the Virgin Mary to one or more people, often children, and almost always from a humble background.[13]

2   *Pilgrimage to a sacred person.* The visionaries of Medjugorie, children at the time the apparitions were initiated in 1981, continue to draw pilgrims to their home village, providing an alternative focus to the sites of the apparitions themselves. In some cases, however, the sanctity of the individual rather than a site associated with an event is sufficient to draw devotees. The Franciscan monk Padre Pio, who received the stigmata (wounds mirroring those Jesus is thought to have received on the cross), attracted growing numbers of pilgrims to San Giovanni Rotondo in Italy, as did another famous priest, the Curé d'Ars in France. In both cases making one's confession and attendance at a Mass was the goal of a pilgrimage for most devotees. In Germany, Mother Meera, a Hindu woman thought by many people to be an *avatar* or manifestation of the divine, draws thousands of people to *darshans* or silent meditations at her home.[14] Pilgrims now need to book some three years in advance in order to attend. Lubavitcher Jews used to make similar pilgrimages to the movement's Brooklyn headquarters in the United States, where their leader, Rebbe Menachem Schneerson, lived until his death in 1994. Some of Schneerson's followers were convinced that he was the *Mosiach* or Messiah and that he would rise from the dead.[15] Within the Christian world there is usually a tension between a holy person (saint or visionary) and the hierarchical structures of the Church. An individual is not easily brought under official control, and if a cult develops after a person's death this is easier to regulate than when they were alive. Turner and Turner (1978, pp. 223–5) provide a vivid picture of one of the visionaries of La Salette in France who, having been educated by the Church following her encounter with the Virgin Mary, wandered around France, Italy, and England, continuously elaborating upon and promoting her apocalyptic message, hungry for the attention of devotees.[16]

3   *Pilgrimage related to a sacred object.* Some sacred objects are fixed in one place (rocks, trees, springs, most buildings), but others are peripatetic.[17] Relics are an obvious example. Within the Roman Catholic, Orthodox, and Eastern or Syriac branches of Christianity it is believed that reception of the Eucharist (the body and blood of Jesus Christ transformed into bread and wine during the Mass) during a person's life sanctifies the body.

Even without this theological justification, any part of a holy person or an object associated with them may be held to contain sacred powers and benedictions. The Crusades to Jerusalem by Western Christians in the Middle Ages led to an orgy of relic hunting – pieces of the "true cross," the "holy nails," the Virgin's breast milk, the burial cloth of Jesus (thought by many to have survived as the Shroud of Turin), as well as the physical remains of the saints and their clothes, all multiplied. This was not a new phenomenon. In Wales in the early Middle Ages, for instance, the dioceses of Saint David's and Llandaf competed with one another, and acquiring saints' relics could add to the status and prosperity of a shrine and its personnel. Some relics changed hands frequently, as different churches and nobles regarded them as trophies, seeking to accumulate as many as possible. By the twelfth century there was no shortage of suppliers. Bodies, organs, or statues that seem to defy normal physical laws, were (and still are) particularly sought after (blood that liquefies, incorruptible or sweet-smelling corpses, weeping or bleeding images, and so on). Statues or images of the Virgin Mary and other saints are often treated as "spiritual power houses," and may be taken on procession at times of crisis. Several are credited with saving the occupants of towns and villages from disaster. Orthodox icons are also mobile and some have acquired reputations of particular sanctity. Within Buddhist and Hindu tradition, sacred objects are also common, whether a tooth or footprint of the Buddha, or a traffic bollard in the Golden Gate Park in San Francisco identified as a Shivite *lingam* (phallus).

4   *Pilgrimage as a sacred text.* The idea of a pilgrimage being based primarily upon a sacred text may seem strange, but this is one way of understanding Christian pilgrimages to the Holy Land. The pilgrims' itinerary and devotions are mapped onto sites identified in the Old and New Testaments. Most Protestant pilgrims, and some Roman Catholics, are likely to have a Bible with them as they travel around Israel and Palestine, and their organized tours will focus exclusively on the holy places identified in the Scriptures (cf. Bowman 1991, 1994). The contemporary political or even religious dynamics of the area are likely to remain invisible to the majority of the pilgrims, and the "correct" location (for instance of the Garden Tomb) is of secondary importance to the events described in the text. The Via Dolorosa, the route through the streets of Jerusalem thought to have been taken by Jesus on his way to Golgotha, the mount of crucifixion, and the allegorical events of the journey (based to some extent on Gospel accounts), are reproduced in every Roman Catholic church and shrine, in the "Stations of the Cross," so that many pilgrims have in fact walked the route devotionally at home many times before they do so physically in

Jerusalem. The *Hajj* is similarly based on a text, the Qur'an, so that pilgrims retrace the significant places and events concerning the foundation of their faith and the life of Muhammad as laid out in the holy book.

5   *Pilgrimage as an allegorical journey.* The Stations of the Cross mentioned above constitute both a physical and spiritual pilgrimage: although they are enacted within the confined space of a church the meditational dimension takes precedence over physical circumambulation of the building. Christian, the hero of John Bunyan's seventeenth-century pietist work, *The Pilgrim's Progress*, represents the apogee of the interiorization of the concept of pilgrimage. All of life and its struggles can be regarded as a journey towards perfection with heaven the goal. Hindu, Buddhist, Islamic Sufi, and Christian traditions have all developed this ideal of the interior pilgrimage. Physical stasis may enhance the inner journey, particularly within Christianity and Buddhism where spiritual perfection has often been sought within cloistered or semi-enclosed communities.[18]

Our Lady of Lourdes

The cult and shrine of Our Lady of Lourdes in southern France provides an example though which we can examine various approaches to the study of pilgrimage, in particular the notion of competing discourses.[19] In 1858 the Virgin Mary is said to have appeared 18 times to a peasant girl, Bernadette Soubirous, at a cave (grotto) just outside the old town of Lourdes. On one occasion the "Lady" instructed Bernadette to wash and drink in a spring where there was only bare earth. Bernadette started to dig with her hands as instructed, and water began to appear. This later developed into a flow of some 32,000 gallons a day, and soon acquired a reputation for miraculous healing.[20] In another utterance the Lady is reputed to have called herself the Immaculate Conception, a theological title officially declared a dogma of the Roman Catholic Church by Pope Pius IX some four years previously. The mid-nineteenth century was a time of increasing secularization in France and diminishing papal power in Italy. Both the local and international Church soon validated the visions and developed the shrine of Our Lady of Lourdes, using its reputation for miracles and its apparent confirmation of theological positions to bolster their causes.[21] The cult has continued to develop, both in Lourdes itself and via associations in various countries. It is still particularly associated with healing although, as we see below, the doctrinal element remains a dominant feature of the Church's official discourse.

Victor and Edith Turner regarded Lourdes as a paradigm of communitas, a moment of anti-structure, stating that: "In Lourdes there is a sense of living communitas, whether in the great singing processions by torchlight or in the agreeable little cafés of the back streets, where tourists and pilgrims gaily sip their wine and coffee. Something of Bernadette has tinctured the entire social milieu – a cheerful simplicity, a great depth of communion" (1978, p. 230). The Turners were concerned to find a descriptive and scientific language to describe religious experience – the warmth, elation, peace, healing, and well-being reported subjectively by hundreds of thousands of people who made the journey to Lourdes. In *Contesting the Sacred*, however, both Dahlberg and Eade attempt to give a more nuanced, but at the same time "flatter," view of Lourdes and its pilgrimages, paying greater attention to the social dimensions of the shrine, but at the expense of giving depth to the spiritual experience of pilgrims. Their contributions to *Contesting the Sacred* contrast elements of structure and communitas, along with "power and resistance, collective discipline and freedom of expression, hierarchy and equality, sacred and secular" (Eade, 1991, p. 75).

Dahlberg and Eade identify two competing discourses associated with Lourdes, the miracle discourse, concerned with miraculous healing, and the suffering discourse, based on a validation of sickness and hardship as a way of sharing in Christ's Passion. They trace a shift in emphasis from the former, particularly during the first century of the shrine's history, to the latter. This is related to wider social trends and to the Catholic Church's attempt to move pilgrims from an individual, ecstatic, female-focused experience to one based on the Church and its sacraments, highly structured and male in orientation. Dahlberg quotes a saying common among European Catholics that "Rome is the head of the church but Lourdes is its heart" (1991, p. 35). The suffering discourse is associated with Rome and with Christ's Passion – the exemplar of suffering. Mary, on the other hand, is believed to be especially present at Lourdes, particularly in the grotto where she appeared to Bernadette, and to communicate directly with pilgrims, offering physical healing and perfection via her prayers and the curative waters from the spring she uncovered. On a pilgrimage for sick and handicapped children, Dahlberg noted that it was only the new helpers who spoke spontaneously about miracle cures, and that the guide book they used and the culture communicated by the more experienced clergy and helpers, as well as the routine of caring for the sick children, "had the effect of deflecting the desire for a miraculous cure from Our Lady of Lourdes and replacing this with an affirmation of the value of physical suffering" (1991, p. 43).

Eade draws on his experience of working as a male helper or *brancardier* at the shrine in order to elucidate the tensions between the rather military-style hierarchy and obsession with order among those who control the shrine, and the aspirations of pilgrims who visit it. One location where conflicts can arise is the baths, where pilgrims are invited to immerse themselves in the icy cold waters piped from the miraculous spring into a covered building. Eade notes a transition from an emphasis on the two female saints associated with the shrine (Mary and Bernadette), invoked through the recitation of the "Hail Mary," the kissing of the Virgin's statue and drinking the water, to "a stress on the sacrament of baptism [that] directs attention away from miraculous cures and towards the institutional authority of the church and the redemptive sacrifice of Christ" (1991, p. 63). As Eade comments: "The shift from miracle to sacrificial discourse implies a shift from a focus on the female, virginal, and maternal elements symbolized by the two female saints and towards a preoccupation with the Son of God and with the male, fatherly qualities of the hierarchical institution of the church" (1991, p. 63).

The recent shift away from the miracle discourse towards the suffering discourse can be seen as an intentional repositioning by the Catholic Church. In the nineteenth century its interests were best served by emphasizing the miraculous. Today the Church attempts to maintain control by highlighting the ecclesial aspects of the pilgrimage. Neither Eade nor Dahlberg claim that these two competing interpretations, the miracle discourse and the suffering discourse, sum up or are sufficient to "explain" the shrine or the experience of pilgrims visiting it. Both describe some of the emotional and spiritual responses that draw people in their millions, many of them year after year. The valuation and virtual sanctification of the sick and handicapped at Lourdes is set by Dahlberg within a broader Catholic natural theology based on an acceptance of God's action in the material world (of which the refusal of artificial means of contraception is another manifestation). The notion of competing discourses, as demonstrated by these two articles, does, however, serve to open up an interpretation of the shrine to multiple perspectives. It is not assumed that the experience of the helpers or the pilgrims are the same, that all pilgrimages are alike, nor even that among the *brancardiers* or helpers is there unanimity. Despite the rhetoric of universal brother and sisterhood and caring, national differences and self-interest may be more in evidence. One could extend the analysis of Lourdes to the impact of the cult on the social and economic life of the region, or look at the tensions within the Church over control of the shine and its finances. In other words, simply to identify an experience of communitas is insufficient. It may be present, but is only one of a number of discourses that can be identified. As Eade and Sallnow state in their Introduction to *Contesting the Sacred*:

> The power of a shrine ... derives in large part from its character almost as a religious void, a ritual space capable of accommodating diverse meanings and practices – though of course the shrine staff might attempt, with varying degrees of success, to impose a single official discourse. This, in the final

analysis, is what confers upon a major shrine its essential, universalistic character: its capacity to absorb and reflect a multiplicity of religious discourses, to
be able to offer a variety of clients what each of them desires. Universalism is
ultimately constituted not by a unification of discourses but rather by the
capacity of a cult to entertain and respond to a plurality. The sacred centre,
then, in this perspective, appears as a vessel into which pilgrims devoutly pour
their hopes, prayers, and aspirations. And in a perfect illustration of the classic
Marxist model of fetishization and alienation, the shrine then appears to its
devotees as if it were itself dispensing the divine power and healing balm which
they seek. (Eade and Sallnow, 1991, pp. 15–16)

The Politics of Religious Synthesis

"The Politics of Religious Synthesis" is the sub-title of an influential collection
of essays published in 1994, under the title *Syncretism/Anti-Syncretism*, edited by
Charles Stewart and Rosalind Shaw.[22] In theological circles "syncretism" is
usually derogatory, suggesting a degenerate or illegitimate form of religion
(usually Christianity). African Independent Churches, for instance, are deemed
to be syncretic if they allow polygynous as well as monogamous marriage, or
adopt other "traditional" practices.[23] Within anthropology the term has not
carried these negative associations. It is assumed that all faiths and cultures
result from a continual process of contact, development, absorption, or conscious rejection of other elements. No society is a cultural island, and no religion
is "pure" in the sense that it can be extracted from its social and cultural milieu.

> **syncretism** – Greek *syn* – "with" and *krasis* – "mixture." The mixing together
> of two or more elements.

What is of interest to anthropologists is not the fact that a religion is
syncretic, but the processes and politics involved in that process. As Rosalind
Shaw and Charles Stewart say in their Introduction, "Simply identifying
a ritual or tradition as 'syncretic' tells us very little and gets us practically
nowhere, since all religions have composite origins and are continually
reconstructed through ongoing processes of synthesis and erasure" (1994,
p. 7). Hence the focus on the politics of religious synthesis and the discourses
around issues of purity, authenticity, and inclusiveness.

Before continuing it is worth saying a word about "anti-syncretism." If a
society or culture develops a discourse of religious "purity," linked to notions
of authenticity, it may consciously reject elements perceived as external to it

and seek to avoid the incorporation of new elements. This process can of course occur in relation to language or any other aspect of culture, not only with religion. As Shaw and Stewart put it:

> If we recast the study of syncretism as the politics of religious synthesis, one of the first issues which needs to be confronted is what we have termed "anti-syncretism"; the antagonism to religious synthesis shown by agents concerned with the defence of religious boundaries. Anti-syncretism is frequently bound up with the construction of "authenticity", which in turn is linked to notions of "purity". In Western religious discourses and scholarship in particular, the implicit belief remains that assertions of purity speak out naturally and transcendentally as assertions of authenticity. (Shaw and Stewart, 1994, p. 7)

A good example of an anti-syncretic religious culture is provided by the Kogi of the Sierra Nevada de Santa Marta in northern Colombia (see chapter 5). Alan Ereira (1990) describes the Kogi as the best preserved pre-Columbian civilization on the American continent, that is, the least affected by Western influences following the arrival of Christopher Columbus in the fifteenth century, despite the fact that the ancestors of the Kogi, the Tairona, were one of the first mainland peoples to encounter the Spaniards. Thanks in part to the mountainous terrain, which discouraged European settlement and allowed the Kogi to "disappear," they were able to select which aspects of Spanish culture they wanted to incorporate (such as metal and domestic animals) and which they wished to reject (including writing, European clothes, and Christianity). Despite various efforts to convert the Kogi, after some five hundred years of contact Christian missionaries have had markedly little success in gaining converts.

Syncretism in Latin America

The mixing of Christian and pre-Christian religious traditions in Central and South America is well documented. In many places the veneer of Catholicism seems to be fairly thin, especially if one takes the numbers of indigenous clergy as a measure. The Roman Catholic Church tended to take over religious sites and festivals from the pre-Columbian era but not in any straightforward or uniform manner. There has been and is a continuous process of negotiation between Latin forms of Christianity and indigenous religions and cultures, and attention needs to be paid to the historical details and social nuances in each time and place.[24] It is certainly the case that the cultural fit between indigenous practices and Roman Catholicism, or what Mary Lee Nolan terms "the permissibility of the familiar" (1991, p. 44) can be extremely close in some cases (although as the Kogi remind us, anti-syncretism is also possible). Inés Sanmiguel, in an article on sacred caves in the mythic system of indigenous Mexicans of Chiapas, for example, claims that:

On the basis of the available data, it is suggested that the Catholic Church was substituted for the cave. The church had in fact replaced part of the cave, and some of the ceremonies, especially the public ones, were moved from the cave to the church approximately 200 years ago. The private ceremonies are still gradually being moved from the cave to the church . . . caves and churches share certain morphological features: both are large, dark places, they both have crosses, incense, flowers, liquid and pine. (Sanmiguel, 1994, p. 170)

One difference between the church and a sacred cave noted by Sanmiguel was the images of the saints present in the church, which the cave does not have. However, anthropomorphic pre-Hispanic figures have been discovered in a cave in the region, suggesting that even the saints' statues would not be entirely unfamiliar.

Nolan warns against attributing all apparently non-Christian aspects of Latin American pilgrimage to indigenous roots. One needs first to examine the religious culture of the missionaries and settlers of a particular area, paying attention to the period of cult formation and the diffusion of ideas. Germanic and Italian folk traditions, as well as Iberian, have influenced Latin American Christianity, and in the Brazilian diocese of Eparquia, for example, pilgrimages reflect the Byzantine Rite traditions of the Ukrainian population, rather than Portuguese or indigenous Indian practices (1991, pp. 46–7).

A degree of cultural fit between a pilgrimage shrine and the indigenous culture helps it to achieve acceptance, as Morinis and Crumrine put it: "This familiarity makes it possible for pilgrims to negotiate the cultural pathways of the sacred centre far from their home parish" (1991, p. 4). But they also make the important point that in order for a shrine to gain acceptance beyond a limited area it must supersede its purely local dimensions, which it does by "claiming to be the repository of the typical ideals of the religious culture, but in their highest, most concentrated form" (pp. 4–5). The local and familiar and more differentiated and intra-regional elements of a pilgrimage tend to be focused on the shrine icons. In Latin America these are typically associated with images of wood or stone. Mary and Jesus are the most popular manifestations of the sacred, and in the pilgrimage shrine the painted or plaster replicas are imbued with life and divine power. Their potency is derived in part from the cosmological significance attributed to pilgrimage in pre-Columbian times. Herman Konrad (1991), for instance, points to the celestial dimension of Andean and Central American pilgrimages.[25] The Maya term usually translated as "pilgrim" actually means "passage and course of the stars" and the main gods were associated with the sun and moon, who were held to have lived on earth before taking up residence in the sky. Pilgrimages to sacred sites constructed in their honor mirror the circumnavigation of the heavenly bodies, linking the individual to the celestial domain. One of the best known Latin American cults, the Virgin of Guadalupe, illustrates well the syncretic fit between indigenous and Catholic beliefs:

> Conversion to Christianity, despite the intentions of the European clerics, did not eliminate the indigenous associations. The emergence of the Virgin of Guadalupe, patron saint of the Americas within the Catholic tradition, can be taken as a case in point. This image of the Virgin Mary miraculously imprinted on the shirt of the Indian Juan Diego hard on the heels of the Spanish conquest of the Aztec Empire in the sixteenth century, shows her standing on the crescent moon. The site of her shrine, on the hillock of Tepeyac, was the location of the Aztec shrine to Coatlicue, terrestrial goddess who had given birth to Huitzilopochtli, the Aztec personification of the blazing sun at noon.[26]

Pilgrimage in the Andes

Michael Sallnow (1991a, 1991b) has also attempted to look at Andean pilgrimages in the light of their historical and cultural context, rejecting Turnerian notions of homogeneity and Eliade's concept of the inherent power of a sacred center. Rather than search for universal meanings attached to a pilgrimage or shrine, Sallnow is interested in the way in which Andean and Spanish Roman Catholic meanings and understandings are superimposed on one another, and the manner in which interpretations change and develop according to social and historical circumstances. Sallnow paints a vivid picture of indigenous attitudes towards the land, while making the important point that Andean culture itself changes, and that non-Christian or pre-Christian elements are not to be viewed in a static sense as "survivals" from the past. Even aspects of belief and practice with very ancient roots are constantly selected and reworked in the present.

> The Andean landscape is imbued with sacredness. Human destinies are in part determined by chthonian powers, localized in the spirits of mountains, rocks, springs, rivers, and other topographic features, and generalized in the earth matrix, Pachamama. The cult of these telluric deities meshes with the cult of the dead, and has as its principal goal the channelling of the variegated powers inscribed in the landscape, pre-eminently the power of fertility, towards the satisfaction of human interests. This indigenous substrate to contemporary Andean religion is emphatically not a cultural survival from the pre-Columbian past, as is so often alleged; on the contrary, it has been actively reproduced and transformed, along with the peasant mode of livelihood which it serves, by the structures of political domination and economic exploitation imposed by the colonial and, later, the republican state. (Sallnow, 1991a, pp. 141–2)

> **apu** – Quechua word for "lord"; applied to mountain deities or spirits.[27]
> **cargo** – circulating ritual office holders or organized pilgrimage groups.
> **chthonic** – of or relating to the underworld.
> **Cusco/Cuzco** – the Inca capital prior to the destruction of the Inca Empire by the Spanish in the sixteenth century.
> **hieratic** – priestly.
> **Pachamama** – Andean (Quechua and Aymara) deity – "mother of earth and time."
> **telluric** – relating to or originating in or on the earth or soil; terrestrial.
> **thaumaturgic** – miraculous.
> **theophany** – manifestation of a deity or the divine to human beings.

Andean cultures have traditions of pilgrimage extending back over three thousand years, which, to borrow Sallnow's expression, can be understood as the "bodily mapping of socio-religious space" (1991a, p. 138). Pilgrimages reached their peak of development in the Inca imperial rituals of the fifteenth century that united all the shrines of the empire through the medium of sacrificial blood. This blood could be transported in sacred vessels, or in living victims, who were led along the extensive network of mountain trails (the metaphoric arteries of the state) that linked Cusco, the sacred imperial capital, with outlying regions. The sacrificial blood circulating around the body of the state was thought to ensure its life, stability, and fertility (while cementing Inca power over the non-Inca population).

Sallnow (1991a, pp. 138–9) traces three stages of religious colonization following the Spanish conquest of the central Andes. Pre-Hispanic pilgrimages were traditionally focused on earth deities (and the sun), and the powers of the sacred, animate landscape, with its power to give and sustain life, were worshiped. Petrification, the merging of wandering divinities into the rocks, thereby becoming part of the landscape, was common and such rocks often became pilgrimage destinations.[28] In the first stage of religious colonization by the incoming Roman Catholic Church, Marian and other saintly images were installed at traditional sacred sites in the hope that the corresponding pagan deities would be superseded. An indigenous Andean response to this imposition of Roman Catholic saints was a millenarian movement known as Taki Onquoy in the 1560s. Neglected Andean deities, formally associated with or lodged in features of the natural landscape – such as crags, mountains, and rivers, came to occupy the bodies of cult adepts, speaking through them and predicting the imminent overthrow of the white invaders and their gods.

After the Taki Onquoy uprising the Spanish tried a different approach, as seeking to replace the local Indian deities with Catholic saints appeared to have failed. They introduced a vigorous campaign for the extirpation of idolatry, and in an effort to reassert control forced the Indians into nucleated villages. They were organized into parishes, each with its own patron saint, feast days, and *cargos* or circulating ritual offices, based on the Iberian model. The hope was that with many small competing localized groups the wider ethnic identities and loyalties would be suppressed. The third and final stage was cult regionalization. From the end of the sixteenth century certain Christian statues and images began to be hailed as miraculous, credited with bringing rain, opening springs, saving people from earthquakes, healing, coming to life, and granting favors. Their shrines, often controlled by religious orders, became new centers of pilgrimage (frequently reconnecting with older pre-Christian sites). These icons and associated sites could be interpreted very differently by the Spanish and Indians, illustrating the conflicting meanings of these new syncretic ritual centers. As Sallnow remarks, miraculous images "enshrined a fundamental theological contradiction" and he goes on to say:

> For the Spaniards, they were the vehicles for displacing the satanic perversions of native religiosity and for reclaiming a foreign land for their faith and their God. For the Indians, on the other hand, they were the means to domesticate the foreign gods, to insert these evidently powerful divine interlopers into the matrix of the animate landscape and through them to reclaim and to reappropriate the extra-local sacred and ritual dimension of their colonized territories. Each group perceived and misunderstood the behaviour of the other through the inverting lens of its own misunderstandings. Thus, the Spanish clergy could and did construe devotional pilgrimage on the part of the Indians as evidence of their conversion to Christianity. The Indians, for their part, construed pilgrimage by Spaniards as demonstrating a tacit recognition by the colonists of the power of the animate landscape. (Sallnow, 1991a, pp. 149–50)

Andean pilgrimages provide a startling example of cultural interchange, religious syncretism, competing discourses and dynamic readjustment to enforced changes. At the mountain shrine known as El Señor de Qoyllur Rit'i (Lord of the Snow Star), for instance, Quechua versus Aymara, and Indian versus mixed race or Spanish identities and loyalties are played out. The shrine, or series of shrines, associated with the appearance of Jesus to a local Indian shepherd boy, Mariano, in the eighteenth century and a miraculous increase in his herd of llamas and alpacas, is linked in the minds of Indian pilgrims with the nearby mountain of Ausankati, home of the most powerful *apu* or mountain spirit in the region (Sallnow, 1991b). The shrine is attended by over 25,000 pilgrims around the feast of Corpus Christi in June, the majority of them Indians, although a *mestizo* religious brotherhood runs

the shrine, and a Spanish Roman Catholic priest is in attendance throughout. The Bishop of Cusco has even presided at the ceremonies, raising the
official status of the shrine.[29] For the majority of the Indian pilgrims the
transportation of a religious image or images from their home village to the
shrine for a blessing and its return are central to the pilgrimage. As well as
devotions to the image of the crucified Christ painted onto a rock,[30] some
pilgrims stage a mock fight on the glacier under cover of darkness, during
which it is accepted that one or more people may be taken by the *apu* as a
sacrifice and fail to return. There is even an element of sun worship, presided
over by the Catholic priest, at the conclusion of the ceremonies.[31]

Conclusion

The early lack of attention paid to pilgrimage by anthropologists is rapidly
being corrected. The challenge of incorporating historical and contemporary
sources, theology and ethnography, political and economic information, as
well as bridging personal, experiential, and social and institutional levels of
analysis, is being attempted by increasing numbers of scholars, whether as a
single or a collective effort. Pilgrimages form part of a continuum of the
practice of visiting sacred sites, and often overlap with secular tourism. We
need be less concerned with precise definitions of what does or does not
constitute a pilgrimage, than with the lessons we can learn from studying this
widespread and enduring aspect of human behavior. A pilgrim travels
through specially constructed time and space. One can make the same
journey as a pilgrim or as a tourist or traveler. We can then ask ourselves
what it is that changes the definition so that one journey is defined as a
pilgrimage while another is not. What are the motivations and expectations
of a pilgrimage that are excluded from more secular journeys? What is the
difference between performing ordinary religious duties and making a pilgrimage? Why do some people or places have the power to draw crowds of
thousands, even millions, of devotees? What are the political, institutional,
and economic dimensions of such cults, and under what circumstances does
their popularity wax and wane? What role do pilgrimages play in reinforcing
or dissolving national, ethnic, and linguistic boundaries? What do pilgrimages reveal about cosmological and environmental attitudes? It is hard to
imagine an atheist or humanist pilgrimage, but how different is the cult of
Elvis Presley or of numerous pop stars and other celebrities from ostensibly
religious cults? For the scholar there is also the practical question: how do you
study a phenomenon that is by its nature transitory and fluid? What are the
different perspectives to be gained studying a pilgrimage locale and actually

making a pilgrimage oneself? How is the ethnographer to combine the study of pilgrims and their networks, the pilgrimage itself and pilgrim sites?

While detailed ethnography can seek to answer at least some of these questions at the local level, we can also try to develop a general framework within which to locate pilgrimages. Jill Dubisch attempts to do this with her statement that:

> In summary, then, pilgrimage depends on (1) the association created within a particular religious tradition of certain events and/or sacred figures with a particular field of social space, and (2) the notion that the material world can make manifest the invisible spiritual world at such places... In addition, a pilgrimage site is connected in complex ways to the non-sacred world around it. It has economic, social, and political ramifications for the local community, the region, and even the nation. (Dubisch, 1995, pp. 38–9)

A pilgrimage, like a rite of passage, is a form of performance. Actually making the journey, whether spiritually from within the cell of a monastery, by measuring one's length across Tibetan passes, or by walking barefoot from the Slipper Chapel to the Holy House in Walsingham, is both a physical and emotional act. The experience of pilgrims may be formed and channeled by their expectations and by companions, or ritual experts, but they are also unique and personal, and therefore remain unpredictable and potentially transformative. Anthropologists vary in the emphasis they wish to place on individual psychology, but we will not achieve a great deal unless we are prepared to consider both the personal and social dimensions of any phenomenon, particularly in the case of pilgrimage in which the body remains central. A pilgrim may aspire to make contact with something beyond everyday experience, to provide a bridge between physical reality and the reality of the spirit (Clift and Clift, 1996, p. 15), but for the anthropologist the task is more complex. Pilgrims are embedded in social relations, they express a particular culture, they may have political goals and aspirations, and their presence has economic implications for a locality. In short, there is still considerable scope for anthropological work, from a variety of perspectives, on this ubiquitous but relatively neglected aspect of religious behavior.

Notes

1   Cf. Stirrat (1991) for an account of Catholic pilgrimage in Sri Lanka.
2   Turner and Turner (1978, p. 230); Eade (1991, p. 76).
3   The number is cited in Morinis (1992a, p. 1). Some pilgrimage destinations now have their own extensive websites, such as Tirupati in Andhra Pradesh (India), and many Marian shrines.

4   All adult Muslims are expected to make the journey to Mecca to take part in the *Hajj* at least once in their lives if they are able to do so (financially and physically).

5   Malcolm X was murdered by his former colleagues for what was regarded as betrayal, although the more open and liberal form of Islam he subsequently stood for has been continued by Wasir Deen Muhammad at his mosque in Brooklyn, New York.

6   See also Turner and Turner (1978).

7   Turner also coined the term "liminoid" to refer to liminal types of activity in industrialized societies. A liminoid activity such as a pilgrimage would be a voluntary activity, unlike a Ndembu initiation ceremony for boys (see chapter 6).

8   For anthropological studies of Walsingham see Coleman and Elsner (1998).

9   Bax (2000) explores the ways in which the politics of pilgrimage in Medjugorje have been used by local Croat-Catholics to "ethnically cleanse" the area of Serbian-Orthodox families, a context lost on the pilgrims who visit the shrine and certainly at odds with the message of peace proclaimed by the Roman Catholic Croat visionaries.

10 Cf. Lyal Watson (1976).

11 An indulgence is a remission of the temporal punishment for sin, granted after performing certain prescribed prayers and rituals, such as visiting a shrine.

12 Nolan and Nolan (1989, pp. 325–8) give figures for sacred trees associated with Christianized shrines, often linked to an image or apparition. Where there is or was a tree, rather than just a legend of a tree, they seldom survive long as most are killed by pilgrims seeking talismans before they can acquire a reputation of sufficient sanctity that to strip it of leaves or bark is considered a desecration, likely to bring misfortune on the talisman seeker. It is unsurprising that in Ireland sacred groves predominate, with the oak by far the commonest species. The pre-Christian druidic tradition of sacred oak groves became incorporated into Christian legends and saints' lives (cf. Davies, 1996).

13 Nolan and Nolan (1989, pp. 268–9) provide data on the distribution, age, sex, and background of visionaries at European apparitional shrines.

14 See Harvey (1991) and Goodman (1998). Mother Meera was born into a poor family in southern India in 1960. Originally named Kamala, she was a sickly child, before being "discovered" and projected onto the world stage (Goodman, 1998). Whether or not she is divine, she certainly has the power to affect people profoundly through her gaze and touch.

15 The Lubavitch are a worldwide movement of Hasidic (ultra-orthodox) Jews, numbering about 200,000 in total (Dien, 1997).

16 The visions at La Salette in France were initiated in 1846.

17 Sallnow (1991b, p. 284) gives one account of the mytho-history of the shrine of El Señor de Qoyllur Rit'i in Peru, in which Christ appeared as a child, and then metamorphosed into the crucified Christ hanging on a tayanka tree. The tree, in the shape of a cross, remained as a sacred image after the vision disappeared. The King of Spain is said to have requested the tree, but failed to return it, so the local

priest commissioned a replica. Even trees, therefore, are far from stable, and this particular replica makes an annual journey as part of the Qoyllur Rit'i pilgrimage.

18 Cf. Muhaiyaddeen's (1998) account of the *Hajj* as an inner journey in the Sufi tradition of Islam and William's (1975) description of discalced Carmelite nuns and the circular journey they trace through time and space within their convent walls.

19 It is worth pointing out that within anthropology the term "cult" is not used in a derogatory sense, but to denote a system of religious beliefs and practices, irrespective of its status or orthodoxy, usually on a smaller scale than a religious faith or culture as a whole. Religious cults often center on a particular person, place, or object. The cult of Our Lady of Lourdes therefore includes the contemporary and historical development of the shrine, its theological understandings, devotional practices, material places and objects, social and organizational structures, and devotees.

20 Turner and Turner (1978, pp. 226–7).

21 Dahlberg (1991), citing an unpublished 1978 thesis by T. A. Kselman on popular religion and the Church in nineteenth-century France.

22 The notion of syncretism also opens the debate as to whether the term should be reserved for religious phenomena, or used more broadly (cf. Werbner, 1994; Yalçin-Heckmann, 1994). The editors of *Syncretism/Anti-Syncretism* point to the difficulties involved in delimiting a category of "religion" separate from "culture" as what is considered one or the other can and does change according to political and social exigencies.

23 Cf. Bowie (1999).

24 Morinis (1992b) gives an interesting account of the re-establishment of a pilgrimage tradition among Canadian Prairie Indians, in which similar issues concerning "traditional" and Christian, Indian, and white relationships and interactions are apparent.

25 Cf. Randall (1982) and Bolin (1998).

26 Konrad (1991, pp. 125–6), who refers to Soustelle (1961, p. 102).

27 A 1608 dictionary lists *apu* as meaning "paramount judge," referring to the most senior office bearers (usually male). Peter Gose has argued that *apu* originally referred to mummified ancestor figures that were destroyed by the Spanish missionaries (Penny Dransart, personal communication).

28 Cf. Salomon and Urioste (1991).

29 The current popularity of the festival, which involves a grueling journey of several days for most pilgrims, may have something to do with the political as well as religious and ethnic tensions in the region, an area in which the terrorist organization known as "Shining Path" (*Sendero Luminoso*) has been active. Pilgrimages often thrive in times of hardship and areas in which inter-ethnic strife is apparent. Medjugorie in Bosnia-Herzegovina is one of the most striking examples, with conflicts between Catholic Croats and Muslims, as well as between the Franciscan clergy and secular priests and bishop.

30 According to local traditions Jesus appeared to Mariano as a shepherd boy and
    spent several days dancing with him (a traditional form of Andean worship)
    while Mariano's flocks increased. He then disappeared into the rock. There are
    numerous other official and unofficial versions of this legend.
31 The syncretic nature of the festival is dramatically portrayed in the BBC film,
    "Return to the Sacred Andes" from their series "Legendary Trails."

References and Further Reading

Bax, Mart (2000) Planned policy or primitive Balkanism? A local contribution to the
    ethnography of the war in Bosnia-Herzegovina. *Ethnos*, 65 (3), 317–40.
Beevers, John (1953) *The Sun Her Mantle*. Dublin: Browne and Nolan.
Bolin, Inge (1998) *Rituals of Respect: The Secret of Survival in the High Peruvian Andes*.
    Austin, TX: University of Texas Press.
Bowie, Fiona (1999) The inculturation debate in Africa. *Studies in World Christianity*,
    5 (1), 67–92.
Bowman, Glen (1991) Christian ideology and the image of a Holy Land: The place of
    Jerusalem pilgrimage in the various Christianities. In John Eade and Michael
    J. Sallnow (eds), *Contesting the Sacred: the Anthropology of Christian Pilgrimage*.
    London: Routledge, pp. 98–121.
Bowman, Glen (1994) Pilgrim narratives of Jerusalem and the Holy Land: a study
    in ideological distortion. In Charles Stewart and Rosalind Shaw (eds), *Syncre-
    tism/Anti-Syncretism: The Politics of Religious Synthesis*. London: Routledge,
    pp. 149–68.
Breitman, George (1967) *The Last Year of Malcolm X: the Evolution of a Revolution*.
    New York: Pathfinder.
Bunyan, John ([1678] 1998) *The Pilgrim's Progress*, edited with introduction by N. H.
    Keeble. Oxford: Oxford University Press.
Clift, Jean Dalby and Clift, Wallace B. (1996) *The Archetype of Pilgrimage: Outer
    Action with Inner Meaning*. New York: Paulist Press.
Cohen, Eric (1992) Pilgrimage and tourism: Convergence and divergence. In Alan
    Morinis (ed.), *Sacred Journeys: The Anthropology of Pilgrimage*. Westport, CT and
    London: Greenwood Press, pp. 47–61.
Coleman, Simon and Eade, John (eds) (2004) *Reframing Pilgrimage: Cultures in Motion*.
    London and New York: Routledge.
Coleman, Simon and Elsner, John (1995) *Pilgrimage Past and Present: Sacred Travel and
    Sacred Space in the World Religions*. London: British Museum Press; Cambridge, MA:
    Harvard University Press.
Coleman, Simon and Elsner, John (1998) Performing pilgrimage: Walsingham and
    the ritual construction of irony. In Felicia Hughes-Freeland (ed.), *Ritual, Perform-
    ance, Media*. London: Routledge, pp. 46–65.
Clift, Jean Dalby and Clift, Wallace B. (1996) *The Archetype of Pilgrimage: Outer
    Action with Inner Meaning*. New York and Mahwah, NJ: Paulist Press.

Crumrine, N. Ross and Morinis, Alan (eds) (1991) *Pilgrimage in Latin America*. New York and London: Greenwood Press.

Dahlberg, Andrea (1991) The body as a principle of holism: Three pilgrimages to Lourdes. In John Eade and Michael J. Sallnow (eds), *Contesting the Sacred: the Anthropology of Christian Pilgrimage*. London: Routledge, pp. 30–50.

Dalby, Jean and Clift, Wallace B. (1996) *The Archetype of Pilgrimage: Outer Action with Inner Meaning*. Mahwah, NJ: Paulist Press.

Davidson, J. W., Hecht, A., and Whitney, H. (1990) The pilgrimage to Graceland. In G. Rinschede and S. Bhardwaj (eds), *Pilgrimage in the United States*. New York: Oxford University Press, pp. 229–52.

Davie, Grace (1993) You'll never walk alone: the Anfield pilgrimage. In Ian Reader and Tony Walter (eds), *Pilgrimage in Popular Culture*. Basingstoke, UK: The Macmillan Press, pp. 201–19.

Davies, J. G. (1988) *Pilgrimage Yesterday and Today. Why? Where? How?* London: SCM Press.

Davies, Oliver (1996) *Celtic Christianity in Early Medieval Wales*. Cardiff: University of Wales Press.

Dien, Simon (1997) When prophecy fails: Messianism amongst Lubavitcher hasids. In Fiona Bowie with Christopher Deacy (eds), *The Coming Deliverer: Millennial Themes in World Religions*. Cardiff: University of Wales Press, pp. 238–60.

Dubisch, Jill (1990) Pilgrimage and popular religion at a Greek holy shrine. In Ellen Badone (ed.), *Religious Orthodoxy and Popular Faith in European Society*. Princeton, NJ: Princeton University Press, pp. 113–39.

Dubisch, Jill (1995) *In a Different Place: Pilgrimage, Gender, and Politics at a Greek Island Shrine*. Princeton, NJ: Princeton University Press.

Durkheim, Émile ([1915]1976) *The Elementary Forms of the Religious Life*. London: George Allen & Unwin.

Eade, John and Sallnow, Michael J. (eds.) (1991) *Contesting the Sacred: the Anthropology of Christian Pilgrimage*. London: Routledge.

Eade, John (1991) Order and power at Lourdes: Lay helpers and the organisation of a pilgrimage shrine. In John Eade and Michael J. Sallnow (eds), *Contesting the Sacred: the Anthropology of Christian Pilgrimage*. London: Routledge, pp. 51–76.

Eickelman, Dale (1990) *Muslim Travellers: Pilgrimage, Migration and the Religious Imagination*. Berkeley: University of California Press.

Eliade, Mircea (1959) *The Sacred and the Profane: the Nature of Religion*. New York: Harcourt Brace.

Eliade, Mircea (1963) Sacred places: Temple, palace, "centre of the world." In *Patterns in Comparative Religion*. New York: World Publishing Company, pp. 367–85.

Ereira, Alan (1990) *The Heart of the World*. London: Jonathan Cape.

Frey, Nancy Louise (1998) *Pilgrim Stories: On and Off the Road to Santiago*. Berkeley: University of California Press.

Gold, Ann (1988) *Fruitful Journey: the Ways of Rajastani Pilgrims*. Berkeley: University of California Press.

Goodman, Martin (1998) *In Search of the Divine Mother: the Mystery of Mother Meera: encountering a Contemporary Mystic.* San Francisco: HarperCollins.

Gose, Peter (1994) *Deathly Waters and Hungry Mountains: Agrarian Ritual and Class Formation in an Andean Town.* Toronto and London: University of Toronto Press.

Harvey, Andrew (1991) *Hidden Journey: a Spiritual Awakening.* London: Bloomsbury Press.

Hertz, Robert ([1913] 1983) St. Besse: a study of an alpine cult. In Stephen Wilson (ed.), *Saints and Their Cults.* Cambridge, UK: Cambridge University Press, pp. 55–100.

Ingoldsby, Mary F. (1978) *Padre Pio: His Life and Mission.* Dublin: Veritas.

King, Christine (1993) His truth goes marching on: Elvis Presley and the pilgrimage to Graceland. In Ian Reader and Tony Walter (eds), *Pilgrimage in Popular Culture.* Basingstoke, UK: The Macmillan Press, pp. 92–104.

Konrad, Herman W. (1991) Pilgrimage as cyclical process: the unending pilgrimage of the holy cross of the Quintana Roo Maya. In N. Ross Crumrine and Alan Morinis (eds), *Pilgrimage in Latin America.* New York and London: Greenwood Press, pp. 123–37.

Lauentin, René (1988) *Learning from Medjugorie: What is the Truth?*, translated by Francis Martin. Gaithersburg, MD: Word Among Us Press.

Lloyd, David W. (1998) *Battlefield Tourism: Pilgrimage and the Commemoration of the Great War in Britain, Australia and Canada (1919–39).* Oxford and New York: Berg.

Martin, David (1990) *Tongues of Fire: the Explosion of Protestantism in Latin America.* Oxford: Blackwell.

McKevitt, Christopher (1991) San Giovanni Rotondo and the shrine of Padre Pio. In John Eade and Michael J. Sallnow (eds), *Contesting the Sacred: the Anthropology of Christian Pilgrimage.* London: Routledge, pp. 77–97.

Millones, Luis (1991) Foreword. In N. Ross Crumrine and Alan Morinis (eds), *Pilgrimage in Latin America.* New York and London: Greenwood Press, pp. xiii–xvi.

Morinis, Alan (1984) *Pilgrimage in the Hindu Tradition: a Case Study of West Bengal.* Delhi: Oxford University Press.

Morinis, Alan and Crumrine, N. Ross (eds) (1991) *La Peregrinación:* the Latin American pilgrimage. In N. Ross Crumrine and Alan Morinis (eds), *Pilgrimage in Latin America.* New York and London: Greenwood Press, pp. 1–17.

Morinis, Alan (1992a) Introduction: the territory of the anthropology of pilgrimage. In Alan Morinis (ed.), *Sacred Journeys: the Anthropology of Pilgrimage.* Westport, CT and London: Greenwood Press, pp. 1–28.

Morinis, Alan (1992b) Persistent peregrination: from sun dance to Catholic pilgrimage among Canadian Prairie Indians. In Alan Morinis (ed.), *Sacred Journeys: the Anthropology of Pilgrimage.* Westport, CT and London: Greenwood Press, pp. 101–13.

Muhaiyaddeen M. R. Bawa (1998) *Hajj: the Inner Pilgrimage.* Philadelphia: Fellowship Press.

Nolan, Mary Lee (1991) The European roots of Latin American pilgrimage. In N. Ross Crumrine and Alan Morinis (eds), *Pilgrimage in Latin America.* New York and London: Greenwood Press, pp. 19–49.

Nolan, Mary Lee and Nolan, Sidney (1989) *Christian Pilgrimage in Modern Western Europe.* Chapel Hill and London: The University of North Carolina Press.

Obeyesekere, Gananath (1984) *Medusa's Hair: an Essay on Personal Symbols and Religious Experience.* Chicago: Chicago University Press.

Pfaffenberger, B. (1979) The Kataragama pilgrimage: Hindu–Buddhist interaction and its significance in Sri Lanka's polyethnic social system. *Journal of Asian Studies*, 38, 253–70.

Peters, Francis E. (1994) *The Hajj: the Muslim Pilgrimage to Mecca and the Holy Places.* Princeton, NJ: Princeton University Press.

Poole, Deborah A. (1991) Rituals of movement, rites of transformation: Pilgrimage and dance in the highlands of Cuzco, Peru. In N. Ross Crumrine and Alan Morinis (eds), *Pilgrimage in Latin America.* New York and London: Greenwood Press, pp. 307–38.

Preston, James J. (1992) Spiritual magnetism: an organising principle for the study of pilgrimage. In Alan Morinis (ed.), *Sacred Journeys: the Anthropology of Pilgrimage.* Westport, CT and London: Greenwood Press, pp. 31–46.

Randall, Robert (1982) Qoyllur rit'i', an Inca fiesta of the Pleiades: Reflections on time and space in the Andean world. *Bulletin de l'Institut Français des Etudes Andines*, 11 (1–2), 37–81.

Reader, Ian and Walter, Tony (eds) (1993) *Pilgrimage in Popular Culture.* Basingstoke and London: The Macmillan Press Ltd.

Robertson Smith, William (1889) *Lectures on the Religion of the Semites.* London: Adam and Charles Black.

Sallnow, Michael J. (1987) *Pilgrims in the Andes: Regional Cults in Cusco.* Washington, DC: Smithsonian Institution Press.

Sallnow, Michael J. (1991a) Pilgrimage and cultural fracture in the Andes. In John Eade and Michael J. Sallnow (eds), *Contesting the Sacred: The Anthropology of Christian Pilgrimage.* London: Routledge, pp. 137–53.

Sallnow, Michael J. (1991b) Dual cosmology and ethnic division in an Andean pilgrimage cult. In N. Ross Crumrine and Alan Morinis (eds), *Pilgrimage in Latin America.* New York and London: Greenwood Press, pp. 281–306.

Salomon, Frank and Urioste, George L. (1991) *The Huarochirí Manuscript: a Testament of Ancient and Colonial Andean Religion.* Austin: University of Texas Press.

Sanmiguel, Inés (1994) A ceremony in the "cave of idolatry": an eighteenth-century document form the Diocesan Historic Archive, Chiapas, Mexico. In David L. Carmichael, Jane Hubert, Brian Reeves, and Audhild Schanche (eds), *Sacred Sites, Sacred Places.* London and New York: Routledge, pp. 163–71.

Shaw, Rosalind and Stewart, Charles (1994) Introduction: Problematizing syncretism. In Charles Stewart and Rosalind Shaw (eds), *Syncretism/Anti-Syncretism: the Politics of Religious Synthesis.* London: Routledge, pp. 1–26.

Stewart, Charles and Shaw, Rosalind (eds) (1994) *Syncretism/Anti-Syncretism: the Politics of Religious Synthesis.* London: Routledge.

Stirrat, Richard L. (1991) Place and person in Sinhala Catholic pilgrimage. In John Eade and Michael J. Sallnow (eds), *Contesting the Sacred: the Anthropology of Christian Pilgrimage.* London: Routledge, pp. 122–36.

Soustelle, Jacques (1961) *Daily Life of the Aztecs on the Eve of the Spanish Conquest*. Stanford, CA: Stanford University Press.

Turner, Victor (1974) *Dramas, Fields and Metaphors*. Cornell, NY: Cornell University Press.

Turner, Victor and Turner, Edith L. B. (1978) *Image and Pilgrimage in Christian Culture*. New York: Columbia University Press.

Tweed, Thomas A. (1997) *Our Lady of the Exile: Diasporic Religion at a Cuban Catholic Shrine in Miami*. New York and Oxford: Oxford University Press.

Urbano, Henrique (1991) Mythic Andean discourse and pilgrimages. In N. Ross Crumrine and Alan Morinis (eds), *Pilgrimage in Latin America*. New York and London: Greenwood Press, pp. 339–56.

Van der Veer, Peter (1994) Syncretism, multiculturalism and the discourse of tolerance. In Charles Stewart and Rosalind Shaw (eds), *Syncretism/Anti-Syncretism: the Politics of Religious Synthesis*. London: Routledge, pp. 198–211.

Watson, Lyall (1976) *Gifts of Unknown Things*. London: Hodder and Stoughton.

Werbner, Richard (1994) Afterword. In Charles Stewart and Rosalind Shaw (eds), *Syncretism/Anti-Syncretism: the Politics of Religious Synthesis*. London: Routledge, pp. 212–15.

Williams, Drid (1975) The brides of Christ. In Shirley Ardener (ed.), *Perceiving Women*. London: Malaby Press, pp. 105–25.

Wolf, Eric (1958) The Virgin of Guadalupe: a Mexican national symbol. *Journal of American Folklore*, 71 (1), 34–9.

Yalçin-Heckmann, Lale (1994) Are fireworks Islamic? Towards an understanding of Turkish migrants and Islam in Germany. In Charles Stewart and Rosalind Shaw (eds), *Syncretism/Anti-Syncretism: The Politics of Religious Synthesis*. London: Routledge, pp. 178–95.

Zimdars-Swartz, Sandra L. (1991) *Encountering Mary: Visions of Mary from La Salette to Medjugorie*. Princeton, NJ: Princeton University Press.

Chapter 10

Myth

Introduction

The term "myth" has a variety of meanings, both in common parlance and within academia. In everyday speech the term is often used pejoratively to refer to a common but erroneously held belief. For a classicist, myth denotes the stories of the Greek or Roman gods, of the Celts or of other ancient peoples. In anthropology and in folklore (ethnology) the focus is often on the stories of origin in an oral culture (cosmological and cosmogonic myths),[1] and the tales that indigenous peoples tell one another to describe and explain the social, natural, and supernatural order. In sociology and cultural studies, as well as in anthropology, the term myth is also used for the ahistorical stories that are used to validate power relationships, which make the social appear natural and pre-existent. Historians are interested in the process by which historical events become imbued with symbolic significance so as to heighten the emotional impact of the story at the expense of verifiable facts. Within psychoanalysis and analytical psychology it is the symbolic rather than the historical aspects of myth that are emphasized. Myths are seen to exist before and beyond history, absorbing historical experience into a language of signs and archetypes, reappearing in dreams and in art as well as in oral and written narratives. Linguists might focus on the structure rather than the content of a myth, noting the limited number of narrative forms that are endlessly recycled. Folklorists deconstruct myths into their constitutive elements or *motifs*, which are numbered and indexed, and look at the ways in which they are arranged and rearranged. Theologians and historians of religion study sacred texts and are concerned with the ways in which people pass on their moral and legal codes, cultural values, and historical experience through these stories, although the notion that any element of a sacred text is mythical rather than historical is seen as offensive and rejected by some believers. These sketches are oversimplified, and the disciplinary boundaries seldom tightly drawn, but they serve to give an idea of the range of meanings and approaches that can be adopted by those who study myth.

While many disciplines use the terms myth, folklore, fairy tale, and legend more or less interchangeably, folklorists and mythographers seek to differentiate these terms.[2] The overall category *folklore* is subdivided into myth, legend, and folk or fairy tale. The term *myth* is reserved for sacred narratives explaining the origin of the world and human beings. *Legends* are narratives that are held to be true, but unlike myths are set in the post-creation era. *Folk tales* or *fairy tales*, on the other hand, are understood to be fictional, and are often introduced with formulae such as "Once upon a time."[3] When studying myths, the reader therefore needs to be aware that the ways the term is being used may vary from one text and one scholar to another. My approach in this chapter is to take a broad rather than a narrow view of myth, and look to folktales, urban legends, and family histories, as well as stories of origin, where these can help to deepen our understanding of the place of myth in human society.

---

mythos (plural **mythoi**), a collection of myths.
motif, a type of myth or **narrative element** within a myth.
Motif-Index, a six-volume work (Thompson, [1932–6] 1955–8), employing letter categories for different types of myth (e.g., A – mythological motifs; A710 – creation of the sun, A740 – creation of the moon). Still widely used by folklorists and mythologists.

Given this wide variety of usage it is difficult to suggest a single definition of myth that can encompass all these perspectives. Robert Segal, in his admirably clear and concise book *Myth: A Very Short Introduction* (2004), divides approaches to myth into questions of origin, function, and subject matter, with a loose definition based on the assumption that the myth is first and foremost a story. It can take place in the past, present, or future, and its main protagonists must be personalities – divine, human, or animal – rather than abstract forces, such as Plato's notion of the Good. These personalities can be either the object or agent of actions. In terms of function, a myth must accomplish something significant for its adherents, and whether considered true or false, it is held to tenaciously by its supporters (Segal, 2004, pp. 3–6).

Although rather minimalist, in that most scholars of myth would wish to add, subtract, or emphasize different elements, Segal's definition has the merit of setting out a lowest common denominator, which might be summed up in the following sentence:

A myth is (1) a story, (2) whose main protagonists are personalities, (3) which accomplishes something significant for its adherents, (4) who hold to the myth tenaciously.

Myth and Ritual

A nineteenth-century debate, that still has resonances in the contemporary study of myth, was between those who held to the primacy of myth in the development of religion and those who thought that ritual was more important. Opinions regarding the exact relationship between these three terms (religion, myth, and ritual) varied, but there was often little acknowledgement of their culturally constructed nature, so that the ideological underpinnings of their use were not fully acknowledged.

To oversimplify once more for the sake of clarity, and to adopt Lévi-Strauss's language of binary oppositions, there was a divide between Idealism and Pragmatism, the German Romantic Idealism expounded by Johann Jakob Bachofen (1815–87) and Max Müller on the one hand, and the French liberal secularism of the Durkheimians on the other. The religion of the Vedas and Indo-European myths were favored by the "myth school," who opposed them to the supposed ritualism of the Hebrew Bible and Semitic religions.[4] They gave priority to myth in the study of religion and associated mythology with the mind, abstracted from particular social forms and studied largely through texts. The "ritual school" on the other hand saw ritual as the primary expression of religion, temporally and methodologically. They favored performed, external forms of religion that could be studied empirically in contemporary societies over narratives that could be disassociated from their original context.

Friedrich Max Müller (1823–1900), an Orientalist and follower of the German Romantic movement. Max Müller's father was the celebrated Romantic poet Wilhelm Müller, whose verses were set to music by Schubert in some of his best known *lieder*. Max Müller studied Sanskrit and his work on Sanskrit linguistics remains a standard text. He became fascinated by the Vedas, the ancient texts of Indian Brahmanical culture, seeing them as at least equal, if not superior, to the Hebrew Scriptures. Based on philological evidence, Müller became convinced that Classical and Northern European cultures were much more closely related to the ancient Indic civilizations than to the Semitic cultures of the Near East, and was the first to use the term *Aryan* to describe this cultural and linguistic affinity, although disavowing the racial overtones the term later acquired. Müller taught at the

University of Oxford in England from 1851 to 1875. In 1868 he become Oxford's first Professor of Comparative Theology, although his own religious impulse was towards pantheistic paganism rather than Christianity. Müller distinguished between "religion-as-such" and the various historical forms taken by religions, the former representing the "true" philosophical root of all religions. Vedic religion was seen as closest to this source of natural religion, and in it myth was thought to play a central role. Belief in the centrality of myth led to a downplaying of the value of ritual.

William Robertson Smith (1843–94), a Scottish philologist and scholar of religion, best known for his classic work *Lectures on the Religion of the Semites* (1889), and his editorship of the *Encyclopaedia Britannica*. Smith lost a teaching position at the Church of Scotland Aberdeen Free Church College for querying the literal truth of the Bible. He subsequently became Professor of Arabic at Cambridge University in England. Smith remained true to his Protestant roots, viewing the personal moral, unmediated approach to God advocated by Calvin as the truest form of religion. Ritualistic "primitive" religions were at a lower point on the evolutionary scale, but nevertheless, the study of ritual was seen as essential if one was to apprehend such religions. Myth was seen as an "explanation of religion," the core of which was comprised of ritual performance, although myths were capable of taking on an independent existence. The earliest religions were thought to have been ritualistic, myths developing at a later stage in human history. Judaism had reached a stage in which myth and ritual combined, but was still relatively primitive, whereas Christianity, and especially Protestantism, were seen as anti-ritualistic and therefore more highly developed.

Sylvain Lévi (1863–1935), a French Orientalist, particularly noted for his dictionary of Buddhism and his opposition to the Idealist school of myth associated with Max Müller. As an observant Jew, Lévi was sensitive to the implicit anti-Semitism in the Aryanist elevation of the Vedas and devaluation of the Hebrew Scriptures. He reacted by asserting the centrality and power of ritual in religion. From 1889 to 1894 he taught in Paris at the Sorbonne, and in 1894 was appointed Professor of Sanskrit at the Collège de France. He is probably best known among Sanskritists and scholars of Hinduism today for his 1898 treatise entitled *La Doctrine du Sacrifice dans les Brahmanas*. One of Lévi's pupils was Marcel Mauss, a member of the new Durkheimian school of sociology, which favored the study of ritual over myth, as ritual represented a form of religion that embodied human relations, which could be studied empirically, rather than one based primarily upon ideas, approached primarily through the study of texts.

For Müller, who held to the idea of an idealized early form of religion that was non-mythic and non-ritualistic, both myth and ritual were degenerate, if necessary, forms of religion. Myth might be more central to religion than ritual, but even so was no more than a "disease of language," a dark shadow that language throws on thought.[5] For Smith, on the other hand, ritual, and subsequently myth, might be primitive, but contained within them the seeds of later, more developed and interior religion. If Müller and Smith shared an evolutionary perspective, others put religion's golden age in the past. For the Protestant founders of religious studies in France, the continued performance of ritual was a sure sign that religion had fallen into "superstition" and was in a state of decline. Mircea Eliade also saw contemporary religion as debased, but for precisely the opposite reason, contending that "modern man" pays insufficient attention to ritual and myth, leading to spiritual impoverishment.

> **Mircea Eliade** (1907–1986). A Romanian by birth, Eliade held a chair in the History of Religions at the University of Chicago from 1957 until his retirement in 1970. Eliade is best known for his works on yoga, shamanism, and Eastern religions. He is associated with the Traditionalist School, founded by the French metaphysician René Guénon, also known as Perennialism or Essentialism, as its teachings are held to be timeless and universal. The key notion of the school is that all authentic religions derive from a single primordial tradition, and that contrary to the modernist idea of progress, the world is in a cycle of spiritual and intellectual decline. When looking at the religious traditions of the world, therefore, Eliade is concerned to discern their original pure form, and to distinguish this from their current debased state.

The view that the links between myth and ritual are not always apparent in modern religious rituals is shared by Amy Simes, who (following Eliade), makes the point that "myths are restricted to either being read out as scriptural stories, or portrayed pictorially in iconographic form in sacred buildings and areas. In other words, the re-enactment of myths tends to be non-participatory. The dramatic re-enactment of myths is much less common" (Simes, 2001, p. 224).[6] An exception to this is contemporary Paganism, in which "participation in mythical re-enactment is almost essential" (ibid.). Although modern Paganism exists in a variety of forms, most are in essence nature religions, central to which is the celebration of the eight seasonal festivals that divide the year into midsummer and midwinter, the spring and autumn equinoxes, and intervening quarter days. Marking the passage of the seasons and the development of an awareness of nature and its cycles is often enhanced by celebrating these rituals out of doors. The "deeper meaning" of these Sabbats is expounded through myths, sometimes read out but more often acted out by all those present. The choice of myth may be eclectic, drawing freely on classical, Celtic, and Northern traditions, perhaps mixed with some elements of Native American or of other "indigenous" mythologies. Some figures with long roots in British culture, such as "the Green Man," may also be identified with classical figures, such as the Greek god Pan.

Although modern Pagans are aware of their own creative processes in their use of myth and in their rituals, and tend to avoid the language of authenticity and tradition, they also note that similar forms of celebration are widespread historically and cross-culturally, and seem to arise naturally from the nature of the celebration. It is hardly surprising that Spring festivals in the Northern Hemisphere, for instance, contain elements such as a chase and symbols of fertility such as a broom, and are generally light-hearted and gay in character. Simes contends that within contemporary Western Paganism, religion could not exist without the performance of ritual. The myths are clearly "borrowed," and although respected are not revered. Their truths are symbolic, and their task is to enhance communal ritual celebrations.

Malinowski and the Function of Myth

Bronislaw Malinowski (see chapter 4) made an important contribution to the anthropological study of myth, and in many ways his theories mediate between the various positions outlined in this chapter. He regarded myth as ultimately false, even if essential to the study of religion. Although his belief in the centrality of myth in human society links him to the "myth school" associated with the Romanticism of Max Müller and the later work of Joseph Campbell, at the same time the method for the study of myth Malinowski outlined was embodied and pragmatic. To this extent his work aligns him with the Durkheimians and the work of Marxist-oriented anthropologists such as Maurice Bloch, who wish to study the *effects* of ritual on social and political life. Malinowski read Freud as a young man, and thought of himself as a Freudian, but he sought to correct the Eurocentric bias of Freudian theory and to challenge its claims to universality (in detail if not in principle) based on his observations of non-Western cultures. In his attempt to see myths through the lens of individual psychological motivations, albeit with a social, collective dimension, Malinowski finds kinship with the work of Jung, Eliade, and Campbell. Like Mary Douglas, and most of the anthropological work on myth stemming from the British structural functionalist school, Malinowski insists on the importance of context in interpreting a myth. It is not enough to take abstract themes and look for human universals – the imperative of biology is worked out in a social context; in other words, although the origin of myths lie in our universal biology, we experience and elaborate them in a particular social, historical context. To use linguistic (Lévi-Straussian) terminology, we need to study myth as *parole*, or observable acts, rather than as *langue*, the abstract notion of a pre-existent language.[7]

Malinowski's theories of myth derive primarily from his detailed knowledge of the Trobriand Islands off the East Coast of Papua New Guinea, where he lived in 1915–16 and 1917–18. He observed the close relationship between myths and magic for the Trobrianders, for whom magic was an everyday necessity, accompanying all practical activities. Malinowski is perhaps best known, in relation to the study of myth, for viewing myth as a "charter for the present." He outlined his position in a talk given in Liverpool in honor of Sir James Frazer in 1925, subsequently published as "Myth in Primitive Psychology."[8]

> There is no important magic, no ceremony, no ritual without belief; and the belief is spun out into accounts of concrete precedent. The union is very intimate, for myth is not only looked upon as a commentary of additional information, but it is a warrant, a charter, and often even a practical guide to the activities with which it is connected. On the other hand the rituals, ceremonies, and social organization contain at times direct references to myth, and they are regarded as the results of mythical event. The cultural fact is a monument in which the myth is embodied; while the myth is believed to be the real cause which has brought about the moral rule, the social grouping, the rite, or the custom. Thus these stories form an integral part of culture. Their existence and influence not merely transcend the act of telling the narrative, not only do they draw their substance from life and its interests – they govern and control many cultural features, they form the dogmatic backbone of primitive civilization. (Strenski, 1992, p. 87)

Malinowski criticizes the view of myth on the one hand as primarily symbolic, and on the other as historical explanation, and dismisses the notion that it is merely a false reading of history. He makes it clear that myths serve a similar function in so-called civilized and primitive societies, stating:

> Myth as it exists in a savage community, that is, in its living primitive form, is not merely a story told but a reality lived. It is not of the nature of fiction, such as we read today in a novel, but it is a living reality, believed to have once happened in primeval times, and continuing ever since to influence the world and human destinies. This myth is to the savage what, to a fully believing Christian, is the Biblical story of Creation, of the Fall, of the Redemption by Christ's Sacrifice on the Cross. As our sacred story lives in our ritual, in our morality, as it governs our faith and controls our conduct, even so does his myth for the savage.[9]

As a pragmatist, Malinowski looked to our experience as embodied human beings as the source of our cultural life, including myths. Societies need myths to codify, express, and enhance their social life. Myths that focus on social themes encode morality and provide practical rules for the performance of ritual and of technical aspects of life, whether it be building a canoe, planting a garden, or deciding who to marry and who to avoid. Myths about the physical world, on the other hand, help reconcile human beings to their natural state. Malinowski accepted from Freud that myths operate below the level of consciousness, arising from our deepest drives and impulses. The most compelling of these instincts, according to Malinowski, is fear of death. For a functionalist it is less important to look at what myths say than at what they do – their function in society – and myths about the spirit world, the afterlife, and communication with deities, whether they are "true" or not (and Malinowski thought not), prevent society from descending into chaos.[10]

Myth and marriage in a matrilineal society

As an illustration of Malinowski's insistence on the importance of context to the study of myth we will look at his essay "Obscenity and Myth," first published in *Sex and Repression in Savage Society* (1927).[11] In his discussion of matrilineal Trobriand society, Malinowski upholds Freud's insight into the close connection between dreams, the unconscious, myths, and sexual obsessions, but rejects Freud's claims for the universality of the Oedipus complex (see chapter 6). In a patriarchal society a boy might dream of having sex with his mother and of killing his father – a figure of power who might castrate him for competing for the mother's attention. In a matrilineal society, such as the Trobriands, however, it is the maternal uncle and not the father who is the figure of power, and the sister rather than the mother who is the forbidden object of desire. The patricidal elements of the Oedipus complex are absent in Trobriand myths, and it is the maternal uncle who appears in legendary cycles as the dangerous villain and oppressive foe.

Every Trobriand sub-clan has its own myths of origin. None feature a man. The ancestral figure is always a woman, sometimes alone, sometimes accompanied by a brother or totemic animal.[12] In most matrilineal societies, where descent is traced through women, physical paternity is less important than the maternal line. In Trobriand myths, as in social life, the husband plays little or no part in producing descendants, and it is a man's sister's children who are his direct kin in terms of authority and descent. In Trobriand myths this social reality is reflected and finds its justification. The ancestral woman is "opened" by a fish while bathing or by water dripping from a stalactite while resting in a cave, and she gives birth to the first clan members without the intervention of a husband or male consort.

Within the Trobriand matrilineal complex a man should pass on his knowledge of magic to his nephew or his younger brother, often for a not inconsiderable payment. He has a duty to protect them, but often does so unwillingly. The relationship between a maternal uncle and his nephews is invariably strained, and there is competition between brothers. Fathers, on the other hand, have no obligation to pass on their magic to their sons, but often do so willingly and without payment. In a fratricidal Trobriand myth these tensions are clearly expressed. A hero figure possesses the most powerful magic in the community. He can construct a canoe so that it can fly, bringing him great success in the all-important trading expeditions. He also possesses the most powerful garden magic, so that his garden alone survives a drought. The other men in the community become jealous and encourage a younger brother (or the maternal nephew), who also possesses the magic, to kill the hero. Unfortunately the younger brother discovers that he possesses only part of the magic, and the ability to make a canoe fly is lost forever. As Malinowski comments, there is a correspondence between the myth and the social experience of living in a matrilineal society:

> Thus in real life, as well as in myth, we see that the situation corresponds to a complex, to a repressed sentiment, and it is at cross variance with tribal law and conventional tribal ideals. According to law and morals, two brothers, or a maternal uncle and his nephew are friends, allies, and have all feelings and interests in common. In real life to a certain degree and quite openly in myth, they are enemies, cheat each other, murder each other, and suspicion and hostility obtain rather than love and union.[13]

Many anthropologists have been concerned not just with the ways in which myths reflect the tensions that exist within society, but have examined what myth *does*, following Malinowski's pragmatic, functional program for the study of myth in observable actions and social relations. One example of the role of myth in enabling and justifying social change is that of the Bori cult in northern Nigeria, to which we now turn.

The Power of Myth

There is a line of argument which states that preliterate societies have myth, but that literate societies have science and history. A variant of this argument holds that all societies think mythically but that in post-Enlightenment societies history has almost replaced myth as a source of authority in thinking about our past, and secular ideologies have trumped religion. Myths become simply (untrue) stories or ways of thinking symbolically about our place in the world. For Sir James Frazer, author of *The Golden Bough*,[14] the myth of the death and regeneration of the king is a primitive way of understanding both natural cycles and political life. Religion, and the myths which form part of it, are false, but they provided an explanation and instructions for our ancestors and "primitive peoples."[15] In his study *Primitive Culture* (1871), E. B. Tylor, the Oxford-based anthropologist,[16] believed that whereas religion becomes a form of metaphysics once its primary explanatory role is usurped by science, myths are "too closely tied to the gods as agents in the world to permit any comparable transformation" (Segal, 2004, p. 17). According to Tylor, therefore, there can be no such thing as modern myths.

The empirical evidence we have cannot support the views of Frazer and more particularly Tylor, with their assumption of the demise of myth. Myths continue to thrive and to exert their power over contemporary societies. As we illustrate in the last section of this chapter, the distinctions between myth and history are not always clear-cut, and feminist scholars in particular have taken an interest in the power of myth to shape our ideas and to legitimate social structure. The Imperial Emperors of Japan justified their absolute power through appeal to divine kingship, claiming descent from the sun-goddess, Amaterasu. In nineteenth-century Germany science and mythology became entangled in the myth of Aryan supremacy, reaching its apogee in the rise of Nazism and the Holocaust. The links between myth and power are sometimes more subtle than in these two examples, but real nonetheless. Peggy Reeves Sanday,[17] in her book *Female Power and Male Dominance*, argues that "there is a congruence between the gender of a people's creator god(s), their orientation to the creative forces of nature, and the secular expression of male and female power" (1981, p. 6). In the case of the Hausa of northern Nigeria, female power, with its muted but subversive potential, is encapsulated in the Hausa creation myth.

Bori spirits and female power among the Hausa

The Hausa were Islamicized in the early years of the nineteenth century. Before this time women could hold political office, own farms, or be self-employed, but with the adoption of Islam women's economic and political status declined. They were regarded as political minors and became secluded within the compound.[18] The segregation of the sexes became extreme and Hausa female power "was pushed underground, where today it remains in the form of a spiritual guerrilla movement" (Sanday, 1981, p. 36).

The Hausa creation story recounted below shows both Islamic and pre-Islamic influences. As with all myths of origin, being set in the past does not imply that the myth itself is unchanging. While some myths may be extremely conservative, altering little over the centuries (even if interpreted differently at different times and places), others incorporate new elements to reflect contemporary social and political concerns.

> A few hundred years ago Allah made the universe from his own dung, and later made humans and animals from the earth's dirt. The first people were Adam and Eve, who were told by Allah to produce many children to present to him. As their offspring increased, Eve suggested to Adam that Allah might destroy all of their children when they were presented. She decided to hide one-half of the children. When Allah called for their presentation he said, "You have hidden one-half of your children. I did not tell you to do this, but since you have hidden them, they shall remain so forever."[19]

We see here a distant and potentially harmful male god, or at least one that women cannot trust. We might also note that in this creation story Eve is not taken from Adam's side, as in the Christian version of the myth in the second chapter of the book of Genesis, giving an equivalence between men and women. The banished children, or child ghosts, belong to a world of spirits that collectively play a central role in Hausa daily life.[20] These spirits or *bori* operate much as witches do in some sub-Saharan African groups (see chapter 8). The banished bori spirit children are central to the operation of the Bori cult, which admits men in minor roles, but which is controlled mainly by women. Onwuejeogwu outlines the clandestine power of the bori spirits, who have the ability to

> inflict illness on hidden and unknown evil-doers; they are the fountains of fortune and misfortune, wealth and poverty, happiness and sorrow. The characters of the individual spirits, as shown in their dance movements, are attributes of particular human beings – anger, envy, love, passion, sensuality, nobility, humility, restraint, ill health, health, violence, etc. The spirits control the moral community by controlling the community's economic activities and its natural environment – epidemics, rainfall, storms, etc. (Onwuejeogwu, 1971, pp. 288–9)[21]

Members of the Bori cult are those who become possessed by these bori spirits, and who form a loose association based on their status as adepts. They have a meeting house where officials of the cult live, where regular possession rituals and other rites can take place, and where female members of the cult can initiate new members. The head of the Spirit Owners is generally a woman, with both female and male assistants.

Sanday contends that it was through the Bori cult that Hausa women consolidated and maintained their power through the years of Islamicization. It gave women space to meet together, gain experience in holding office, and to organize politically. Claims to religious experience, be it spirit possession, visions, or locutions, are a common way in which women who are denied authority by virtue of their sex gain access to political power.[22] The creation myth explained and justified this irregular form of female power: "Through Bori and spirit possession, women wield their lost power. Because the spirits are beings of great force and must be treated with submissiveness and subservience, possessed women can defy not only the domestic authority of their husbands, but also that of the political authorities" (Sanday, 1981, pp. 36–7). The corollary of this is that without a myth that authorizes such female power, it is much harder for women to legitimate their claims to any form of equality with men. The relative paucity of female images in the creation myths and sacred scriptures of Judaism and Christianity has led some feminist scholars, as well as the Western pagans described above, to create their own myths, to reclaim female deities, or to rewrite versions of patriarchal myths so as to empower women spiritually and socially.

The coming of Lilith

Many people who don't read the Hebrew Scriptures or Christian Old Testament are nevertheless familiar with the account of God's creation of Adam and Eve in the Book of Genesis, although perhaps less aware that there are two version of the story, one in the plural (Genesis 1: 26–31) in which God creates human beings, the other in the singular (Genesis 2:7–25), which places the first man and woman in the Garden of Eden. Most Christians are also unfamiliar with Jewish traditions of Lilith, Adam's first, rebellious wife who quarreled with Adam, refusing to be subservient (to "lie beneath") him. When Lilith saw that they could not get along with one another "she uttered the Ineffable Name and flew off into the air of the world."[23] Adam complained to God that Lilith had left him, and God sent three angels to bring her back, saying "If she wants to return, good and well, and if not, she will have to take it upon herself that every day one hundred of her children should die."[24] Lilith chose not to return, preferring to drown in the sea rather than be subservient to Adam. The story goes on to explain the origin of the protective amulets bearing the image of the three angels worn by newborn babies to protect them from Lilith's curse (or rather God's curse on Lilith). Like the bori ghost children, Lilith is thought to be of particular danger to women and infants.[25] Eve is then created not from the earth, like Adam, but from his side, so that she is subservient to him.

In a popular Jewish feminist midrash (commentary) on Lilith and Eve, Judith Plaskow (and others) rewrote the creation story in a way that validated the female characters, rather than using Lilith as a means of frightening women into obedient submission.[26] As in the earlier Jewish versions of the story, Lilith leaves the garden because of Adam's refusal to accept their equal status. Eve "occasionally sensed capacities in herself that remained undeveloped" but was basically satisfied with her role as Adam's companion and helper, despite a disturbing closeness between God and Adam that seemed to exclude her. Adam had persuaded Eve to help him strengthen the walls of the Garden in order to keep Lilith at bay, telling her "fearsome stories of the demon Lilith who threatens women in childbirth and steals children from their cradles in the middle of the night." However, in a battle between Lilith and Adam, Eve caught a glimpse of her, and saw that she was a woman, like herself. One day Eve climbed the apple tree she and Adam had planted, and swung herself over the wall. Lilith was waiting on the other side, and they talked for many hours, "laughed together, and cried, over and over, till the bond of sisterhood grew between them." Adam told God about Eve's comings and goings, and her changed attitude towards him. God too was confused, "Something had failed to go according to plan." The God in this feminist version of the creation story is a God of process theology,[27] able to change and to reflect on His unfolding creation: "I am who I am . . . but I must become who I will become." The midrash ends with the words: "And God and Adam were expectant and afraid the day Eve and Lilith returned to the garden, bursting with possibilities, ready to rebuild it together."

A myth is often distinguished from fiction and other forms of narrative in not having an attributable author, but the genres become blurred when dealing with texts that may have authors attributed to them (Moses, for instance, is held in Jewish and Christian tradition to be author of the Pentateuch, the first five books of the Hebrew Bible), although they contain elements, such as stories of creation, that by most definitions would be described as myths. Whatever their age and provenance, myths can be, and are, used to justify the status quo, and creating new myths and rituals can be experienced as liberating for those who listen to and participate in them.

The Structural Study of Myth

Claude Lévi-Strauss is associated with a school of thought known as *structuralism* (see chapter 1). His work seeks to answer a question we can look at from two angles. Why, if human beings are infinitely creative, do they draw on a limited cultural vocabulary when organizing their social life, their kinship systems, their myths? And, looked at from another perspective, what are the common elements or structures that can help us to make sense of the bewildering variety of cultural forms that we do find? Are they merely an arbitrary jumble, or is there a discernible pattern to them? The answer comes from the human body and its basic, slightly asymmetrical, binary form. We experience ourselves as a single entity, but in two parts – with a left and a right brain, two arms and legs, two hands, two eyes and ears, as well as in two genders, male and female. As with computer binary code which has two modes, on and off, which through a variety of arrangements can generate the most complex programs, so too the human mind makes sense of the world through understanding similarity and difference. The purpose of anthropology, according to Lévi-Strauss, is not to understand what societies "are" in their own terms (as Franz Boas sought to do), but to discover how they differ from one another – following linguistics, looking for contradictive or distinguishing features (Lévi-Strauss, 1977, p. 63).

An illustration of Lévi-Strauss's use of binary oppositions can be seen in his analysis of a myth from western Canada concerning the skate (a species of flatfish) and the South Wind. In a time before the creation of the distinction between humans and animals, all were extremely bothered by the winds, which blew all the time making it impossible for them to fish or to gather shellfish from the beach. The skate played a key role in capturing the South Wind, who was liberated on condition that he promised to blow only at certain periods or every other day, so that in between times creatures could go about their activities. Lévi-Strauss argues that the choice of a skate is not arbitrary. It has very precise characteristics, being very large seen from above or below, but extremely thin when viewed from the side. It can easily evade capture by turning to present its thin side, creating a very difficult target. Like a modern computer, the skate has two discontinuous states, one positive, one negative. A skate might not appear to have much in common with a wind, but both have a similar relationship with a binary problem. If the South Wind blows one day in two it is "yes" one day and "no" the next. There is, according to Lévi-Strauss, a logical affinity (like Saussure's linguistic *associative relations* or paradigms) between the South Wind and the skate (Lévi-Strauss, 1995, pp. 21–3).

While Lévi-Strauss draws indirectly on the work of his friend Roman Jakobson (1896–1982), the Russian linguist and co-founder of the European movement in structural linguistics known as the Prague School,[28] it was reading the Swiss linguist and founder of semiotics, Ferdinand de Saussure, that provided Lévi-Strauss with the tools he need to realize his project.

Ferdinand de Saussure (1857–1913) was interested in the study of language as a system of signs, which he called *semiology*. His lecture notes, published posthumously as *Course de linguistique générale* (Course in General Linguistics) in 1916, was one of the most influential works on linguistics of the twentieth century. Saussure saw language as a system of signs that have meaning only in relation to one another. Just as we distinguish words by their phonetic differences from one another, so too we distinguish the ideas to which they correspond through distinctions. The sign itself is arbitrary – there is no intrinsic reason why we might say "dog," "le chien," or "das Hund." There is no essence of "dogness" in the sign (as Plato might have held). What these sounds have in common is what they refer to or signify, the idea or concept of an animal in the category we label canine.

$$\text{sign}\begin{cases} \text{signified} = \text{concept} \\ \text{signifier} = \text{sound-image} \end{cases}$$

For Saussure language is social, we are born into a pre-existing language or languages that we learn as a child. We may innovate and make individual contributions to that language, but we are only understood by others insofar as we obey the pre-existing rules of that language.

la langue (language) = whole linguistic system
parole (speech) = individual speech acts

Language can be studied in two ways, *diachronically* in relation to its historical development, or *synchronically*, by looking at its different components and their interrelations at a given moment in time.

The ambitious project realized by Lévi-Strauss in his four-volume *Mythologiques* (1964–72) (in English *Introduction to a Science of Mythology*, 1970–1982), and in other shorter books, lectures, and essays, is to "crack the code" of myths by looking for and making sense of their components, and seeing how these relate to one another both within a single myth and as part of a much wider complex of myths across a broad cultural area (such as the whole of the Americas). For Lévi-Strauss myths are an attempt by human beings to resolve or mitigate the contradictions that are basic to our existence. They give us a sense of understanding the world, even if the basic dilemmas addressed (such as life/death, the exercise of power/dependence, male/female) are not capable of outright resolution.

A related idea, of importance to Lévi-Strauss's analysis of myth was the idea of *associative relations* or *paradigms*, represented by a vertical axis, and horizontal or temporal relations, known as *syntagms*. The basic grammatical structure of a language is determined by its syntagmatic structure, such as the subject-verb-object relationship in a sentence such as *the woman had a baby*. Paradigmatic analysis looks at the rules of substitution within a grammatical category, so we could change the meaning but not the structure of the sentence by substituting the subject, verb, and object to say *the man bought a cow*. Within a myth this can mean that we have two parallel version of a plot, which represent a single *mytheme* or narrative unit:

the man tricked his brother	*relations within the mytheme*
↓ ↓ ↓	↓ paradigmatic
the nephew killed his uncle	→ syntagmatic

In "Harelips and Twins: The Splitting of a Myth" (1995, pp. 25–33), Lévi-Strauss notes the widespread association between twins, hares, feet, the weather, and trickster figures/gods in many American myths. He dismisses the claim that myths can only be understood within a specific localized cultural and historical setting, treating the various narrative units of the stories as elements that can be transferred and transformed over time. By comparing myths from different parts of the continent Lévi-Strauss succeeds in constructing a logical association between seemingly unrelated elements. There is apparently a general belief among Native Americans that twins result in the splitting of the body fluids that solidify to form a child. The hare is an incipient twin – the slit lip representing the potential splitting of the individual into two separate halves. Twins are in a race to be born first, and therefore a birth where the feet appear first, which endangers the life of both mother and child or children, is often feared and mother and child/children may be killed. The hare as an ambiguous character, somewhere between an individual and a twin, may be seen as a wise deity or a trickster. Whereas for Mary Douglas (see chapter 2) an anomalous figure who defies or contravenes symbolic boundaries is often seen as powerful or dangerous, or both, for Lévi-Strauss an anomaly is to be sought as a mediator between boundaries, which are the site of contradiction. The hare mediates between twins and singletons although, as Douglas observed, its status as mediator remains ambiguous.

It is not by looking for an original, authentic version of a myth that we find its meaning, according to Lévi-Strauss, but by accumulating as many versions as possible and looking for the metaphoric (paradigmatic) and metonymic (syntagmatic) relationships between their various elements that we come to an understanding of the whole.

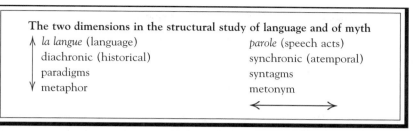

The two dimensions in the structural study of language and of myth

la langue (language)	*parole* (speech acts)
diachronic (historical)	synchronic (atemporal)
paradigms	syntagms
metaphor	metonym

While many nineteenth-century thinkers were concerned with the question of origins (see chapter 1), Lévi-Strauss is more concerned with systematic comparison. He does not, like Eliade, posit an original complete myth that is subject to degeneration, any more than one might look for a perfect language. Rather than try to reconstruct a composite mythical narrative from a number of versions or, on the other hand, see each version of a myth as an isolated story to be interpreted only from within its particular context, Lévi-Strauss is interested in the transformations and substitutions that exist within a mythical complex. It is more like trying to understand a conversation by collecting different versions of an event, each of which helps to throw light on the whole, but without supposing the existence of an original "authentic" version of the story. He is not insensitive to history or to cultural specificity, as his critics sometimes claim. It is rather that the anthropology that interests Lévi-Strauss is what he terms "the elaboration of that *logic of the concrete*" (1977, p. 65) that goes beyond a phenomenological description of a society. By using a rigorous methodology (outlined below), the ethnographer can hope to go beyond or beneath emic descriptions of a society and discover the "hinges of the 'true' system" which can "carry the investigation beyond the limits of consciousness" (1977, p. 67).

Lévi-Strauss's method for the study of myth:
A myth must never be interpreted in isolation. No privileged explanation exists, for any myth consists in an *interpretation* of several explanatory levels.

1 A myth must never be interpreted individually, but in its relationship to other myths which, taken together, constitute a transformation group.
2 A group of myths must never be interpreted alone, but by reference: (a) to other groups of myths; and (b) to the ethnography of the societies in which they originate. For, if the myths transform each other, a relation of the same type links (on a transversal axis) the different levels involved in the evolution of all social life. These levels range from the forms of techno-economic activity to the systems of representations, and include economic exchanges, political and family structures, aesthetic expression, ritual practices, and religious beliefs.[29]

Despite the influence of structuralism on Anglo-American, as well as French, anthropology, particularly in the 1970s and 1980s, its popularity as a method of interpretation has declined, and Lévi-Strauss himself admits that he represents a school which has few followers today, although the renewed interest in cognitive anthropology can be seen as a continuation of the broader project that seeks universal structures rather than particular description. The results of the structural analysis of myth, with its mathematical symbols and seemingly endless detail does not always repay the effort involved. As Wendy Doniger put it in her largely sympathetic Foreword to the 1995 edition of *Myth and Meaning*, "We must jump off Lévi-Strauss's bus one stop before he does. And once we have jumped off, we usually find that we are not there yet. We have to get on another bus (theological, psychological), or, indeed, several buses. We need a lot of transfers on the mythic journey. But if we know where to look, Lévi-Strauss provides those transfers, too" (1995, p. xiv).

Joseph Campbell and the Monomyth

One of the most influential writers on myth in the English-speaking world is Joseph Campbell. Although he had an excellent knowledge of many cultures, and a lifelong interest in the native peoples of America, Campbell was a theorist and a storyteller rather than an ethnographer. Like Mircea Eliade, Réne Girard, or Claude Lévi-Strauss, he was interested in looking for ultimate truths and meanings behind ethnographic details, and wished to embrace the whole of human history in his purview. While he did not follow either uncritically, the psychoanalytic ideas of Sigmund Freud[30] and more particularly Carl Gustav Jung,[31] play a major role in Campbell's writing.

Joseph Campbell (1904–87). Brought up as a practicing Roman Catholic in New York, Campbell became fascinated by Native American culture as a boy. He studied languages and read widely in comparative mythology, retaining an interest in many disciplines from archeology and anthropology to psychology and art, as well as English literature, the subject he taught at Sarah Lawrence College from 1934–72. Campbell established his reputation as an original thinker through the publication in 1949 of *The Hero with a Thousand Faces*, in which he posits the existence of a *monomyth* – a universal pattern that lies beneath the heroic tales of all cultures. Campbell went on to publish a four-volume study of mythology, *The Masks of God* (1959–68), and numerous other books, articles, and edited works as well as lectures and broadcast interviews, on the subject of comparative mythology. One of his phrases, "follow your bliss," which expressed his belief in a guiding force in individuals' lives, became a catch phrase among a generation of North Americans.

The search for a grand scheme and unifying theory, which remained part of Campbell's goal and his popular appeal, has generally been greeted with suspicion by anthropologists, who feel on more secure ground when looking at the differences between cultures rather than possible underlying similarities. In the Foreword written on completion of the four-volume *The Masks of God*, Campbell sets out the all-embracing scope of his study, which:

> ...has been the confirmation of a thought I have long and faithfully entertained; of the unity of the race of man, not only in its biology but also in its spiritual history, which has everywhere unfolded in the manner of a single symphony, with its themes announced, developed, amplified and turned about, distorted, reasserted, and, today, in a grand *fortissimo* of all sections sounding together, irresistibly advancing to some kind of mighty climax, out of which the next great movement will emerge. (Campbell, 1991, p. 5)

The myth of the hero

The notion of a hero is central to virtually all cultures, and embodies a society's ideals. In *The Hero with a Thousand Faces* ([1949] 1990), Campbell argues that certain archetypal patterns recur, and may indeed point to a single, original myth that evolved over time. Borrowing a phrase from the Irish novelist James Joyce, Campbell refers to the hero's journey as the monomyth.

The hero's journey can be divided into three stages,[32]

Departure (or separation) → Initiation → Return

This basic pattern of the hero myth (further elaborated below) involves introducing the hero to us in the ordinary world where he (or she) receives a call to adventure, often through a meeting with a mysterious or miraculous messenger. At first the hero is reluctant to accept the call, but is encouraged by a wise old man or woman to venture forth and cross the first threshold (Victor Turner's "liminal space"), where he or she endures various tests and hardships, meets with fabulous creatures, helpers, and obstacles. On reaching the innermost cave the hero endures the supreme ordeal, and seizing the prize is pursued back to the ordinary world. The returned hero, now a citizen of both worlds, has the power to bestow blessings, treasure, or some boon on fellow human beings.

> **Vladimir Propp** (1895–1970), a member of the Russian formalist school, who studied folktales though breaking them down into narrative units or *narratemes* in the way that formal linguistics breaks down sentences into morphemes. Propp was particularly interested in Russian folktales, and identified 31 generic narratemes. While not all were necessarily present in each folktale, their sequence is unvarying. Propp's exposition of narrative sequences, outlined in his work *The Morphology of the Folktale* (1958), is one of a number of attempts to describe an underlying pattern of hero myths. Other examples are Otto Rank's *The Myth of the Birth of the Hero* ([1909] 2000), Lord Raglan in *The Hero* (1936), and Joseph Campbell's *The Hero with a Thousand Faces* (1949).

While the hero myths of many cultures, as Campbell amply demonstrated, follow this basic pattern, it can also be seen in novels, film, and other artistic media. Tolkien's *Lord of the Rings* is one obvious example from the world of literature, with the hobbit, Frodo Baggins, and the man, Aragorn, both taking parallel, intertwined heroic roles. Many artists pay tribute to Campbell's monomyth as the direct inspiration for their own creations, including George Lucas, creator of the science fiction *Star Wars* films; Richard Adams, author of *Watership Down*, in which the hero is a rabbit; and the Wachowski brothers in their film *The Matrix*. It may not escape the reader's notice that in each of these instances the hero is in fact male. The monomyth is primarily, if not exclusively, a male story.

Stages of the hero's journey

Although the details may vary, some sequences may be left out and others elaborated, there is a basic pattern seen in many if not all hero myths and the fictional tales derived from them. As noted above, the hero's journey replicates the threefold pattern of a rite of passage, with movement from structure to anti-structure, and back to structure. The characters in the monomyth have universal appeal because they depend not on any one individual's external experiences or particular historical events, but upon universal archetypes linked to inner psychic growth and the development of humanity as a whole.

Although the sex of the hero is unspecified, the sequence clearly presupposes a male hero, and at the level of psychological integration the journey only makes sense from a male perspective.[33] While Campbell gives female as well as male examples of heroes, the stages of the journey suggest that he is indeed committed to a male hero. There is the stereotypical conquering nature of heroism that dictates a male hero, but also in the

---

The Hero's Journey

I   Separation (departure)
    1   The hero is introduced in the ordinary world of structure.
    2   There is a call to adventure, which is initially refused.

    3   The hero is encouraged by a wise old man or woman to accept the call.
    4   The hero then crosses the first threshold into a fabulous world.
    5   There are adventures and trials in which the hero meets various helpers.
    6   The hero finds him/herself in what is sometimes termed "the belly of the whale" or the "innermost cave."

II   Initiation
    7   The hero encounters a woman or women in the form of a goddess and/ or temptress.
    8   There is some reconciliation or integration with the figure of the father.
    9   The hero undergoes an ultimate test or endures a supreme ordeal.
    10   He wins the sword, treasure, or boon, or gains esoteric or self-knowledge.

III Return
    11   The stage of the return is initiated, but may at first be refused in a mirror image of the initial call to adventure.
    12   There is a magical flight during which the hero is pursued by malign forces.
    13   The hero is rescued by an external force or agency.
    14   The hero crosses the threshold into the ordinary world of structure, transformed by the experience of the journey.
    15   As master of two worlds, the hero has the power to live in both, and can dispense the benefits of this knowledge, or of the treasure or boons won, to those in the ordinary world.

---

second or middle stage of the journey the hero meets (and has sex with) a female god or temptress, and achieves reconciliation with the rival male god/ father figure.

Carl Gustav Jung (1875–1961), Swiss founder of Analytical Psychology. Jung rejected Freud's emphasis on the *libido* and the dominance of sexuality in human motivation, and developed a view of the human psyche based on the notion of the *collective unconscious*, a common psychological disposition, which works through dreams, myths, and symbols. According to Jung the mind works with a limited number of *archetypes*, to which other ideas and experiences are assimilated in a "complex."

The four basic archetypes outlined by Jung are:

- The shadow
- The anima
- The animus
- The self

The unconscious mind also works with a number of common symbolic forms, which may be found as recognizable types in the dreams, myths, and stories from many different cultures.
These symbolic types include:

- the Child
- the Superman
- the Hero
- the Great Mother
- The Wise Old Man
- The Trickster or Joker

Jung believed that psychological health is dependent upon being attentive to and integrating these archetypes and symbols, and that we should therefore take seriously the dreams, myths, and religious inspiration of our own and other cultures.

The gender of the hero

While heroes can in theory be of either sex and of any age, they are predominantly young males (Luke Skywalker in *Star Wars*, Frodo Baggins in *The Lord of the Rings*), even if adherence to Jungian principles would dictate that they are undertaking the journey of the second half of life. Adult men may also feature as heroes, or share this role with a younger protagonist (as Aragorn shares the hero role with Frodo Baggins). Where the hero is female she is almost always pre-pubescent (Alice in Wonderland, Dorothy in *The Wizard of Oz*, or Lucy in C. S. Lewis's *The Lion, the Witch and the Wardrobe*). It is as if the hero role is inimical to mature femininity.

If the woman is the hero the story may be more complex with rather different messages. In many primate species it is young males who are the most curious, who band together in single-sex groups, and journey farthest from their natal home, before returning to take over the role of "husband" and "father." The hero of the monomyth fits a male life-course more easily than a characteristic female one. Female chimpanzees, for instance, learn primarily from their mothers and become more proficient tool-users than their brothers, who have a shorter concentration span and spend more of their time with their male age-mates. Women in human societies are usually given a more constricted geographical and social range than their male counterparts, and take on adult domestic roles at an early age, helping to fetch water, cook, farm, look after younger children, and so on. Bruce Lincoln suggested that van Gennep and Turner's stages of a rite of passage (see chapter 6) fits male initiation more closely than female, and proposed an alternative pattern, namely

enclosure → metamorphosis/magnification → emergence

representing a greater continuity between childhood and adulthood than is the case for males. Initiation for women often reinforces a domestic role in which they are subject to husbands, fathers, and older women (Lincoln, 1991) – this might be heroic, but does not involve the type of outward journey and return characteristic of the monomyth.

Writing on medieval women mystics, Caroline Walker Bynum (1987) observes that the life trajectories of medieval women saints and mystics are less marked by sudden and dramatic conversions and reversals than those of their male counterparts, and that a high proportion of female saints had decided on a religious life in early childhood. Unlike male saints, whose heroic journeys often involve a dramatic call and conversion (one might think of Saint Paul being struck blind when he heard Jesus calling him on the road to Damascus, or Saint Francis stripping off his fine robes before the Bishop of Assisi), women tend to grow slowly into their vocation. This may be because men in most societies and at most times have had greater power than women to shape the course of their own lives. Both men and women in the Middle Ages in Europe tended to see female saints as models of suffering and male saints as models of action.[34]

Where women do embark on a heroic journey they often do so in disguise. They need to find some strategy to deny or detract attention from their sex (as with Joan of Arc, who dressed and lived as a man), or they may stress their harmless female nature so as to divert attention from their actions (as many women mystical writers did, including the twelfth-century Rhineland abbess, Hildegard of Bingen).[35] Virginity or celibacy may be stressed (as with Queen Elizabeth I of England, the "Virgin Queen"), rejecting or surmounting accepted female role models. As women are seldom authorized to teach or hold positions of authority, they commonly need to wait until they are post-menopausal, or use the authority of visions or claims to supernatural guidance in order to bestow the boon or share the wisdom that they have won on their journey.[36]Women can and do change the world, but their heroism often has more to do with the qualities of endurance, patience, determination, and compassion, than with dramatic feats of bravery and magical intervention. A woman in myth is more likely to be cast in the role of goddess or temptress, wise woman or witch, than hero of the tale.

A version of the heroic journey that is intended to be more inclusive than those of Campbell, Rank, or Raglan is Carol Pearson's schema, which further develops Jung's notion of Archetypes. Pearson is the author of numerous books aimed at popularizing the concept of Archetypes, making them relevant to people in their everyday lives. In *The Hero Within* (1999) Pearson chooses six of the commonest Archetypes that relate both to personality types and to the stages of the hero's journey (our life's journey from infancy through maturation to old age). They are framed so as to be equally relevant to women and men. As well as a plot structure, each narrative unit/Archetype is associated with the gifts and tasks that we recognize from the monomyth. The six Archetypes presented here can also be divided by pairs into the stages of Separation (Orphan, Wanderer), Initiation (Warrior, Altruist) and Return (Innocent, Magician).

The Heroic Journey[37]

	Archetype	Plot Structure	Gift	Task
Birth	Orphan	How I suffered or survived	Resilience	Survive difficulty
	Wanderer	How I escaped or found my own way	Independence	Find yourself
	Warrior	How I achieved my goals or defeated my enemies	Courage	Prove your worth
	Altruist	How I gave to others and how I sacrificed	Compassion	Show generosity
	Innocent	How I found happiness or the promised land	Faith	Achieve happiness
Death	Magician	How I changed my world	Power	Transform your life

Anthropologists have, by and large, paid less attention to the psychological, symbolic aspects of myth that so fascinated Carl Jung, Joseph Campbell, and Carol Pearson, and have focused more on questions of structure, function, context, and memory.

History, Myth, and Memory

For Lévi-Strauss mythology is static – the same mythical elements are combined over and over again in a closed system, whereas history is open (1995, p. 40). This distinction is not, however, as rigid as may at first appear. History may contain mythical elements which, through various arrangements, can be used to form an original account. Lévi-Strauss looks at the example of two books written by Tsimshian chiefs from the Pacific coast of Canada recording the history of their respective groups. *Men of Medeek* (1962) is a supposedly verbatim account collected from Chief Walter Wright and the other is a book by Chief Kenneth Harris (1974). They can be contrasted with works based on data collected from the Tsimshian, but structured by a non-native, such as Boas and Tate's *Tsimshian Mythology*. In works organized by anthropologists we have an arrangement of material that starts with cosmological and cosmogonic myths, and only much later legendary tradition and family history. Wright's and Harris's works, on the other hand, start with a mythical, or perhaps historical, account of the destruction of a city and the scattering of its inhabitants. The accounts share an "explanatory cell" – a fight and murder arising from adultery, but the protagonists and details vary. Lévi-Strauss calls this a "mini-myth" in which different (metaphoric) transformations occur. When one element is transformed, the other elements should be rearranged (metonymically) to fit. Both histories are also highly repetitive with the same type of event used several times. In each account these similar events take place at different places, affect different people, and may refer to different historical periods.

Lévi-Strauss refers to these accounts as representing an intermediary level between myth and history: "It shows us that by using the same material, because it is a kind of common inheritance or common patrimony of all groups, of all clans, or of all lineages, one can nevertheless succeed in building up an original account for each of them" (1995, pp. 40–1). By trying to simply put together a "hodge-podge" of traditions and beliefs belonging to many different peoples, much as Frazer did in *The Golden Bough*, the historical character of the material is lost. As Lévi-Strauss makes clear:

> This makes us lose sight of a fundamental character of the material – that each type of story belongs to a given group, a given family, a given lineage, or to a given clan, and is trying to explain its fate, which can be a successful one or a disastrous one, or be intended to account for rights and privileges as they exist in the present, or be attempting to validate claims for rights which have since disappeared. (Lévi-Strauss, 1995, p. 41)

This tendency to historicize our myths and to mythologize our history is not unique to indigenous peoples and traditions, although Lévi-Strauss does see myth in pre-literate and history-literate societies as serving different purposes. Mythology in societies without writing seeks to ensure that, "the future will remain faithful to the present and to the past. For us, however, the future should always be different, and ever more different, from the present" (ibid., p. 43).

Structural studies of myth had a brief spell of popularity within British anthropology. One of the foremost proponents of structural methods of analysis was Edmund Leach in Cambridge who applied Lévi-Strauss's prescriptions, tempered with English common sense. Biblical myths were analyzed in terms of a set of (unconscious) binary oppositions, such as life and death, mortal and immortal, with a mediating category (virgin mothers, incarnate gods), which is "unnatural," "holy," the focus of taboo and ritual observance.[38] Using the analogy of computer language, with its elements of *redundancy* (repetition of the same basic plot with different details), and of the "bit" (the narrative unit of information that can be reused in different contexts), and of psychoanalysis, with the assumption of unintelligibility at the conscious level, the role of the structural anthropologist is to "crack the code" by laying bare the underlying structure of the stories. Leach takes the view that myths can be understood as "the expression of unobservable realities in terms of observable phenomena,"[39] but that whereas for believers there is a "sender" of the message, at least when talking about the Bible, for anthropologists there are only "receivers."[40]

The importance of context

As can be seen from the discussion of the Tsimshian above it is clear that Lévi-Strauss does not, as is sometimes claimed, ignore the role of history in his analysis, but he is less concerned with the historical and ethnographic context of a particular myth than most anthropologists, or the context he refers to privileges culture over contemporary interests in political concerns. A very similar point concerning the "butterfly collecting" approach to myth that characterizes so much of the field of mythology was made by Mary Douglas (1996, p. 48). In her account of the tale of Little Red Riding Hood, Douglas aims to demonstrate the sensitivity to cultural and historical detail necessary to "interpret other people's myths" (ibid.), and to critique theorists who "like to gather up the materials of so-called myths from here and there and anywhere, without regard to sources or to how or why the stories were told, to say nothing of how and why they have been preserved or collected" (ibid.).

Douglas, like William Robertson Smith before her, wants to know the context of a myth before interpreting it: "Who tells it? To whom? On what occasion? What sort of ceremonial is it used to explain?" (Douglas, 1996, p. 39). In other words, to what genre does the myth belong? The Red Riding Hood story is strictly a fairy tale rather than a myth, but it is useful in illustrating the sort of information needed in order to make sense of myths. In the version of the tale told as a child's bedtime story a little girl takes cakes to her grandmother, and on the way meets a wolf who asks her where she is going. The wolf runs ahead to kill and eat the grandmother, taking the old lady's place in bed. When Little Red Riding Hood arrives a conversation ensues in which the child remarks on the differences between the grand-mother and the wolf: "Grandmama! What big ears you have!" "Grandmama! What big teeth you have!"– at which point the wolf jumps out of bed to eat her, but Little Red Riding Hood is saved by the appearance of a woodcutter, who kills the wolf, and splits open its stomach to rescue the grandmother.

According to Verdier (1980, cited in Douglas, 1996), however, in the original nineteenth-century French versions of the tale the wolf and the girl take turns in eating parts of the grandmother (and the girl does not have a red hood). In fact, the wolf's role is rather minor and accidental. In each of the versions of the tale recorded there is a choice of routes to the grandmother's house. The girl, or young woman around the age of puberty, is given the choice of the way of pins or the way of needles, a well-understood metaphor in its original context for the choice between girlhood (associated with pins) and mature womanhood (associated with needles, with its sexual innuendo of threading the needle). The conversation with the wolf can also be inter-preted as a passage to womanhood. The wolf invites the girl to get into bed with him, and she complies, noting how big, strong, and hairy he is (Douglas, 1996, p. 43). As well as eating her grandmother, the girl performs various domestic tasks, much as she would in her own kitchen. The story would have been understood as a form of female initiation, but also acknowledges that there is a time when the grandmother can no longer thread the needle, and her place is taken (she is consumed by) the younger woman. Without such historical and cultural details of peasant life in nineteenth-century France interpretations of the tale remain impoverished.

Myth and memory

If Lévi-Strauss has demonstrated the ways in which Tsimshian chiefs create personal histories that make use of what appear to be mythical motifs, we might ask what role memory plays in the creation of such stories, and where and how history becomes myth. Literacy does not seem to preclude the incorporation of mythological elements in recorded histories. In my own family we possess a family tree that confidently traces back one line of forebears for several generations, before declaring "... descended from Adam." This was a common trope in the nineteenth century, a Scottish and Welsh variant of which was to record descent from St Anne, the maternal grandmother of Jesus. Genealogical studies have shown us the ways in which in literate and oral traditions generations become telescoped, individuals merged and split, minor lines become assimilated into major lines, and some individuals disappear while others assume a greater prominence. One study that can help us to understand the way in which historical events and experiences become mythologized and ritualized is Rosalind Shaw's accounts of the slave trade among Temne-speaking communities in Sierra Leone, West Africa (1997, 2002).

Slave trading among the Temne is rarely mentioned in verbal accounts, but survives in historical memory in the form of rogue spirits, witches, the visions of ritual specialists, and the imagery of divination techniques. Witchcraft among the Temne is not a "traditional" phenomenon but, in its present form, thoroughly modern, receiving its shape from the historical experience of the transatlantic slave. In Temne cosmological thinking there are three invisible places that intersect with the visible world – the "Place of the Dead," the "Place of Spirits," and the "Place of Witches." When Shaw asked about these three invisible worlds, the former two elicited little specific description. The Place of Witches, by contrast, was consistently described as "an urban world of wealth and rapid global mobility" (Shaw, 1997, p. 875). It was envisaged as

> a prosperous city where skyscrapers adjoin houses of gold and diamonds; where Mercedes-Benzes are driven down fine roads; where street vendors roast "beefsticks" (kebabs) of human meat; where boutiques sell stylish "witch gowns" that transform their wearers into animal predators in the human world... where electronic stores sell tape recorders and televisions (and more recently, VCRs and computers); and where witch airports dispatch witch planes – planes so fast, I was told, that "they can fly to London and back within an hour" – to destinations all around the globe. (Shaw, 1997, p. 857)

At one level these images draw on motifs found in much of sub-Saharan Africa. Corrupt regimes consume large amounts of the country's resources while the poor die for lack of basic necessities. Wealth is acquired at other people's expense – and witchcraft is the idiom commonly used to explain this "eating" of one's neighbor, one's family, one's people, with whom one should by rights share.[41] There is also a more specific historical dimension to the Temne witch-cities. In much of Cameroon Mount Kupe is seen as a place of witch-markets and zombies, which has its roots in the experience of planta-tion workers, stripped of their autonomy and forced to work for a master. Among many peoples in Sierra Leone, technology is thought to result from witchcraft powers, which Europeans have learnt to exploit in order to achieve material success. Development requires not less witchcraft but more – Africans too need to discover the secret of harnessing such powers. The problem is that Europeans are unwilling to share their knowledge,[42] or anything else for that matter. Among the Temne the term for "European-ness" "designates a range of anti-social behavior – living a secluded life, exchanging abrupt greetings, not stopping to talk, not visiting others, eating large quantities of meat, and eating alone without inviting others... Such qualities of seclusion, selfishness, and greed are also precisely those that characterize witches" (Shaw, 1997, pp. 860–1).

European contact with the Temne goes back four or five centuries. Their people had been reduced to consumable entities, exchanged for wealth in the European slave trade. Much of the capital that fueled the Industrial Revolu-tion in Britain and the rest of Europe, and the growth of the American colonies, came from the wealth generated by New World plantations depen-dent on African slave labor. Local wealth in Sierra Leone was created by the exchange of raw materials, and in particular slaves, with European traders. While the earliest accounts of divination in the region from the late fifteenth century make no mention of witchcraft, by the seventeenth century it appears that diviners would identify the relatives of a sick or dead person as witches, many of whom, particularly those from poorer families, would be enslaved. The African slavers were thereby "absolved," as the witch-victim of the slave trade had been transformed into the aggressor. The role of divination in supplying "witches" for the international slave trade was noted by English agents, but they reversed the direction of influence, seeing witchcraft and divination as cause rather than effect. With the abolition of slavery the practice of identifying and enslaving witches declined, and spirits rather than witches were more often named as the cause of sickness or death.

Shaw suggests a parallel between the European slavers, consuming the local population, the diviners, and other wealthy locals who benefited from the slave trade, and today's elites who, self-evidently witches by virtue of their wealth, are not those publicly accused of witchcraft. Now as in the past, it is the poor and powerless who are convicted of being witches. It is said that although they "may appear weak and unimportant in this world... they are 'big persons' in the invisible city" (Shaw, 1997, p. 868).[43] Shaw concludes that: "Built into the Temne imagination through an extended historical experience that has tied transregional commercial flows and foreign commodities to a traffic in human lives, the witch-city is a Sierra Leonean 'cosmology of capitalism' (Sahlins, 1988) that 'remembers' this experience in its construction as a startling commentary on global modernity" (Shaw, 1997, pp. 869–70).

Although it may seem as if we have strayed a long way from the tales of gods and heroes that are commonly the subject of mythology, Shaw's analysis provides an important pointer to the ways in which historical events are incorporated into a people's cultural memory. The Place of Witches, the fabulous witch-city, described by the Temne may seem to be the stuff of fables and dreams – a mythological place if ever there was one, but has its roots in a complex set of relationships that are modern, global, and grounded in recent historical experience. While the Tsimshian Native American chiefs used literary narratives to produce their mytho-histories, the Temne use oral narrative and ritual to reproduce their memories of slavery.[44]

The urban myth

Urban myths have much to teach us concerning the ways in which narratives can slide between myth and history. They usually have a clear narrative structure – a plot, characters, a time and location – with enough extraneous detail to add authenticity to the tale. Many urban myths contain elements that have the quality of a Jungian archetype, such as the stranger/angel who appears in time of trouble and leads the traveler though a place of danger to a place of safety before disappearing. Whatever the mode of transport the basic form of the narrative, repeated in numerous times, places, and cultural settings, is the same. Other tropes are more culturally specific. The belief that shaking the hand of a stranger can make a man's penis disappear causes periodic panic in parts of West Africa. Other urban legends, such as the story of the person who wakes after an encounter with a stranger to find that a kidney has been removed, are persistent and widespread.[45]

The urban myth or legend is a form of folklore often taken as fact. Stories are repeated verbally, in newspapers and other media and, increasingly, by email. Urban myths are not based on direct experience but believed as they come from a trusted source. The incidents described are often said to have happened to a "*friend of a friend*" (FOAF). The term "urban" is used to distinguish such tales from "traditional folklore," although it is not a very useful distinction as there is considerable continuity between "traditional" and "modern" forms of the genre, with evidence of such tales dating back to the work of the fifth-century Greek historian Herodotus.

The concept of the urban legend was popularized by the work of Jan Harold Brunvand in his 1981 book *The Vanishing Hitchhiker: American Urban Legends & Their Meanings.*

Urban myths play on or reflect people's fears, often fear of change, new technology, or encounters with strangers. They may well have a basis in fact. Just as Sierra Leonean politicians and elites, and the experience of the slave trade may be mediated by the image of the witch, so the commercial world of organ transplants and international trade in body parts, and a loss of individual control within an increasingly technological health system, is mediated by the image of the seducer-stranger who removes the innocent victim's kidney. Nancy Scheper-Hughes (2002), in her account of the illegal trade in organs for transplant, recalls how rumors of body-snatching among the poor of Recife in Brazil had precisely the character of an urban legend. Scheper-Hughes initially wrote of them in this fashion, as a reflection of "the normal, accepted, everyday violence practiced against the bodies of the poor and the marginal in public medical clinics, in hospitals, and in police mortuaries, where their ills and afflictions were often treated with scorn, neglect, and general disrespect" (2002, p. 34).[46] The rumors of organ theft began to appear with variations from many other parts of South and Central America, then from Africa, India, Asia, and Europe. In Poland and Russia it was said that poor children's organs "were being sold to rich Arabs for transplant surgery" (p. 35). In sub-Saharan Africa the tales were of blood-sucking vampires stealing organs. It was said that firemen or paramedics driving red combi-vans would drive around "looking to capture unsuspecting people to drug and kill in order to drain their blood or remove their organs and other body parts – genitals and eyes in particular – for magical medicine (*muti*) or for more traditional medical purposes" (ibid.).[47] In Italian versions of the story the kidnap vehicle is a black ambulance. These metaphoric substitutions, as Lévi-Strauss would put it, do not alter the basic story line and, as with other myths, by collecting all the possible variants a picture emerges that is not just psychologically relevant but, as Scheper-Hughes demonstrates, points to all too real practices.

> [Organ-stealing stories] were told, remembered, and circulated because they were true at that indeterminate level between the real, the surreal, and the uncanny. They expressed an intuitive sense that something was amiss, signaling the chronic "state of emergency" of the world's subcitizens living in a negative zone of existence where lives and bodies are experienced as a constant crisis of presence (hunger, sickness, injury) on the one hand, and as a crisis of absence and disappearance on the other. (Scheper-Hughes, 2002, p. 36)

By paying attention to the timing, geopolitical distribution, and specific details (mythic variants) of the stories, Scheper-Hughes noted that the stories circulated in times of upheaval and crisis. Evidence began to emerge, reported in respectable medical journals, of a global, illegal trade in human organs and other body parts. As Scheper-Hughes notes, "Indeed, wild rumors, like metaphors, do sometimes harden into 'ethnographic facts' "(p. 38).

Conclusion

The relationship between myth and history is evidently complex. The notion of myth itself and its study as a discrete phenomenon is dependent upon a view of history as recorded fact and the development of a post-Enlightenment view of the world to which myth can be opposed. Myths appear to gain salience when they have both psychological relevance and possibly some basis in fact. They then take on easily remembered, stereotypic forms. While there are specific cultural details and resonances to myths, such as cannibalistic witches in Africa, werewolves in Northern Europe, angels in white among Christianized peoples, or trickster hares in the Americas, they are also capable of crossing cultural, religious, and geographic boundaries. Literacy and history have not, as sometimes supposed, "done away with myth" or rendered myths obsolete. On the contrary, human societies constantly refigure their history so as to resemble myth, condensing some details, elaborating others, using repetition and formulaic devices that are simultaneously flexible and conservative. Myths become reservoirs of human experience. They are reflections of our present and our past, a mirror to our fears and anxieties, and a guide to our hopes for the future.

Notes

1   See chapter 5, p. 108, for definitions of these terms.
2   For standard, folkloristic definitions of these terms see Bascom (1965).
3   See Dundes (1996).
4   This distinction is related to the stereotypical distinction often made by Christian (especially Protestant) theologians between Judaism as a religion of ritual and Christianity as a religion of faith. Judaism is seen as a form of externalized religion, Christianity as an "inner" religion (within which contemplation is regarded as its highest expression).
5   See Strenski's discussion in *Myth and Method* (1996, pp. 56–7).
6   It could be argued that the celebration of the Mass or Eucharist within Christianity is the dramatic re-enactment of a myth, but that participation is usually

formal and restrained, internal rather than expressive, and most believers would probably resist the designation of the Eucharistic celebration as myth.

7 For a discussion of these terms see the section on "The Structural Study of Myth," p. 281.

8 Reproduced in *Magic, Science and Religion and Other Essays* (1954), edited by Robert Redfield, and in *Malinowski and the Work of Myth* (1992), edited by Ivan Strenski.

9 Strenski (1992, p. 81).

10 For a good discussion of Malinowki's pragmatism, as well as other aspects of his work on myth, see Strenski's introductory essay in *Malinowski and the Work of Myth* (1992).

11 Reprinted as chapter 4 in Strenski (1992).

12 Cf. the discussion of Peggy Reeves Sanday's work in chapter 5, which also stresses the parallels between myth and social structure.

13 Strenski (1992, p. 66).

14 See chapter 1, pp. 13–14.

15 Segal (1994, p. 75) makes the interesting point that for Smith, as for Frazer, myth serves to explain ritual, whereas for the French literary scholar René Girard, author of *Violence and the Sacred*, the function of myth is to disguise and not explain. The myth-ritual of the scapegoat disguises the tensions within society by focusing them on an acceptable victim (see chapter 6, pp. 163–4).

16 See discussion of Tylor in chapter 1, p 13.

17 See discussion of Sanday's work in chapter 5, pp. 118–22.

18 Onwuejeogwu (1971, pp. 288–9) in Sanday (1981, p. 35).

19 Faulkingham (1971, pp. 104–5) in Sanday (1981, p. 36).

20 Tremearne (1968).

21 Cited in Sanday (1981, p. 35).

22 Cf. Bowie and Davies (1990); Petroff (1986).

23 Louis Ginzberg (1913), in Ruether (1985, p. 71).

24 Ibid.

25 According to Tremearne (1968, p. 243), "[Bori spirits] are ready for their human victim before his birth, and will be certain to get him in the end."

26 Judith Plaskow, "The Coming of Lilith," originally written at the Feminist Theologizing Conference, Granville, Ohio, 1972. Reprinted in Ruether (1985, pp. 72–4).

27 Among the classic texts of process theology is Alfred North Whitehead's (1978) *Process and Reality*.

28 Jakobson also read the work of Ferdinand de Saussure, and sought to develop a structuralist understanding of the ways in which a language's structure serves its basic communicative function. In 1949 Jakobson moved to Harvard University, and in the 1960s developed a broader interest in communication science as a whole.

29 *Structural Anthropology, Volume II* (1977, p. 65). Robert Segal makes the point that Lévi-Strauss is a kind of myth-ritualist, but with a twist. Instead of seeing

myth and ritual as parallel expressions, he sees them as binary opposites (personal communication).

30   See chapter 6, pp. 161–3 for a discussion of Freud.

31   As he paid lavish tribute to Jung, Campbell is sometimes identified as more straightforwardly Jungian than is actually the case. Jung saw the task of the second half of life as integrating the external world of adulthood with the internal world one left behind as a child. Campbell's monomyth ostensibly follows a Jungian conception of an adult rather than a childhood journey, although this is not followed through consistently.

32   Cf. Arnold van Gennep's threefold stages of a rite of passage, separation-transition-incorporation (see chapter 6, p. 147ff.).

33   As Segal notes (personal communication), the hero's journey fits and symbolizes the journey of the discovery of the collective unconscious that is at the heart of Jungian psychology (albeit, nominally at least, for both genders).

34   Bowie (1989, p. 33), Bynum (1987, p. 131).

35   See Bowie and Davies (1990).

36   Elizabeth Petroff has a very interesting discussion on the role of visions and the sense of the self in her introduction to *Medieval Women's Visionary Literature* (1986).

37   From Pearson (1999).

38   Leach, "Genesis as Myth" (1969, p. 11). See also the discussion of Mary Douglas and anomalies in chapter 2, pp. 45–6.

39   A quote from the German theologian J. Schniewind, in Leach's essay "Genesis as Myth" (1969, p. 7), originally published in 1962.

40   Cf. Bowie (2003) for a discussion of the personal beliefs and attitude to religion of anthropologists who study religion.

41   Bayart (1993), refers to the "politics of the belly" to describe the metaphoric link between politics and cannibalism, mediated through the image of the witch. See also Geschiere (1997), Mbembe (2001), and chapter 8.

42   There are parallels here with the "cargo cults" of Oceania, which sought to discover the magic key that would unlock the secret of European technological dominance. See Lawrence (1964) and Trompf (1991).

43   Girard refers to this process as "scapegoating." (See the discussion in chapter 6 on ritual violence.)

44   For Lord Raglan the mythic heroic pattern is specifically defined as that which is non-historical, and is contrasted with the pattern of indisputably historical heroes (Segal, personal communication).

45   Some myths are both persistent and harmful, such as the widespread belief that having sex with a child or a virgin can cure a man of HIV-AIDS.

46   French folklorist Campion-Vincent also wrote of these rumors as the "literary inventions of semiliterate people who lack the skills to sort out the credible and realistic from the incredible and fantastic" (quoted in Scheper-Hughes, 2002, p. 36).

47   The use of children's body parts in "traditional" African ritual has gained increased visibility after the discovery of the torso of a child in the River Thames

in London in September 2001. The boy, named Adam by the police investigating the murder, was believed to be the victim of a *muti* or voodoo murder. From forensic evidence Adam was traced to a village in southwest Nigeria. There is a growing realization that many African children who enter the UK simply disappear from official view, and that some at least may, like Adam, have been brought into the country expressly to be sacrificed.

References and Further Reading

Bachofen, J. J. ([1954] 1992) *Myth, Religion and Mother Right: Selected Writings of J. J. Bachofen*, Preface by George Boas, Introduction by Joseph Campbell, trans. Ralph Manheim. Princeton, NJ: Princeton University Press.

Bascom, William (1965) The forms of folklore: prose narratives. *Journal of American Folklore*, 78, 3–20.

Bayart, J. F. (1993) *The State in Africa: the Politics of the Belly*, trans. M. Harper, C. and E. Harrison. London: Longman.

Bowie, Fiona (ed.) (1989) *Beguine Spirituality*. London: SPCK; New York: Crossroad.

Bowie, Fiona and Davies, Oliver (eds) (1990) *Hildegard of Bingen*. London: SPCK; New York: Crossroad.

Bowie, Fiona (2003) Belief or experience? The anthropologists' dilemma. In Cyril G. Williams (ed.), *Contemporary Conceptions of God: Interdisciplinary Essays*. Lewiston, Queenston, Lampeter: The Edwin Mellen Press, pp. 135–60.

Brunvand, Jan Harold (1981) *The Vanishing Hitchhiker: American Urban Legends & Their Meanings*. New York: W. W. Norton.

Bynum, Caroline Walker (1987) Religious women in the later Middle Ages. In J. Raitt (ed.), *Christian Spirituality: High Middle Ages and Reformation*. London: Routledge, pp. 121–39.

Campbell, Joseph (1988) *The Inner Reaches of Outer Space: Metaphor as Myth and as Religion*. New York: Harper and Row.

Campbell, Joseph ([1949] 1990) *The Hero with a Thousand Faces*. Princeton, NJ: Princeton University Press.

Campbell, Joseph ([1959–68] 1995) *The Masks of God: Creative Mythology*, 4 vols. London and New York: Penguin.

Campbell, Joseph (2004) *Pathways to Bliss: Mythology and Personal Transformation*. Novato, CA: New World Library.

Coupe, Laurence (1997) *Myth*. London and New York: Routledge.

Doniger, Wendy (1995) Foreword. In Claude Lévi-Strauss, *Myth and Meaning: Cracking the Code of Culture*. New York: Schocken Books.

Douglas, Mary (1996) Children consumed and child cannibals: Robertson Smith's attack on the science of mythology. In Laurie L. Patton and Wendy Doniger (eds), *Myth & Method*. Charlottesville and London: University of Virginia Press, pp. 29–51.

Dundes, Alan (1996) Madness in method, plus a plea for projective inversion in myth. In Laurie L. Patton and Wendy Donniger (eds), *Myth & Method*. Charlottesville and London: University of Virginia Press, pp.147–59.

Eliade, Mircea (1963) *Myth and Reality*, trans. Willard R. Trask. New York: Torch Books.

Eliade, Mircea (1968) *The Sacred and the Profane*, trans. Willard R. Trask. New York: Harvest Books.

Eliade, Mircea ([1954] 1989) *The Myth of the Eternal Return: Cosmos and History*. London and New York: Arkana.

Ellwood, Robert S. (1999) *The Politics of Myth: a Study of C. G. Jung, Mircea Eliade, and Joseph Campbell*. New York: State University of New York Press.

Faulkingham, Ralph Harold (1971) *Political Support in a Hausa Village*. Doctoral thesis, Michigan State University. Ann Arbor, MI: University Microfilms, Microfilm 71–18201.

Geschiere, Peter (1997) *The Modernity of Witchcraft: Politics and the Occult in Postcolonial Africa*. Charlottesville and London: University of Virginia Press.

Ginsberg, Louis ([1913] 1981) From *The Legends of the Jews, vol. 3*. In Rosemary Radford Ruether, *Womanguides: Readings Toward a Feminist Theology*. Boston: Beacon Press, p.71.

Hill, Jonathan D. (ed.) (1988) *Rethinking History and Myth: Indigenous Perspectives on the Past*. Urbana and Chicago: University of Illinois Press.

Lawrence, Peter (1964) *Road Belong Cargo*. Manchester, UK: Manchester University Press.

Leach, Edmund (1969) *Genesis as Myth and Other Essays*. London: Jonathan Cape.

Lévi-Strauss, Claude (1963) *Structural Anthropology*. New York: Basic Books.

Lévi-Strauss, Claude (1977) *Structural Anthropology, Volume II*. London: Penguin Books.

Lévi-Strauss, Claude (1970–82) *Introduction to a Science of Mythology*, 4 vols. London: Jonathan Cape. New York: Harper and Row (1969–81).

Lévi-Strauss, Claude ([1978] 1995) *Myth and Meaning: Cracking the Code of Culture*, Foreword Wendy Doniger. New York: Schocken Books.

Lincoln, Bruce (1991) *Emerging from the Chrysalis: Rituals of Women's Initiation*. New York and Oxford: Oxford University Press.

Malinowski, Bronislaw ([1925] 1954) Magic, science and religion. In *Magic, Science, Religion and other Essays*, ed. Robert Redfield. Garden City, NY: Doubleday Anchor Books, pp. 17–92.

Malinowski, Bronislaw ([1926, 1927] 1992) Myth in primitive psychology, and Obscenity and myth (1927). In Ivan Strenski (ed.), *Malinowski and the Work of Myth*. Princeton, NJ: Princeton University Press, pp. 77–116, 58–73.

Mbembe, Achille (2001) *On the Postcolony*. Berkeley, Los Angeles and London: University of California Press.

Middleton, John (ed.) (1967) *Myth and Cosmos: Readings in Mythology and Symbolism*. New York: The Natural History Press.

Müller, Friedrich Max ([1856] 1867) Comparative mythology. In *Chips from a German Workshop*. London: Longmans, Green.

Onwuejeogwu, Michael (1971) The cult of the *Bori* spirits among the Hausa. In M. Douglas and P. Kayberry (eds), *Man in Africa*. New York: Doubleday, pp. 279–305.

Patton, Laurie L. and Doniger, Wendy (eds) (1996) *Myth and Method*. Charlottesville and London: University of Virginia Press.

Pearson, Carol S. ([1986] 1999) *The Hero Within: Six Archetypes We Live By*. San Francisco: HarperSanFrancisco.

Petroff, Elizabeth Alvida (ed.) (1986) *Medieval Women's Visionary Literature*. New York and Oxford: Oxford University Press.

Pelton, Robert D. (1989) *The Trickster in West Africa: A Study of Mythic Irony and Sacred Delight*. Berkeley: University of California Press.

Plaskow, Judith (1985) The coming of Lilith. In Rosemary Radford Ruether, *Woman-guides: Readings Toward a Feminist Theology*. Boston: Beacon Press, pp. 72–3.

Propp, Vladimir ([1958] 1968) *Morphology of the Folktale*, trans. Laurence Scott, 2nd edn, rev. and ed. Louis A. Wagner. Austin: University of Texas Press.

Raglan, Lord (1936) *The Hero*. London: Methuen.

Rank, Otto ([1909] 2000) *The Myth of the Birth of the Hero: a Psychological Exploration of Myth*, trans. Gregory C. Richter and E. James Lieberman, Introduction Robert A. Segal. Baltimore: Johns Hopkins University Press.

Robertson Smith, William (1889) *Lectures on the Religion of the Semites*. Edinburgh: Black.

Sahlins, Marshall (1988) Cosmologies of capitalism: the trans-pacific sector of "the world system." *Proceedings of the British Academy*, 74, 1–51.

Samuel, Raphael and Thompson, Paul (eds) (1990) *The Myths We Live By*. London and New York: Routledge.

Sanday, Peggy Reeves (1981) *Female Power and Male Dominance: On the Origins of Sexual Inequality*. Cambridge, UK and New York: Cambridge University Press.

Scheper-Hughes, Nancy (2002) Mind(ing) the body: on the trail of organ-stealing rumors. In Jeremy MacClancy (ed.), *Exotic No More: Anthropology on the Front Lines*. Chicago and London: University of Chicago Press, pp. 33–63.

Segal, Robert (1990) *Joseph Campbell: an Introduction*. New York: Penguin.

Segal, Robert (ed.) (1998) *The Myth and Ritual Theory*. Oxford: Blackwell.

Segal, Robert (1999) *Theorizing about Myth*. Amherst: University of Massachusetts Press.

Segal, Robert (ed.) (2000) *Hero Myths: a Reader*, Oxford: Blackwell.

Segal, Robert (2004) *Myth: a Very Short Introduction*. Oxford: Oxford University Press.

Shaw, Rosalind (1997) The production of witchcraft/witchcraft as production: memory, modernity, and the slave trade in Sierra Leone. *American Ethnologist*, 24 (4), 856–76.

Shaw, Rosalind (2002) *Memories of the Slave Trade: Ritual and the Historical Imagination in Sierra Leone*. Chicago and London: University of Chicago Press.

Simes, Amy (2001) Children of the gods: the quest for wholeness in contemporary paganism. In Alaine Low and Soraya Tremayne (eds), *Women as Sacred Custodians of the Earth?* New York and Oxford: Berghahn Books, pp. 219–37.

Strenski, Ivan (1992) *Malinowski and the Work of Myth.* Princeton, NJ: Princeton University Press

Strenski, Ivan (1996) The rise of ritual and the hegemony of myth: Sylvain Lévi, the Durkheimians, and Max Müller. In Laurie L. Patton and Wendy Doniger (eds), *Myth & Method.* Charlottesville and London: University of Virginia Press, pp. 52–81.

Thompson, Stith ([1932–6] 1955–8) *Motif-Index of Folk-Literature: a Classification of Narrative Elements in Folktales, Ballads, Fables, Mediaeval Romances, Exempla, Fabliaux, Jest-Books and Local Legends,* 6 vols, rev. and enl. Copenhagen: Rosenkilde and Bagger.

Tremearne, Major A. J. N. ([1914] 1968) *The Ban of the Bori: Demons and Demon Dancing in West and North Africa.* London: Frank Cass.

Trompf, G. W. (1991) *Melanesian Religion.* Cambridge, UK: Cambridge University Press.

Tyler, Edward Burnett (1871) *Primitive Culture,* 2 vols. London: Murray.

Verdier, Yvonne (1980) Le petit chaperon rouge dans la tradition orale. *Le Débat,* 3.

Whitehead Alfred North (1978) *Process and Reality.* New York: The Free Press.

Appendix: Film and Video Resources

The following films and videos are a representative selection of those that could be used for teaching and independent learning. They have been selected because they illustrate points made in the chapters, or expand on related topics. They include both ethnographic and commercial films made for television in the United Kingdom.

The information is taken primarily from the Royal Anthropological Institute Film Library Catalogue (two volumes, 1982 and 1990, with a supplement published in May 1998), and the Cambridge University Department of Social Anthropology Video Catalogue (available online). The first line is the title of the film/video, and below this, where applicable, is the series title. Additional information on the producer, date, and length, if available, is given in parentheses. Most films made for television series, such as Everyman or Under the Sun, are approximately 50 minutes in length. The RAI Film and Video Library is administered by Concord Video and Film Council Ltd, 201 Felixstowe Road, Ipswich, Suffolk IP3 9BJ.

Chapter 1 Theories and Controversies

Everything is Relative

(*Director André Singer. 1985*)

Strangers Abroad
W. H. R. Rivers's work in the Torres Straights and Melanesia, including among the Todas.

Firth on Firth

(*By Rolf Husmann, Peter Loizos and Werner Sperschneider. 1993. 49 minutes*)
In a series of interviews at his London home and the London School of
Economics (LSE), Sir Raymond Firth talks about his life and some of his
personal views. The film focuses on his Maori studies, social anthropology
under Malinowski at the LSE, and Firth's fieldwork in Tikopia. In an inter-
view together with Lady Rosemary Firth, they talk about their common
fieldwork in Malaya.

Off the Verandah

(*Director André Singer. 1985*)

Strangers Abroad
Bronislaw Malinowski's work in the Trobriands, Papua New Guinea.

The Shock of the "Other"

(*Public Broadcasting Video. 1992*)

Millennium
The fieldwork encounter with Xavante Indians in Amazonia.

Tracking the Pale Fox

(*Filmmaker and anthropologist Luc de Heusch. 1983. 48 minutes*)
The film tells the history of the research on the Dogon in West Africa since
the famous 1931 expedition of Marcel Griaule. The film establishes the
original expedition in the context of French anthropology at the time. Jean
Rouch, celebrated filmmaker and an anthropologist who worked with the
Dogon, narrates part of the story, and interviews Dogon elders and veteran
expedition member Germaine Dieterlen.

Waiting for Harry

(*Director Kim McKenzie. Anthropologist Les Hiatt. 1980. 57 minutes*)
The film was planned around the final mortuary rites for Les Angabarraparra,
a member of the Anbarra people of northern Australia. The presence of the
dead man's maternal uncle, Harry, is essential for the mortuary ritual. The
interaction of the film is based around the absent Harry, the anthropologist,

Les Hiatt, and Frank Gurrmanamana, instigator and narrator of the film and classificatory brother of the dead man. The film is therefore about fieldwork, the filmmaking process, and relations with anthropological subjects, as much as it is about Australian mortuary rituals.

Chapter 2 The Body as Symbol

All Dressed Up

Body Styles
Clothing and fashion, style, and the symbolism of clothes.

Bird of the Thunderwoman

(Director David Parer. Anthropologist Paul Silitoe. 1980. 55 minutes)

Australian Broadcasting Corporation
An exchange ceremony in the Southern Highlands of Papua New Guinea, showing the fusion of myth and drama. The Thunderwoman is the mythological guardian of cassowaries, birds at the center of a ritual exchange that takes place only once every fifteen years. The film can be used to illustrate the role of myth and symbol.

Body and Soul

(Director David Cordingley. Anthropological consultant Jean La Fontaine. 1978. 55 minutes)

Face Values
Five different societies are compared and contrasted: the gypsies of California, the Kayapo of Central Brazil, the Swahili of Chole Island, Tanzania, the Balinese, and the Maltese. In this episode, which focuses on the body, there are discussions of ritual symbolism and the relationship between religious behavior and rationality.

The Inner Journey

The Healing Art
Techniques involving the mind and spirit in healing the body, including relaxation and pilgrimage.

Kataragama – a God for All Seasons

(*Director Charlie Nairn. Anthropologist Gananath Obeyesekere. 52 minutes*)

Disappearing World. Granada Television
Sinhalese of all religions (Muslim, Christian, and Buddhist) turn to Kataragama, a Hindu God, in times of trouble and desperation. The pilgrims' dramatic acts of physical penance are placed within an understandable social context. (Also suitable for chapter 9.)

Principles of Caste

(*Director Tom Selwyn. 1982. 24 minutes*)

Open University
The film explains the fundamentals of the Indian caste system, including the relations between castes. It is based on the field research of Tom Selwyn in the village of Singhara in Madhya Pradesh in central India. A central event of the film, a marriage ceremony, illustrates how theoretically exclusive castes interact. Mary Douglas uses the caste system as an example of symbolic classification and the maintenance of symbolic and physical boundaries. (Also suitable for chapter 3.)

Were Ni! He is a Madman!

(*Directors Francis Speed and Raymond Prince. 1963. 30 minutes*)

An ethnopsychiatric film showing the management of psychiatric disorders by the Yoruba of Nigeria through herbalists and "possession." The film can be used to illustrate relationships between the mind, body, and society.

Chapter 3 Maintaining and Transforming Boundaries: the Politics of Religious Identity

The Common Bond

(*Director David Cordingley. Anthropological consultant Jean La Fontaine. 1978. 55 minutes*)

Face Values
This film examines the way in which the ceremonies and rituals that punctuate everyday life serve to reinforce cultural identity and say something

about the attitudes and beliefs of the participants and their relationship to the world around them.

Everything in Its Place

(*Director David Cordingley. Anthropological consultant Jean La Fontaine. 1978. 55 minutes*)

Face Values
This episode shows that drawing boundaries is a universal human occupation, although the nature of these divisions depends on what is important to the people concerned. The main focus of the film in order to make this point is religious life on Malta and Bali.

Gypsies: a People Apart

(*Director Peter Ramsden. Anthropologist Anne Sutherland. 1982. 30 minutes*)

Other People's Lives. BBC Television
The aim of this film is to show how one group of Californian Gypsies (Rom) maintain the boundary that separates them from non-Gypsies, with whom they have daily contact. The leader acts as an intermediary with the outside world, operating with a set of values that defines marriage or sexual relations with outsiders as "dirty," and that seeks to protect the "purity" of the ethnic group.

Gypsyland – It Doesn't Exist

(*Director Ludi Boeken. 1982*)

People to People
A look at the origins and culture of Gypsies and their place in a changing Britain.

Heal the Whole Man

(*Director Paul Robinson. Anthropologist Jean Comaroff. 50 minutes*)
The film examines Barolong (Tswana) religious syncretism in South Africa in the context of the modern sociopolitical situation. The main religious division shown is between the mission churches and the so-called Zionist churches. The film also explores the impact of Christian dogma on indigenous ideas. Seemingly irrational belief and action make sense when viewed in

context, and the apparently bizarre syncretistic religion of the Barolong can be seen as part of the universal human quest to impose order and meaning upon everyday experience. (Also suitable for chapter 6.)

Mistaken Identity

Millennium (*1992*)
Concepts of identity in different societies.

A Veiled Revolution

(*Directors Marilyn Gaunt and Elizabeth Fernea. 1982. 25 minutes*)
This film looks at the politics and gender of dress in Egypt, one of the first Arab countries where women cast off the veil, but in which many women are now readopting "Islamic dress" out of choice. Some of the older women interviewed see the return to the veil as abandonment of a hard-earned freedom, but younger women often regard Islamic dress as a way of reasserting Egyptian Muslim identity, and a means of seeking freedom through their own Islamic tradition. A study guide by Elizabeth Fernea is available from Elizabeth Fernea, Centre for Middle Eastern Studies, The University of Texas at Austin, Texas 78712–1193, USA.

Chapter 4 Sex, Gender, and the Sacred

Chole Island – a Woman's Place

(*Director Peter Ramsden. Anthropologist Pat Caplan. 1982. 30 minutes*)

Other People's Lives. BBC Television
The film is designed to show the relations between men and women that seem to conform to the Islamic ideal of segregation. Men and women keep apart and there is a division of labor along sex lines: men are concerned with religious and political affairs, while women occupy themselves with children, cooking, and the performance of customary, as opposed to Islamic, rites and ceremonies. The film features a wedding celebration. A study guide accompanies the film.

El Sebou: the Egyptian Birth Ritual

(*Director F. El Guindi. 1986. 27 minutes*)
An ethnographic account of the birth ritual in Egypt called El Sebou, "the seventh," celebrated on the seventh day following the birth of a child, by Coptic Christian and Muslim families. Traditionally, this was an occasion for naming newborn children, circumcising boys, and piercing the ears of girls. Character-istic of the Egyptian ritual depicted in the film is the gender-linked imagery reflected in the ceremonial clay pot and the cosmological symbolism embedded in the numerical value "seven." The ceremony is presented as a key rite of passage, as newborn children cross the threshold into gender and status. (Also suitable for chapter 6.)

Our Way of Loving

(BBC, 1994)
Under the Sun
Hamar women of Ethiopia talk about their perceptions of love and courting.

The Women's Olamal

(*Director Melissa Llewelyn-Davies, BBC, 1982*)
Diary of a Masai Village
The organization of a Masai fertility ceremony. The women argue for holding the ceremony against the men's wishes.

Chapter 5 Religion, Culture, and Environment

The Axing of the Himalayas

The World about Us (1982)
Attempts by hill people to prevent wholesale felling of trees in their homeland, with reference to the celebrated environmentalist Chipko Move-ment.

Dances at Aurukun

(*Director Ian Dunlop. 1962. 29 minutes*)
An account of eight different totemic increase ceremony dances performed by the Wikmungkan of Cape York, Australia, at Aurukun, a Presbyterian mission station. Each dance acts the legendary history attached to a particular clan totem.

From the Heart of the World: the Elder Brothers' Warning

(*Producer and director Alan Ereira. Anthropologists Graham Townsley and Felicity Nock. 90 minutes*)
BBC Television
The Kogi of Colombia's warning to the "Younger Brother" of the devastating environmental effects of our current lifestyle. The film includes a short sequence documenting the reaction of the Kogi Mamas to the screening of the film, which was made at their instigation. The film is available from the Tairona Heritage Trust: e-mail tairona@lamp.ac.uk.

Gelede: a Yoruba Masquerade

(*Director Francis Speed. 30 minutes*)
Among the Yoruba of Western Nigeria and Dahomey, the Gelede cult honors the earth spirits, the ancestors, and especially the Great Mother. The festival filmed here emphasizes the status of women and placates their potentially dangerous mystic powers. The commentary emphasizes that the annual Gelede festival serves a cathartic role by paying respect to women in a patriarchal society.

The Mehinacu

(*Director Carlos Pasini. Anthropologist Thomas Gregor. 52 minutes*)

Disappearing World. Granada Television
The Mehinacu live in the Xingu National Park in Central Brazil. The film focuses on a series of rituals concerned with the planting and harvesting of the piqui tree, in the context of the social relations between the sexes. In one sequence a Mehinacu elder tells of the origin myth of the sacred flutes, illustrating the relationship between myths and social structure, sex roles and ritual.

My Country Djarrakpi

(*By Ian Dunlop. 1981. 16 minutes*)
Paintings, together with their related songs, dances, and ritual events, form an integral part of the religious life of the Yolngu people of Northeast Arnhem Land in Australia. Every painting or design is owned by a particular clan and tells of events in a clan's ancestral past.

Never Stay in One Place

(*ABC-TV, 1983*)
The Natural World
Australian Aboriginals attempt to keep to a traditional way of life in their remote northern homeland.

The Noble Savage

Horizon
Asks whether indigenous peoples really are good ecologists.

The Red Bowman

(*Director Chris Owen. Anthropologist Alfred Gell. 1981. 50 minutes*)
A record of the Ida ceremony performed in Punda village in the West Sepik province of Papua New Guinea. The film shows the villagers' ambivalent attitude toward the bush: it is life giving, providing them with sago, yet it is also full of danger and sorcery. The country is infertile and malarial, and the people have little political power. The dominant interest of the villagers is securing their demographic survival in the face of a difficult environment, yet much of their daily life is also oriented toward the preparation of the Ida ritual.

Sacred Boards and an Ancestral Site

(*Part Three of People of the Australian Western Desert. Director Ian Dunlop. Anthropologist Robert Tonkinson. 1965. 7½ minutes*)
In this film an Aboriginal shows the crew his sacred carved boards hidden at a totemic site. The boards are thought to link directly with the Dreamtime when the ancestors carried similar boards. The commentary recounts a

legend in which the ancestors of the Dreamtime circumcised a boy at the totemic site.

Stonehenge and the Druids

Modern Druids in Britain and their attempts to re-enact ancient traditions, often leading to conflict with the civil authorities.

Ten Times Empty

(*Directors James Wilson and David Tristram. 1977. 21 minutes*)
Set on the Greek island of Symi, off the Turkish coast in the Aegean Sea, an idyllic paradise where tourists come only for a few hours a day and the only cars people have seen are on television. Unfortunately the paradise is dying because the fish are too few and agricultural cultivation on the barren, almost waterless, island is even more difficult. The text that describes the customs, religion, national celebrations, funeral ceremonies, and general life is narrated by Vassilis, a local 12-year-old boy.

Chapter 6 Ritual Theory, Rites of Passage, and Ritual Violence

The Ainu Bear Ceremony

(*Director Neil Gordon Munro. c. 1931. 27 minutes*)
The Ainu of Japan used to live by hunting and gathering, and the bear ceremony, now no longer performed, was the most important of their rituals. It has much in common with bear ceremonies among other northern peoples. The film shows how a specially reared animal was reverently killed and its flesh and blood eaten by the participants.

The Axe Fight

(*Director Timothy Asch. Anthropologist Napoleon Chagnon. 1975. 20 minutes*)
The film focuses on a brief single event, a fight among the Yanomamo of Venezuela, giving three views of the event, each view increasing insight into both the event itself and the process of filmmaking. The second view places the fight in its ritual context. A study guide accompanying the film is available from Documentary Educational Resources, 101 Morse Street, Watertown, MA 02172, USA.

Bali – Cremation
Bali – Down from the Mountain

(*Director Peter Ramsden. Anthropologist Anthony Forge. 1982. 30 minutes each*)
Cremation describes the sequence of events of a cremation in Bali, as well as exploring the ritual itself and the implications of the cremation for those involved. *Down from the Mountain* examines some of the social uses of water in Balinese culture, including the use of holy water for washing away pollution and ensuring well-being. (Also suitable for use with chapter 2.)

Benin Kingship Rituals

(*Directors R. E. Bradbury and Francis Speed. 20 minutes*)
Until the British conquered it in 1897, the city of Benin, in what is now Nigeria, was the center of a powerful kingdom. Its rulers, the Obas of Benin, were mysterious, secluded figures who spent much of their time in the performance of rituals designed to enhance their own power and to ensure the prosperity of their subjects. The film shows some of the most significant moments in the rituals. In the Igwe Festival, in which the Oba's divine powers are strengthened and renewed, the object of worship is the head of the living Oba, the seat of his ritual energy, on which the well-being of the nation is thought to depend.

A Celebration of Origins

(*By Timothy Asch, Patsy Asch and E. Douglas Lewis. 1993. 45 minutes*)
A realistic portrayal of a rarely performed cosmogenic ritual in Indonesia. It evokes the contested nature of ritual, demonstrating how ritual performance implicates delicate political relationships based on pragmatic alliances, festering antipathies, or developing jealousies. Conflict is the thread that weaves together the disparate themes of the film.

Chole Island – Circumcision

(*Director Peter Ramsden. Anthropologist Pat Caplan. 1982. 30 minutes*)

Other People's Lives. BBC Television
Circumcision rituals in Tanzania, demonstrating the mixture of Islam and customary ritual. A study guide accompanies the film.

The Dervishes of Kurdistan

(*Director Brain Moser. Anthropologists Ali Bulookbashi and André Singer. 52 minutes*)

Disappearing World
This film explores the unusual manifestations of Qadiri Dervish faith – followers of an ecstatic, mystical cult of Islam. In rituals presided over by their leader, Sheikh Hussein, the Dervishes have the power to carry out acts that would normally be harmful, such as having electricity passed through their bodies, eating glass, handling poisonous snakes, and skewering their faces.

Emu Ritual at Ruguri

(*Director Roger Sandall. Anthropologist Nicolas Peterson. 1966 and 1967. 35 minutes*)
The film portrays traditional Australian art and ritual practice among the Walbiri of the Central Desert. The painting of sacred designs on the cave walls and the construction of an elaborate ground painting and other emblems are important components in the ritual.

Goodbye Old Man

(*Director David MacDougall. 1977. 70 minutes*)
The family of the Australian Aboriginal Mangatopi family of Snake Bay, Melville Island, wished to make this film as a tribute to the head of the family. The film centers on the pukumani ceremony to put the dead man's spirit at rest and to readjust to the imbalance his death has created. The family seeks to make the viewer understand the ceremony and the reasons behind it.

Imbalu: Ritual and Manhood of the Gisu of Uganda

(*Filmmaker Richard Hawkins. Anthropologist Suzette Heald. 1989. 69 minutes*)
A male circumcision ritual among the Gisu of Uganda. The narrative follows two male participants though the ritual and contrasts their hopes and anxieties with the expectations of the rest of the village.

Madarpa Funeral at Gurka'wuy

(*Director Ian Dunlop. Anthropologist Howard Morphy. 1979. Part 1, 42 minutes. Part 2, 44 minutes*)
A detailed explanation of a funeral among the Yolngu people of Northeast Arnhem Land. The links between the kinship structure, religious belief systems, and current social relationships between various related Aboriginal groups are shown. There is an accompanying monograph by Howard Morphy (see bibliography for chapter 6).

Masai Women and Masai Manhood

(*Director Chris Curling. Anthropologist Melissa Llewelyn-Davies. 53 minutes each*)

Disappearing World. Granada Television
The Masai are cattle herders living in the East African rift valley. Their main wealth is composed of cattle. Both films include initiation ceremonies, by means of which young women and men reach adulthood.

The Sakuddei

(*Director John Sheppard. Anthropologist Reimer Schefold. 53 minutes*)

Disappearing World. Granada Television
The Sakuddei are a small and ethnically separate community living on the island of Siberut off the west coast of Sumatra in Indonesia. Their distinctive way of life and elaborate religious ceremonies, centered on the *umah* (ceremonial house), are under threat from the Indonesian government, which wishes to "civilize" them. The first part of the film contains scenes of ritual life in the *umah*.

The Shilluk of Southern Sudan

(*Director Chris Curling. Anthropological consultants Paul Howell, Walter Kunijwok, and André Singer. 1975. 52 minutes*)

Disappearing World. Granada Television
Divine kingship rituals among the Shilluk in Southern Sudan. This film can be used to complement Evans-Pritchard's 1948 text *The Divine Kingship of the Shilluk*.

Shorinji Kempo – the New Way

The Way of the Warrior
A fighting religious cult in Japan, founded by the late Doshin So, who was succeeded as leader by his daughter.

Spirits, Ghosts and Demons

Beyond the Clouds
Childhood, spirit beliefs, and rituals in modern China.

Towards Baruya Manhood

(Director Ian Dunlop. Anthropologist Maurice Godelier. 1972. 465 minutes)

Australian Commonwealth Film Unit
The Baruya of the eastern Highlands of Papua New Guinea allowed an entire set of male initiation rituals to be filmed, on condition that the series never be shown in Papua New Guinea. The initiation, which takes place every two years, is in four stages, beginning when a boy is nine and ending when he is about twenty.

Walbiri Ritual at Gunadjari

Walbiri Ritual at Ngama

Emu Ritual at Ruguri

(Three films directed by Roger Sandall. Anthropological consultant Nicolas Peterson. 30 minutes, 23 minutes, and 35 minutes)

Australian Institute of Aboriginal Studies
These films give a vivid account of traditional Australian Aboriginal ritual in the Central Desert. The sacred sites, songs, and paintings are related to the ancestors and the Dreamtime.
(Also suitable for use with chapter 5.)

Ways of the Middle Kingdom

(Director Hugh Gibb. Consultant Marjorie Topley. 50 minutes)

BBC Television
Made in Hong Kong, this film is a wide-ranging study of traditional Chinese religion and custom. Domestic, monastic, and communal rituals are presented.

Chapter 7 Shamanism

A Balinese Trance Séance

(*Directors Timothy and Patsy Asch. Anthropologist Linda Connor. 1980. 30 minutes*)

The film follows a Balinese spirit medium, Jero Tapakan, who goes into a series of trances at the request of a family who wish to learn from their dead son the cause of his death and his needs for his cremation ceremony. In a second film, *Jero on Jero: a Balinese Trance Séance Observed*, the Aschs and Linda Connor film Jero's reactions to herself on film.

Drums of Flight

Drums of Asia
Shamanism, Buddhism, and healing rituals in Mongolia.

The Herders of Mongun-Taiga

(*Director John Sheppard. Anthropologist Caroline Humphrey. 1989. 51 minutes*)

The film looks at the lives of the Tuvinians of the Mongun-Taiga or "sacred wilderness" in Central Asia. It includes methods used by the herders to protect children from destructive spirits, shamanic beliefs, the worship of mountain spirits, purification by the water of sacred springs, sacrifice, and the use of animals in exorcism, omens, and divination.

Magical Death

(*Directed by Napoleon Chagnon and Timothy Asch. 29 minutes*)

A Yanomamö shaman in Venezuela, Dedeheiwä, uses hallucinogenic snuff to cure his co-villagers and send sickness to enemy villages. The film illustrates how religion serves political ends and how shamans can manipulate the spirit world to demonstrate their allegiance to allies.

The Meo: Laos

Disappearing World. Granada Television
An account of the Meo of Laos, including shamanism, opium, agriculture, and the effects of war.

To Find our Life: the Peyote Hunt of the Huichols of Mexico

(*Director Peter T. Hurst. 65 minutes*)
A film about a pivotal event in the religious and ritual life of the Huichol
Indians of Mexico, a pilgrimage led by a shaman to obtain peyote, a hallucinogenic drug from a cactus, used in religious rituals. (Also suitable for
chapter 9.)

N/um Tchai: the Ceremonial Dance of the !Kung Bushmen

(*Filming and direction John Marshall. Ethnography Lorna Marshall. 1950s. 20
minutes*)
The medicine dance of the Nyae Nyae !Kung (south-west Africa) is used to
heal the sick and ward off evil. Medicine men may go into a light trance as
they lay their hands on people in order to draw out manifest sickness and
unknown ills. A Study Guide by L. Marshall and M. Biesele accompanies the
film (published by Documentary Educational Resources, 101 Morse Street,
Watertown, MA 02172, USA).

Taiga Nomads

(*Director Heimo Lappalainen. 1992. Three films of 50 minutes each*)
A series of three films about the Evenki (Tungus), a nomadic people of
eastern Siberia, who live under harsh conditions in the taiga. The films
give a picture of everyday life, following the fortunes of one family.

Chapter 8 Witchcraft and the Evil Eye

Cakchiquel Maya of San Antonio Palopo

Disappearing World. Granada Television
With wealthy outsiders moving to Lake Atitlan in Guatemala the local Maya
Indians either welcome the outside world, or try to drive it away with
witchcraft.

States of Mind

Jonathan Miller interviews American anthropologist Clifford Geertz on the
magical rites of preliterate peoples, and the attitudes these express to the
world around them.

Strange Beliefs

(*Director André Singer. 1985*)

Strangers Abroad
Sir Edward Evans-Pritchard's work in Congo and the Sudan among the Azande and Nuer.

Witchcraft among the Azande

(*Director André Singer. Anthropologist John Ryle. 1981. 52 minutes*)

Disappearing World. Granada Television
Set in Zaire, the film shows that the Azande continue to refer to oracles, much as described by Evans-Pritchard, and that Christianity has had little impact on witchcraft beliefs.

Witches and Women

Burning Embers
Discussion of the persecution of women caused by their relationships with the Church and medicine, and their fight for power in the modern world.

Chapter 9 Pilgrimage

Cuyagua

(*Filmmaker Paul Henley. 1987. Part I, 52 minutes. Part II, 56 minutes*)

Useful for teaching about religious syncretism. The people of Cuyagua on the Venezuelan Caribbean coast are descended from African slaves. In their celebration of major Catholic feast days they have conserved clear traces of African cultural traditions. Part I – Devil Dancers – focuses on a male ritual celebrated on the feast of Corpus Christi. Part II – The Saint with Two Faces – focuses on celebrations of the feast of John the Baptist, a predominantly female affair. The feast is an extraordinary conjunction of the sacred and profane, of celebration, and of mourning.

Kataragama: a God for All Seasons

(*Film-maker Charlie Nairn. Anthropologist Gananath Obeysekere. 1973. 52 minutes*)

Once a year pilgrims make the journey to Kataragama's shrine in southeast Sri Lanka (Ceylon) to fulfill vows by performing acts of penance and worship in payment for a favor received. Kataragama is called on to help with a wide range of problems (unemployment, sickness, examinations, personal relationships) and is appealed to by people of all social backgrounds, notably the growing middle class and urban dwellers. A good third of the film is concerned with the annual festival and the often sensational acts which the pilgrims perform. These penitential performances are interwoven with the story of a peasant family whose son has disappeared, leading them eventually to seek help from Kataragama.

Return to the Sacred Ice

(*Executive director Peter Furbrook. Narrator Nicholas Shakespeare. 1989. 55 minutes*)

Under the Sun series. BBC2
The film focuses on a group of Quechua pilgrims attending a ceremony at the rural shrine of El Senor de Quoyllur Rit'i ("Lord of the Snow Star"). Although ostensibly a Catholic shrine, older elements such as the propitiation of the mountain gods or *apu*, and human sacrifice for the fertility of the llama herds are still evident. The whole is bound together by the haunting music that forms a backdrop to the pilgrimage.

Umbanda

(*Producer and Director Stephen Cross. Anthropologist Peter Fry. 1977. 50 minutes*)

Umbanda is a syncretic religious movement combining elements from orthodox Catholicism with submerged African and indigenous Indian spiritual beliefs.

The Quechua

(*Director Carlos Pasini. Anthropologist Michael Sallnow. 1974. 51 minutes*)

Set in the Peruvian Andes, *The Quechua* explores religious and secular life. The first part shows a pilgrimage to a Christian sanctuary, illustrating the syncretism of Catholic and pre-Hispanic local religious traditions. The second part of the film shows a fertility rite for sheep.

Chapter 10 Myth

Bird of the Thunderwoman

(*Filmmaker David Parer. Anthropologist Paul Sillitoe. 1980. 55 minutes*)

This film, made for the Australian Broadcasting Corporation, unravels an exchange ceremony of the Wola people of the Southern Highlands of Papua New Guinea. The fusion of myth and drama makes this portrait of their ceremonial exchange featuring the cassowary (a large flightless bird) both powerful and informative.

Kayapo – Fire of the Jaguar

(*Director Peter Ramsden. Anthropologist Terence Turner. 1982. 30 minutes*)

Other People's Lives. BBC Television
Study guide available. The film tries to show how a complex and powerful set of ideas (a whole philosophy of human nature and society) is communicated and brought to bear on everyday events in Kayapo society. The opening scene shows the telling of the myth of the jaguar. Myths in Kayapo society are potent instruments of socialization.

The Lau of Malaita

(*Director Leslie Woodhead. Anthropologist Pierre Maranda. 1987. 51 minutes*)

Disappearing World. Granada Television
The film focuses on the people of the Lau Lagoon in the Solomon Islands and the themes of change and conflict. The concept of "custom," the traditional way of life with its myths, rituals, and practices, is being undermined by the presence of Christian converts.

Index